Career Counseling
A Developmental Approach

Career Counseling
A Developmental Approach

Robert J. Drummond
University of North Florida

Charles W. Ryan
Wright State University

Merrill,
an imprint of Prentice Hall

Englewood Cliffs, New Jersey   Columbus, Ohio

Library of Congress Cataloging-in-Publication Data

Drummond, Robert J.
  Career counseling : a developmental approach / Robert J. Drummond,
Charles W. Ryan.
    p.   cm.
  Includes bibliographical references and index.
  ISBN 0-02-330675-0
  1. Vocational guidance. I. Ryan, Charles W. (Charles William),
II. Title.
  HF5381.D68 1995
  158.6—d20   94–16162
                                                              CIP

Cover art: Byron Gin
Editor: Kevin M. Davis
Production Editor: Stephen C. Robb
Text Designer: EDH
Cover Designer: Jill E. Bonar
Production Buyer: Pamela D. Bennett
Electronic Text Management: Marilyn Wilson Phelps, Matthew Williams, Jane Lopez,
    Karen L. Bretz

This book was set in Kuenstler 480 and Swiss 721 by Prentice Hall and was printed and
bound by R. R. Donnelley & Sons Company. The cover was printed by Phoenix Color
Corp.

 © 1995 by Prentice-Hall, Inc.
A Simon & Schuster Company
Englewood Cliffs, New Jersey 07632

Printed in the United States of America

10 9 8 7 6 5 4 3 2 1

ISBN: 0-02-330675-0

Prentice-Hall International (UK) Limited, *London*
Prentice-Hall of Australia Pty. Limited, *Sydney*
Prentice-Hall of Canada, Inc., *Toronto*
Prentice-Hall Hispanoamericana, S. A., *Mexico*
Prentice-Hall of India Private Limited, *New Delhi*
Prentice-Hall of Japan, Inc., *Tokyo*
Simon & Schuster Asia Pte. Ltd., *Singapore*
Editora Prentice-Hall do Brasil, Ltda., *Rio de Janeiro*

DEDICATION

We both learned from our interactions with these significant people in our lives. Their influence lives on.

To Gloria E. Drummond (1942–1992), my wife, who loved her work as a housewife and church secretary

To Cornelius F. Ryan (1906–1993), my father, a self-taught engineer who loved ideas and who taught me the meaning of work

To Catherine B. Ryan (1897–1987), my mother, who loved working with people

PREFACE

There are many challenges to career counselors: corporate mergers, down-sizing, rapidly changing technology, a world employment market, and changing demographics of the work force, among other variables. Clients range across the age span from teenagers seeking part-time and summer employment to retired workers wanting to reenter the labor market. Clients vary in gender, gender preference, ethnic membership, and cultural heritage. Career, employment, and life-style are salient issues with everyone, including individuals with disabilities. Career exploration, career choice, career decision making, job placement, job-seeking skills, job-keeping skills, and self-understanding are important constructs to the career counselor. Career counselors have to master the techniques and methods that will be effective with clients across the life span.

PURPOSE

The purpose of this text is to help learners understand the skills, abilities, and knowledge needed by career counselors. The text shows the dynamic relationship among theory, research, and practice when working with different types of clients across the life span. Counselors need to be alert to sources of career information and the most effective and efficient ways in guiding individuals with different types of learning styles to develop a good knowledge base for decision making. Case studies and suggested activities are included to help readers apply the concepts and reflect on them. (Note to instructor: The instructor's manual contains a variety of classroom activities and additional cases for discussion.)

STRUCTURE

The book is divided into four sections. The first section focuses on career and life-style planning and the world of work. The first chapter analyzes the career counseling process and various theoretical approaches. The second chapter introduces various philosophical and conceptual ways of understanding work and career. Stress and job satisfaction are also included in this chapter. The third chapter presents labor market trends and projections and describes various systems of classifying occupations.

The second section emphasizes career development theory and practices of individuals and groups across the life span. Chapter 4 looks at students in grades K to 5; chapter 5, middle school; chapter 6, the high school; chapter 7, community college, college, and postsecondary students; chapter 8, early adulthood; chapter 9, middle adulthood; chapter 10, older adults; chapter 11, individuals with disabilities; and chapter 12, individuals from other ethnic and cultural groups.

Part III covers types of career information. Chapter 13 explores the various types of career information resources, and chapter 14 looks specifically at computer-assisted guidance systems and other applications of technology in career counseling. Chapter 15 presents an overview of testing and other assessment techniques, such as the use of the portfolio.

The fourth section emphasizes current practices and future trends. Chapter 16 reviews developmental counseling strategies, and chapter 17 focuses on where we have been, where we are, and where we might be in the future.

ACKNOWLEDGMENTS

The writing of a major text is not a task easily accomplished by one or two persons alone. We are deeply indebted to the following individuals for editorial review: Aneneosa Okocha, University of Wisconsin at Whitewater; Dale Grant, Georgia Southern University; John C. Dagley, University of Georgia; Susan Whiston, University of Nevada at Las Vegas; Patricia Wolleat, University of Wisconsin at Madison; James Daniel Romero, California State University at Hayward; Susan D. Phillips, State University of New York at Albany; Harry Drier, Career, Education & Training Associates, Inc.; Angelo V. Boy, University of New Hampshire; James J. Muro, University of North Texas; Scott Wilson, Central Ohio Technical College; Lawrence K. Jones, North Carolina State University; Stephen Feit, Plymouth State College.

The following individuals at Wright State University contributed: Bonnie Trzaska for typing and stylistic editing, Debbie Ratliff for typing; and Dr. Donna J. Cole for reviewing selected chapters and providing well-focused comments. At Jacksonville, Robin Drummond typed and checked the references.

THE AUTHORS

Robert J. Drummond is professor in the counselor education program at the University of North Florida, Jacksonville. He earned a bachelor's degree in English from Waynesburg College, master's in English from Columbia University, and master's in educational psychology and doctorate in educational and psychological measurement and evaluation from Teachers College, Columbia University. He is a Fellow of the American Psychological Association and the American Association of Applied and Preventative Psychology and a member of the American Counseling Association.

Dr. Drummond has published more than sixty articles in journals, more than fifty research and evaluation monographs, and five chapters in books. He also is the author of *Appraisal Procedures for Counselors and Helping Professionals, Second Edition.*

Charles W. Ryan is professor of educational leadership and counselor education at Wright State University, Dayton, Ohio. He earned a bachelor's degree in history from Slippery Rock University, a master's in history and counselor education from Colgate University, and a doctorate in counselor education from the University of Toledo.

Dr. Ryan is the author of fifty-three articles, five chapters in published books, four monographs, and twenty-three book reviews. In addition, Dr. Ryan has had twenty-nine externally funded research projects that have focused on career counseling programs, intervention strategies for minority groups, and drug education through portfolios within the public school and university sector. He has also lectured at more than fifteen major colleges and universities and has served as a consultant in the development of career education programs at the university level. Among his published books are *Career Education: Kindergarten through Grade Twelve* (three volumes) with Saltzman and Wysong and *Career Education: A Handbook for Funding Resources.*

BRIEF CONTENTS

CONTENTS

CHAPTER 8   Early Adulthood: Developing Career Identity

150

CHAPTER 14   Computer Applications in Career Counseling   284

CHAPTER 15   Assessment in Career Counseling   306

PART IV   Contemporary and Future Practices, Trends, and Issues   331

CHAPTER 16   Counseling Strategies   332

CHAPTER 17   Context of Current Trends and Issues   360

I

CAREER COUNSELING AND THE WORLD OF WORK

CAREER COUNSELING

A Process for Human Development

A wide variety of approaches have been developed to help us understand the processes of career development and decision making. Anthropologists, sociologists, educators, economists, psychologists, and philosophers have all studied vocational behavior and have provided us with insights into the processes. Field-based counselors and practitioners are concerned with knowing what type of counseling practices are effective to help individuals achieve their full potential.

Theories have been developed by Super (1984), Holland (1985), and others to try to help provide a conceptual framework for us to understand career development. These theories have led to the development of assessment strategies, counseling techniques, and the creation and structuring of information sources to assist a variety of clients. This book can help workers in career counseling and development to develop new insights and techniques to facilitate the career decision making and career choice of their clients.

LEARNING OBJECTIVES

After studying this chapter, you should be able to do the following:

- Discuss the theoretical framework for career counseling and development in various counseling settings
- Explain the contribution of career development theories to career counseling and human development
- Identify cognitive theories and approaches used to deliver career counseling and development services
- List and discuss the roles and competence needed to be an effective career counselor
- Identify the major theorists and describe their theories of career counseling
- Evaluate the strengths and weaknesses of different career counseling approaches
- Discuss the value of understanding theories for the counselor
- Identify the current trends and issues in career development theories

HISTORICAL EVOLUTION OF CAREER GUIDANCE AND COUNSELING

It is difficult to pinpoint with accuracy when individual or group career guidance and counseling services were first provided through a recognized institution. The division of labor occurring in industry, the growth of industrial technology, the spread of democratic forms of government within the United States, and the evolution of the public school system during the period 1850 to 1900 created a need in American schools to help young people determine what type of career path they wished to follow. Another contributing factor was the development of vocational education within the old classical academy or public school.

In the post–Civil War period from 1865 to 1900, the United States witnessed the most rapid growth of urbanization and industrial development than any time period prior. In essence, the Industrial Revolution ushered in a need for all major industries to find workers who had certain skills and aptitudes to perform well and successfully in various occupations. There were also an increasing number of conflicts in the urban areas with wave after wave of immigrants arriving from various foreign countries—the attendant social problems that occur when people are crowded into neighborhoods that lacked the social services to assist them in achieving personal fulfillment.

An accompanying issue was the abuse of children in the labor force. Some estimates indicate that in 1900 over 500,000 boys and 200,000 girls in the 10-to-13 age bracket were employed in the factories of the United States. To counteract this abuse, a number of states began to establish minimum age laws as early as 1848 (Pennsylvania). The absence of clearly identified career counseling centers with staff skilled in testing and career assessment was a critical variable. Young people had no referral sources to seek career counseling and find help in dealing with issues of child abuse in the labor force. Public schools lacked the specialized staff to assist young people with issues of career planning, personal problems, and adjustment to adulthood. In short, children who were abused by the labor market system had few sources of personal or career counseling to turn to for help.

Frank Parsons, who is often considered the father of vocational guidance, is regarded as a major voice in the development of early efforts to provide career counseling. Parsons worked in the Boston area and was extremely concerned about the lack of assistance provided young people in determining what type of career path to follow. Parsons described career counseling in 1909 as the analysis of the individual, the study of occupational information, and counseling. As conceived at this early date, career counseling consisted of individual analysis by means of questionnaires and interviews in order to ascertain the nature of a person's abilities, interests, and background. It is from these humble beginnings that we have witnessed a truly staggering evolution of career counseling and guidance services that range from work in preschool to comprehensive programs in grades K–12 and a variety of efforts at the postsecondary level.

As a result of Parsons's work, the first national conference on vocational guidance was held in Boston in 1910. A number of prominent speakers, including Charles W. Elliott, president of Harvard University, emphasized a need for school personnel who had an interest in guidance. An increasing number of publications dealing with worker productivity in the industrial sector occurred as a result.

From 1900 to 1940, there was an increasingly strong interest in measurement and its relationship to career guidance efforts. James Cattell's work was influential in studying individual differences. There was interest in testing individual abilities as they relate to large groups of people who were being selected for military service and needed some type of classification and subsequent training. Within the industrial sector there was a correlated effort to assess people for their abilities and aptitudes as it related to job placement.

The period from 1900 to 1940 is often called the Measurement Period in the evolution of career guidance services due to the strong emphasis on intelligence, aptitude, and ability testing that evolved in both the private sector, institutions, and at the university level. The works of Lewis Terman, Louis Thurstone, Arthur Otis, and Robert Woodworth are exemplary examples of the testing movement. In 1928, Clark Hull published *Aptitude Testing*, which was devoted to the interpretation and use of aptitude test batteries for vocational guidance. It is this early identification of matching human traits with job requirements that became a cornerstone for the trait factor movement that characterized early career guidance efforts.

A number of federal initiatives also contributed to the development of the career guidance movement from 1917 to 1940. The Smith-Hughes Act (1917), the George Dean Act (1936), and the Wagner-Peyser Act (1933) were highly influential. In addition, the federal government established the Works Progress Administration (WPA) and a civilian conservation corps in the mid-1930s to provide employment for people during a period of national economic stagnation. In 1939, *The Dictionary of Occupational Titles* was published by the U.S. Employment Service, and this has continued to be a benchmark reference for those in the area of career guidance.

The evolution of career guidance continues from 1940 to the present with the development of a number of major counseling publications, significant federal programs, the evolution of career development theory, the development of career education, the professional training of school counselors and others, and advances in career technology. It is during this period that we note a variety of significant contributions by researchers such as Donald Super, David Tiedeman, E. G. Williamson, Carl Rogers, Eli Ginsberg, and John Holland, to cite a few. There also was a shift in the approach of career counseling from directive to nondirective and social/psychoeducational. We have also witnessed increasing professionalization of the counseling movement through the continued development of the current American Counseling Association and its attendant divisions. Considerable career emphasis is also located in state-related national occupational information coordinating committee with subsequent locations in each of the 50 states.

Career counseling and career guidance were developed to help individuals choose vocations, but it was recognized by leaders such as Herr, Drier, Hansen, and others that this was not enough. The mere imparting of career information did not address issues of psychological deviance, social problems, and other societal needs that plague people. As we move into the future and survey the past, we note a continual need commencing in the elementary school to provide students with experience in career planning, trying out occupational roles, understanding the role of work in our society, and developing responsible behavior patterns to help them be successful. At the junior high/middle schools, we have developed guidance programs that are more exploratory and focus on helping students develop basic work skills, develop decision-making skills, and have early field experience in the world of work. As students enter high school and prepare for postsecondary training and education, they need continued career exploration and to develop a portfolio of career skills as they explore the wide range of career options in our culture.

Although this brief summary does not tell of all of the major efforts that occurred in the last 100 years, it does provide a quick overview of the development of career counseling from a narrow focus of finding a job to a more substantial and extending concept of career counseling over the life span. In later chapters of this book, we provide suggestions for dealing with special populations, integrating career technology into counseling, and other trends and issues related to providing modern career counseling and guidance services.

CAREER COUNSELING AND DEVELOPMENT

Career counseling and development are processes in which counseling activities, strategies, and interventions are used to work with people who seek help in making career exploration, planning, and transition decisions. Career counseling and development consider both the people and the environments in which they learn and work. They facilitate positive and human change and recognize that family, community, school, and other sociocultural systems must be taken into account when working with individuals and groups. Counselors recognize that developmental change occurs within a cultural milieu that requires multicultural awareness of group and individual differences. Career counseling and development counselors use a holistic approach to assist the process of human development in schools, colleges, and human service agencies.

Career counseling and development professionals recognize and accept the importance of the educational-developmental model as a framework to guide their practice. On the national level, the change in the names of counseling organizations and the journals they publish reflect this model. The American Personnel and Guidance Association became the American Association for Counseling and Development in the 1980s and changed the title of its major journal to *Journal of Counseling and Development.* The *Vocational Guidance Quarterly* is now *The Career Development Quarterly,* a journal of the National Career Development Association. Ivey and Van Hesteren (1990) state that the counseling and development model is:

. . . holistic and considers both the physical (medical) and the mental health (psychological) models as important to education. Education (from the Latin *educare*) is about drawing out what is already there in the person or system. Development (from the Latin *dis* plus *villuppare*) concerns the gradual unfolding of what is the "germ" of a person. The educational-developmental model attempts to heal the mind/body split and recognize that individuals live and grow in families, groups, organizations, and cultures. The educational-developmental model is more ecological and focuses on interdependence of individuals and systems. (p. 534)

The core of career counseling and other behavioral sciences is the educational-developmental framework. Counselor educators advocate that developmental theories be one of the cornerstones of counselor training programs. Career counselors have the need to acquire and enhance their own developmental competencies and skills in this educational domain.

ROLE OF THEORY

In every discipline there are three dimensions that influence our behavior as practitioners. First, there are usually a number of theories that have been adopted or adapted from the social and behavioral sciences. Second, there is a research base. Third, there is a base of successful practices. Career counselors find that some of the theories have been adapted from other disciplines such as social learning theory, behavioral theory, psychoanalytical theory, and developmental theory. Career counselors can perform more effectively in a professional position if they have mastered the knowledge and theory on which that profession is based. Knowledge of theory, research, and practice leads to proficiency. Counselors need to have a repertory of skills and be able to select the most appropriate strategy for a given situation and know why they made the choice. They need to know what types of information sources would be most effective for a client and why.

Theories provide a framework for counselors to observe, collect, and organize data. They define parameters of what is important and structure how knowledge is organized. They guide individuals in the interpretation and understanding of the data of behaviors in question. Theories provide bridges between the phenomena observed and hypotheses to test and guide us in the predictions we have to make about individuals and behavior. Theories help us summarize and generalize a body of information on career development and decision making. They stimulate further research and exploration.

Some career development theories are not mature theories (Roe, 1956) and have gone through a number of changes (Super, 1984; Holland, 1985). Their data bases have been updated to reflect societal changes, such as the changing patterns of family and work. Some counselors feel that the value of theories has been overestimated. In the practical and real world technology has changed workers' as well as the counselors' roles. Computer guidance systems, for example, definitely have changed the role of the counselor in providing information. There are constraints in the workplace that limit the freedom of both counselors and clients in how they function and make decisions. For example, clients often lack access to current job openings in their community or region.

Some critics feel that the career development theories are limited and have numerous shortcomings, for example, not being relevant for minority groups and women. Theories sometimes focus on just narrow phases of the total process such as decision making or developmental stages. We stress holistic approaches and the need to look at total development and life choices rather than just career choice. Many career development theories fail to focus on differential aspects of the individual and the individual's total environment.

TYPE OF THEORIES

Career development and decision-making theories reviewed in this chapter are organized into three categories, presented in Table 1.1.

Social Science Theories

Sociology and economics are two of the social sciences that have explored work and career development. Hotchkiss and Borow (1990) point out that sociologists look at work from a social and institutional framework. They investigate such topics as the status hierarchy of the occupational culture. Sociological theories assign greater importance to institutional and impersonal market forces that constrain decision making and fulfillment of career decisions than the role of the individual in decision making. Sociologists are interested in institutional factors such as formal rules, norms, and supply-and-demand factors that affect the settings in which one works.

The Wisconsin Model developed by Sewell, Haller, and Ohlendorf (1970) and Blau and Duncan (1967) have developed status attainment theories. These status attainment models hypothesize that the parents' status affects the occupational level sought by their children. Parents and significant others affect the attitudes children have toward their education, career plans, and occupational status level. Mental ability is also included as a component in some models.

The process of career development can also be viewed from an economic framework (Ginzberg, 1972). Human capital research suggests that individuals invest in their own productivity similar to the way investments of physical capital are made. Individuals make investment decisions such as going to college or technical school that affect not only their current earnings but also future earnings. People also spend money on noneducational factors such as moving to another geographical area of the country because they hope to improve their earning power. Individuals attempt to maximize their productivity by matching their profile of skills and ability with those in the job market. The dualistic theory classifies businesses into two sectors, core and periphery. Large companies

TABLE 1.1
Structure of career development and decision-making theories

Category	Example	Basic Tenants
Social science	Economic	Choice is a function of supply and demand; knowledge of the workers, of opportunities, and job outlook; ability; and the availability of training.
	Sociological	External forces such as social background, number of job openings, monetary rewards, and so on influence the career choices people make.
	Chance and Accident	Chance and accidental happenings are the major source of most occupational decisions.
Psychology of Interpersonal Differences	Appraisal	Individual differences in aptitudes, skills, achievement, and personality exist and can be measured. Jobs require certain traits and skills. Best choice requires a match between individual and job characteristics. It is important to match a person's interest and abilities with the environment of the job.
	Developmental	Career decisions take place a number of times during the course of one's life. Career decisions begin in childhood and end in late adulthood.
	Personality	Career choice is a function of one's personality. Personality dynamics such as needs and motives affect choice. Occupations are an expression of one's personality.
Psychology of Learning	Cognitive	Counselors need to focus on information processing and the structure of knowledge. Cognitive structure of the individual defines how one views oneself, others, and the environment. The way one thinks determines how one behaves.
	Decision Making	Decision making is related to one's ego and value development and decision-making ability. Counselors need to help individuals see decision-making activities in the proper perspective and to think out their decisions.
	Social Learning	Career decisions are made through reinforcement, modeling, and contiguous pairing. Learning leads one to make occupational choices, not interests.

belong to the core sector and offer higher wages, job stability, and opportunity for advancement, and periphery firms are small and do not provide the same level of benefits. Salaries tend to be lower and the risk of unemployment high.

Race and gender are also important job-finding variables. Both have an effect on the salaries individuals make and their level of employment. Minorities hold a large percentage of low-status jobs and earn less than whites. Women find employment in a more limited band of occupations and make lower salaries than men. However, intensified career counseling efforts have opened career doors for women and minorities through improved personal assessment, job search strategies, and enhancing educational skills.

Some sociologists such as Miller and Form (1951) feel that chance enters into how most occupational choices are made. Because many people follow no set pattern in their career history, chance seems to help explain the progression from one job to another.

Psychology of Interpersonal Differences Theories

Trait-and-Factor Theory

The trait-and-factor theory has been one of the major theories used in career counseling. Frank Parsons (1909)—considered the father of the trait-and-factor theory—felt that there were three factors needed to make a wise vocational choice. First, individuals needed to have a clear understanding of themselves, their aptitudes, abilities, interests, ambitions, resources, limitations and causes. Second, they need to know the requirements and conditions of success, advantages and disadvantages, compensation, opportunities, and prospects in different lines of work. Third, they needed to explore the relationship between their knowledge of themselves and their knowledge of different jobs.

There were others who were influenced by Parsons's ideas. D. G. Paterson was very much involved in designing instruments to help individuals gain an understanding of their aptitudes and abilities. Paterson and his associates developed tests such as the Minnesota Rate of Manipulation test and the Minnesota Test of Spatial Relations. The group also published books on assessment procedures and counseling techniques.

There is some disagreement among measurement experts and psychologists about what traits are. Traits were defined as enduring psychic and neurological structures located in the mind (Hogan, DeSoto, & Solano, 1977). Other well-known trait theorists include R. B. Cattell, H. Eysenck, J. P. Guilford, and H. Murray.

The terms *factor* and *trait* were often used interchangeably. There are also terms used to describe the construct validity of standardized tests. Some developmental psychologists feel that traits are learned not inherited. Regardless, a number of traits appear to be stable over time.

The trait-and-factor method is based on assumptions such as the following:

- Individuals have a unique set of traits that have validity and reliability.
- There are patterns of traits necessary for success in a given field.
- To be successful on a job the worker has to have the pattern of traits required by the job.

The closer the match among the three sets of requirements, the greater the chance for job satisfaction and productivity.

Williamson (1939) advocated a six-step counseling process:

1. Analysis
2. Synthesis
3. Diagnosis
4. Prognosis
5. Counseling
6. Follow-up

This model was in vogue up through the sixties and has been gradually replaced by more client-centered approaches, such as a verbal process model.

The counselor collects data about the client and synthesizes or organizes the data. Usually tests, inventories, and questioning take place and provide information on the interest, aptitudes, and achievement of the client. Diagnosis involves identifying the strengths and weaknesses in order to identify the client's problem and to discover the possible causes. Prognosis is used to predict the degree of success the client might have. The question asked is How successful will the client be in achieving his or her vocational goals?

Williamson advocated the use of a variety of counseling techniques. For clients who were making unwise choices, the counselor should recommend that the client not make the choice and advocate alternative choices. The counselor might need to teach the client decision-making skills. For clients with no occupational choice, the counselor should administer interest inventories and provide occupational information and some direct advice. The counselor should ask the client to respond and react to a number of occupational choices. If there is a discrepancy between aptitudes and interests, the counselor is expected to assist the client in thinking of alternative approaches.

The counselor encourages the client to discover more about jobs by seeking information sources, field trips, and interviews with workers in the fields being considered. Self-awareness is aided by the use of tests and assessment instruments as well as interactions with the counselor. The counselor assumes the role of teacher at times and provides instruction in decision-making strategies.

Testing is an important component of the trait-and-factor approach. Counselors guide clients in normative interpretations of the results. Clients can, for example, compare their performance or scores to national and local norms and make certain judgments about the possibilities of success in an educational program. Trait-and-factor counselors tend to use actuarial approaches, predictions based on the relationships between the scores of the client and workers in the field being compared.

Personality and Career Choice

One of the theorists who has postulated that there is a relationship between personality theory and occupational classification is Anne Roe (Roe & Lunneborg, 1984), who stated that her "purpose has been to view the whole range of occupations in terms of their relationship to individual differences in backgrounds, physical and psychological variables, and experiences" (p. 31). She found Maslow's (1954) hierarchy of needs to be a useful approach for personality theory because it provided a framework to discuss the relevance of occupations to the satisfaction of basic needs, in short, a need-theory approach to career counseling and choice.

The eight levels of Maslow's hierarchy are as follows:

1. Physiological needs
2. Safety needs
3. Need for belongingness and love
4. Need for importance, respect, self-esteem, and independence
5. Need for information
6. Need for understanding
7. Need for beauty
8. Need for self-actualization

Roe found that the standard occupational classification systems were confusing and overlapping and did not have a psychological basis. She developed groups of occupations that could be arranged on a continuum based on the intensity and nature of interpersonal relationships. She developed eight groups (which are described in Chapter 2): Service, Business Contact, Organization, Technology, Outdoor, Science, General Culture, and Arts and Entertainment. She included six levels in each group based on the degree of responsibility, capacity, and skill required.

The theory is a two-level approach to career counseling. The first level relates to five propositions on the origin of interests and needs and the second level to how the basic needs are affected by childhood experiences. The propositions deal with genetic inheritance, the influence of experiences, and the patterns of how interests, attitudes, and other personality patterns are developed. Roe postulates that the eventual pattern of psychic energies in terms of attention directedness, is the major determinant of interests. She believes that the intensity of these needs and of their satisfaction and their organization are the major determinants of the degree of motivation that reaches expression in career accomplishment.

Roe hypothesizes that there are two basic orientations, either toward or not toward persons. This orientation is formed by early childhood experiences. Career choice is influenced by the orientations developed in early childhood.

Roe does not specifically address the role of the counselor in career development. If her propositions were supported by research evidence, then parenting classes would have to address career choice practices and values held by parents.

Discussions of parental career needs and how this is transferred to children would require class discussion and analysis. The research base to support Roe's contentions is sparse at this time throughout the career literature.

It is interesting to note that many approaches to career education have objectives related to parent involvement. In self-assessment, counselors should explore the need structure of clients and use this type of information to help clients find satisfying jobs. Roe and Lunneborg (1990) conclude that economic and chance factors are important determiners in career decision making. Counselors need to consider using the labor market materials and approaches that have been developed and put more emphasis on entrepreneurship and possibly risk taking in working with clients.

A Theory of Vocational Personalities: John Holland

Holland (1985) states that his theory of vocational personalities provides explanations for three common and fundamental questions:

1. What personal and environmental characteristics lead to satisfying career decisions, involvement, and achievement, and what characteristics lead to indecision, dissatisfying decisions, or lack of accomplishments?
2. What personal and environmental characteristics lead to stability or change in the kind of level and work a person performs over a lifetime.
3. What are the most effective methods for providing assistance to people with career problems? (p. 1)

Holland thinks the primary concern of his theory is to explain vocational behavior and to suggest to individuals across all levels how to select jobs, change jobs, and attain vocational satisfaction. His theory also focuses on personal competence, educational and social behavior, and personality.

Holland sees personality type as a model against which counselors can measure individuals. He identifies six types:

1. Realistic
2. Investigative
3. Artistic
4. Social
5. Enterprising
6. Conventional

Types are viewed as a product of interaction among culture, personal views, peers, biology, parents, social class, and the physical environment by individuals as they grow. The interests and competencies of individuals create a personal disposition that leads them to think, perceive, and act in certain ways. Individuals have a characteristic repertoire of attitudes and skills for coping with environmental problems and tasks. Holland feels that individuals foster certain environmental influences and reject others. He feels that each type of environment is dominated by a given type of personality, and the environment presents opportunities as well as problems. Individuals tend to seek environments and individuals congruent with their own interests, competencies and perceptions.

Individuals tend to seek environments that will let them exercise their skills and abilities, express their attitudes and values and assume roles and problems that are agreeable to them. From the individual's personality types, counselors could predict the individual's choice of occupations, educational and social behavior, and competencies and achievements.

Second, Holland (1985) assessed assumptions relate to consistency, differentiation, identity, congruence, and calculus. Holland points out that within a person or an environment, some pairs of type are more closely related to each other than others. Realistic and investigative personalities are more closely related or consistent than conventional and artistic. Differentiation of environments or persons who are more clearly defined than others needs to be considered. Some individuals resemble all of the six types and others more closely resemble one type. The same applies to environments, which might be dominated by a single type.

Third, identity provides an estimate of the clarity and stability of an individual's identity. Some clients have a clear and stable picture of their goals, interests, and talents. Some organizations and environments have clear, integrated goals, tasks, and rewards that are stable over time.

Congruencies relate to one of the six types preferring a consistent environment that meets their personal needs. Incongruence happens when individuals are in an environment foreign to their preferences and abilities. This type of mismatch often results in worker dissatisfaction with the current job.

To Holland, calculus describes the relationships between and within types of environments. Holland used a hexagonal modal to represent the relationships among the six types.

Principles   Holland (1985) postulates that the choice of a vocation is an expression of personality. His second postulate is that interest inventories are personality inventories. Vocational interests are an expression of personality. Third, vocational stereotypes have reliable and important psychological and sociological meanings. Holland claims that interest inventories are based on the assumption that individuals perceive occupations and the activities required by the occupation are relatively the same over time. Fourth, workers within a given vocation have similar histories of personal development. Fifth, people within a vocational group will react and respond to situations and problems in a similar way. Sixth, vocational satisfaction, stability, and achievement depend on the congruence between the individual's personality and the environment in which he or she works.

Holland's theory is not developmental, but he believes that a child's interaction with environmental influences assists in developing an increasing differentiation among preferred activities, interests, competencies, and values, which leads to the development of personality type. No discussion is given to how or when this takes place but it is a blending of self-concept, perceptions of the environment, values, achievement and performance, differential reaction to environmental rewards and stresses, preference for occupation and occupational role, coping style, personality traits, and repertories of skills. The types are presented in Table 1.2.

Holland's Classification   Holland's system of classification is used to classify people, occupations, or environments as types or substyles. Individuals are assessed by completing the Self-Directed Search or the Vocational Preference

TABLE 1.2
Holland's personality types

Type	Descriptors	Values
Realistic	Asocial, conforming, frank, genuine, hard-headed, inflexible, materialistic, natural, normal, persistent, practical, self-effacing, thrifty, uninsightful, uninvolved	Money, power, status
Investigative	Analytical, cautious, complex, critical, curious, independent, intellectual, introspective, pessimistic, precise, rational, reserved, retiring, unassuming, unpopular	Scientific and mathematical abilities
Artistic	Acting, artistic, complicated, disorderly, emotional, expressive, idealistic, imaginative, impractical, impulsive, independent, introspective, intuitive, musical, nonconforming, open, original, sensitive, speaking-oriented, writing-oriented	Aesthetic qualities
Social	Ascendant, cooperative, empathetic, friendly, generous, helpful, idealistic, kind, patient, persuasive, responsible, sociable, tactful, teaching-oriented, understanding, warm	Social, ethical
Enterprising	Acquisitive, adventurous, agreeable, ambitious, domineering, energetic, excitement-seeking, exhibitionistic, extroverted, flirtatious, likes to lead, optimistic, self-confident, sociable, talkative, speaking	Political, economic
Conventional	Careful, clerical, conforming, conscientious, defensive, efficient, inflexible, inhibited, methodical, numerical, obedient, orderly, persistent, practical, prudish, thrifty, unimaginative	Business, economic, achievement

Inventory or the Strong Interest Inventory, and the highest rank or score becomes the primary code, the next becomes the second highest, and then the third. The letters of the three highest types are used.

Occupations are also classified by the three-letter codes. For example, actor/actress is ASE, which means that the actor or actress most resembles people in the artistic occupations, the social occupations somewhat less, and the enterprising scales still less.

Some examples of selected occupations with the specific occupational code by the realistic type are included in Figure 1.1.

Psychodynamic Model of Career Choice: Edward S. Bordin

Bordin (1984) proposes a psychodynamic theory that proposes that the participation of personality and work and career is rooted in the role of play in the human life. The spirit of play is correlated with spontaneity. There are seven major propositions in this theory that are of help to the practicing counselor.

1. This sense of wholeness, this experience of joy, is sought by all persons, preferably in all aspects of life, including work.
2. The degree of fusion of work and play is a function of an individual's developmental history regarding compulsion and effort.
3. A person's life can be seen as a string of career decisions reflecting the individual groping for an ideal fit between personal needs and work.

Type/Occupation/Dictionary of Occupations Classification/Educational Level

RIA   (Realistic, Investigative, Artistic), Dental technician, (712.381-018), 4
RIS   (Realistic, Investigative, Social), Baker, (526.381-010), 3
RIE   (Realistic, Investigative, Enterprising), Petroleum engineer, (010.061-018), 6
RIC   (Realistic, Investigative, Conventional), Piano tuner, (730.361-010), 4
RAI   (Realistic, Artistic, Investigative), Bookbinder, (977.381-010), 3
RSE   (Realistic, Social, Enterprising), Taxi driver, (913.463-018), 3
RSI   (Research, Social, Investigative), Appliance repairer, (637.261-018), 4
REC   (Realistic, Enterprising, Conventional), Supervisor, natural gas plant, (542.130-010), 4
REI   (Realistic, Enterprising, Investigative), Ship pilot, (197.133-026), 4
RES   (Realistic, Enterprising, Social), Fish and game warden, (379.167-010), 5
RCI   (Realistic, Conventional, Investigative), Carpenter, (860.381-022), 4
RCS   (Realistic, Conventional, Social), Bricklayer, (861.381-018), 3
RCE   (Realistic, Conventional, Enterprising), Tractor-trailer truck driver, (904.383-010) 3

FIGURE 1.1
Examples of occupations by type

4. The most useful system of mapping occupations for intrinsic motives will be one that captures life-styles or character styles and stimulates or is receptive to developmental conceptualizations.

5. The roots of the personal aspects of career development are to be found throughout the early development of the individual, sometimes in the earliest years.

6. Each individual seeks to build a personal identity that incorporates aspects of father and mother, yet retains elements unique to oneself.

7. Sources of perplexity and paralysis at career decision points will be found in doubts and dissatisfactions with current resolutions of self.

Compulsion in this context is defined as the internalization of external pressures. Effort is characterized by intensity and directedness. Compulsion and effort are related in that the greater the effort, the longer the activity endures and the stronger the psychological and physical pressure toward cessation and rest. As the individual matures, the more complex play becomes.

One of the key elements to Bordin's approach is to seek understanding at each turning point of a career path of what provides self-fulfillment for the individual. Work provides an outlet for sublimated wishes and impulses. Bordin, Nachmann, and Segal (1963) relied heavily on Freud's stages of psychosexual development and focus on the physiological and socially based sources of satisfaction.

Bordin (1984) states his approach is best applied to individual career counseling, but he also sees it as useful in self-awareness programs designed to aid individuals in exploring themselves and in decision making. He also sees his approach as having application to the work environment, in redesigning jobs to permit greater satisfaction and improving the quality of work life, and to aging and retirement issues.

Developmental Theories

Developmental theories are important to career counseling and development specialists because they provide a framework to describe, explain, and develop human behavior (Jepsen, 1990). Piaget's (1952) work, for example, provides a model for describing an individual's cognitive development. Erikson's (1963) theory of psychosocial development of the individual helps us to explain and understand the psychological development of the individual. As counselors, we seek to guide positive development and ask how the individual's capacities can be enhanced to overcome problems and make better life and career decisions. It is important that individuals be provided career assessment through counseling to clarify critical life stage needs, for example, transitions from high school to post-secondary education.

Baltes, Reese, and Lipsitt (1980) help us to remember the complexities of human development and remind us that human development is a lifelong process not just focused on infancy, childhood, or adolescence. Development can be viewed only by understanding the individual's past history, as people are influenced by the interactions and experiences with others during their lives. Development is complex and is influenced by factors both within and without the person. As Baltes, Reese, and Lipsitt (1980) point out, development in any one phase can be best understood in the context of the whole life span. As counselors, we need to know what factors influenced the present situation, for example, how individuals resolved each of their previous developmental crises.

The work of Storm, Bernard, and Storm (1987) summarizes the knowledge about development in a different manner, and reminds us that development is continuous and sequential. Growth follows a systematic and sequential process, and educational or occupational training can influence development. During development there are numerous factors that contribute to the formation of behavior and personality. Growth is a process of interaction between the organism and the environment and is most rapid during the early stages, birth to age 5. The drive to relieve tensions and maintain equilibrium affects development in several ways. For example, individuals have a drive for heterostatic activity as they like to explore, to learn about, and to satisfy their curiosity. People have the simultaneous and compatible processes of differentiation and integration.

Career and Life Development: Donald E. Super

Donald E. Super (1984) sees his efforts as a loosely unified set of theories dealing with specific aspects of career development, taken from developmental, differential, social, and phenomenological psychology, and held together by the self-concept or personal-construct theory. Super was influenced by the works of Buehler (1933) and Rogers (1951). Super distinguishes between a career and a vocation. A *career* is the sequence of things that a person does during the course of a life-time, which includes preoccupational, occupational, avocational, and postoccupational roles—all of the positions that a person occupies. A *vocation* is defined as something a person wants to do to earn a living.

Super (1953, 1957, 1984) has redefined his theoretical model, but it stills includes the following constructs:

- People differ in their abilities, interests, and personalities.
- People are qualified, by virtue of these characteristics, for a number of occupations.
- Each of these occupations requires a characteristic pattern of abilities, interests, and personality traits, with tolerances wide enough to allow both some variety of occupations for each individual and some variety of individuals in each occupation.
- Vocational preferences and competencies, the situations in which people live and work, and hence their self-concepts, change with time and experience, although self-concepts are generally fairly stable from late adolescence until late maturity, making choice and adjustment a continuous process.

- This process of change may be summed up in a series of life stages (or maxicycle) characterized as growth, explorations, establishment, maintenance, and decline, and these stages may in turn be subdivided into (1) the fantasy, tentative, and realistic phases of the exploratory stage and (2) the trial and stable phases of the establishment stage. A smaller cycle takes place in transitions from one stage to the next or each time an unstable or multiple-trial career is unstabilized, which involves new growth, reexploration, and reestablishment.
- The nature of the career pattern—that is, the occupational level attained and the sequence, frequency, and duration of trial and stable jobs—is determined by the individual's parents' socioeconomic level, mental ability, and personality characteristics, and by the opportunities to which he or she is exposed.
- Development through the life stages can be guided partly by facilitating the maturing of abilities and interests and partly by aiding in reality testing and in the development of self-concepts.
- The process of career development is essentially that of developing and implementing self-concepts; it is a synthesizing and compromising process in which the self-concept is a product of the interaction of inherited aptitudes, physical make-up, opportunity to play various roles, and evaluations of the extent to which the results of role-playing meet with the approval of superiors and fellows.
- The process of synthesis of or compromise between individual and social factors, between self-concept and reality, is one of role-playing, whether the role is played in fantasy, in the counseling interview, or in real-life activities such as classes, clubs, part-time work, and entry jobs.
- "Work satisfactions and life satisfactions depend on the extent to which the individual finds adequate outlets for abilities, interests, personality traits, and values; they depend on establishment in a type of work, a work situation, and a way of life in which one can play the kind of role that growth and exploratory experiences have led one to consider congenial and appropriate" (Super, 1953, pp. 189–190).
- The degree of satisfaction people attain from work is proportionate to the degree to which they have been able to implement self-concepts.
- "Work and occupation provide a focus for personality organization for most men and many women, although for some persons this focus is peripheral, incidental, or even nonexistent, and other foci, such as leisure activities and homemaking, are central" (Super & Bachrach, 1957, pp. 11–12). (Social traditions, such as sex-role stereotyping, racial and ethnic biases, and the opportunity structure as well as individual differences are important determinants of preferences for roles such as those of worker, leisurite, and homemaker.)

Developmental and Life Stage Career Theory   Super defines career maturity as the readiness to cope with the developmental tasks appropriate to one's life stage. Super (1957, 1963, 1981) has developed a model of life stages and sub-stages, which are presented in Table 1.3 for counselor use.

TABLE 1.3
Stages and substages of Super's developmental model

Stage	Age range	Substages
Birth/Growth	0/0–14	
	4–7	Fantasy
	7–11	Interest
	11–14	Capacity
	14–18	Tentative
Exploration	14–25	Trial transition
		Implementing
		Specifying
		Crystallizing
Establishment	25–40	
	25	Beginning of stabilization
	30–40	Advancement or frustration and consolidation
Maintenance	45–60	Innovation, stagnation, or updating
Decline	60–death	
	60	Beginning deceleration substage
	60–65	Specialization/disengagement or retirement
		Planning and living

Super (1980) melded the concept of life stages and role theory to a Life-Career-Rainbow synthesis. The outer perimeter of the arc represents the life stages and ages and the inner part of the rainbow represents the major roles and individual plays. There are six roles: child, student, leisurite, citizen, worker, and homemaker. These roles vary in importance from one stage to another, and their relative importance is indicated by two dimensional bar type graphic representation.

Super (Super & Thompson, 1981) states ages at each transition point are flexible, and the possibility of recycling through a stage does exist. The life stages are growth, exploration, establishment, maintenance, and decline. For example, in moving from birth to older adulthood we progress through the following stages:

Early adulthood
Growth—learning to relate to others
Exploration—finding opportunity to do desired work
Establishment—settling down in a permanent position
Maintenance—making occupational position secure
Decline—reducing sports participation

The self-concept portion of this theory is essentially a matching theory in which individuals look at their own attributes and the attributes required by the occupations. Super's self-concept construct is developmental and fashioned through the exploratory activities that help provide feedback to the individual.

Super (1984) sees the application of theory to education, assessment, and counseling. He sees career development theory as being the foundation for any career education program. Super has made important contributions to career assessment and has authored a variety of career inventories such as the *Career Development Inventory, Work Values Inventory, Adult Career Concerns Inventory,* the *Values Scale,* and *The Salience Inventory.* His tests have been developed to assess career maturity, work salience, and work values.

Psychology of Learning Theories

Cognitive Approaches

In addition to roots in developmental psychology, career counseling and development has roots in developmental psychology and has ties to cognitive psychology. Van Hestern and Ivey (1990) state the cognitive viewpoint in their work as the following:

> The theoretical orientation bringing this group together is grounded in the belief that each person constructs his or her thoughts, meanings, and behaviors in a unique fashion over time. Within this perspective, personal developmental history over the life span is assumed to deeply influence how the individual (or family/community) makes sense of experience and how meaning structures are translated into behavioral action. (p. 526)

Huffman and Nead (1983) advocate a general contextual approach in the cognitive sciences. As this approach is translated to the field of career counseling and development, counselors need to focus on the total counseling sequence in which the client is involved. We have to look at the situational demands, the characteristics of the client and counselor, developmental perspectives, contextual aspects, family, community, group membership, the counseling intervention, and the purposes of the client. The contextual approach requires careful analysis of environmental influences and their impact on client behavior.

Cognitive Models

Knefelkemp and Slepitza (1976) propose a cognitive developmental model of career development. The theory emphasizes the cognitive processing that takes place as individuals' develop. They include four stages in their model:

1. Dualism—Students think that there is only one right career.
2. Multiplicity—Students recognize that they are capable of entering several career fields.

3. Relativism—Individuals move from an external focus of control to a more internal focus of control. They now recognize that they are the ones responsible for making their decisions but are not just ready to make a final commitment.
4. Relativism with commitment—Students become concerned about their identity and making a commitment.

Decision Making

Tiedeman and O'Hara (1963) have postulated a vocational decision-making model of career development. They note that career development grows out of a continuous differentiating and reintegrating of ego identity as it forms and re-forms from experience. It is influenced by an individual's early childhood experiences with the family unit, the resolution of psychosocial crises, and the consistency between societal values and ideas and those of the individual.

They propose a two-stage decision-making process: anticipation and implementation. Each of the stages has several phases. The four steps of anticipation or preoccupation are exploration (awareness), crystallization (of something), choice (felt being), and clarification (objectification). The implementation stage has three steps: induction, reformation, and reintegration.

Tiedeman and Miller-Tiedeman (1984) illustrate the process by a counselor who is feeling burned out and is exploring new job possibilities.

1. *Exploration*
    Talking with people
    Visiting potential workplaces
    Conducting information interviews
    Reading everything available on possibilities
    Thinking about new places to live
2. *Crystallization*
    Seeing patterns evolve in form of alternatives and their consequences, ordering and considering the information
3. *Choice*
    Making a choice from the alternatives
4. *Clarification*
    Organizing and clarifying the decision
5. *Induction*
    Beginning to work at choice
6. *Reformation*
    Feeling good about doing it
    Getting proficient at the work
7. *Reintegration*
    Advocating the choice

They consider the seven steps in their decision-making process as neither instantaneous nor irreversible. They postulate that career development occurs not only with one decision but also as the result of many decisions, and that how persons make decisions influences their actions in decisions they are currently making, or making in the future, or have made in the past.

They find that individuals are presented with stress or change points in their life that present them with problems to be solved, such as selecting a part-time job while in school and afterward, selecting courses in junior or senior high school, selecting a college, junior college, or technical school, or selecting their first full-time position. Tiedeman's theory has been integrated into career-information services through books and curriculum materials to help individuals in decision making. For example, Tiedeman developed a paradigm to assist counselors in leading clients through problem solving. This paradigm includes *anticipation* (exploration, crystallization, choice, and clarification) and *adjustment* (induction, reformation, and integration). Suggested interpretations are provided for each stage of the paradigm, for example, choice—a career goal is chosen and behaviors to attain the goal specified. There are other decision-making models. Gelatt (1962) has a model that takes into consideration the cyclical nature of decision making as well as the sequence. He considers decision making as a continuous process ranging from immediate to intermediate to future decisions.

Social Learning Theory

Krumboltz, Mitchell, and Gelatt (1975) developed a theory of career choice based on social learning theory. Their theory emphasizes four factors: genetic endowments and special abilities, environmental conditions and events, learning experiences, and task-approach skills. The theory also draws on cognitive learning theory and looks at the role of cognitive processes such as problem solving. Individuals' learning experiences over their life-span development have a direct influence on their occupational decisions and career selection, especially their learning through observation of models and other direct experiences. Career decision making is a product of the individual's learning. Career-education programs, instruction in decision making, and the counselor's role are important in this approach.

Clients need help in career decision making. Many have made decisions based on faulty beliefs and generalizations and unrealistic expectations. They do not know all their alternatives and tend to use approaches that they have used in prior job search situations.

CONTEXTUAL MODEL OF CAREER COUNSELING

Career counseling and development involve the use of cognitive processes and information processing (Peterson, Sampson, & Reardon, 1991). Counselors can apply the model in Figure 1.2 to develop a career counseling process for clients with different career needs.

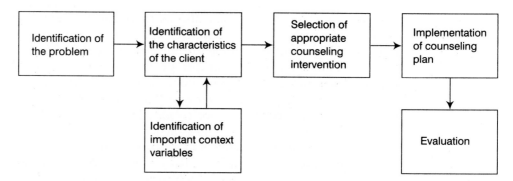

FIGURE 1.2
Contextual Model of career counseling procedures

The model illustrates a framework to review the career counseling process and implement a plan for human growth. The first step is the identification of the problem. A client might state a variety of problems ranging from the complex to the simple. The problems might be psychological as well as career problems, and the stated problem might not be the real problem. In any event, the counselor needs to have a clear understanding of the problem or problems of the client.

The second step is to identify the salient characteristics of the client. Characteristics of the individual that might influence the strategy and types of intervention to be used are age, gender, cultural background, role salience, values, cognitive level, self-concept, work history, personality traits and types, motivation, needs, learning styles, and employment status. The counselor must know not only the stages of cognitive, psychological, and career development of the client, but also the important life experiences that have shaped the individual's perceptions and attitudes. Niemeyer, Pritchard, Berzonsky, and Metzler (1991) stated that clients' characteristic way of approaching problems influences their vocational exploration.

The third step requires the counselor to identify the important context variable. Variables to be considered are labor market information, local/regional, and state employment trends, educational and training programs available, as well as socioeconomic level of the community, environmental and climatic preferences, and type of opportunities available in the community. The counselor needs to be familiar with the industries and institutions in the region. The problem might relate to job enrichment, job redefinition, or person-environment-fit as it relates to career planning.

The fourth step involves the selection of the most appropriate counseling strategy or intervention. The previous three steps influence what takes place in this step, and counselors have a wide range of theories and practices that are appropriate for career counseling. They also have a wide variety of sources of information available to them. For example, continuing educational opportunities, interaction with colleagues, and professional literature provide a variety of approaches and successful practices. The spectrum covers counselor-free, computer-assisted counseling approaches to counselor-led interventions.

The fifth step is using the information from the previous steps to implement a counseling plan. The sixth step is evaluation, which can be used in each step of the process not only in determining whether the intervention brought about the desired outcomes but also whether the counselor identified the real problem. Other questions that can be answered are as follows:

Did the counselor identify the salient characteristics of the client?
Did the counselor identify the important context variables?
What was the client's perspective of the counseling?
What cognitive processes were used? Were they effective?
Was a plan of career action implemented?

STAGES OF COUNSELING

The counselor can also examine the career counseling process in terms of stages. Three stages are pictured in Figure 1.3.

Before Counseling

Two of counselors' major tasks before career counseling are first, to have a good understanding of the characteristics and needs of the clients they are working with, and second, to have knowledge of labor market information. The counselor needs to be familiar with appropriate assessment instruments and techniques and have knowledge of the available literature and information sources.

The counselor wants to choose the most appropriate mode of input in order that the information is easily encoded. If information is needed to expand the client's knowledge and understanding or to challenge irrational beliefs, it first has to be encoded in the client's memory.

There are many examples of specific skills that the client might need to learn, such as interviewing and writing resumes or where the responses or behaviors must become a part of the client's repertoire. The learning requires the use of repetition, contiguity, rehearsal and reproductive phases. The attitudes, skills, or behavior to be learned have to become a part of the client's self-regulatory behavior. Besides consideration of the appropriate mode of intervention, the counselor needs to focus the attention of the client on the goals and objectives in the counseling plan. The counselor works at identifying the client's needs and

Stage 1   Stage 2   Stage 3
Before Counseling _____ During Counseling _____ After Counseling

FIGURE 1.3
Stages of career counseling

decides what incentives are motivating for the client. The counselor works to enhance the self-concept of the client.

During Counseling

The counselor identifies the client's problem during the initial session. In order to proceed, the counselor needs to know what goals and objectives need to be accomplished and to establish a work plan. Counselors assess developmental characteristics of the client with whom they are working. The counselor recognizes that there are different strands of human development—the biological, the cognitive, and the social—that are interwoven to make up an integrated person. The counselor, in choosing the most appropriate counseling intervention, recognizes that any counseling plan has to take into consideration the client's socioeconomic status, educational level, age, gender, and cultural background.

A holistic picture of the client is gained through additional knowledge of the values, role salience, self-concept, personality type, stage of career, and psychosocial development of the client. The client's job history, educational level, and family situation are important practical issues in deciding what type of intervention is to be used. Some issues are the cost, time restraints, number of clients to be served, and type of resources available, for example, computer guidance systems. Family variables are important, too. Some family theorists say we are what our families are; factors such as divorce and separation have had an effect on the family. The number of single-parent families is increasing and will call for different career counseling strategies. Jepsen (1991) states that developmental counselors listen for indications of the general roles and purposes clients are trying to fulfill and acquire a general sense of where they are in their career development.

Counselors need to integrate the information about clients, the economic trends, labor market forecasts, and the important context variables and decide the type of counseling intervention that they feel will be most effective. The counselor recognizes the limitations of the current theories, practices, and research in career counseling. As we attempt to summarize the variety of reports that have focused on these issues, some sense of direction seems to emerge. It is important to consider our role in a global community and to recognize that solutions to a variety of problems are not the responsibility of the counselor in isolation, but will require a multiteam approach.

After Counseling

After counseling, it is necessary to evaluate what occurred during the sessions. The clients can provide an immediate assessment of the value they see from the counseling and what they plan to do. Counselors can evaluate their success by asking whether the goals and objectives of the intervention were met. The final test, however, is what did the client do as a result of the intervention. For example, was there positive human development? Did the individual have a greater knowledge of the different occupational fields available? Did the client make an appropriate career choice? Was the client successful in writing a resume, improving her interviewing skills, getting and keeping a job, gaining admission to a school or training program?

INFORMATION PROCESSING APPROACHES

Career counseling and development involves information processing and includes several stages: Input and Information, Encoding and Attention, Memory and Thinking, and Language and Behavior. The information-processing model presented in Figure 1.4 consists of four phases.

Input and Information

Counseling can be thought of as a component of the learning process and a process to guide learning. The counselor decides the most effective way of inputting the information to clients for their decision or action. It could be learning about jobs in other fields that require the same types of skills that their present positions require or the best direction for career change. Will the counselor select a computerized guidance system such as CHOICES, GIS, or DISCOVER? Will the counselor suggest job shadowing or scheduling an interview with a successful worker in a given field? Will the counselor schedule the client to participate in a group to discuss job change and work together as a team? Will the counselor use assessment instruments to help clients understand themselves? Or will the counselor suggest clients read career guides and self-help books? The text, *What Color Is Your Parachute* (Bolles, 1991), has proved very popular as a self-help career guide and is recommended. As you can see, there are varied approaches to input information.

Encoding and Attention

Information has to be encoded to be used. The input has to get the client's attention. The individual's needs influence how the individual perceives the information source. For example, it may be hard to get persons who have been

Input ——— Information	Encoding ——— Attention	Memory ——— Thinking	Language Behavior
Phase 1	Phase 2	Phase 3	Phase 4

FIGURE 1.4
Learning phases of career counseling

unemployed to look at values and self-awareness when their self-concept is low and they are faced with seeking food, shelter, and safety.

Clients differ in their learning styles and in how they process information. Keefe and Languis's (1983) definition of learning style can be adapted for counseling situations. They define learning styles as the composite of characteristic cognitive, affective, and physiological factors that serve as relatively stable indicators of how a client perceives, interacts with, and responds to the counseling environment. Cognitive styles reflect the information-processing strategies of the individual, how the individual perceives, thinks, remembers, and solves problems. Attention, expectancy, and incentive help arouse, direct, and sustain the individual's behavior. Physiological styles are biologically based modes of response such as personal nutrition and health and reactions to the physical environment.

Individuals have different perceptual preferences. Some prefer auditory and verbal modes, others prefer visual or spatial modes, and still others prefer tactile or kinesthetic modes. Therefore, individuals react differently to various types of counseling interventions. For example, some may prefer to read about jobs and others may prefer to interview persons who are working on that job. Another preference may be to complete a job shadow to see if they like the type of job. Some people may be selective listeners and are not able to process oral or auditory information correctly. Clients need to develop a readiness to attend and to receive information. Career research suggests clients perform better in processing information if they see that the information is important to them and to their immediate needs.

Memory and Thinking

Cognitive and affective input has to be encoded into long-term memory and used to be effective. The information has to be organized in order to be stored. Individuals tend to speak to themselves in internal dialogues and in images, fantasy, and dreams based on the experiences they have stored in their memory. They also have learned physiological reactions to different situations. For example, certain situations might cause people fear, anxiety, or stress. Both the cognitive and affective input affect not only the content of our thinking but also the process of our thinking. Clients may have irrational beliefs or faulty thinking styles and arrive at erroneous conclusions; selective attention based on isolated experiences; conclusions based on one or more isolated incidents; overgeneralizing, magnifying, and distorting the processing of an event; and relating events to oneself when there is no basis for the association or connection. People also use dichotomous thinking (right, wrong; good, bad). Counselors need to check on the validity of the information the client has memorized. Thinking is also influenced by learning style. Corcos and McChesney (1991) utilized Kolb's (1984) model, which is based on two major dimensions: concrete experience versus abstract conceptualization and active experimentation versus reflective observation. Four types of learners emerge: accommodators, divergers, convergers, and assimilators. In career decision making, accommodators might prefer to be out on job tryouts or cooperatively exploring and exposing themselves to new experiences.

Language and Behavior

The ultimate goal of the career counseling intervention is to develop or change the behavior of clients so they accomplish the goals agreed on by them and their counselor. Clients are guided to act on the basis of the intervention. For example, the self-language needs to be changed for some people from "I can't do anything right" to "I can do what I set out to do." Clients might have a surface knowledge of what to do, say, and behave in an interview session but now have to practice through role-playing interview situations so that the behavior becomes natural. If the client has irrational beliefs, thought processes, or decision-making skills, more appropriate cognitive beliefs and strategies have to be substituted and practiced. Clients are guided so that they develop proficiency in the new processes. They need to rehearse by using imagery and modeling.

ISSUES AND TRENDS

There have been a number of issues raised about the validity of the theories of career choice and development. Some of the major issues are the following:

- Are the theories applicable to minority groups, women, and the poor?
- Are we overemphasizing career aspects of life and not focusing on the total individual?
- Are theories rather static because they are not reflecting the changes in our society—for example the role of women, corporate takeovers, the labor market, and so on?
- Are the theories practical and useful to counselors in their day to day work? Are there assessment instruments, modules, manuals, and computerized software for participants and counselors?
- Do the theories take into consideration the chance factors as well as the sociological factors?
- Are the theories valid? Can you translate the postulates into hypotheses that can be tested?
- Are the theories practical? Can the principles be related to counseling strategies and supportive materials that help the individual?

The theories appear to reflect the prevailing trends in the behavioral sciences. Current theories by researchers such as Knefelkemp and Slepitza (1976) and Krumboltz (1979) were influenced by cognitive psychology. Roe and Lunneborg (1990) and Bordin (1990) were influenced in part by the psychodynamic movement. Super (1984) was influenced by both the trait-and-factor psychologists and the life-span developmentalists. Holland (1985) is called by some a neo-trait-and-factor psychologist. The theorists were also influenced by the prevailing work and economic situations of their times. Choosing a career for one's lifetime is no longer the mode as it was at the time Ginzberg, Ginsburg, Axelrad, and Herma (1951) and Super (1957) originally proposed their theories. The family situation has changed dramatically in our society from when Roe (1956) developed her theory.

The strengths and weaknesses of these theories are compared in Table 1.4.

SUMMARY

Certain basic assumptions are integrated within this text. First, counselors need to have a life-span developmental focus. They need to know as much as possible

TABLE 1.4
Strengths and weaknesses of selected career development theories

Theory	Strengths	Weaknesses
Ginzberg, Sociological	Helps explain external factors in career development	Does not explain why same factors have different effects on different individuals
Roe, Need	System for classifying occupations	Difficult to research
Holland, Birds of a feather	Easily understood Broad research base Has useful assessment instruments	Does not explain process of career choice Deals primarily with external factors Does not explain how types are developed
Williamson, Trait and factor	Stimulated work in measurement Statistical prediction better than clinical prediction Large research base Basis for DOT	Too cognitive and mechanistic Valid instruments not always available for minority groups. Does not explain process of career choice
Super, Self-concept components	Comprehensive theory Availability of assessment instruments Provides explanation of the birth to death process of career development	Consists of a number of constructs that are not well integrated
Krumboltz, Social learning	Explains constructs well Has developed materials Integrates economic and social factors	Theory not developmental More emphasis on choice than on adjustment Research base needs to be longitudinal

about the characteristics and behavior of people at all age levels—not just the one at which they expect to be working. They often have to work with the family, as well as the worker, and the parents, as well as the students. Understanding the past development of the client helps us to develop insight regarding the current developmental stage of the client. The focus of counseling and development has to be on the total person, including the cognitive, social, emotional, psychological, biological, and career-development stages. Counselors have to work with the total person. Work and career are only one part of the individual's world and are not highly valued by all individuals.

The counselor needs to know and understand local, national, and world labor markets and economic trends and projections. The counselor needs to recognize the changing nature of work and the work force as we move to a multicultural society. Hispanic, Asian, and African-American populations cannot be neglected as we plan career counseling programs in both rural and urban areas. As a multicultural society, and non-Hispanic counselors, for example, will need to be conversant with the language and culture of different cohort groups (Ryan, 1990).

Successful counselors will use a wide assortment of career strategies in both individual and group counseling to be successful. This may mean that we become increasingly *eclectic* in our approaches. We need to be up-to-date with information sources, career development theory and research, and decision-making and problem-solving strategies. We need to focus on action research and evaluation to see what theories, practices, technology, and information sources work best for our clients and us. Blustein (1992) advocates continued research is needed to enhance our understanding of career exploration.

REVIEW QUESTIONS

1.   Read the following five situations and apply the model of career counseling presented in this chapter. What additional information would you need in each situation?

(a) My company has had a record of declining revenue and is trying as its first alternative to reduce its work force. I am 57 and have had 25 years with the company. They have offered me early retirement—in some ways they have stated I'd better take it or I won't have a job—but I do not know what I will do. I really am not financially set for retirement. I do not know what type of job I would be able to get. The last time I was in school was when I went to technical school after high school.

(b) We were just taken over by that Japanese company. The first thing they decided to do was to reduce all the executives. I have my month's notice. My wife and children love this area of the country. The children are doing so well in school. There are not any similar corporations in this area that would have a job opening for me. Everything was going so well for us and now . . .

(c) Here I am 35 years old and cannot do anything. Thought I had a good marriage going and all of a sudden he leaves me for another woman. We were high school sweethearts and married right after graduation. I stayed home to take care of our children. I have never had a real job. I need a job badly to support my kids.

(d) I'm 16 and have to drop out of school. I have to work at least part time to support my two kids. Just can't go back to my school. My aunt says for me to get a job and help pay for my living with her and child care.

(e) I do not know why they don't want people over 70 to work. I know how to do the job much better than those crazy teenagers. They are not reliable and they are not good workers.

2.   Have students write a short reaction paper on the following statement by Lois E. Berger, president of the National Employment Counselors Association, 1989–90, published in the Spring 1990 *NECA Newsletter:*

> I firmly believe that we must become advocates for improving our professional image. We need to be more strident in informing others of what we do. We must ask for what we need to be more effective in providing assistance to those we counsel. The role of the employment counselor is not understood. The role of employment counselor in relation to getting the unemployed back into the work force apparently is not understood by our governors, legislators, and appointed commissioners and their staff. If they understood our role and its significance to the work force certain decisions probably would not have been made . . . state cutbacks in funding for training. . . . Certainly we should be concerned. I think we have a responsibility to enlighten our elected officials and politically appointed officials.

After discussion of the reaction paper consider the following: Should competencies in public relations, communication skills, and above all, political action be added to the NCDA competencies?

3.   How would you define developmental career counseling?

4.   How does the concept of career counseling fit within the mission of your specific school, college, or human service agency?

5.   What levels of career counseling skills do you need for providing effective service?

6.   What are the career counseling needs of youth? Adults? Minorities? Women?

7.   Why are theories important to career counselors?

8.   Do you think career development and career decision-making theories will be helpful to you as a counselor? Why or why not?

9.   Do you think career counselors should be systematic in their approach and utilize one theory—for example, Holland's or Super's?

10. Do any of the theories seem to provide a good explanation of your career development?

11.   How important were your family and early childhood experiences in determining what you are doing today?
12.   Was chance a factor in your career history and career decision making? How important were factors such as geographic location, nearness to family, climate, and so on in your job history?
13.   What instruction did you receive in decision-making skills? Were any applications given to making career decisions?
14.   How important do you think it is to have a match between the person and the environment in the workplace? Why or why not? Is there a match between your personality traits and types and the characteristics of your job?
15.   Do you think that there should be a special career development theory for women and for minority groups? Why or why not?

SUGGESTED LEARNING ACTIVITIES

1.   Interview several career counselors and find out what theory or theories they use if any and why or why not.
2.   Write a paper on one of the theories introduced in this chapter.
3.   Write an analysis of how your career history fits the theories outlined in this chapter.
4.   Construct your own personal career development theory model.
5.   Become involved in action research in evaluating the theories of career development and decision making. Theories should stimulate the forming of hypotheses that can be tested with your clients.
6.   Read "Getting Down to Cases" section in the *Career Development Quarterly*. Several counselors present how they would handle the case. Have several counselors present how they would approach each after considering the issues or facts. Look at practical issues in deciding your approach. Certain theoretical orientations have more support materials for the career counselor and assessment instruments.
7.   Get several counselors to meet for coffee or lunch each week and go over problem cases as a group.
8.   Try writing your theory of career counseling or decision making. The exercise will help you develop a conceptual framework for what you do.
9.   Keep up on the new theories that are being developed. Take time to read the current literature in your field. Career development and decision making is not a static field.
10.   The National Vocational Guidance Association (now called the National Career Development Association Professional Standards Committee) (1992) identified six general areas in which the career counselor needs to be competent: (1) counseling, (2) career resources and information, (3) individual and group assessment, (4) manage-

ment and administration, (5) implementation skills and strategies, and (6) consultation. Have each student complete the checklist found in the Exercise.

EXERCISE

Complete the following career counselor's competency checklist. Use "+" to indicate strengths and "-" to indicate where more training is needed.

General Counseling Skills

____ Shows knowledge of counseling theories

____ Shows ability to establish rapport

____ Uses appropriate strategies to assist in career choice and life/career decisions

____ Assists client in understanding the role of personality, values, interests, aptitudes, and motivation in making life and career decisions

____ Can guide clients to relate self-understanding to effective career and life decisions

____ Assists client in analyzing the role of family, friends, educational opportunities, and finances in career decision making

____ Helps client understand and clarify career decision making

Information

____ Shows knowledge of education and training sources

____ Knows employment and labor market trends

____ Knows information sources available on job tasks, functions, salaries, requirements, and future outlooks

____ Understands career pathing and career patterns

____ Uses career development and career decision-making theories

____ Shows awareness of the changing roles of women and men and the linkage of work, family, and leisure

____ Knows computer software and packages for disseminating career and vocational information

Assessment

____ Demonstrates knowledge of the use of appraisal techniques

____ Knows appropriate aptitude, interest, values, and personality tests

____ Shows ability to assess job performance

____ Identifies appropriate appraisal procedures for specific situations and populations

____ Evaluates tests in terms of their reliability, validity, and appropriateness for race, sex, age, and ethnicity

____ Administers tests in the proper way

____ Interprets appraisal data so clients can understand it

____ Help assists clients in appraising quality of life

Management and Administration

____ Knows program designs that can be used in the organization of career development

____ Implements needs assessment techniques and practices when needed

____ Knows performance objectives used in organizing career development programs

____ Demonstrates leadership and knowledge of management techniques

____ Demonstrates problem-solving ability

____ Prepares budgets and time lines for programs

____ Designs, compiles, and reports on the evaluation of career programs within the unit

Implementation

____ Knows how to adapt and change programs when needed

____ Identifies personal and environmental barriers that can affect the implementation of career development programs

____ Conducts individual and group programs in career development for specified populations

____ Implements a public relations effort on career development activities and services

____ Knows how to organize and set up a career resource center

____ Implements pilot programs in career areas where needed

Consultation

____ Knows consultation strategies and models

____ Works effectively in consultation roles with parents, teachers, employers, community groups and general public

____ Provides career development consultation to business, industry, or professional groups

____ Conveys program goals and achievements to key personnel in positions of authority, such as legislators, executives, and so on

____ Provides data on the cost effectiveness of career counseling and career development

CASE STUDY

The Traveler

By the age of seven I had seen half the world and had the opportunity to interact with people from many different countries. I had the rare opportunity to see many cultures and observe many customs. By the age of 23 I had visited or lived in every state in the Union with the exception of Alaska. I have been working since I was 14. My positions have included laborer, military soldier, food service worker, security guard, machinist, tractor trailer driver, heavy equipment operator, welder, plumber, electrician, salesperson, mechanic, woodworker, corporate supervisor, business owner, teacher, counselor, and consultant. This varied job experience has enabled me to actually participate in the cultures of the areas where people live and work. My career history was difficult and interesting. I felt relatively without direction even at the age of 25 when I was in such a responsible position as corporate supervisor for a very large company. In this position I was responsible for over thirty employees and millions of dollars worth of products. At this time I had earned an AA degree and the corporation was putting the pressure on me to complete my bachelor's degree. The corporation did not care what the degree was in; they simply indicated that I should get one. I attempted history, political science, art, and finally was advised to see a counselor. The counselor, who had a degree in business, advised me to go into any field except psychology because there were no jobs and no money. I immediately tried psychology and I knew I was home. I completed my bachelor's by the time I was 30.

Case Questions

1. What career theories can best be used to interpret this career autobiography?
2. Interpret the career progression using Holland's theory.
3. Does this person's pattern correlate with the stages proposed by Super?
4. What career field would you predict this individual would choose next? Do you feel that this individual will remain in any position for any length of time?
5. How does the pattern of career choice correspond to career decision theories?

SUGGESTED READINGS

Arthur, M. B., Hall, D. T., & Lawrence, B. S. (Eds.). (1989). *Handbook of career theory*. New York: Cambridge University Press.

The book contains chapters on new directions in career theory, the utility of adult development theory in understanding career adjustment processes, developmental views of careers in organizations, exploring women's development implications for career theory, counseling, and so on. There are three sections to the book. The first is current approaches to the study of careers; the second, new ideas for the study of careers; and the third, future directions for the development of career theory.

Bolles, R. W. (1991). *What color is your parachute? A practical manual for job-hunters and career changers.* Berkeley, CA: Ten Speed Press.

This book was written to help job hunters, job changers, and persons seeking assistance with career planning. It contains practical, step-by-step instructions for individuals who are able to follow instructions and work independently. It is particularly helpful for adults who wish to determine their job objectives and career goals.

Ryan, C. W. (1990). "Career decision making: Enhancing life work options" in S. Thompson (Ed.), *A study of work family integration issues.* Augusta: Maine Occupational Information Coordinating Committee.

The content of this book focuses on child and parent/family interactions as related to school planning for education or career and presents a number of strategies. The text has a strong section on career needs of rural youth, career interest assessment, and preparing adolescents for future job roles.

2

WORKING

Implications for the Future

Work has been a significant part of our past, our present, and will be a significant part of our future. Work has many meanings that are influenced by the values and philosophies of the individuals involved. We spend a large portion of our time in preparing for work and doing work. The American Dream begins and ends with a job that permits development of social status and participation in the leisure activities of our culture.

LEARNING OBJECTIVES

After studying this chapter, you should be able to do the following:

- Define and discuss the meaning of work from a personal perspective
- Compare and contrast the different types of work ethics
- Recognize the developmental aspects of career development and the need for life-style development
- Discuss the problems of job dissatisfaction and stress

CONCEPTS OF WORK

There are terms that deal with the time and effort aspects of work, such as *labor, employment, leisure,* and *play.* There are terms that deal with the content of work, such as *task, positions,* and *occupations.* These terms define the role of work in the culture of the United States. Gowler and Legge (1989) conclude that *work* and *employment* have become synonymous terms and that *employment* means a contractual agreement whereby individuals are rewarded for work. They feel that the concept of *career* should be embedded in the notion of work as employment. Work can serve many purposes. Work can benefit the individual, the family, and also society. Traditionally, work has been viewed from economic, psychological, and social perspectives. The categories are not mutually exclusive, and very few individuals would just work for one purpose. For most people the critical questions relate to identifying a career path and determining how they climb the career ladder. How do they acquire the skills needed to progress in a chosen career field?

Work satisfies our psychological needs. Our self-esteem and career self-concept can be enhanced through work. Some theorists such as Holland (1985), Super (1990), and Crites (1981) feel that career choice reflects our self-concept, and we develop personal identity through our career choice.

WORK IN AN EVOLVING SOCIETY

Historically, work has had a variety of meanings to people at different times and places. Some think work is play; others think play is work. The National Vocational Guidance Association (NVGA) glossary of terms defines work as a conscious effort, other than having as its primary purpose either coping, or relaxation, aimed at producing benefits for oneself or others (Sears, 1982). Super (1980) defines work as "the systematic pursuit of an objective valued by oneself (even if only for survival) and desired by others; directed and consecutive, it requires the expenditure of effort" (p. 142). It may be compensated (paid work) or uncompensated (volunteer work or an avocation). The objective may be intrinsic enjoyment of the work itself, the structure given to life by the work role, the economic support that work makes possible, or the type of leisure allowed United States has its roots in the Protestant work ethic. The ethic emphasizes that through work individuals can achieve religious peace and spiritual salvation. Luther preached that all work was God's work and all work was important. The Protestant Reformation elevated work to a new status. Work attained spiritual dignity, but it was not until the Renaissance that work was recognized as a source of joy and creative fulfillment. The philosophy of work during the Reformation was that one should work industriously and hard. Hard work was translated into worldly achievements, high profits, and individuality (Kanchier, 1991). The ethic is also reflected by our contemporary attitudes toward the unemployed and those on welfare.

Another work ethic is materialistic, which means that a job is more satisfying and more positive for an individual if it has a higher prestige rating than other jobs and provides for a higher level of salary. The materialistic ethic postulates that career success will generate life satisfaction and that one cannot have life satisfaction without materialistic career success. Individuals bring their own interests, attitudes, and needs to the work situation. In seeking self-fulfillment each individual's unique attempt to satisfy both physiological and security needs are acted out in the work environment.

Another work ethic is self-growth. A job has to have personal significance to the worker, ask for the worker to use a variety of skills, be important according to the values of society, and provide autonomy for the worker. The more workers make their own decisions, the more autonomy they have, and the more meaningful the job is to them. Feedback systems are also important in developing employee performance. Feedback tells individuals how well they are doing and helps individuals feel the job is important. Now, workers seek satisfaction of their own desires in their work, which they feel is an expression of their personal values and needs. Gorman (1993) states that the term *values* describes "the attitudes, beliefs, opinions, hopes, fears, prejudices, needs, desires, and aspirations that taken together govern how one behaves, and that one's internal set of values finds holistic expression in life-style" (p. 19).

Ludeman (1989) has another view of current work ethics and describes the *worth ethic* as adults coming to the workplace with new expectations and expecting work to include personal satisfaction, a chance to be their best selves on the job, and an opportunity to make a contribution. Workers influenced by this ethic choose job satisfaction over job security. Kanchier (1991) states that as traditional career paths are being altered currently, people have to learn new attitudes and patterns of coping, new values, and new skills. More workers are influenced by the total self—body, mind, emotion, and spirit—and judge work by personal criteria and satisfaction and less by money and status.

Different ethics have been accepted by different groups. Blue-collar workers may tend to be governed by the Protestant work ethic and younger professionals and recent college graduates by self-growth ethic. Professionals and executives over 35 may tend to be more materialistic. Conflict among the three ethics can generate innovation and lead people to clarify their views and see how others think and feel. Fyock (1990) points out that values and ethics are largely a product of the time in which the individual grew up. The values of older workers differ from those of younger workers, "traditionalists" versus "challengers." Challengers, for example, often display little regard for authority and openly criticize authority figures.

Work is continuing to change and so might work ethics. One problem is that there are conflicting philosophies toward work. Some groups say, Why work? Work does not lead to satisfaction. Many of the jobs that will be available in the year 2000 will be low-paying, routine types of jobs that will be repetitious. We suspect that individuals following the self-growth ethic will not be motivated or interested in working in these jobs.

Yankelovich (1982) asked workers to choose which of three career concepts most closely matched their personal view. They ranked first that people work only because they would not otherwise have the resources to sustain themselves, which represents a materialistic ethic. They ranked third that work has a moral imperative to do one's best apart from the practical necessity or financial remuneration, and is more reflective of the Protestant work ethic. As counselors our role is to help individuals deal with motivation, commitment, and personal need when making a career choice. Jobs and attendant rewards do affect performance and ultimately personal satisfaction. Rank what your values are by taking the Personal Values Inventory found in the exercises.

DEFINITION OF CAREER

The word *career* is derived from the French word *career,* which means *road* or *racetrack.* Sometimes we think of ourselves as being on a race track. Careerists are persons interested chiefly in achieving their own professional ambitions to the neglect of other things. Normally a career is defined as "an occupation or profession which one trains for and pursues as a life work" (Guralnik, 1980, p. 214).

Arthur, Hall, and Lawrence (1989) define career as the "involving sequence of a person's work experience over time" (p. 9) and show that different disciplines in the social sciences can be used to view the concept. These are listed in Table 2.1.

Kanchier (1991) points out that life-long careers are disappearing. People change careers a number of times during their lifetime. A combination of psychological and sociological factors affect how and when career change takes place. The changes in family structure through death, divorce, the empty nest, and separation have forced individuals to reexamine their goals, values, and careers. People are also living longer. The change in family roles—dual-career couples, Mr. Mom households, and the like—has affected career decisions. Many

TABLE 2.1
A discipline procedure for categorizing careers

Social Science	Perspective
Anthropology	Career as a status
	Career as a rite of passage
Economics	Career as a labor market function
Geography	Career as a response to geographic factors
History	Career as a correlate of historical outcomes of people and events
Psychology	Career as a vocation
	Career as a means for self-realization
	Career as a function of developmental stages
Sociology	Career as a social mobility
	Career as the unfolding of social roles

highly educated adults rather work in career fields that provide them an opportunity to express themselves and make meaningful contributions to society. With recessions and downsizing and the like, many workers can only consider basic survival needs and have to make rapid and sweeping changes in their lives.

Super (1976) defines career as the sequence of major positions occupied by persons throughout their preoccupational, occupational, and postoccupational life. Super examined the various career roles persons occupy during their life, such as student, worker, homemaker or family member, leisurite, and citizen.

FACTORS THAT DETERMINE CAREER PATHS

Careers of individuals consist of different roles and, many times, working in a number of different occupations. Careers are influenced by economic, sociological, political, and psychological factors.

Economic Factors

Technology has had a great impact on the manufacturing and agricultural fields. Automation has caused a reduction in the number of workers needed. The cost of wages and salaries has been a factor also. The reduced labor costs in third-world countries has had an impact on many American industries such as auto, steel, and textile. We see the influence of the world economy on trends in our work force. Although there are no seers or crystal balls to accurately predict the future, it is essential for counselors to understand trends and develop strategies to assist clients with career choices.

Sociological Factors

Hotchkiss and Borow (1990) conclude the institutions within our society provide perceptions of what is acceptable in a career. Careers are viewed as movement from a specific occupation to another within a job market structured by status and differing role expectations by workers in a specific category. The family has an important influence on career choice as well as on the educational and occupational level children attain. Socioeconomic level is also a factor. Upper-socioeconomic-level families prepare their children for entering a profession and not for unskilled or low-level occupations. The support systems are not available for children from lower socioeconomic families. Family socialization has an influence on the work preferences and values of children. For example, Anglo-European families stress the development of autonomy, independence, and competitiveness. Native Americans stress cooperation and group work.

Employers are also very influential. They define the work roles that are acceptable for their workers. They establish codes of behavior and may even define how they expect employees to dress. They may move or transfer employees from one section of the country or world as economic trends demand. An example of this is the armed services.

Professional organizations, licensing boards, and other similar groups often specify codes of ethics and behavior. Apprenticeships are often limited and the labor union determines how many and what type of person is going to be accepted. College and universities also influence who and how many will be admitted to a program.

Political Factors

Governmental bodies and agencies make laws and regulations that affect individuals, such as safety and minimum wage laws. They make decisions about taxes and the regulation of commerce, work, and public ownership. Some governmental decisions may increase jobs in some sections and decrease jobs in others; for example, legislation of environmental protection may increase the number of jobs in that area. Also, legislation creates new or revised jobs in relation to the demand for compliance with the law.

Psychological Factors

Our values, aptitudes, achievements, skills, and competencies set parameters on what we may be able to accomplish. Our interests and aptitudes guide us in choosing certain environments that we prefer, certain educational options, and career decisions. People have to become more introspective and aware of their assets and limitations, their likes and dislikes, and the realities of their environment.

DEVELOPMENTAL ASPECTS

Careers are usually thought of in a developmental context in that they build on what people have done in their lives, what they presently are doing, and what they hope to do. Super (1990) provided an outline of career stages as a guide to understanding events over time (see Table 2.2). The ages are approximate and vary depending on the individual. The process may have to be recycled because people might not remain in one field all their lives. Career stages continue and overlap, but one stage may be dominant at a certain age period.

JOB SATISFACTION

Job satisfaction is a difficult construct for career counselors to understand because it has numerous dimensions. The word *satisfaction* has a Latin root and means "to make enough." Individuals might be happy with the type of work they

TABLE 2.2

Career stages

Stage	Age	Qualities
Growth	0–14	Elementary and junior high students learn positive work attitudes and habits. They think about the future and imagine themselves in different occupations. They develop self-confidence in their ability to do a job well and get along with people.
Exploration	15–24	Individuals explore their interests, abilities, and goals and form vocation aspirations. They identify a group of occupations, and learn what is needed to obtain a job in that occupation group.
Establishment	25–44	Individuals establish their careers and stabilize their occupational positions. They settle down in their jobs, learn how to get things done, and how to get promoted.
Maintenance	45–64	Many people maintain positions that they have achieved, and others reestablish themselves in new positions. They find ways of being enthusiastic and learn new ways of doing things.
Disengagement	65–	Individuals reduce their workload and devise easier work methods. They explore new hobbies and participate in community activities.

do but unhappy with the conditions, coworkers, supervision, or pay. The factors might then relate to the job content or the job context. Dawis (1992) reports that 75% to 80% of workers report that they are satisfied with their jobs; nevertheless, 40% to 50% also say that they would change their occupation if they had a chance. Dawis points out, however, that job satisfaction is different from occupational satisfaction.

Herzberg, Mausner, and Snyderman (1959) proposed a two-factor theory of motivation: (1) hygiene or issues within the working environment such as salary, technical supervision, working conditions, company policies and administration, and interpersonal relations or (2) motivators or intrinsic issues such as recognition, advancement, possibility of growth, achievement, and work itself. When workers governed by the latter motivation are asked about what makes them feel good about their work, motivators might say their jobs give them feelings of achievement or their work is interesting. Those governed by the former motivation might say to the same questions a good salary or working conditions.

Locke (1976) postulated that individuals were satisfied with their jobs when their work was related to their work values, was mentally challenging and interesting, had attainable goals, had fair rewards, was not overly fatiguing, had environments conducive to the attainment of the work goals, and was rewarded by high wages, promotions, and self-esteem. O'Toole (1973) identified nine areas in which satisfaction with work was related to constructs such as prestige, change, security, working environment, and the reward system. Dawis (1992) proposed a composite rank of the things that people look for in the job over the years: type of work, security, reputation of the company, advancement, coworkers, pay, supervision, working hours, benefits, and working conditions.

Different career theorists analyze job satisfaction in different ways. Super (1990) wrote that work satisfaction depends on the extent to which individuals can find adequate outlets in their jobs for their abilities, interests, values, and personality traits. The degree of satisfaction individuals attain from their work is related to the degree to which they have been able to implement their self-concept in their work. Satisfaction from a psychodynamic approach focuses on whether the needs of the worker have been met. Holland (1985) focuses on the person-job fit.

Healy (1982) concluded that career satisfaction is related to life satisfaction. Individuals who become workaholics or overemphasize their careers over their personal lives often become frustrated and unhappy. The relationship between satisfaction and motivation is unclear; other factors may result in job satisfaction for one person and job dissatisfaction for another.

JOB STRESS

Stress can be both good and bad depending on its nature, duration, and resources available to respond to it. A stress experience is a process that occurs when a person is confronted by a demand that is perceived to exceed the emotional or physical resources available to effectively respond to it (Zaccaro & Riley, 1987). Stress is the actual process—the fight-or-flight response. It is associated with the awareness of a potential threat and is defined on a physiological level as the sympathetic response of the autonomic nervous system. Shore (1992) classifies stress at work into three categories: biochemical, physical, and psychosocial. An example of biochemical stress is exposure to chemical and biological substances that interfere with normal body functioning. Physical stress includes noise, ventilation, heat, pace of production, time of shift. Psychosocial stress occurs as a result of a potential or actual conflict between a worker and some aspect of the worker's company. Examples are conflicting job demands, negative patterns of supervision and communication, lack of respect and recognition, racism, sexism, and the like. Different jobs vary greatly in the amount of stress they produce. Of those who experience stress, some will feel it to a slight degree, and others may be incapacitated.

Sometimes stress can have a positive effect on an employee group, especially if it is a cohesive group, and can lead to higher overall performance and meeting quotas and deadlines. Other times the strain caused by the stress can lead to psychological reactions such as job dissatisfaction, depression, burnout, and anxiety, or physiological reactions such as high blood pressure, exhaustion, and headaches, or behavioral reactions such as smoking and drug and alcohol abuse. As these factors affect individuals, they are less capable of responding to task demands. The job strain reduces the motivation of the individual as well as the task performance. Individuals try to escape from the situation through tardiness and absenteeism.

Lazarus and Folkman (1984) advocate changing cognitive and behavioral efforts to manage specific external or internal demands that are appraised as taxing or exceeding the resources of the person. Also, the ability to handle stress is limited to the following characteristics: First, a person's personal work style and personality are linked to how we interpret and respond to stress. Second, the amount and quality of social support from family, friends, and colleagues during stressful events. Third, the physical make-up of a person is linked to one's ability to ward off colds, nervous reactions, and other psychosomatic illnesses. Finally, each individual's health practices are important in reducing the harmful effects of stress, for example, avoiding excessive use of drugs, alcohol, and tobacco. In sum, our hardiness is related to our work commitment and life, rather than being alienated from them. Positive people have a sense of control rather than powerlessness when confronted with change and problems.

Shore (1992) states that counselors can help workers understand how work stress affects them by getting them to analyze and identify the parts of their job that are sources of stress, by helping them learn their own stress reactions, and by helping them determine what they can do about job stress. He states that long-range strategies for dealing with stress involve how the workers view their work and how the work environment changes. Often stress can be reduced when the organization defines the work roles and responsibilities more clearly; provides career development and counseling services, social support systems, and meaningful stimulation; redesigns jobs to allow workers to use their skills; reduces work loads; rethinks work schedules; and involves workers in decision making.

PERSON-ENVIRONMENT-FIT MODEL

The person-environment-fit theory (Holland, 1985) postulates that the behavior of people in organizations and in other social situations is a function of transactions between the person and the environment. Caplan (1987) points out that research on the attributing of blame and responsibility clearly demonstrates that we tend to simplify the world by attributing the cause of success to ourselves (P) and the cause of failure to external circumstances (E). Individuals tend to look at the mistakes of others as due to their own ineptitude. There are different types of fits: the fit between the employee's needs and the job's supplies or resources for meeting these needs (needs-supply fit) and the fit between the job's demands and the person's abilities (demands-abilities fit). A subjective fit is what is perceived by the person. An objective fit is one not influenced by bias and includes facts about the job environment and the person that are not perceived by the person. This theory provides us a way of looking at job satisfaction as well as job placement.

LIFE-STYLE MANAGEMENT

There appears to be a relationship among life-style, stress, mental health, and job satisfaction. The theme of the American Association for Counseling and Development (AACD) convention at Reno in 1991 was wellness. Hettler (1986) includes six dimensions in his model: physical, spiritual, emotional, social, intellectual, and occupational. The career counselor can have an input on lowering stress and increasing job satisfaction by providing career and individual counseling if necessary. Group sessions might be valuable also. Some of the key components of a planned program can be found in Figure 2.1.

SUMMARY

Certain events occur with relative predictability over the course of a person's career. It is essential for career counselors to understand these events and to take an active role in helping individuals manage their careers. Early career experiences may have included formation of unrealistic expectations and reality shocks when coupled with unsatisfactory job experiences. Stress is part of organizational

---

* Teaching clients to manage their personal work environments by developing planning skills, time management skills, learning to say *no,* and possibly switching jobs, varying routines, taking a leave of absence, or leaving their job
* Teaching clients life-style management by helping them to prioritize their goals, maintain a balance in the roles as a worker, family member, leisurite, and so on, eat a balanced diet, get involved in regular exercise, find leisure activities they like, use caffeine and alcohol moderately, and avoid drugs
* Teaching clients to manage their personal perceptions of stress by teaching them the power of constructive self-talk, how to recognize realities, dispute cognitive distortion, disassociate themselves psychologically from the situation, and change their type-A behavior patterns
* Teaching them to use relaxation methods such as meditation, self-hypnosis, biofeedback and progressive relaxation
* Teaching clients to seek emotional outlets such as joining support groups, participating in role-playing and psychodrama, and keeping a diary or notebook of their feelings
* Having clients seek medical assistance such as having check-ups, seeking medication, and so on
* Encouraging them to seek counseling or psychotherapy if there seems to be evidence that they need specialized help

---

FIGURE 2.1
Objectives for a planned program in life-style management

life, and individuals need to develop response patterns for dealing with job demands and coworkers.

The starting point for individual career planning is to understand what one wants from work, career, and life. Career counselors can propose strategies to assist individuals in systematic career planning.

REVIEW QUESTIONS

1. What is your definition and philosophy of work? Which work ethic represents your view of work?
2. What factors influence your career? How do you view your career? By a sequence of positions? By a sequence of roles?
3. Discuss the developmental aspects of your career? Can you identify stages in your career development? Do they parallel the stages that Super has identified?
4. What factors have influenced your job satisfaction? Can you classify these factors into categories. Into existing theories?
5. Do you feel stress on your current job? What types of stress? What are the causes of your stress?
6. How does person-environment-fit theory apply to you and your work situation? Do you see a correlation between your characteristics and the characteristics of your working environment?
7. Do you feel business and industry should offer seminars on life-style management? Have you taken any seminars in life-style management? If so, what was your reaction to the seminar? What did you learn as a result of the seminar?

SUGGESTED LEARNING ACTIVITIES

1. Interview a variety of workers from different levels and types of work and have them tell you what their definition and philosophy of work is. What type of ethic are they expressing?
2. Interview several workers from different levels and types of work and question them on their satisfaction with their work. What causes the workers to be satisfied? Dissatisfied?
3. Interview several workers from different levels and types of work and question them on job stress. What causes the workers to have psychological or physiological stress? How do your results fit the current theories and research on stress?
4. Review several syllabus or curriculum guides to seminars or courses on life-style management. What topics were included in these seminars? What techniques were suggested for teaching the seminars?

EXERCISES

Personal Values Inventory (PVI)

Read each statement and decide the extent to which you agree using the following key: SA = strongly agree, A = agree, U = uncertain, D = disagree, and SD = strongly disagree.

1. Hard work makes individuals better persons.	SA A U D SD
2. A good indication of individuals' work is how they do their jobs.	SA A U D SD
3. Individuals who have failed on a job have not tried hard enough.	SA A U D SD
4. Work can be a means for self-expression.	SA A U D SD
5. Work should be challenging.	SA A U D SD
6. Work needs to be meaningful.	SA A U D SD
7. Before taking a work assignment individuals need to ask what is in it for them.	SA A U D SD
8. Individuals should refuse tasks that are dull.	SA A U D SD
9. Salary and advancement are the most important factors in work.	SA A U D SD

Responses to the PVI should suggest how you view the importance of work in meeting self-esteem issues such as achievement, competence, and personal reward.

Work Goals and Values

Rank in order the following work values as to how important you feel they are in your work. Select the most valuable value and rank it 1. Next choose the value that is second in importance to you and rank it 2. Continue to rank all 11. Don't have any ties.

_____ A lot of opportunity to learn new things

_____ Good interpersonal relationships with supervisors and coworkers

_____ Good opportunity for upgrading or promotion

_____ Convenient work hours

_____ A lot of variety

_____ Interesting work that you really like

_____ Good job security

_____ Good match between your job requirements and your ability and experience

_____ Good pay

_____ Good physical working environment—light, temperature, and so on

_____ A lot of freedom that allows you to decide how to do your work.

CASE STUDIES

The Hard Worker

My first job was with my father, who was a building contractor. He lived to work. He got pleasure out of creating the buildings he completed. I had to work afternoons and weekends. I was 15 when I started. I had to lift 75 and 100 pound bags of cement and plaster and mix mortar and plaster and carry it when needed. I helped rake concrete when they were pouring it. Boy, it was heavy work—dusty and dirty, too. I hated the work. It did provide me money for movies and dates.

The Helper

I went to college and decided that I wanted to be a teacher. I wanted to help children learn the skills and competencies they needed to be successful in life. I majored in elementary education, and my first job was as a third grade teacher. It was an exciting year. I loved the kids and the school.

Tired of Routine

I am tired of the same routine day after day. Get up at 5:30 and go to the clinic and pull and file medical records all day. They got us a computerized system, but who wants to sit in front of a screen all day. We are so busy and coworkers don't stay long here. The inexperienced help are always misfiling or losing the records.

Case Questions

1. What type of work ethics are being illustrated in each of the cases?
2. How are the individuals defining work?
3. Discuss how you would use Ludeman's approach with one of the cases in this section or with your own situation. Ludeman (1989) suggests that you can guide an individual to achieve the worth ethic by using the following steps:

   C Create a concrete description of the desired change
   H Honestly examine the motivation to change
   A Abandon the old behavior in one's imagination
   N Name the change positively

G Give attention to the payoffs or what reinforces old behavior
  to stay in place
I Imagine the past and see how one behaved
N Nail down the new behavior using mental rehearsal
G Graduate to the new behavior

4.   How do these cases illustrate job satisfaction? Dissatisfaction?
5.   How did these jobs meet social needs? Self-esteem needs? Physical needs?

The Stressed-out Worker

Sally is a customer representative for one of the Fortune 500 corporations. She began missing one to two days of work a week. Usually she would call in to let her supervisor know. She complained of headaches and shortness of breath. Customers have complained to the company recently about how discourteous she was to them. Sally is a 28-year-old single parent with two young children, a boy 5 years old and a girl 3 years old. She graduated from the local state university with a degree in elementary education and taught one year but was surplussed the next year. After her divorce two years ago she took her current position. Her parents are retired and have moved to Arizona.

The supervisor has recommended that Sally see the employee assistant counselor at work. Sally agreed and has been having sessions with the counselor. Recently Sally agreed to take the *Occupational Stress Inventory* (Osipow & Spokane, 1987). Her profile on the test is as follows:

Scale	T Score	Interpretative Comments
Occupational Roles		
Role Overload	75	Work viewed as unreasonable; too much
Role Insufficiency	70	Poor fit between skills and performance
Role Ambiguity	49	
Role Boundary	45	
Responsibilities	35	
Physical Environment	40	
Personal Strain		
Vocational Strain	70	Poor attitude toward work
Psychological Strain	75	Feels depressed, unhappy, anxious
Interpersonal Strain	60	Quarrels, dependency on family
Physical Strain	40	
Personal Resources		
Recreation	39	
Self-Care	43	
Social Support	35	Low social support; no close friends
Rational/Cognitive	50	

SUGGESTED READINGS

Cameron, C., & Elusorr, S. (1986). *Thank God it's Monday: Making your work fulfilling and finding fulfilling work.* Los Angeles: Jeremy P. Tarcher.
   The authors present suggestions on how to achieve greater satisfaction in their jobs. How the worker perceives the work environment is extremely important.

Holland, J. L. (1985). Making vocational choices: A theory of careers, 2nd ed. Englewood Cliffs, NJ: Prentice Hall.

Super, D. E. (1957). The psychology of careers. New York: Harper and Row.

3

OCCUPATIONAL ENVIRONMENTS

Preparing for Change

The role and function of the career counselor are changing as a result of the shift from an industrial to an information-centered society. Economic conditions affect career choices. Career counselors need to be alert to labor market and economic conditions in the world and appropriate information sources that are both relevant and accurate. Youths growing up in our society can no longer count on working in one job or career during their lifetime. Many youths are not prepared to make important career decisions. Technology is also changing, and different types and modes of information are now available to help youths make important educational and vocational decisions.

LEARNING OBJECTIVES

After studying this chapter you should be able to do the following:

- Explain current employment trends and projections for the future
- List and evaluate different ways of classifying jobs
- Identify some of the problem areas that career counselors will have to face during the 1990s and early 2000s
- Know if the following statements are true or false:

T F 1. In the year 2005 the work force will number 118 million.

T F 2. The fastest-growing region in the United States is the West.

T F 3. Three out of five jobs by the year 2005 will be in the service sector.

T F 4. Women will account for two-thirds of the labor force in the year 2005.

T F 5. The percentage of youth in the labor force in the year 2005 will increase over the number in 1995.

T F 6. The percent of jobs in manufacturing has remained relatively the same from 1960 to 1990.

T F 7. The numbers of jobs available in the agricultural services industries will grow.

T F 8. The number of jobs available in state and local government agencies will decrease significantly by the year 2005.

T F 9. The demand for computer operators, programmers, and systems people has peaked and will decline in the 1990s.

T F 10. The largest number of new jobs from 1990 to 2005 will be in retail sales.

THE GROWTH OF THE WORK FORCE

The size of the work force in our country in the year 2005 is projected to be 151 million as compared with 125 million in 1990. This is a growth of approximately 21% (U.S. Dept. of Labor, 1991). The make-up of the labor force is also changing with the increasing composition of minorities and women. Women will account for 43% of the work force in the year 2005, and minority groups will account for about 16.4% of the labor entrants' growth between 1990 and 2005. Hispanic entrants will number 8.7 million and account for 15.7% of all entrants, and African Americans will account for 13% or 7.2 million workers. See Table 3.1 for the breakdown of labor-force entrants by ethnicity.

There will be 26 million jobs added to the U.S. economy by 2005, and career counselors need to be familiar with these new jobs and the requirements for entry. The counselor also needs to know where these jobs will be located, as there are geographic shifts in population. Currently, the western United States is the fastest growing region in the country, and the local job market may not parallel the regional or national market.

The shift from a goods-producing economy to a service-producing economy is continuing, and 60.6% of the jobs by the year 2005 will be in the service sector as compared with 18.5% in the manufacturing sector. Counselors need to be knowledgeable about the labor market and work to improve the school-to-work transitions of young adults. A summary of the characteristics of the work force in presented in Figure 3.1.

POPULATION TRENDS

The Bureau of Labor Statistics (1991) has identified these population trends in the period 1990 to 2005: The U.S. population will grow more slowly but with a steady increase in demand for goods and services. There will be a smaller proportion of children and youth but a greater proportion of those aged 25 to 54, and 55 and older. Minorities and immigrants will make up a larger part of the population in 2005 than in 1990. Some sections of the West and Southeast will be the fastest-growing areas. The Midwest is projected to remain the same and the Northeast to decline slightly.

TABLE 3.1
Ethnic composition of labor-force entrants in 2005, by percent

	Women	Men
African American	6.8	6.2
Hispanic	6.6	9.1
Anglo-European	33.1	32.2
Asian	3.0	3.0

* The number of civilian workers will be 151 million as compared with 139 million in 1990.
* African Americans will increase their share in the labor market from 10.7% to 11.6%; Hispanics from 7.7% to 11.1%; Asians and others from 3.1% to 4.3%.
* Minorities will constitute about 35% of the labor-force growth between 1990 and 2005.
* Women will account for over 49% of the entrants in the labor force between 1990 and 2005.
* The number of older workers 55 and over is expected to be about 14.7% in 2005.
* The youth share in the labor market in 2005 will be 16%.
* Three out of four workers in 2005 will be between 25 and 54. The baby boomers, people born between 1946 and 1964 in 2005 will be concentrated in the 45-to-54 age group and make up 23.8% of the work force.
* The decline in the birthrate in the late 1960s will cause a decline in the 25-to-34 age group between 1990 and 2005 and will drop from 28.8% to 21%.
* The percentage of four-year college graduates will rise to 21%.

FIGURE 3.1
Characteristics of the work force in the year 2005

EDUCATIONAL TRENDS

The educational trends are changing in our society because of growth in areas such as executive, managerial, professional, and technical, all requiring high levels of education and skill. The proportion of workers with college backgrounds has increased substantially in the past 20 years. Only 14% of the labor force had college degrees in 1972 as compared with 21% in 1986. Only 14% had at least some college (1 to 3 years) in 1972 as compared with 20% in 1986. Shelley (1992) projects that the number of new graduates that will enter the labor force between 1990 and 2005 will total 16.5 million, with the annual average being 1.1 million. Jobs for college graduates have become less available with negative economic conditions, and many graduates find that it takes longer for them to secure a job. Many accept jobs in which they are overqualified educationally. Hecker (1992) points out, however, that there are problems with data on college graduates. He says that many facets have to be taken into account, such as the evidence for a surplus, the difficulty of classifying occupations according to the education they require, the employment data for underutilized college graduates, relative earnings, and the evidence of a shortage by industry.

INDUSTRIAL TRENDS

Olney (1988) summarized the major shifts in employment in industry since 1900 and concluded that goods-producing industries have declined in importance as employment sources although they contribute substantially to the gross national product (GNP). He cites that 18.5% of all the jobs in 1959 were in manufacturing, but only 5.1% in 1984. The U.S. Department of Labor (1992–93) predicts that there will be a continual decline in manufacturing jobs, a loss of 600,000 from 1990 to 2005.

Current projections call for an increase of jobs in the construction area. There will be an increase of 18%; the number of workers is projected to increase from 4.9 million in 1986 to 5.7 million in 2000.

Manufacturing positions are expected to decline by 4% from 19 million jobs to 18.2 million jobs. Part of the reason for the decrease of jobs in this sector is the use of technological advances to increase productivity, for example, robotics. More of the job losses will be in the manufacturing of durable goods and fewer in the manufacturing of nondurable goods. The steel and textile industries will have the most job losses. Some industries are projected to have gains such as electronics, computing, and medical instruments and supplies.

Mining employment is expected to show a 7% decline, partly because of the impact of technology and partly due to foreign import competition. There were 800,000 employed in mining in 1974 as compared with 700,000 in 1990. The projection for 2005 is the same as employed in 1990.

Agriculture's share of employment continues to drop. Olney (1988) reports the drop over a 25-year period from 8.2% to 3.1%. The number of jobs in 2000 will decline 14% from 3.3 million to 2.9 million. There will be growth in the agricultural services industries, though in 2005 the Department of Labor projects 1.9 million jobs in agriculture, forestry, and fishing.

SERVICE-PRODUCING INDUSTRIES

The Bureau of Labor Statistics projects that four out of five jobs by 2005 will be in industries that provide service: banking, data processing, education, health care, insurance, and management consulting. Jobs in this area are expected to rise from 37.5 million in 1990 to 50.5 million in 2005 for a 35% increase (13 million more jobs).

Employment growth in the business-service industries is projected to grow by 2.4 million and account for 11% of the growth. There will be a demand for a variety of services including computer and data processing services (710,000), miscellaneous business services (590,000), personnel supply services (510,000), services to buildings (186,000), miscellaneous equipment rental (13,000), advertising services (107,000), and credit collection (61,000).

Occupations in the health services industry will continue to rapidly rise. Health services accounted for 7% of the total wage and salary workers employed in 1975, 8% in 1990, and will probably account for 9% in 2005. Demographic trends such as the increase of population 75 and older, the baby-boom health-care needs, and new medical technology will increase the need for health-care workers.

Employment in the public and private educational services industry will grow by 2.3 million, almost 10% of the total job growth (U.S. Department of Labor, 1992–93). There will be 40% increased need for special education teachers, 36% for registered nurses, 33% for teacher's aides and educational assistants, 29% for vocational education teachers, 24% for educational administrators, 23% for elementary teachers, 23% for preschool and kindergarten teachers, 21% for speech and language pathologists, and 19% increased need for college faculty.

TRENDS FOR NEW JOBS

There are two ways of looking at where jobs will be: occupations with the largest absolute growth and occupations with the fastest growth rate. The Bureau of Labor Statistics (1993) has identified the 20 job categories as showing the largest absolute growth:

The top 20 occupations with the largest projected increase are:

Sales personnel	887,000
Registered nurses	767,000
Cashiers	685,000
General office clerks	670,000
Truck drivers	617,000
General management	598,000
Janitors/cleaners	555,000
Nurses aides/orderlies	552,000
Food counter/fountain	550,000
Waiters/waitresses	449,000
Teachers/secondary	437,000
Receptionists/information	422,000
System analysts	366,000
Food-preparation workers	365,000
Child care workers	363,000
Gardeners/groundskeepers	348,000
Accountants/auditors	340,000
Computer programmers	317,000
Elementary teachers	308,000
Guards	298,000

The fastest-growing occupations include those shown in Table 3.2.

The fastest-growing categories of occupations that require a college degree are system analysts, physical therapists, operations research analysts, medical scientists, psychologists, computer programmers, occupational therapists, management analysts, marketing/advertisement/public relations managers, podiatrists, and teachers—preschool, kindergarten, and special education.

TABLE 3.2
Projected fastest-growing
occupations from 1990 to
2005

Occupation	Increase
Home-health aides	92%
Paralegals	85%
System analysts	78%
Personal/home care aides	77%
Medical assistants	74%
Operations research analysts	73%
Human-service workers	71%
Radiation technologists/technicians	70%
Medical secretaries	68%
Physical/corrective therapists and aides	64%
Psychologists	64%
Travel agents	62%
Corrections officers	61%
Data-processing equipment repairers	60%
Flight attendants	59%
Computer programmers	58%
Occupational therapists	55%
Surgical technologists	55%
Medical records technicians	54%
Management analysis personnel	52%

OCCUPATIONAL TRENDS

The *Occupational Outlook Handbook* (U.S. Dept. of Labor, 1992–1993) provides the following statistics on the number of workers employed in the various fields and the projections of how the job market will be in the 1990s (see Table 3.3).

CHANGING WORK FORCE

After examining the occupational employment trends to the year 2000 as presented in the U. S. Department of Labor monthly *Labor Review* Hoyt (1988) identified ten major problems and needs:

1.   The rate of job growth between 1986 and the year 2000 will be only half as great as it was during the 1972–1986 period.
2.   The percentage of 16- to 24-year-olds in the total labor force will decline from 20% in 1986 to 16%, and the percentage of 25- to 54-year-old workers will increase from 67% in 1986 to 73% in 2000.
3.   Skill levels required for occupational success will increase with both the content and complexity of jobs being modified by technological change.
4.   A higher percentage of new jobs will demand some form of postsecondary education, and a sharp decline will occur in the percentage of new jobs requiring less than a high school education.

5. Almost five in six of the 21 million new labor market entrants will be minority persons, women, or immigrants. Only 8% of the increase in 1986 to 2000 will be nonminority.
6. Women, minority persons, and immigrants in today's labor force are underrepresented in those occupational areas experiencing the greatest job growth and overrepresented in those areas experiencing the least amount of job growth.
7. Women and minority persons are currently less well prepared for occupational success by the existing educational system than are non-Hispanic white men.
8. African Americans, Hispanics, and Asians account for a rising proportion of the school population.

TABLE 3.3
Current and future prospects for occupations

Occupation	Employed in		Job Outlook 1990–2005 Change	
	1986	1990	%	Number of New and Replacement Workers Needed
Accountants/auditors	945,000	985,000	34	340,000
Construction/building inspectors	50,000	60,000	19	11,000
Cost estimators	157,000	173,000	24	42,000
Educational administrators	288,000	348,000	24	85,000
Employment interviewers	75,000	83,000	23	19,000
Financial managers	638,000	701,000	28	193,000
General managers and top executives	2,400,000	3,086,000	19	598,000
Health-service managers	274,000	257,000	42	108,000
Hotel managers and assistants	78,000	102,000	44	45,000
Inspectors/compliance officers	125,000	156,000	30	46,000
Managerial analysts/consultants	126,000	151,000	52	79,000
Marketing, advertising, public relations managers	323,000	427,000	47	203,000
Personnel trainers, labor specialists, and managers	381,000	456,000	32	144,000
Property and real estate managers	128,000	225,000	34	76,000
Restaurant and food service managers	470,000	556,000	32	177,000
Underwriters	99,000	105,000	24	25,000
Wholesale and retail buyers	192,000	361,000	19	68,000
Aerospace engineers	53,000	73,000	20	15,000
Chemical engineers	52,000	48,000	12	5,600
Civil engineers	199,000	198,000	30	59,000
Electrical and electronics engineer	401,000	426,000	34	145,000
Industrial engineers	117,000	135,000	19	26,000
Mechanical engineers	223,000	233,000	24	56,000

9. Minority youth and family households headed by women under the age of 25 are likely to find employment problems greatly compounded by the fact that they are poor.
10. Both African-American and Hispanic youths have higher dropout rates than nonminority youth, which contributes to their difficulties in career development.

Local communities and regions have problem areas, too. For example the Jacksonville Florida Community Council (1990) identified seven major problems related to developing future work force needs:

1. Lack of a focal point for planning activities to meet future work-force needs in northeastern Florida
2. Insufficient local work-force data to plan for future work-force needs
3. High-school dropouts and even many graduates who have not mastered literacy and employability skills required in the labor market
4. Extremely high unemployment among youth and minorities made worse by insufficient work training and employment opportunities
5. Stigma attached to illiteracy, which deters people from seeking literacy education needed for work-force success
6. Destructive effects of illegal drug use in the workplace
7. Increasing work-force diversity, changing family needs of employees, and changing employee expectations

FASTEST DECLINING JOBS

The U. S. Department of Labor (1992–93) has also identified the fastest-declining jobs. It is not surprising that half of the declining occupations are in manufacturing. Some of the jobs are farmers, bookkeepers, accountants, auditing clerks, child-care workers, sewing machine operators, electric and electronic assemblers, typists, word processors, cleaners, servants, farm workers, textile draw-out and winding machine operators, machine tool-cutting operators, telephone and cable operators, statistical clerks, packaging and filling machine operators, bank tellers, grinder and polishers, and lathe-turning machine tool setters.

STRUCTURE OF WORK

The world of work is becoming increasingly complex with the impact of technology on society and the change from a manufacturing-based to an information-based society. New jobs are constantly being developed and old jobs discarded or eliminated through legislative or scientific invention. Our society is becoming more service-oriented than product-oriented. It is estimated that there are roughly 20,000 service occupations in our country today. A major question for career counselors is how can these occupations be grouped or classified to make sense of all these options?

There have been several classification systems developed to order occupations, and many of these systems were designed for specific purposes. Several were developed by governmental agencies such as the U.S. Department of Labor. Others have been developed by career theorists such as John Holland and Anne Roe. Each system makes a unique contribution and has its advantages and disadvantages. Career counselors need to be aware of the different systems of classifications in order to know when to apply them, how to use them, and how to compare them with other systems that have been developed. First, the counselor has to assess why the information will be useful before deciding what source would be best to use. The structure provides a framework for counselors to use to put the whole picture together. One has to go beyond the title and recognize the patterns of interest, skills, abilities, education, income, prestige, work, environment, and other variables that accompany the job.

OCCUPATIONAL HANDBOOKS AND TOOLS

Dictionary of Occupational Titles

The *Dictionary of Occupational Titles (DOT)* (U.S. Department of Labor, 1991) is well known and used by career counselors as a source of job analysis and occupational information. The first edition of the DOT was printed in 1939 to provide employment counselors with a standardized occupational information system to assist in the placement, counseling, and career guidance of clients. The current edition proposes four major uses: classifying job applicants, classifying job orders, matching workers to orders, and assisting special groups. The authors point out that the important thing is not the job title, but the skills and abilities required by the applicant whose experience and aptitudes are matched to an occupation never considered before. Counselors who use the DOT must be familiar with the occupational code number as it provides educational and physical demand data about all listed jobs.

The DOT number assigned each occupation has nine digits divided into three sections, with three digits in each section. The first set of three numbers classifies the category, division, and the group in which the occupation is classified. For example, the first digit is assigned to the following occupational categories:

0/1	professional, technical, and managerial occupations
2	clerical and sales occupations
3	service occupations
4	agricultural, fishery, forestry, and related occupations
5	processing occupations
6	machine trade occupations
7	bench work occupations
8	structural work occupations
9	miscellaneous occupations

The second number refers to a division within the field described in the first number; for example, 0/1 represents professional, technical, and managerial occupations; the 04 represents occupations in the life sciences; and the 09 represents occupations in education.

The third digit refers to the occupational group. For example, under 00/01 occupations in architecture, engineering, and surveying 001 signifies architectural occupations and 002 aeronautical engineering occupations.

The middle set of digits represents the worker functions ratings of the tasks performed in the occupation. These functions are data (fourth digit), people (fifth digit), and things (sixth digit). The codes for data, people, and things are listed here:

Data (4th digit)	People (5th digit)	Things (6th digit)
0 Synthesizing	0 Mentoring	0 Setting up
1 Coordinating	1 Negotiating	1 Precision working
2 Analyzing	2 Instructing	2 Operating
3 Compiling	3 Supervising	3 Driving-operating
4 Computing	4 Diverting	4 Manipulating
5 Copying	5 Persuading	5 Tending
6 Comparing	6 Speaking-signaling	6 Feeding
	7 Serving	7 Handling
	8 Taking instructions-helping	

The continuum ranges from 0 "most complex" to 8 "least complex."

The final set of three digits indicates the alphabetical order of the titles within the six digit code group. There may be other jobs that have the same first six digits but only one job that has the last three digits.

Remember, first three digits specify the occupational areas in which the work is done and the second three indicate what the worker does.

The following procedures are suggested in using the manual: Use the information obtained from the job seeker and make a tentative selection of an occupational code and title, then review the requirements of the occupation. Select and match them against the past experience, training, job experience, and the like of the applicant. Counselors then have to take into consideration the labor market information and the achievement and ability of the client. Counselors can find a good match when they know the job tasks workers are required to perform, the purpose of the work, the machines tools, equipment or work aids used, the materials, products, subject matter or services involved, and where the work is located.

Each entry in the occupational group arrangement section includes the occupational code number, the job title, the industry designation, alternate titles if any, the summary of the occupation, the summary of the tasks done by the worker, and other duties and undefined related titles if any. The citation for 045.107-010 counselor is cited as an illustration (*Dictionary of Occupational Titles*).

045.107-010 Counselor (profess. & kin.):

Counsels individuals and provides group educational and vocational services; collects, organizes, and analyzes information about individuals through records, tests, interviews, and professional sources to appraise their interests, aptitudes, abilities, and personality characteristics, for vocational and educational planning. Compiles and studies occupational, educational, and economic information to aid counselees in making and carrying out vocational and educational objectives. Refers students to placement services. Assists individuals to understand and overcome social and emotional problems. May engage in research and follow-up activities to evaluate counseling techniques. May teach classes. May be designated according to area of activity as Academic Counselor (Education), Career Placement Services counselor (Education); Employment Counselors (Government Service); Guidance Counselor (Education); Vocational Advisor (Education).
GOE 10.01.02 Strength:5 GED: R5 M5 SUP:7 DLV: 81. (p. 51)

The DOT is a valuable resource to the counselor and client because it is more comprehensive than the computerized guidance systems. Because the DOT is organized by occupational groups, it is an excellent source for identifying related jobs. The DOT also lists the industries in which the occupation is found and is a good resource for helping unemployed skilled workers find similar jobs in different industries. The related jobs at the end of each definition also are a useful source. The coding system simplifies the work of employment counselors who need to match worker's qualifications with available jobs. One caution: Clients may have a psychological block to using the DOT. It requires effort by the client to analyze data and relate it to career plans.

Guide for Occupational Exploration

The *Guide for Occupational Exploration* (GOE) is a publication by the United States Employment Service (USES) to provide job seekers with information about fields of work that match their aptitude and interest areas. There are 12 interest areas used in the guide: artistic, scientific, plants and animals, protective, mechanical, industrial, business detail, selling, accommodating, humanitarian, leading-influencing, and physical-performing. The GOE uses 66 work groups and 348 subgroups. The work groups are the jobs suitable for exploration by clients who may have a given area of interest.

For each of the 66 work groups, a description provides a general overview of the occupational area and the following questions are provided to guide client exploration: What kind of work would you do? What skills and abilities do you need for this kind of work? How do you know if you would like or could learn to do this kind of work? How can you prepare for and enter this kind of work? What else would you consider about these jobs? The description also includes a list of DOT codes.

The GOE has four appendixes that provide useful information for career counseling. Appendix B, for example, discusses the related use of the USES interests and aptitude tests. Appendix C includes information on how to use the guide in organizing occupational information. Appendix D has an alphabetic arrangement for the occupations, with related DOT and GOE code numbers.

Counselors use this guide as one of the tools in career exploration. The guide can also be related to results on the General Aptitude Test Battery (GATB) and Holland's Self-Directed Search. The guide was developed as part of a coordinated assessment and occupational exploration system by USES for use in the counseling process. The GOE is intended for use with people who want assistance in determining their career goals, with or without the assistance of the counselor.

Standard Occupational Classification Manual

The *Standard Occupational Classification Manual (SOC)* arranges all the occupations defined in the DOT into groups according to the type of work performed. There are 22 broad occupational divisions identified, shown in Table 3.4.

The SOC is not easily converted by clients into career plans. The SOC is broken into four levels: division, major group, minor group, and unit group. The manual contains titles and descriptions of occupational groups. Detailed information is given for the 22 divisions and 60 major groups.

Counselors should use SOC to identify potential jobs for which a client may already be trained or might require additional training. Some counselors use the SOC structure as a way to arrange their files of occupational materials or classify information sources in career resource centers. The *Occupational Outlook Handbook* is organized by the major SOC divisions.

Standard Industrial Classification Manual

The *Standard Industrial Classification Manual* (SIC) classifies business establishments by the type of activity or type of product or service in which they are engaged. There are ten major divisions. The four goods producing industries are Agriculture, forestry, and fishing, Mining, Construction, and Manufacturing. The remaining six are service producing industries: Transportation, communication, electric, gas and sanitary services, Wholesale trade, Retail trade, Finance, insurance, and real estate, Services (including agricultural services), and Public administration. Each division is subdivided into additional categories. For example, 83 would represent Educational Services and 833 Job Training and Vocational Rehabilitation Services.

TABLE 3.4
SOC occupational divisions

* Executive, administrative, and managerial
* Engineers, surveyors, and architects
* Natural scientists and mathematicians
* Social scientists, social workers, religious workers, and lawyers
* Teachers, librarians, and counselors
* Health-diagnosing and treating practitioners
* Registered nurses, pharmacists, dietitians, physicians' assistants, therapists
* Writers, artists, entertainers, and athletes
* Health technologists and technicians
* Technologists and technicians, except health
* Marketing and sales
* Administrative support, including clerical
* Service
* Agriculture, forestry, fishing
* Mechanics and repairers
* Precision-production
* Construction and extractive
* Production working
* Transportation and material moving
* Handlers, equipment cleaners, helpers, and laborers
* Military
* Miscellaneous

Counselors can use the system to help clients with job placement. Similar occupations can be found in similar industries. The counselor can study the type of industries and the type of employment opportunities within the region.

Occupational Employment Statistics Program

The Occupational Employment Statistics (OES) program provides information by industry on the number of workers employed by occupation and is used in forecasting the future employment requirements by industry and occupation. There are seven divisions in this system: managerial and administrative; professional, paraprofessional, and technical; sales and related occupations; clerical and administrative support; service; agriculture, forestry, fishing, and related occupations; and production, construction, operating, maintenance, and material-handling occupations. The information helps counselors use employment trends and forecasts in planning career counseling programs for their clients.

Census

The national census has been conducted every ten years since 1790 with the household as the unit of study. Each responding individual's industry and occupation is classified and an alphabetical index of industries and occupations developed. The index includes approximately 20,000 industries and about 30,000 occupational titles. Census data provide the counselor with comprehensive demographic information on the population and data about single-family homes, career plans, educational goals, and the like. The census uses the Standard Industrial Classification System and its 11 categories to classify the type of industries represented in the survey data. Occupations are classified into categories such as managerial and professional specialty occupations, service occupations, and technical, sales, and administrative-support occupations. The census periodically provides a current distribution of workers in each of the occupational categories and in each type of industry.

USOE Cluster

The United States Office of Education developed a 15-cluster taxonomy, which was popular during the 1970 and 1980 career education movement, and is used by many career education materials developers. In each cluster there is a hierarchy of jobs covering the range from unskilled to professional: business and office, marketing and distribution, communication and media, construction, manufacturing, transportation, agribusiness and natural resources, marine science, environment, public services, health, recreation and hospitality, personal services, fine arts and humanities, and consumer and homemaking education. The system has been criticized because many occupations could be classified in more than one cluster and it is considered difficult to use.

PSYCHOLOGICAL CLASSIFICATION SYSTEMS

One of the most widely used systems of classification of occupations is the type theory developed by John L. Holland (1985), who postulated that there are six personality types: realistic, investigative, artistic, social, enterprising, and conventional, with corresponding occupational environments.

Realistic types prefer activities that entail the explicit, ordered, or systematic manipulation of objects, tools, machines, and animals and acquire manual, mechanical, agricultural, electrical, and technical competencies.

Investigative types prefer activities that entail the observational symbolic, systematic, and creative investigation of physical, biological, and cultural phenomena in order to understand and control such phenomena and acquire scientific and mathematical competencies.

Artistic types prefer ambiguous, free, unsystematized activities that entail the manipulation of physical, verbal, or human materials to create art forms or products and acquire language, art, music, drama, and writing competencies.

Social types prefer activities that entail the manipulation of others to inform, train, develop, cure, or enlighten and acquire human relations and interpersonal competencies.

Enterprising types prefer activities that permit manipulation of others to attain organizational goals or economic gain and acquire leadership, interpersonal, and persuasive competencies.

Conventional types prefer activities that entail explicit, ordered, systematic manipulation of data such as keeping records, filing materials, reproducing material, organizing written and numerical data according to a prescribed plan, operating business machines and data processing machines to attain organizational or economic goals and develop clerical, computation, and business system competencies.

All occupations are classified by Holland's three-digit letter system. For example, a diesel mechanic is classified as RIE. This means that the personality type that most corresponds to this occupation is realistic. The next closest match would be enterprising. Holland provides a single digit number to show the educational level necessary for the position. RIE 4 for the diesel mechanic means that a high school education is needed along with some college, technical, or business training. Holland also provides the DOT number for each occupation. The type theory has been adapted by several major interest inventories such as the Strong Interest Inventory to provide a system of classification. The system is less complex to order and classify jobs and is more manageable than some of the other systems.

Roe (1956) classified work in a two-dimensional model. She had eight fields: service, business contact, organization, technology, science, outdoor, general culture, arts and entertainment. Each of these fields had six levels: professional and managerial I, professional and managerial II, semiprofessional, small business skilled, semiskilled, and unskilled. Within each of the eight fields the classifications show a continuum of functioning:

Group/Level	Occupation
Service/Professional and Managerial (higher)	Director of agency
Service/Professional and Managerial (regular)	Social worker
Service/Semiprofessional	Welfare worker
Service/Skilled	Practical nurse
Service/Semiskilled	Waitress
Service/Unskilled	Chambermaids

Roe's (1956) six levels represent differences in the amount of training or education required, challenge, prestige, and salary. The work groups may vary but within levels there are many similarities of the amount of education and training required, the salary, the degree of challenge and responsibility, and the degree of autonomy.

OCCUPATIONAL PRESTIGE AND STATUS

Occupations can also be classified by status or prestige. In their review of the literature on individual's status rating, Parker and Chan (1988) concluded that prestige ratings are correlated with occupations that were predicted to have the fastest growth rates. The top ten occupations by status and prestige in their study were physicians, lawyers, electrical engineers, computer system analysts, computer programmers, accountants and auditors, mechanical engineers, registered nurses, civil engineering technicians, and physical therapists. Ranked 55th were building custodians, 54th kitchen helpers, 53rd guards and doorkeepers, 52nd delivery and route workers, and 51st fast food workers.

The National Opinion Research Center (1947) identified the following prestige hierarchy:

Governmental officials
Professional and semiprofessional workers
Proprietors, managers, and officials (except farm)
Clerical, sales, and kindred workers
Craftspeople, supervisors, and kindred workers
Farmers and farm managers
Protective service workers
Operatives and kindred workers
Farm laborers
Service workers (except domestic and protective)
Laborers (except farm)

OTHER SYSTEMS OF CLASSIFICATION

A number of interest inventories based on other systems of classification have been developed to assess and clarify interest of clients and occupational clusters. The clusters are designed to be appropriate for both the vocationally oriented individual and the college-oriented individual. One such system is included on the Career Occupational Preference System Interest Inventory. Some clusters are included in Table 3.5.

VALUES OF CLASSIFICATION SYSTEMS

One of the major purposes of classification systems is to provide a framework to help counselors present to clients and students the occupational structure of today's society. All clients need to know the myriad possibilities, but not become overwhelmed with the large number of occupations available. The system needs to aid understanding of the interrelatedness of the occupations. Also, knowing the organizational structure is helpful in planning programs and workshops or developing curriculum materials on occupational fields.

TABLE 3.5
COPS career clusters

Cluster	Occupational Examples and Description
Science Professionals	Astronomer, marine biologist, and mathematician. Requires research, planning, and knowledge of science
Science Skilled	Laboratory technician, dental assistant, and x-ray technologist. Requires observation, classification, and assisting scientists in a laboratory situation
Technology Professionals	Engineer, mechanical engineer, and computer systems engineer. Requires responsibility for engineering or designing functions
Technology Skilled	Auto mechanic, brick layer, and machinist. Requires use of hands in a skilled trade in construction or manufacturing
Consumer Economics	Baker, carpet layer, and food service supervisor. Requires extensive use of hands and fingers, or hand tools and machines
Outdoors	Farmer, groundskeeper, and park ranger. Requires activities to be performed primarily outdoors
Business Professional	Accountant, bank manager, and trust officer. Requires high responsibility and skills in finance, accounting, or management
Business Skilled	Buyer, administrative secretary, and sales representative. Requires activities in sales, promotion, or marketing
Clerical	Cashier, teller, and computer operator. Requires attention to details and keeping records
Communication	Copywriter, editor, and lawyer. Requires use of language skills and competency in written and oral communication
Arts Professional	Actor, fashion model, and musician. Requires creative or musical talent
Arts Skilled	Graphic designer, photographer, and display artist. Requires artistic skills in the fields of photography, graphic arts, and design
Service Professionals	Teacher, counselor, and social worker. Requires responsibility in caring for the personal needs and welfare of people
Service Skilled	Housekeeper, cosmetologist, and bus driver. Requires providing personal, social and health services, or protection and transportation

SUMMARY

Although several different classification systems were illustrated in this chapter, they do not represent all systems available to help counselors to organize occupational information. Counselors need to explore computer systems, such as CHOICES, Guidance Information System (GIS), and DISCOVER, as they plan programs for a variety of clients. Occupational trends and projections were presented to show the changing nature of society and the labor market.

REVIEW QUESTIONS

1. What impact do you think the change in the work force from a producing to service economy will have on us as helping professionals? What services do we need to provide?
2. What job fields would you advise youths to enter? Why?
3. How has technology and the age of information affected you and your work?
4. What are some of the major ways to classify jobs and structure the world of work? How important do you think it is for career counselors to know these sources?

SUGGESTED LEARNING ACTIVITIES

1. Make an analysis of the want ads in your daily newspaper. What jobs are most often advertised? What type of jobs did you find least represented? Do the same review of the jobs posted on the computer network from your state department of employment and labor.
2. Interview state employment counselors or other employment counselors from the private or public sector and have them identify the work trends they are seeing in your community. Do they match the trends on the national level?
3. Write a paper or make an oral presentation on one of the topics in this chapter such as trends for new jobs, the changing work force, or the like.
4. Use several sources that are used to classify the structure of work such as the *Dictionary of Occupational Titles.* How easy was it for you to use the sources? What were some of the good features about the sources used? What were some of the problems you had with the classification systems?

CASE STUDIES

A Competent Teacher

Ms. Johnson, a middle-grade (science, math, reading, English, social studies, physical education, art, music) teacher, wants to show students that what they are learning is related not only to skills and competencies they need in everyday living but also in the workplace after they graduate.

Case Questions

1. What resources, reference sources should Ms. Johnson use with the students?

2.   Would you use any of the sources with the students discussed in this chapter? What ones would you choose? If you would not choose some of the sources, why not?

Searching for a Job

John has had a great time going to college but now, the semester he is planning to graduate, he decides he needs to research out what he will do after he graduates. He has read in the student newspaper some articles on the tight job market for college students. He concludes after some preliminary study that a lot of the jobs are the same but have different job titles in different industries.

Case Question

What sources, if any, would you use that were mentioned in this chapter?

SUGGESTED READINGS

McDaniels, C. (1989). *The changing workplace.* San Francisco: Jossey-Bass.

The book is divided into four parts. Part one discusses what to expect in tomorrow's workplace. Part two describes three scenarios on the future of work and their implications for career counseling. Part three reviews wild cards in the changing workplace and new career possibilities. Part four centers on career counseling for work and leisure.

McDaniels, C., & Gysbers, N. C. (1992). *Counseling for career development: Resources and practice.* San Francisco: Jossey-Bass.

The purpose of this book is to assist counselors with client career development. It provides theory, resources, and information about work structure and strategies for using this information in counseling.

CAREER DEVELOPMENT THEORY AND PRACTICE

4

DEVELOPMENTAL THEORIES IN GRADES K–5

Personality theories such as the psychodynamic emphasize the importance of early childhood experiences in formulating the personality and attitude of adults. Children do tend to make initial career decisions during this period. They are greatly influenced by the environment, the community they live in, their socioeconomic status, their family situation, and the significant adults in their life among other factors. Their initial attitudes and knowledge about the world of work are also shaped by television. Career preparation during this period focuses on developing the awareness of occupations and guiding students in developing greater self-knowledge.

LEARNING OBJECTIVES

After reading the chapter, you should be able to do the following:

- Identify the key theories of cognitive, career, personality, and social development that are essential to understanding the child during this period
- Discuss the roles of the elementary school counselor in career counseling and career preparation programs
- Discuss the goals and objectives of career preparation programs in grades K–6
- Discuss the types of career counseling approaches that would be appropriate to use with K–6 grade students
- Identify the type of assessment instruments that would be appropriate for counselors to use at this level

COMPETENCIES

The counselor needs to have knowledge of career development theories, theories of cognitive development, personality development, and social development and be able to use this knowledge to work with children in this age group. The counselor needs to know the resources available and be able to evaluate their appropriateness. The counselor needs to be able to consult with administrators, teachers, and parents and guide them to start an effective career education program for children in this age group.

The career guidance movement had as one of its basic assumptions "since both one's career and one's education extended from preschool through the retirement years, career education must also span almost the entire life cycle" (U.S. Office of Education, 1975, p. 4).

The input and communication among classroom teachers, the business-labor-industry community, home and family member counseling, guidance personnel, school administrators, and school board members are an important part of the career education movement process. The assumption is that the infusion of career education could be accomplished by existing personnel with some minor role changes. Teachers had five tasks in the comprehensive career education model. These are to do the following:

1. Devise and/or locate methods and materials designed to help pupils understand and appreciate the career implications of the subject matter being taught
2. Utilize career-oriented methods and materials in the instructional program, when appropriate, as one means of educational motivation
3. Help students acquire and utilize good work habits
4. Help students develop, clarify, and assimilate personally meaningful sets of work values
5. Integrate, to the fullest extent possible, the programmatic assumptions of career education into their instructional activities and teacher-pupil relationships.

Parents and guardians of the students were also to have a role in career education. They were to do the following:

1. Help students acquire and practice good work habits
2. Emphasize development of positive work values and attitudes toward work
3. Maximize, to the fullest extent possible, career development options and opportunities for themselves and for their children. (Office of Education, 1975, p. 10)

Administrators and school board members were asked to be involved in the following tasks:

1. Emphasize career education as a priority goal
2. Provide leadership and direction to the career education program
3. Involve the widest possible community participation in career education policy decision making
4. Provide the time, materials, and finances required for implementing the career education program
5. Initiate curriculum revision designed to integrate academic, general, and vocational education into an expanded set of educational opportunities available to all students. (Office of Education, 1975, p. 10)

Counselors also had their specific responsibilities:

1. Help classroom teachers implement career education in the classroom
2. Serve, usually with other educational personnel, as liaison between the school and the business-industry-labor community
3. Serve, usually with other educational personnel, in implementing career education concepts within the home and family structure
4. Help students in the total career development process, including the making and implementation of career decisions
5. Participate in part-time and full-time job placement programs and in follow-up studies of former students (Office of Education, 1975, p. 9)

THEORETICAL BASES

Career counseling and development activities for preschool and elementary-aged children have a broad theoretical base. Plato, Jesus Christ, Alexander Pope, Wordsworth, and Freud all emphasized the importance of early experiences on later behavior. For example, Plato pointed out that in the early years any impression we choose to make leaves a permanent mark on the child. Freud emphasized that the child is the father (or mother) of the man (woman), and his or her early experiences are extremely important influences on later life.

DEVELOPMENTAL TASKS

Career counselors need to be familiar with what the traditional developmental tasks are for preschool and primary-school-aged children. According to Havighurst (1972), developmental tasks are tasks that arise "at or about a certain period in the life of an individual, successful achievement of which leads to his happiness and to success with later tasks, while failure leads to unhappiness in the individual and disapproval by society, and difficulty with later tasks (p. 2)." The five tasks for early childhood are the need to learn sex differences and sexual modesty; the need to achieve physiological stability; the need to form simple concepts of social and physical reality; the need to learn to relate oneself emo-

tionally to parents, siblings, and other people; and the need to learn to distinguish right and wrong and to develop a conscience. The tasks for middle childhood are to learn physical skills necessary for ordinary games; to build whole-
some attitudes toward oneself as a growing organism; to learn to get along with
age-mates; to learn an appropriate masculine or feminine social role; to develop
fundamental skills in reading, writing, and calculating; to develop concepts necessary for everyday living; to develop conscience, morality, and a scale of values;
to achieve personal independence; and to develop positive attitudes toward social
groups and institutions. Seligman (1980) suggested that six additional goals
should be added to broaden the list so that it would address the issues of career
development better:

1.   To develop a broad, flexible, and satisfying sex role identity
2.   To develop attitudes that are conducive to competence, cooperation,
      and achievement
3.   To develop self-awareness and a positive self-concept
4.   To acquire knowledge about workers, their roles, and the value of work
5.   To develop some understanding of the relationship of interests and
      values to occupational choice
6.   To develop an awareness and appreciation of one's own interests, val-
      ues, abilities, and personal qualities.

Cognitive Development

There are several stages of cognitive development in elementary students. Children between 2 and 5 are moving from using preoperational to concrete operational thought. Their thinking tends to focus on one quality. They have the
inability to reverse, and so exhibit one-track thinking. They have difficulty taking
another's point of view. The 6- to 12-year-old group uses concrete operational
thinking, which is characterized by decentration, classification, and seriation.
They can use socialized thinking, which shows the beginning of their awareness
of others and self-consciousness. Differences in cognitive styles also appear during the ages of 6 to 12. Some students want to give quick answers or are impul-
sive thinkers, and others tend to mull things over before responding and are
reflective thinkers. Some tend to focus on details and are analytic and others may
report general patterns and themes. Counselors need to know that the cognitive
level or understanding of the child may affect how he or she understands and
structures the knowledge being presented. This information is also valuable when
determining whether counseling materials are appropriate for the age group.

Relationships with Others

Sullivan (1953) emphasizes the importance of interpersonal relationships in the
formulation of one's personality. Preschool children's personalities are influ-

enced by their relationships with their parents. For example, children who have authoritative parents tend to be self-reliant and competent and children who have authoritarian parents tend to be insecure and hostile. Children with permissive parents become dependent and immature. Peers also serve as models and as reinforcing agents. Other significant adults such as teachers are important role models. Primary grade students' family structure may have an important influence on their development. Boys from father-absent homes may have problems in acquiring masculine traits and act immature. Single parents are often forced to play multiple roles. Children often have problems in identifying appropriate sex-role behavior. The divorce rate has increased to where one out of every two marriages ends in divorce. Children are often greatly influenced by the change in family structure. The impact of divorce depends on factors such as the age of the child, the sex of the child, and the attitude the mother and father have toward each other.

Personality Development

An important aspect of personality development is psychosocial development. Erikson (1963) postulated that personal identity grows out of the crises we have in our psychosocial development. Preschool and primary-school-aged children have three crises that occur. The first is autonomy versus shame and doubt, which occurs in early childhood. Children constantly test their parents and environment to learn what they can control and what they can not. Ideally children can develop a sense of self-control without having a negative self-esteem. Over-control by parents might lead to feelings of doubt of their abilities.

The second crisis is initiative verses guilt, which occurs in middle childhood. The development of initiative and the consequent experience of guilt begin to form the conscience. If teachers and parents block initiative too often, children will feel guilty and constricted.

The major crisis that occurs between kindergarten and puberty is accomplishment versus inferiority. If children are not able to achieve, they will develop feelings of inferiority and inadequacy. Teachers and parents need to structure experiences in order that the child does achieve.

Between 2 and 5 children develop a cognitive map of sex roles by imitating the behavior of multiple models. Society has different expectations for both sexes, and numerous environmental factors help shape sex-stereotyped behavior.

Career Development Theories

Career development theorists see this age period as important in beginning career exploration. Super (1981) identified the ages of 4 to 14 as the tentative period in which children start thinking about careers and themselves. They use fantasy in their play and act out career roles. They become more aware of their interests, and by the age of 11 and 12, their interest are strong determinants of the activities they choose and the aspirations they consider.

Ginzberg, Ginsburg, Axelrad, and Herma (1951) have identified the period from birth to age 11 as the fantasy period. The stage is valuable for children to participate in because they can picture themselves in a variety of adult roles without any risk and have fun doing it.

Self-Concept Development

Self-concept development is important at this period and begins to have an influence on career development. Lynch and Lynch (1990) postulated that self-concept is a cognitive variable and has a cognitive set of rules. They concluded that these rules operate as an executive monitor similar to ego control functions in information processing models of cognition. Children go through stages of self-concept development and at each stage there are major emphases on rule development. The set of rules that affect the self-concept of children in early childhood are the self-esteem rules that are related to their evaluating their self-worth. Lynch says that the period from 6 to 12 years is marked by the development of idealized self-rules.

CAREER PREPARATION

Career preparation is important for preschool children as well as for elementary school students. Children's perceptions of work and occupations are based on what they see and hear at home, in their neighborhood, and community or what they see and hear on television.

CAREER PREPARATION OBJECTIVES FOR GRADES K-3

The scope and sequence of career preparation activities depends on the priority the program has within a school district as well as the availability of appropriate materials and trained personnel. The goals for three programs for K–3 students are compared in Table 4.1.

The program goals in the three programs include objectives relating to awareness of self, awareness of decision making, and awareness of competencies needed as building blocks for positive career development.

Students in grades K–3 are to be guided to develop an appreciation for and a positive attitude toward work. They can be presented situations in which they have to identify and discuss different types of workers. They should be able to demonstrate that they understand the importance of jobs in the community and are able to understand the importance for preparing for a job. Students can also

TABLE 4.1
Comparison of goals of three career-preparation programs for K–3

Portland, OR	Iowa	Riverside, CA
Identify and develop attitudes toward the world of work	Develop inter-personal relationships	Develop self-awareness
Acquire knowledge about world of work	Discover relationship between education and life planning	Develop occupational awareness
Identify their individuality and relate it to occupational roles	Learn educational competencies necessary to survive in changing world	Attitude development
Develop decision-making skills	Develop appreciation and positive attitude toward work	Develop economic awareness
Develop physical and mental skills related to occupational goals	Be actively involved in the career development process Get family involved in student's career decision making	Learn basic life and survival skills

be expected to discuss work-related activities necessary in the home and school, important community workers, and how these workers help everyone.

They can also be guided to develop skills to help them locate, evaluate, and interpret information about vocational and career opportunities. They can be expected to describe the work of members of their family, as well as jobs that are unique to their community. They can begin to identify the work activities that appeal to them as students.

Students in K–3 are also instructed in decision-making skills. They are able to discuss the choices they make and show that they know the simple strategies and steps used in problem solving. They are able to discuss the importance of learning skills for decision making, even though they are still young.

Students in K–3 are instructed in employment-seeking skills, too. They can be presented activities in which they are guided to recognize the interdependence of jobs and facts about the economy. They can study local employers and the skills necessary for workers being hired by these employers. They can learn about the different working conditions or work environments related to the jobs they study.

It is important to involve the family in the career decision-making process of their children. In order to accomplish this goal the family has to gain an understanding of the student's interests, abilities, and achievement. The family has to be willing to assist their children in developing responsibility for themselves and their learning. The parents need to help their children develop interest in learning.

Characteristic Activities

Counselors and teachers use a wide variety of activities to help children develop occupational awareness. The students in this age range do prefer concrete experiences and active participation.

Passive listening and lecture techniques are ineffective. The activities also need to relate to their world and what they are familiar with.

The developmental objective of occupational awareness is to have students learn about different jobs in the community, the working conditions, and the functions, duties, and titles of the workers. The counselor might use the activities listed in Figure 4.1.

Infusion of Career Preparation into the Curriculum

Students should have an instructional program that infuses self-concept, career development, and technological awareness activities into the curriculum. Sometimes the objectives can be a part of the basic curriculum that primary children have in the language arts, social studies, mathematics, or science areas. Counselors then are facilitators and help the teacher infuse occupational preparation activities into the curriculum; for example, if the objective were to focus on the roles of family members, both on the job and at home. The unit may be infused in the language arts curriculum. Students could be asked to write a paragraph of what mom and dad do at work. They could make a booklet about themselves

---

* Field trips to local businesses, industries, and governmental agencies, for example, police, fire, mayor, etc. The teacher or class could make a video if equipment was available for other and future classes.
* Outside speakers, especially parents, talking about their job field
* The students dress or use pantomime or pictures or role-playing to depict occupations and have the other students guess.
* Identify and use tools. A variety of either pictures of tools or real tools could be used and discussed of typical occupations in the area. The students could be asked what occupations use each tool.
* Dramatic presentations. The students could dress up as workers or family members and demonstrate the roles, responsibilities, or duties of that person.
* Puppets. They could use puppets to role-play duties and responsibilities of school personnel or family members.
* Films, pictures, or other visuals, worksheets. The activities could include experiences in which they have to describe the worker, classify the job, or some features of the job environment.

FIGURE 4.1
Activities to develop occupational awareness for K–3 students

and tell about their jobs and responsibilities around their home, their school, and also tell about their parents.

They could write a paragraph and illustrate it with drawings about the type of jobs they do at school and at home. They could write a story about a job they would like to do or a worker they would like to be like.

In mathematics they could work with birth dates of each family member, count the number of duties they are responsible for doing at home, or at school.

THE MIDDLE GRADES

Middle grade students are guided to focus on the same general themes as the K–3 students—self-awareness, occupational awareness, attitude toward work, educational awareness, economic awareness, and learning basic life and survival skills—but at a higher cognitive level. Typical objectives for middle grade career guidance programs are included in Figure 4.2.

Parents should also be involved in the career development of their children. The family needs to take interest in as well as to develop understanding of the

---

Decision Making
See the need to establish goals
Use decision-making skills in working with school-related problems

Self-awareness
Be aware of individual strengths and weaknesses
Relate strengths and weaknesses to job choices

Educational Awareness
Investigate the relationship between educational skills and individual success

Economic Awareness
Understand the process of production and distribution of products and services
Understand the law of supply and demand
See the relationship between economic conditions and jobs available

Occupational Awareness
Be able to classify occupations according to several types of systems
Recognize how careers influence one's roles in life
Discuss the advantages and disadvantages of jobs considered

Work Attitudes
Learn the rights and responsibilities of a worker
Recognize the role of work in our society

FIGURE 4.2
Career guidance goals for middle grade students

student's interests, abilities, and achievement. They can be instrumental in assisting the student in developing the responsibility for learning to learn. They can instill in their child the concept that learning is a lifetime process.

Sometimes career preparation for the middle grades consists of just a brief unit. Pugh (1986) had 15 objectives on a unit on occupations, which are listed in Figure 4.3.

The Iowa State Department of Education (1986) has suggested five developmental outcomes focused under personal and social development for fourth- to sixth-graders:

1. Be able to demonstrate concern and respect for feelings and interests of others
2. Be able to distinguish between self-characteristics and group characteristics

---

1. After learning about occupations, students will be able to match personal attributes with occupational areas.
2. Students will demonstrate ability to use the library to do research.
3. Students will be able to write open-ended questions pertaining to occupations, which they will use to conduct interviews and write letters.
4. Given an occupation, students will be able to name a personal attribute and level of education for that occupation.
5. Students will be able to set short- and-long term personal goals and be able to revise them.
6. Students will be able to name qualities of a good worker.
7. Students will interview persons about their occupation using open-ended questions.
8. After studying this unit, students will be able to name a variety of occupations.
9. Students will state that one advantage of choosing an occupation in the United States is freedom of choice.
10. Students will give an oral presentation on an occupation having gained information through research, interviews, and written letters.
11. On a quiz at the end of the unit, students will list three qualities that are common to the responsible worker and the responsible student.
12. Students will state the advantages of being educated.
13. Students will state that in the United States occupation is a matter of personal choice.
14. On a quiz at the end of the unit, students will be able to name types of education available to them.
15. In class discussions, students will state their determination to accomplish their life goals.

FIGURE 4.3
Objectives for a unit on occupations

3. Be able to demonstrate tolerance and flexibility for interpersonal relationships in group situations
4. Be able to demonstrate contributing competencies in group situations
5. Be able to relate values to interpersonal communication

Students are expected to grow in their educational development also by being able to realize the influence of their educational planning for living a responsible and self-fulfilling life. They are expected to be able to discuss the different factors that influence their learning as well as accept their responsibility for developing their potential and recognize that making mistakes is an important part of learning. They also are guided to identify the relationships between learning and various careers.

The career development objectives for fourth- through sixth-graders under Learning to Make a Living are that the student is expected to be able to discuss a variety of occupations and jobs and show an understanding of the importance of personal characteristics to these jobs.

Students at this grade level are also expected to develop an appreciation for and a positive attitude toward work. They are expected to be able to describe the relationships between the needs of society and work and how jobs satisfy individual needs. They need a broad-based knowledge of jobs and occupations.

Fourth- through sixth-graders begin to need skills for locating, evaluating, and interpreting information about career opportunities. They need to be exposed to the ways occupations are classified and be able to identify a number of jobs within an occupational classification. They need to be guided to use school and community resources to help them learn about occupations. They need to begin to examine the relationship of personal values and abilities to occupational interests.

Students also need to be able to work on their career decision-making skills by being able to identify goals and then outline steps for establishing a plan of action in decision making. They need to be able to assess their skills for making decisions and recognize what their personal values are and how they affect decision making. They need to begin to understand that career and vocational development is a continuous process.

Students need to start to develop job-seeking skills. They need to start to explore the demand for workers in various careers and note the changes in supply and demand for employees in different occupations. They need to see how their skills are related to occupations.

Evaluation skills are also necessary. Students need to be familiar with the businesses and industries in their area and be cognizant of the working conditions in these places of work.

ASSESSMENT INSTRUMENTS

There are a number of career assessment instruments that are appropriate for administration within the lower primary and middle grades. It may be helpful to counselors and teachers to know what self-concept, interest, and career knowledge tests are appropriate for this age group. The test information can be used to help facilitate planning or tell the staff where is a good place to start class or group sessions. The tests are listed in Table 4.2.

Assessment instruments provide a structured approach to help counselors understand the interests, self-concept, and attitudes of the students with whom they are working. The instruments can be used effectively in individual, group, or class situations.

CAREER PREPARATION ROLES OF THE COUNSELOR

Miller (1989) identified three major career preparation roles of the counselor in grades K–6: (1) to enhance the child's self-awareness, (2) to promote self-skills needed later in life (e.g., playfulness, cooperation), and (3) to present general information about occupations and the world of work. He cautions counselors about providing too specific career information at this grade level and reminds us that time perspective is not centered on what might happen when they are 18, 20, or 25.

The counselor's role involves coordination of the program to ensure continuity of the themes through K–6 grades. Are the materials, tests, work sheets, audiovisual aids ordered and/or scheduled? Are the classrooms scheduled? The counselor's role also requires consultation skills. Teachers might need to seek help if the program is to be infused into the curriculum rather than being the direct responsibility of the counselor. They might want to discuss the suggested activities and content. The counselor also may be in charge of professional development activities and be involved in direct instructions of topics to the teaching staff.

The counselor uses group guidance techniques to present the topic of the day in a classroom situation and utilizes hands-on experiences, role-playing, dramatization, class discussion, as well as audiovisual aids to present the topic.

COUNSELING APPROACHES

Miller (1989) feels at the elementary school level the introductory stage of career development should include activities that target the students' awareness of self, feelings of autonomy and control, need for playful behavior, and desire for exploration.

Some of the activities Miller suggests are as follows:

This Feels Like a Peach
These are a series of Gestalt-theory-based classroom exercises designed for classroom groups from kindergarten through the sixth grade (Remer & Schrader, 1981). The exercises focus on learning how to be aware of oneself and ones environment.

TABLE 4.2

Career development assessment instruments for K–6 students

Category/Instrument Interests/Attitudes	Beginning grade level	Description	Publisher
Wide Range Interest–Opinion Test	5	Assess perceptions of ability, aspiration level, and social conformity for use in vocational and career planning and counseling	Jastak
Career Maturity Inventory Attitude Scale & Competency test	6	Assesses students' attitude and competencies regarding career decisions	CTB/McGraw-Hill
COPSystem Interest Inventory Form R COPSystem Intermediate Inventory	6	Assesses interest related to occupational clusters	Educational & Industrial Testing Service
Explore the World of Work	4–6	Assesses vocational interests for students in grades 4–6	CFKR Career Material, Inc.
Hall Occupational Orientation Inventory (Intermediate)	3–7	Assesses psychological needs related to worker's traits and job characteristics	Scholastic Testing Service
Individual Career Exploration	3–12	Assesses general career areas of interest	Scholastic Testing Service
Safran Students Interest Inventory Level 1	5–9	Measures occupational interests and school subject interests	Nelson Canada
Career Awareness Inventory Attitudes	3–12	Measures how much students know about careers and their own career choices	Scholastic Testing Service
Arlin-Hills Attitude Surveys	K–12	Measures attitudes toward teachers, learning, language, and arithmetic	Psychologists and Educators
Survey of School Attitudes	1–8	Measures student's attitudes toward reading and language arts, science, social studies, and math	The Psychological Corporation
Values Inventory for Children	1–4	Assesses values of children and their relations to other children, parents and authority figures	Sheridan Psychological Services
The Affective Perception Inventory	1–12	Measures students attitude toward self and school and specific subject areas	Soares Associates
Martinek-Zaichkowsky Self-Concept Scale for Children	1–8	Assesses global self-concept and physical, emotional, and behavioral aspects of self-confidence	Psychologists and Educators
SCAMIN: A Self-Concept & Motivation Inventory	Preschool-K 1–3 3–6	Early elementary forms Assesses achievement investment, role expectations, achievement needs, and self-adequacy	Person-O-Metrics, Inc.
Coopersmith Self-Esteem Inventory—School form	3–12	Assesses attitudes toward self, school, family, and peers	Consulting Psychologists Press
Culture Free Self-Esteem Inventory	3–+	Measures general self-esteem school, peer, parent, self	Special Child Publications
Piers-Harris Children's Self-Concept Scale	4–12	Assesses student self-concept in six areas: behavior, intellectual and school status, physical appearance and attributes, anxiety, popularity, happiness, and satisfaction	Western Psychological Service

What Do Your Parents Do?

Parents can be a valuable source of information about the world of work. Students can interview their parents and find out what they do, where they work, what kinds of clothing they wear to work, what they like or dislike most about their jobs, how they decided on the type of work, and what other types of jobs they would like to do.

How Does McDonald's Affect My Life

Students are asked to identify all the workers that affect their lives between the time they get up in the morning to the time they go to bed at night, such as the mail carrier, paper distributor, radio disc jockey, breakfast food manufacturer, and so on. Groups could be formed to determine whether one category of workers was more important than another and discuss their reasons for this choice.

I've Got A Great Plan

Miller suggests that the class can be involved in real situations as well as imaginary or simulated situations in planning and decision making. Planning skills are needed to plan class parties and other school activities. He feels that any activity that reinforces students' ability to plan and use decision-making competencies are beneficial.

Hey! It's Story Time!

Guided reading of bibliotherapy can be used to help students gain an understanding of themselves and their environment but also can be used to accomplish career development objectives.

IMPORTANT CHARACTERISTICS OF ELEMENTARY SCHOOL CHILDREN

There are a number of important characteristics of elementary school children that the counselor needs to be reminded to consider in developing any career development program:

- Children's self-concept is determined by what others say about them and expect of them. Parents and teachers are highly influential in the development of children's self-esteem.
- Teacher expectations may have a negative effect on some students especially minority and nonachieving students.
- Children begin to develop their ability to show empathy and move through several stages of moral development during this period.
- During middle childhood sex identification becomes stronger and friendships are formed with members of the same gender.

- Some experts feel that television inhibits the social development of children and encourages them to be passive recipients of information rather than to be actively involved in the discovery of knowledge.
- In this developmental period children decrease in their involvement in free play, and replace it with hobbies, reading, organized team sports, and other activities.
- School is a powerful socializing influence.
- Boys are normally heavier and taller than girls throughout their lives but during middle childhood girls become heavier and taller than boys for a brief period.
- Some children are mastery oriented and accept the responsibility for their actions and for the outcomes of their behavior. Others are helpless and attribute their successes and failures to factors over which they have no control and tend not to change their estimates of their capabilities when presented with success.

SUGGESTIONS FOR COUNSELORS

1. Work with teachers to help them identify stud∶nts who are not achieving and developing a success identity so that interventions can be designed to help these students early on.
2. Work with at-risk students individually and in small groups to help them develop positive self-concepts. Early intervention will prevent dropouts later and assure that the students learn the basic skills that they need to survive in our changing society.
3. Work with teachers to get them to infuse career guidance objectives into the classes they are teaching. Have a bibliography of resources for teachers to use. Provide suggested activities for them to use. Showing application of what the students are studying to real-life applications makes learning more meaningful.
4. Learning is more effective if students are actively involved. They learn by doing, seeing, and hearing. Encourage the use of field trips, laboratory activities, and outside speakers.
5. Use parents and individuals from the community in career guidance activities. Students are more impressed with seeing successful role models than by reading about them.
6. Work at expanding the horizons of girls and minority group members. Stereotyping starts early.

REVIEW QUESTIONS

1. What are the typical roles and duties of the elementary guidance counselor?

2.   Are career guidance activities an important part of the counselor's work? Why or why not?

3.   In choosing career guidance activities for the primary grades, what aspects of development does the counselor need to take into consideration? For the middle grades?

4.   Should the counselor be responsible for and deliver the career guidance program or should the teachers be responsible for it by infusing the objectives into the subjects they teach? Take a position and discuss the rationale for your decision.

5.   What elements would you include in a career guidance program for kindergarten students? For first-graders? For second-graders? For third-graders? For fourth-graders? For fifth-graders? For sixth-graders?

6.   What type of strategies would you use to help both boys and girls avoid sex stereotyped views of occupations and the world of work?

7.   Would you use career assessment inventories as part of your guidance program? Why or why not? If yes, when would you use them and how would they be used?

SUGGESTED LEARNING ACTIVITIES

1.   Interview several elementary counselors and find out what priority career guidance has in their work and what type of career education and guidance activities they do with the students.

2.   Collect several career guidance programs from different states or districts and analyze the similarities and differences in them.

3.   Interview children in grades K–6 and find out their career and educational plans. You could construct a brief questionnaire or interview schedule to find out about their plans and interests and how they relate to their parents educational and occupational backgrounds.

4.   Get permission from the parents of a student and administer one of the career assessment instruments. Interview the test taker and find out his or her reaction to the test and to its results.

5.   Watch television programs that are normally watched by this age group. What are the occupations of the main adult characters in the programs? What are their attitudes toward work? What kind of impact do you think television has on occupational interest?

6.   Review several basal readers from this grade level. What are the occupations of the main adult figures in the story? Are these adults working in nontraditional career fields? Is there sex stereotyping in the stories?

7.   Review several commercial programs designed for this grade level. Make a critical analysis of these materials. Do the materials take into consideration the developmental characteristics of the students the materials were designed for?

8. Interview several different elementary teachers and find out if and how they infuse career guidance objectives into their curriculum.

9. Work with teachers to get them to infuse developmental counseling objectives into the classes they are teaching. Have a bibliography of resources for teachers to use. Provide suggested activities for them to use. Showing application of what the students are studying to real life applications makes learning more meaningful.

10. Learning is more effective if students are actively involved. They learn by doing and seeing and hearing. Encourage the use of field trips, laboratory activities, and outside speakers.

11. Use parents and individuals from the community in career guidance activities. Students are more impressed with seeing successful role models than by reading about them.

12. Work at expanding the horizons of girls and minority group members. Stereotyping starts early.

CASE STUDIES

Girl Engineers?

"Designing and building space stations sounds like an exciting field for the 21st century," Mary, a fifth-grade student commented. Before she could continue, Albert said, "Girls do not become engineers. They need us men. We know more science and math."

Case Questions

1. Would you interrupt the discussion and make some comments? How would you respond?
2. What would you do as a counselor to discourage sex stereotyping and encourage consideration by students of nontraditional career fields?

Boring Field Trips

You are walking down the hall and overhear the conversation of a third-grade student who says, "to the fire station again. All we do ever is take trips to the same stupid places."

Case Questions

1. Would you interrupt and ask why the student did not like the field trip? What would you do?
2. How would you work with teachers to make field trips more exciting and include some career preparation objectives?

George in Trouble

You were asked by a teacher to have a conference with a student and his mother. George is from a single-parent family whose father recently left George's mother for another woman. George refuses to do any homework and his mother works two jobs to make ends meet. He is left alone at home part of the time while his mother works. George feels rejected and has also developed a negative identity at school because he is failing his reading and math in third grade. He received B's and C's on his report card the year before. He scored in the average range on the Stanford Achievement Test.

Case Questions

1. What additional information would you need to have to help George?
2. How would you help him develop a positive identity and meet the goals at his stage of development?

SUGGESTED READINGS

Development during middle childhood. (1984). Washington, DC: National Academy Press.

    The book presents essays on what is currently known about families, peers, self, problems, and disturbances of students during their elementary school years.

Strom, R. D., Bernard, H. W., & Strom, S. K. (1987). *Human development and learning.* New York: Human Science Press.

    The book presents a life-span approach to learning and includes chapters on maintaining health and wellness, developing intellectual abilities, supporting emotional growth, pursuing lifelong learning, facilitating positive motivation, coping with stress, acquiring social competence, and fostering effective communication. Each chapter has sections that discuss aspects of infancy, early childhood, middle and later childhood, adolescence, early and middle adulthood, and later adulthood.

5

CAREER COUNSELING OF MIDDLE SCHOOL CHILDREN AND JUNIOR HIGH STUDENTS

An important transition period for students is the end of childhood and the beginning of adolescence. These students are moving from elementary school to middle school and are required to make decisions about what courses they have to take. The educational decisions they make can affect their later vocational opportunities. They need assistance in developing decision-making skills. They need to work on increasing their vocational awareness and exploring and planning for their future. Career education during this period focuses more on career and educational awareness, exploration, and tentative planning.

LEARNING OBJECTIVES

After reading the chapter, you should be able to do the following:

- Identify the key theories of career development, personality development, and social development that are essential to understanding the child during this period
- Discuss the role of the counselor in working with middle school students
- Critique the practices, methods, procedures, and career and developmental counseling activities that are currently used with middle school youth
- Discuss the goals of career education for the middle school student
- Use skills to gather, process, and act on information to plan a middle school career program

CHARACTERISTICS OF MIDDLE SCHOOL CHILDREN

As parents and teachers know, this age group possesses limitless energy, among a number of other characteristics. At grades five and six, girls tend to be taller than boys and experience their growth spurt just before the event of puberty. They usually begin their growth spurt about 2 years earlier than boys. The average age at which American girls reach menarche is between 12 and 13. Boys reach puberty on the average at 14. Sex-typing becomes more marked during this period.

Students are gaining more personal independence as well as the ability to think and reason at higher conceptual levels. They grow less self-centered and proceed through stages of moral development from conventional to postconventional morality. The physical growth spurt, or lack of growth, may influence their self-concept development. They have begun to develop body control, strength, and endurance. They want to make decisions, assume responsibility, take initiative, and have independence regarding activities they see as important.

DEVELOPMENTAL TASKS

The Carnegie Task Force on Education of Young Adolescents (1990) identified five characteristics that they want every young adolescent to know, to feel, and to be able to do:

1. Become an intellectually reflective person
2. Be enroute to a lifetime of meaningful work
3. Be a good citizen
4. Be a caring and ethical individual
5. Be a healthy person

Havighurst (1972) identified 10 developmental tasks that span across adolescence. The list includes the same themes as the Carnegie report but adds additional social and psychological tasks such as achieving new and more mature relations with peers of both sexes, accepting one's physique and using the body effectively, and achieving a masculine or feminine social role.

Overall, the developmental tasks relate to changing cognitive, social, emotional, and physical self of students in this age period. They are expected to develop internal locus of control, to be guided by intrinsic rewards and demonstrate a degree of personal and social responsibility. Early adolescents are expected to develop and use decision-making skills and have the ability to plan.

Cognitive Development

Early adolescence marks the movement from the concrete operational stage to the formal operational stage. In the formal operational stage adolescents demonstrate the ability to think about possibilities, to think ahead, to think about thoughts, and even think beyond limits as well as to think about plans to solve problems rather than the use of trial-and-error learning (Keating, 1980). The transition from one stage to another might not take place abruptly. It may be characteristic of the individual's thinking in one subject but not another. Some individuals never achieve the full progression to the formal stage of operations even when they are in college.

Traditionally, the following is thought: Girls tend to excel in verbal ability and boys tend to excel in visual-spatial ability and mathematics. Boys exhibit more aggressive behavior than girls. Block (1976) found evidence that boys are better at solving insight problems than girls, are more dominant, and have stronger self-concepts than girls. Girls tend to be more fearful and compliant than boys.

Early adolescents tend to become egocentric again and use their new cognitive skills to analyze themselves in an introspective fashion. They project this interest in introspection to their peers and this causes them to be self-conscious.

The morality of cooperation, that is, the stress on agreements, is important to early adolescents. They also begin to understand that they might have to make allowance for intentions and see how their actions influence other individuals.

Personality Development

Erikson (1968) postulated that personal identity grows out of crises the individual has in psychosocial development. The failure to resolve crises can cause personality regression. The crisis accomplishment versus inferiority was central in the preadolescent school years. If this crisis is successfully resolved, then students have developed their cooperation skills and value working. Adolescence marks the crisis of identity versus role confusion. The important goal of this period is for individuals to establish a sense of identity. If individuals are unable to come to an understanding of themselves, the lack of identity leads to role confusion. The search for identity is not often resolved during early adolescence but at a later age. What adolescents want to do and who they are are questions they start to try to resolve.

Sullivan (1953) felt that the significant others in our lives help shape our personality. Peers become more important than do parents or other adults in the early adolescent period. A friend of the same sex becomes an important figure going into puberty.

Most adolescents fall into Selman's (1980) level 3, the mutual perspective-taking. Adolescents become able to develop points of view that take all individual perspectives into account. They are able to see themselves and others as if they were a third person. They are limited in their interpersonal understanding because they are able to integrate only those perspectives they have experienced and may develop one-sided views of social life.

Lynch and Lynch (1991) described middle childhood as the period when individuals focus on developing idealized self-concept rules. This period is labeled *the idealized self.* Rules for setting expectations and standards are set. The period from 12 to 18 years is labeled *the empathic self.* Rules for social interactions, social acceptance, independence, ego-identity, and sex-orientation are being developed.

Career Development

Ginzberg (1972) has identified the age between 11 and 17 as the tentative period. This stage is divided into four stages: interest, capacity, value, and transition. Children initially consider what they like to do and are interested in doing. They realize that they have to take into consideration their aptitudes because there are some things they can do more skillfully than others. Next, they develop an awareness that there are some activities that have more extrinsic or intrinsic value than others, and they include this value factor in the decisions they make or think about making. They start to consider their interests, aptitudes, and values in their vocational decisions. The interest stage evolves around ages 11 and 12; the capacity stage, between 12 and 14. The value stage follows and is usually during middle or late adolescence. The transition stage is the last part of the tentative period and occurs approximately at age 18.

Early adolescents approach the tentative stage in Super's (1980) model. They are still in the growth stage in which they are exploring their interests and their aptitudes. The students in this age period will be making some important career and educational decisions, developing the discipline of work, and acquiring respect for others and the work they do.

IMPORTANT CHARACTERISTICS OF THE STUDENTS

In review, the important characteristics a counselor should keep in mind when working with junior high–aged students are the following:

- Early adolescents are egocentric and greatly concerned about the reaction of others to them.
- Personal appearance becomes extremely important.
- Early maturing boys tend to have higher self-esteem and self-confidence than late-maturing boys.
- Most students arrive at the formal cognitive stage although formal thinking may not be used in all subjects.
- The rapid rate of development in girls as compared with boys is evident in the marked differences in the social orientation and maturity of the sexes.
- Cognitive subabilities (such as spatial, verbal, memory, induction, deduction) begin to sharpen.
- Students want to have autonomy.

CAREER PREPARATION GOALS AND OBJECTIVES

The variety and type of current programs vary from school district to district and state to state. Some states have comprehensive career education plans to provide structure for the individual school districts. Ohio has recently mandated an individual career plan commencing for all students in the seventh grade.

Usually the first major component of a career education program at this level is the focus on the personal and social development of students. They are expected to develop an appreciation for others that will enrich their interpersonal relationships. Counselors can guide students to demonstrate concern and respect for feelings and interests of others as well as distinguish between self-characteristics and group characteristics in interrelationships. They can help students to demonstrate tolerance and flexibility for interpersonal relationships and group participation, to contribute in group activities demonstrating competencies interrelating with group members, to relate values to the process of interpersonal communication, and to begin to identify their own value system.

A second goal is to help students learn to learn. They are to be guided to realize the influence of their education in planning for and in living a responsible, self-fulfilling life. This goal can be accomplished through helping students understand the different factors that influence learning, understand the concept of accepting responsibility for developing their own potentials, and understand that success and failure in academic areas are important aspects of learning. They can be exposed to advantages and disadvantages of different types of post-secondary educational and training programs and can be asked to study the requirements for entering secondary education and training programs.

Students must develop an understanding of the importance of minimum educational competencies in order to be able to function in a rapidly changing society. Students are expected to acquire skills in order to understand what effect a changing society has on occupations. They need to be able to relate changing occupations to continued education and study and know how to assess the skills needed to cope with changing job markets.

Not only does the career education program have outcomes related to learning to learn but also about learning to make a living. Students are expected to develop an appreciation for and a positive attitude toward work. Middle school students need to be able to discuss the variety and complexity of occupations and jobs, demonstrate an understanding of how each job is important and has its place in society, demonstrate an understanding of the importance of personal traits to job success, and relate self-knowledge to a variety of jobs and occupations.

They also have to understand how the needs of society and the work performed by the members of society are related, discuss how every occupation has appealing aspects, and demonstrate knowledge of how occupations and jobs contribute to society.

Career awareness requires students to know how to locate, evaluate, and interpret information about career opportunities. The students need to be instructed to identify various ways occupations can be classified as well as to identify a number of jobs within an occupational classification. They must be able to demonstrate skills in using available school and community resources to learn about occupations. Discussing the relationship of personal values, abilities, and skills to occupational choice is critical to career decision making at this time.

Middle school students are expected to be actively engaged in planning their career and vocational development process. In doing this they are guided to see that career and vocational development is a continuous process with a sequential series of choices. Attention has to be given to assisting students with their decision-making skills. Students are asked to clarify their personal values and explain how their values affect decision making. Through discussions and exercises students begin to distinguish between essential and nonessential skills in decision making. As a result, they begin to use decision-making skills in the selection of courses and in setting tentative career goals. One way to accomplish this is to have a group of students design a project that would establish a mini business or industry in the classroom. Students would have to determine what goods or services people in the community need from a company and provide the service.

Early adolescents are expected to develop skills in securing employment. In the middle school setting, students need to be able to interpret terms and concepts used in describing employment opportunities and conditions, identify the demand for workers in various occupations, and recognize the influence of change in supply and demand for employees in different occupations at the local, state, and national level. In conjunction, they assess their salable skills for making educational choices. They also need to be familiar with the desirable aspects of working conditions of local occupations and jobs.

Students at this level need to learn to use the available placement services. Based on their interests, capabilities, and skills, they are expected to be able to select vocational exploratory and introductory programs, demonstrate knowledge of the training provided by the various programs that teach salable skills, and demonstrate knowledge of information related to employment opportunities. Students have to be able to choose instructional programs that will best meet their needs.

The career development of the students and their career decision-making skills will be enhanced if the family becomes involved in the process. Four outcomes that focus specifically on the family are the family needs to gain an understanding of the student's interests, abilities, and achievements, assist the student in yearly course selection and registration and in the career decision process, as well as to assist the student in understanding the relationship between school courses and occupational choices. It is also important to understand how parents make a living and what careers they are involved in.

The goal for sixth-graders in the *Florida Blueprint for Career Preparation* (1988) is a program of personal assessment and technology literacy instruction. It advocates that emphasis should be placed on assisting students with the assessment of personal aptitudes, abilities, and interests prior to orientation and exploration of careers. The plan includes representative competencies such as developing and using a positive self-concept for career development; understanding the emotional and physical development required for proactive career decision making; understanding the values of personal responsibility, good work habits, and planning for career opportunities; comprehending the significance of technology in the world of work; identifying career opportunities in the field of technology; and demonstrating technological literacy.

The *Florida Blueprint for Career Preparation* (1988) has career orientation and exploration as the goal for grades 7–8. Students are to identify goals for which they are striving and recognize that they may change as further experiences are obtained. Students are expected to develop a 4-year plan for grades 9–12 using input from students, families, and school advisers. The plan is to be evaluated annually and revised as requirements change or students' goals become clearly defined. Some of the competencies expected of this grade group are relating educational achievement to career opportunity; understanding the attitudes necessary for success in work and learning; applying skills to locate, understand, and use career information; identifying types and levels of work performed across a broad range of occupations; relating careers to the needs and functions of the economy and society; choosing alternatives and making decisions to plan and pursue tentative educational and career plans; understanding how sex-role stereotyping, bias, and discrimination limits career choice, opportunity, and achievement; and assessing personal aptitudes, interests, and abilities relative to the career clusters.

DEVELOPING A CAREER PORTFOLIO

The portfolio process helps students prepare for the high school experience, as well as assist them in setting goals for the future. In the fifth grade, all students can develop a portfolio for designing a life—a program of empowerment. The objectives of such a portfolio program are as follows:

- Students will gather information regarding their learning styles, personal competencies, present and future vocational interests, and their parents' expectations.
- Students will evaluate the data gathered and formulate choices through instruction on decision making, use of decision trees, and group discussions.
- Students will design and build an actual portfolio stating learning strengths and weaknesses, academic and vocational interests, social interests, and immediate and possible future goals.

Selected counselor-directed activities could include field trips to career centers, completing the Coopersmith Self-Esteem Inventory (School Form), and small group instruction on decision making. The portfolio will provide an opportunity to involve parents in helping to design the student's individual portfolio. In sum, the portfolio will assist students in determining individual preferences as related to educational and career interests. Also, it will stimulate the decision-making process as tied to later outcomes. Content for the portfolio should include a self-portrait section, a career plans area, and a section focusing on educational and academic accomplishments.

ROLE OF THE COUNSELOR

Middle schools are characterized as flexible, exploratory, and transitional. Currently, many states are moving from the junior/senior high school model to a middle school (grades six to eight) and a high school (grades nine to 12) type of structure. In either case, the counselor is faced with a diverse population of students with marked individual differences in physical, emotional, cognitive, and social growth.

Bergmann (1991) lists the following roles for the middle school counselor

- Be a good role model and caring adult
- Establish peer groups
- Involve students in community service
- Encourage students in decision making
- Establish wellness programs for both students and teachers
- Establish a CARE (Concern about Reaching Everyone) team
- Sponsor age appropriate social activities for at-risk students
- Conduct needs assessments of the students

The counselor is one of the important team members in the school and has to work with teachers, parents, and administrators to develop academic programs that stress skill learning for each student as well as to help develop exploratory and enrichment experiences for the students (Williamson & Johnson, 1991). Much emphasis is placed on teacher/student guidance and advisory programs. The counselor is a part of the interdisciplinary or multidisciplinary teams that are established in the school. Cooperative learning rather than competitive learning is stressed along with strategies to increase the students independence, responsibility, and self-discipline. Students are guided in formulating their personal values and standards during this time. In order to be effective, counselors have to assess local needs and resources, establish priorities and clear program objectives, build in evaluation procedures, communicate effectively with school staff and the community, and work closely with staff members as a cohesive team.

COUNSELING STRATEGIES

Group counseling is an effective intervention strategy at this level. Group participation provides the youth with a chance to practice communication skills, try out new behaviors, and receive feedback from their peers and the counselor. The focus of the groups can be on the developmental issues that they face and can be more preventative. The priority is to develop positive interpersonal relationships, as they make group work more positive.

When students are faced with specific problems such as divorce, child or sexual abuse, or substance abuse problems, special groups might be necessary. Developmental issues such as self-awareness, self-esteem, personal relationships, social skills, moral behavior, conformity, sexual and sex-role behavior, decision making, values clarification, academic performance, study skills, and career and vocational concerns are the usual topics of the groups.

Peer-facilitator programs are growing in popularity. Bowman and Myrick (1987) indicate that there are significant benefits for both the facilitators who are trained in one-to-one and group skills as well as for the peers with whom they work. These facilitators address both academic and nonacademic issues. They also are in contact with their peers both in class and out of class and even out of school. The counselor can use a variety of steps to design, implement, and evaluate a program, for example, identifying the goals of the program, devising the criteria to select peer facilitators, providing training for those selected, monitoring and meeting with the facilitators periodically, providing additional training when necessary, and devising a plan to evaluate the program. Evaluating the program and reporting the results is critical for revising the program to make any needed changes in procedures or selection criteria.

Establishing parent education groups is also an important function of the counseling program at this developmental stage. Students grow in their independence from their parents and become more influenced by peers, thereby presenting challenging situations to many parents. Effective parenting groups, developmental parenting groups, or some type of support group might be helpful to parents with children in this stage of development. There are a number of established programs marketed by publishers for this group. Huhn and Zimpher (1984) found that the most effective programs used a behavioral approach and taught parents how to improve their communication skills and know how to apply behavior management techniques.

COUNSELING ACTIVITIES TO PROMOTE CAREER DEVELOPMENT

Miller (1988) suggested the following specific activities that have proved to be effective in getting students at this level to think about career exploration.

Just How Important Is Prestige.   Counselors have students discuss in small groups what is prestige, and then rank order any list of 10 occupations in terms of prestige or status. Counselors can also ask students to discuss the impact of family and socioeconomic status on prestige. Miller feels that these discussions can result in intensified awareness of how the standards of others can affect how individuals look at occupations as well as how they make decisions.

Let's Play Cards.   The Occ-U-Sort (Jones, 1983) or a similar card sort can be used to help individuals see how the world of work is organized. Students are given the cards with a title on the front and a job description on the back and asked to sort them in several ways. The Occ-U-Sort uses Holland's typology, and individuals can study the codes of the occupations they might want to pursue.

What Is Important to Me.   Students are divided into groups and asked to discuss how factors such as income, education, social class, race, and prestige might affect their future life-style. They are then responsible to take two of the factors and do some research from sources such as television, ads, commercials, newspapers, and literature on two of the factors and show how these influence life-style. They also can discuss or write about how these factors relate to the life-style of their own families.

The World Outside of School.   Miller suggests that it is the counselor's responsibility to provide the students with relevant educational and vocational information. He suggests the using of Holland's (1984) typology of classifying environments and occupations. He feels that this can be done through field trips as well as from interviews or writing a report on an occupation and presenting this report to the group.

Debunking Occupational Myths.   Miller suggests that a productive idea is giving the students a quiz that addresses widely held myths about career development. The quiz allows the counselor to use a cognitive behavioral approach to challenge irrational beliefs. Some of the sample questions that Miller uses for illustration are as follows:

T   F   Once a decision has been made it should be pursued to the end.
T   F   The main purpose of an interest test is to be able to tell a student what occupation he or she should choose. (p. 177–178).

St. Clair (1989) reviewed the middle school counseling research and reported that counselors can be instrumental in promoting self-esteem, achievement motivation, and career knowledge through a career exploration program. These programs also help to discourage sex stereotyping.

COUNSELING MIDDLE SCHOOL GIRLS

Kahnweiler (1984) feels that one of the major goals of the counselor with this age group is to combat sex-stereotype attitudes. She feels this can be accomplished partly by a career education program in which counselors work with teachers to infuse concepts such as identifying women and men in new or unusual occupations, the type of compromises a woman or man may have to make in choosing an occupation, and identifying the discriminatory practices in the work environment that one might help to change.

Hands-on experiences are also an important component of such programs. Girls are encouraged to engage in hands-on activities that include doing experiments, trying out new equipment, and the like. They are encouraged to interview women who are successful in nontraditional fields as well as women in traditional fields. Girls might be able to find mentors or role models who would be willing to provide them assistance in their current stage of career development.

Fitzgerald and Crites (1980) encourage counselors to be activists and question the values and career and life-style choices of their students. They need to be able to help students compare and contrast their choices and especially choices between traditional and nontraditional occupations. Counselors need to be alert to sex biasness on many of the standardized tests.

SUMMARY

This chapter details the emotional and physical changes that are critical to the career development of children in the middle school. Career counselors must relate the appropriate career development theories to the personality and social needs of children in this age bracket. It is an exciting opportunity for counselors, and we recommend the use of varied methods, for example, field trips, job shadow, role models, and up-to-date curriculum materials in the career education program.

REVIEW QUESTIONS

1. What is the role of the counselor in the middle school?
2. What should the counselor know about the social, psychological, physical, cognitive, and career development of students at this level?
3. What are the developmental tasks of early adolescents? What psychosocial crises do they face?
4. What are the career education goals for students at this level?
5. What counseling and teaching strategies and techniques seem to be most effective for this level?
6. Do you feel that the reform movement in education has placed too much emphasis on academics to the expense of preparing students for the working world?
7. What would you say to teachers who take the position that it is not their job to infuse career education into their courses?
8. What kinds of strategies can we use to increase the career knowledge and awareness of youth in this age period?

SUGGESTED LEARNING ACTIVITIES

1. Interview counselors in middle schools and report to the class on their philosophies about guidance and counseling, their job duties and responsibilities, and the percent of time they devote to each duty.

2. Interview counselors about the career education and counseling programs available at their school. Report to the class what you found out about their programs.

3. Request career guidance curriculum guides from your state department of education, bureau of career guidance. Present an oral report or paper to the class on key points.

4. Construct a survey or interview schedule to find out the career interests of students in the middle school. What type of occupations do they choose? What type of educational plans and expectations do they have? How do the job choices relate to the employment needs during the upcoming century? Do students tend to choose traditional or nontraditional fields?

5. Interview several parents with students in the middle school. How are they helping their children with their career development? Does the school their children attend have a seminar or program for them on career development?

6. Make a review of the career guidance programs for middle schools included in ERIC. Analyze the common as well as unique features of these programs. Do these programs take into consideration the developmental characteristics of the students they have been designed for?

SUGGESTIONS FOR COUNSELORS

1. Place emphasis on career exploration and planning activities in the middle school.

2. Work with teachers and students on the importance of course selection. Teachers need help in learning advisement strategies. Students need to recognize the consequences of the courses they choose on their educational goals and career plans.

3. Work with the faculty on infusing career education goals and objectives into their courses.

4. Encourage teachers to invite people from the community to talk about how the skills the students are learning are related to the world of work and specific occupational fields. Students are more motivated if they can see that what they are required to learn is related to survival skills in the real world.

5. Conduct several career exploratory groups for parents. They in turn will be helped themselves and better able to help their children.

6. Bring in graduates from the school who have gone on to be successful in attaining their educational and career objectives. Role models of individuals employed in nontraditional fields are important in addition to successful minority group members.

CASE STUDIES

Profile of a Potential Dropout

Name: Rose Ireland
Age: 15
Grade: 7
School: Shaw Middle School

Background

Rose is now attending Shaw Middle School. She lives with her mother and grandmother. Her mother is 31 and on public assistance. Rose had a good attendance record through grade six; however, her attendance record in grade seven is poor and she is frequently absent several times a week. Her grandmother works part-time for a fast food restaurant and her mother is unemployed.

Her grades in school range from D to B. She makes C's and D's in her mathematics and science classes and C's in reading and language arts. She makes B's in physical education and fine and practical art classes.

Assessment Information

Rose took the Otis Lennon Scholastic Ability Test in seventh grade and had a score of 98. Her seventh grade scores on the Differential Aptitude Test were as follows:

Verbal	35%
Numerical	15%
Abstract	25%
Spatial	35%
Mechanical	5%
Sentence	28%
Spelling	55%
Clerical Speed	85%

At Shaw Middle School, she was given a self-concept test, The Culture Free Self-Concept Scale. She scored 35% on the General Self Scale, 75% on the Social Self, 48% on the School Self, and 15% on the Personal Self scale.

When asked what she would like to be when she finishes school, she says pediatrician or gynecological nurse.

Case Questions
1.   What additional types of information would be useful to you as her counselor?
2.   How can the assessment information be used? Is additional assessment information needed? If so, what?
3.   How would you work with this student? What type of career counseling services and interventions would be most useful to this student?
4.   How would you use the developmental theories to analyze Rose's stages of development?
5.   How would you handle her unreal career aspirations?

The Shoplifter

The school has asked that all students who wish to participate in field trips bring money to purchase school insurance. Reba does not want to admit to the teacher that she can't ask her mother for the money. A woman has left her wallet on the store counter. Reba slips the wallet into her purse and calmly walks out the door. However, she is caught by the store clerk.

Case Questions
1.   How would you have handled this problem?
2.   What would you do if you had this problem?
3.   Pretend you are the injured party in this case. How would you explain your feelings to your best friend?

The Troublemaker

Tom has come to class, taken out paper, and begun to draw cartoons. He obviously is not listening to the teacher's assignment, and Ms. S. obviously is getting annoyed. She has asked him to put his cartoons aside, but he has ignored her. Now she tells him again to stop drawing and pay attention. Reluctantly, he puts his paper into his desk and begins to whistle softly. At this point Ms. S. orders Tom out of the room and to the principal's office.

Case Questions
1.   What are the possible causes of this conflict and how could they be resolved?
2.   How could Tom have prevented this conflict?

SUGGESTED READING

Capelluti, J., & Stokes, D. (1991). *Middle level education: Policies and practices.* Reston, VA: National Secondary School Principals Association.

Clark, S. N., & Clark, D. C. (1990). *Schools in the middle: Theory into practice.* Reston, VA: National Secondary School Principals Association.

These are two short books that provide readers with a good overview of the philosophy and programs advocated for middle schools. They are published by the secondary principals association.

Cole, C. C. (1981). *Guidance in the middle school: Everyone's responsibility.* Fairborn, OH: National Middle School Association. (ED 219 7000)

Huhn, R., & Zimpfer, D. G. (1984). The role of middle and junior high school counselors in parent education. *The School Counselor, 31*(4), 357–365.

The article discusses approaches the counselor can use to conduct parent education groups and the benefits of such programs.

6

HIGH SCHOOL

A Transition Period

S enior high students vary considerably in their career development and career maturity. One of their major goals is to specifically plan what they are going to do about a job or education choice after graduation. It is estimated that 30% of senior high students already have had work experience, sometimes in low status, minimum wage–paying jobs, and have developed attitudes toward work and different career fields. Adolescent vocational development requires an understanding of school programs and graduation requirements. School counselors are often not viewed as helpful and important people when adolescents think about their career field and seek employment because students tend to get their first jobs through family and friends. Vocational education, career education programs, and work-experience programs have attempted to help youth in this period of transition by providing technical training and intensive career counseling.

LEARNING OBJECTIVES

After reading the chapter, you should be able to do the following:

- Discuss the goals of secondary school developmental guidance and the roles of the counselor
- Identify the key theories of career development, personality development, and social development that are essential to understanding the adolescent
- Describe goals of career counseling and career guidance during senior high school
- Identify the current practices, methods, and procedures used in career counseling with adolescents in senior high school

SECONDARY DEVELOPMENTAL GUIDANCE

Secondary guidance is directed to the developmental stages of adolescence. In an early study Erikson (1963) identified the key crisis as identity versus role diffusion. The primary roles for the counselor are organize and integrate through the teaching staff guidance-related goals into the secondary curriculum such as self-concept development, career choice and planning, and social relationships; to organize and make available comprehensive educational and occupational information students need for their planning and decision making; to assist adolescents with assessment of their competencies, interests, aptitudes, needs, and career maturity so that they can make educational and vocational decisions both during and after high school; and to provide remedial interventions and alternative programs for adolescents showing adjustment problems, vocational maturity, or negative attitudes toward personal growth in school (ASCA, 1981).

ROLES OF THE COUNSELOR

Secondary counselors generally focus their attention on four major roles:

1. The guidance curriculum (classroom guidance, group guidance, group teacher advisement, and peer programs)
2. Individual planning (individual advisement, placement, and individual appraisal)
3. Responsive services (group counseling, consultation, information giving and dissemination, and referral)
4. System support (program development and evaluation, staff development, parent education, testing programs and community relations) (Georgia State Department of Education, 1984).

The traditional school counseling programs developed in the 1950s, with their emphasis on appraisal, group guidance, educational/occupational planning, and placement, will no longer suffice in a rapidly changing world. We need school counselors to adopt a model encompassing personal counseling, informational counseling, consulting, teaching training in human relations, parent training, and pupil personnel team participation. In addition school counselors need career support for retraining and revising the existing services to meet the needs of clients in the year 2010.

Peer (1985) recommended that counselors establish a broad-based steering committee to direct and evaluate the guidance and counseling program, develop a plan to teach all students a guidance curriculum, and make secondary guidance part of statewide education.

It is essential for counselors to be able to assess local needs and resources. Annual needs assessments are seen as a must. Counselors need to establish priorities and clear objectives for the guidance program and work as a team with the school staff in order to accomplish the goals of the program.

THEORETICAL BASES

Adolescence is a period of rapid change for young people sometimes marked by confusion and uncertainty (Eccles et al., 1993). They are moving from a period of dependency on parents to a period in which they will have to function independently. Adolescents tend to confide more in their peers than to parents or other adults. Middle adolescence is marked by insecurity of teens about friendships. Personal appearance and popularity are what they look for in a partner. Later, they consider dependability and sensitivity to be more important. The rate of maturation tends to be an important factor; for example, early-maturing boys are self-confident and late-maturing boys compensate by seeking attention. Both early-maturing boys and girls tend to develop into self-confident adults (Siegel, 1982).

DEVELOPMENTAL TASKS

The developmental tasks cited in Chapter 5 for junior high students are also appropriate for senior high students. Developing social intelligence and learning how to develop and foster interpersonal relationships are important for this age group. They need to develop autonomy and independence not only from parents and teachers but also from their peer group. They need to come to grips with themselves and develop a positive sense of identity and self-concept. In addition developing their coping skills so that they are better able to handle everyday problems of living is a high priority.

High school students need to know themselves, their capabilities and limitations, develop a positive self-concept, and identify their interests, aptitudes, values, and achievement. It is vital that they develop skill in self-evaluation and tie it to knowledge of the world of work. Formulating tentative but realistic career plans is a priority.

To become responsible citizens this age group must know their roles and responsibilities in society. They need to develop practical intelligence and the practical skills necessary to survive in society. They need to think about their preferred life-style and work toward the way of life that they would find rewarding.

LEVELS OF DEVELOPMENT

Cognitive Development

Studies by Ginsburg and Operr (1988) suggest that most adolescents become at least partially capable of formal thought and are able to form hypotheses and problems and engage in complex mental operations. However, adolescents tend to concentrate more on possibilities than realities, and egocentrism arises again but in a different form than in childhood. High school students become introspective and are concerned about the reactions and thoughts and feelings of their peers. They initially tend to take the other person's point of view to an extreme degree, but later realize that other people are more concerned with themselves and their problems, and not with others.

Personality Development

Erikson (1968) called the period from 12 to 18 years identity versus role confusion. The senior high student is forced to make decisions that will lead to commitments for life. Identity to Erikson is a feeling of acceptance of oneself and knowing where one is going. It is characterized by inner assurance and reinforced by recognition from the significant people in one's life.

The roles and appropriate behaviors accepted by society of males and females have changed drastically. Cosse (1992) concluded that the developmental pathway for females is based on interpersonal, empathic relatedness and is driven by both qualities; therefore, they develop empathic understanding. Males follow a pathway leading to autonomy. Males learn to think and stand alone and follow an internalized set of rules applicable to all situations. There has been, however, a blurring of roles and movement toward unisex views or androgyny instead of the traditional or conventional roles. The differential treatment of boys and girls by parents and educators influence their role expectations and career choices.

Erikson reiterates that occupational choice has a great impact on teenagers' sense of identity. He feels that the occupations they select influence other aspects of their lives more than any other single factor. The decision is one of the biggest commitments the adolescent has to make. The rapid changes in the job market and technology make this difficult for adolescents.

Erikson (1968) found that career choice posed a threat to many adolescents' personal identity. Instead of making a firm commitment and then feeling overwhelmed and unable to act, it may be desirable for adolescents to take a psychosocial moratorium. The moratorium is a period in which the adolescent does not make a choice or commitment but postpones this to a later time. The experience can be positive or negative. If the adolescent uses this time for exploration of possibilities, it might lead to good choice and positive results. If adolescents cannot resolve their inner conflict, they may develop negative identity and become involved in defiant and destructive behavior.

Career Development

Early studies by Ginzberg, Ginsburg, Axelrad, and Herma (1951) identified the period from 11 to 18 years as the tentative period. The period consists of four stages: the interest, the capacity, the value, and transitional. During their 15th and 16th years (sophomore year), senior high students pass through the values stage. One of the dominant values in this period is altruism. They begin to think about the idea of service to society and think less about satisfying their own needs and the prestige level of the occupation being considered. They also begin to consider the life-style implications of jobs they are considering. They see that a medical doctor would have a different type of life than a life insurance agent or a computer operator. Other changes take place during this stage also. Adolescents begin to be aware that they might be able to choose a career field that would use their special abilities and skills. They also develop a broader perspective of time than what they had before. They see that a career involves a day-to-day life pattern.

The transition stage occurs in their junior and senior years, or age 17 or 18. They realize that they have to make timely, concrete, and realistic decisions about their vocational future and also have to assume the consequences of their decisions. Students feel an increase in independence and greater freedom to seek new surroundings in which they can try out their skills and talents. They consider the practical factors such as kind of preparations necessary for the job and the amount of salary that can be expected.

Other studies by Super (1969a, 1990) call the period from 14 to 25 years the exploratory stage. The period has three substages: tentative, transitional, and trial. Adolescents operate in the tentative and transitional stages. The developmental tasks in this period are crystallization, specification, implementation, stabilization, and consolidation. Crystallization is a process that is characterized by high school students formulating ideas about work that might be appropriate for them. This task is considered the primary career development task of the adolescent years. High school students begin to explore resources to help them in their decision making. They give less time to their hobbies (Super, 1990). They are able to differentiate their values and interest and formulate general preferences. They recognize the time perspective necessary in their planning. They begin to work toward the task of specification and verify their current occupational choice. They seek information concerning the preferred occupation and begin to plan and learn more about opportunities in their fields of choice. The implementation, stabilization, and consolidation stages usually are implemented after they complete high school and during the early adulthood period. In short, they develop a realistic self-concept.

CAREER MATURITY

The goal of career guidance and career counseling programs is to have individuals attain the proper position on the continuum of vocational development as to their life stage of development and age (Super, 1990). Crites (1978) proposed a model that helps in understanding the factors and variables affecting a person's degree of career development. He included factors such as consistency of career choice, career choice content, realism of career choice, career choice competencies, career choice process, and career choice attitudes.

CAREER GUIDANCE GOALS

The goals of a career guidance program depend in part on the priority and support the program receives within the state and school district. Sometimes the program is a formal program with credit assigned for participation; other times, the program is informal and voluntary. The career guidance competencies set for students in the State of Florida are presented in Figure 6.1.

High school students could be encouraged to start a career portfolio, which includes these competencies:

- School activities. The clubs, offices held, honors and awards received, and athletics they participated in
- Their hobbies and leisure activities
- Abilities, skills and/or special talents (out of school). Profiles from ASVAB, PSAT, and other tests
- Work experience. The type of jobs they held during summer, part-time, or during school hours—paid, volunteer, or credit
- Activities log. Record of the field trips taken, job observations, speakers, interviews, and so on
- Educational courses completed
- Career plans and information received about vocational programs at the high school level, for example, business education, work-study program, and so on
- Record of interviews held with counselor and topics discussed
- Brochures, catalogs of postsecondary schools reviewed
- Completed resume

Competencies for Grades 9–12

- ★ Developing a marketable skill
- ★ Making decisions and choosing alternatives in planning and pursuing educational and career goals
- ★ Understanding the interrelationship of life roles and careers
- ★ Understanding the continuous changes in male and female roles and how they relate to career decision
- ★ Applying skills to revise the students' career plan
- ★ Understanding the relationship between educational achievement and career planning, training, and placement
- ★ Using positive attitudes toward work and learning
- ★ Researching, evaluating, and interpreting information about career opportunities
- ★ Locating, obtaining, maintaining, and advancing in a job
- ★ Understanding how societal needs and functions influence the nature and structure of work

---

FIGURE 6.1
Florida career guidance competencies

In Figure 6.2, a sample of items that are typically included on a career education needs assessment for high school students is provided. It is recommended they be considered prior to sampling student needs.

The objectives can be organized under several different headings: living skills, learning skills, and learning to make a living skills. They also could be classified under career planning and decision-making skills, interpersonal skills,

---

Directions: Circle the number of the item you would like to know more about or have more experience in doing.

1. Learn how to function more effectively in small groups
2. Learn appropriate social skills needed for group activities
3. Improve my ability in self-control
4. Show respect for others
5. Learn to modify my value system based on feedback from interpersonal relationships
6. Learn to demonstrate knowledge and skills of societal interdependence
7. Locate and use available resources for reaching my potential
8. Learn how to improve my educational performance so that I will able to attain my educational and career goals
9. Learn strategies on how to cope with success as well as failure
10. Acquire knowledge of steps required for entrance into postsecondary educational and training programs
11. Evaluate personal assets and limitations for meeting requirements for postsecondary education and training programs
12. Understand how education relates to entering the job market
13. Accept lifetime learning as a way of life
14. Attain skills to change and adapt to constantly changing requirements for occupations
15. Learn general skills that can apply to a variety of occupations
16. Study the positive contributions all occupations make to our society
17. Understand the relationship between occupational roles and life-styles
18. Learn how the requirements of entry-level occupations are related to my high school program of study
19. Understand and make use of available handbooks and materials published by national, state, and local agencies and commercial publishers on jobs, careers, and so on
20. Learn the different clusters or systems of classifying jobs and know what jobs are included in each cluster
21. Design a workable guide for beginning the formulation of goals and plans that reflect the ability to locate, evaluate, and interpret information about career and vocational opportunities
22. Learn more effective time-management skills
23. Identify alternate courses of action in a given decision-making situation

---

FIGURE 6.2
Career guidance needs assessment

educational awareness, occupational and career awareness and knowledge, job-seeking skills, and attitudes toward work.

CAREER DECISION MAKING CHARACTERISTICS

Miller (1987) identified four major career decision-making characteristics counselors need to consider when working with adolescents. First, adolescents want to know and to be better informed about the world of work and the type of training and educational requirements of different occupations. Many adolescents are unfortunately making their decisions on limited or inadequate data.

Second, the values of adolescents become a more important factor in their career decision making, and implicit values such as security dominate their thinking. Challenge and interest are not as strongly considered. Third, parents still have a strong influence on their career choice and are perceived by adolescents as helpful in the process. Fourth, their personal experiences in school become more important in the decision making of adolescents.

ACTIVITIES FOR CAREER DECISION MAKING

Miller (1987) suggested that there are a number of activities the counselors should use to stimulate the thoughts adolescents have toward making career decisions. A practical way of doing this is to develop instruments that provide feedback to adolescents on how they make decisions. He suggested the use of the type of process provided by Hesketh (1982) that requires students to become aware of their decision-making styles. The students are required to rank statements of how they make their job choice. For example,

_____   Based on my feelings of what I like or want (emotional)

_____   Based on my feeling that this choice is right or inevitable (intuitive)

_____   Based on my feeling at this moment of time. I have not given it much thought. (no thought)

_____   Based on what my parents or peers or other adults expect of me (complaint)

_____   Based on my analysis of all the possibilities I have considered that fit in with my ideas (logical)

_____   Based on my comparisons and analysis I am not ready to commit myself at this time. (hesitation)

The counselor would ask the group of students about which type of decision-making style they use in what types of situations and the advantages and disadvantages of each type of style (Miller, 1987).

Miller and Knippers (1992) suggested designing a career "Jeopardy" game to highlight for students the important aspects of career development. Students learned from the game the important aspects of career development and the process of risk taking.

Miller feels that pressures from parents need to be addressed in individual and group sessions. He suggests questions should be asked such as do the adolescents feel constrained by their family values and what and how much pressure they feel is being experienced from the family about their career decisions. Miller (1987) suggested having a series of orientations for parents and providing them information on the process of career development, the myths surrounding occupational choice, the tremendous influences they have over their adolescent's career outlook, and the process of risk taking.

Programs need to help students look at who they are. Miller suggests the use of assessment and personality instruments such as the *Myers-Briggs Type Indicator*, the *Edwards Personal Preference Inventory*, the *Self-Directed Search*, and the *Work Values Inventory*. He feels that the scores on these tests can be related to Holland's type theory and provide a way of synthesizing the test information.

To increase the adolescents' knowledge of career fields, Miller suggests they become involved in volunteer work. There are many organizations such as schools, hospitals, museums, charities, churches, animal care facilities, recreational programs, and nursing homes that need volunteers. Sometimes the volunteer work can lead to part-time employment during the school year and full-time summer opportunities.

Adolescents can interview workers in the fields they are considering. The students can validate what they have learned with the individuals they interview. The students must individually decide whether the information they gained is realistic and accurate. They can ask the workers what advice they would give them if they were going to choose that specific occupation. Grubb (1989) suggested counselors encompass programs to integrate work with school and feels that there needs to be a union of vocational education, career education, counseling and guidance, worker training programs, and work experience programs. He sees youth unemployment as a major problem and has questions about the viability of the goals and roles of education in adolescence.

Miller (1987) suggests that the counselor can use televisions as a way of getting students to examine societal values as related to various jobs. The students can be assigned to compile a list of the occupations that they see most frequently on television—through the shows and in the commercials—and record the aspects of the jobs they consider desirable. They can also use magazines and newspapers to do the same study and can display their findings through a montage and discuss the information they gained.

ASSESSMENT INSTRUMENTS AND STRATEGIES

Assessment instruments and procedures can be used to help adolescents gain a better understanding of their aptitudes, interests, and values. Some of the instruments that are used in working with high school students are included in Table 6.1.

TABLE 6.1
Assessment instruments to measure aptitudes, interests, and values

Title	Description	Publisher
Armed Services Vocational Aptitude Battery	Evaluates vocational interests and aptitudes	Department of Defense
ACT Assessment Program	Measures academic achievement and used to help students develop postsecondary plans	American College Testing Program
Differential Aptitude Test	Assess aptitude in eight areas for educational vocational guidance purposes	Psychological Corporation
COPSystem Aptitude Battery	Quick measure of eight aptitudes	
Career Maturity Inventory	Measures attitudes and competencies related to career decisions	CTB/McGraw-Hill Educational and
Career Orientation Placement & Evaluation (COPES)	Assesses personal values related to work	Industrial Testing Service
Work Values Inventory	Measures 15 intrinsic and extrinsic values inherent in work	Riverside Publishing Co.
Career Assessment	Contains 22 interest scales and 91 occupational scales	National Computer Systems
COPSystem Interest Inventory	Assesses interests in professional and skilled job clusters	Educational and Industrial Testing Service
Harrington-O'Shea Career-Decision-Making	Measures interests and abilities of students	American Guidance Service
Jackson Vocational Interest Survey	Gives profile of interest in 10 areas	Research Psychologist Press
Kuder Preference Record, Vocational	Assesses interests in 10 general areas	Science Research Associates
Occupational Aptitude Survey & Interest Schedule	Measures aptitudes and interests of high school students for various occupations	Pro-Ed
Ohio Vocational Interest Survey (OVIS)	Measures vocational and occupational interests	Psychological Corporation

Table 6.1 represents a representative sample of the large number of tests available to help students with self-assessment. The tests usually have coordinated support materials that can be used by the counselor and students. Some use the *Occupational Outlook Handbook* and others have correlative books and manuals available to provide occupational descriptions for the students to read and study. Some of the computer-assisted programs are described in Chapter 14.

COUNSELING ADOLESCENT GIRLS

Career counseling of adolescent girls needs to focus on expanding their career and educational horizons. Many girls tend to still see themselves in traditional feminine roles and following formerly traditional sex roles, although their aspirations for higher-status professional occupations has increased. However, more young women are entering the labor force earlier and remaining there longer than in the 1970s and 1980s. The projection is that the percentage of females in the work force will increase and be equal to that of males (W. T. Grant Foundation, 1988). Studies are beginning to show changes in stereotypes. Post-Kammer (1987) found that girls had significantly higher scores on achievement and variety than did boys, whereas boys had significantly higher scores on independence, economic returns, and living their lives in their own way. Studies have shown that females take fewer mathematics courses than males (Pallas & Alexander, 1983). Because lack of mathematics and science courses limits career choice in many areas, counselors need to work with teachers and students to help girls develop more positive attitudes (Fennema & Peterson, 1987). Cooperative and small group instruction help to increase the achievement of girls in these subject areas. Self-concept of adolescent girls tends to be lower for girls than boys. Because self-concept is important in career and educational decision making, counselors need to provide activities and interventions to enhance self-concept.

SUMMARY

Some of the key points for counselors to consider when working with adolescents are the following:

- Physical, cognitive, and social changes in high school students have an impact on parent-student relationships.
- Family structure changes when students are adolescents if there is parental marital dissatisfaction, economic crises, career revaluation, or concern about health. These problems affect the relationship of teens with their parents and affect the teen's self-concept.
- Adolescents ability to reason effectively is closely linked to familiarity with content.
- Adolescents spend a higher proportion of their time in leisure activities than in work, school, or study (Zaslow & Tukanishi, 1993).
- Divorce is a stressful experience for teens and influences the social and emotional behavior of teens.
- There is strong pressure to conform to peers and peer culture.
- Worldviews and concern for others become more important to the adolescent in the late adolescent period.
- Danger in resolving the psychosocial conflict during this period leads to uncertainty about who one is and what one is to become.
- Adolescents need motivation to use their assets and talents.
- Adolescents pursue autonomy but need both the support of peers and parents.
- Social and intellectual development of teens are influenced greatly by their achievement in school.

- One quarter of all adolescents in the United States are poor or near the poverty level.
- One half of black, Hispanic, Latino, Native American, and Native Alaskan adolescents are poor or near the poverty level.

REVIEW QUESTIONS

1. What are the goals of developmental counseling for high school counselors?
2. What are the major roles of the secondary school counselor?
3. What does the counselor need to know about the social, psychological, physical, cognitive, and career stages of students at this level?
4. What are the developmental tasks of adolescents? What psychosocial crisis do they face?
5. What are the career education goals for students at the high school level?
6. What kinds of strategies and activities can counselors use to increase the career knowledge and awareness of youth at this level?
7. Did the high school you attended have a career guidance curriculum? Did your teachers infuse career guidance activities into their teaching? Who helped you make your educational and career decisions? Your counselor? Your teachers? Your parents?

SUGGESTED LEARNING ACTIVITIES

1. Interview several high school counselors and report to the class on their philosophies about career guidance and the priority they give career counseling. What are their job duties and responsibilities and what percent of time do they devote to each duty?
2. Interview counselors about career education and find out whether they have developed a local curriculum or use a state module. Give a report on your findings to the class.
3. Collect career guidance curriculum guides and modules from your state and local school district. Compare the goals and objectives and the type of activities suggested. What are the common features? What are the unique features?
4. Construct a survey or interview schedule to find out the interests and career plans of students in the senior high. What types of occupations do they choose? What type of educational plans and expectations do they have? How do the choices relate to the employment needs at the beginning of the next century? What kinds of work experience have they had?
5. Interview several parents of high school students. How are they helping their children to develop career maturity and make the

choices they have to make at this time? If the school offers one, have the parents sent their children to a seminar or program for parents on career development? Have parents used counselors outside of the school system to provide career counseling for their children?

6. Interview several teachers at the high school level and find out if they infuse career education into their teaching.

7. Develop a module to infuse career guidance goals and objectives into a course that you are currently teaching.

8. Start an idea notebook and collect activities and strategies that would be helpful to you when you become a counselor.

9. Interview some local businesses that hire teens and find out the types of experiences available, the requirements for getting a job with the business, the pay offered, and the number of hours teens can be employed. Find out what the businesses consider to be the major problems with employing teens.

10. Interview high school students who are currently working part- or full-time. What do they think about their working experience? What do they see as the disadvantages of the experience? The advantages? How do the experiences fit in with the student's values and interests?

SUGGESTIONS FOR COUNSELORS

1. Remember, the focus is to help students examine career and educational plans. These are important decisions and little attention is placed on them in most of the traditional school curriculum.

2. Be innovative in your attempts to reach the students. Offer brown bag seminars during their lunch period and short video presentations that they can see while they are changing their classes. Also take your life in your hands and try several sessions on the bus runs.

3. Recruit and train peer facilitators and counselors to help in the career counseling and guidance program. Recent graduates who have been successful in their career and educational efforts are excellent presenters.

4. Develop ties with business and industry for student work-experience programs.

5. Provide practical seminars in interviewing techniques, writing a resume, how to find a job, assertiveness training, and so on in addition to the traditional career and college days or nights.

6. Invite parents and community members to become involved in career and life-planning seminars. Use them as speakers.

7. Get faculty to infuse career education content into the curriculum. Show them how they can use the computer guidance system to demonstrate the career fields related to the subjects they are teaching and how their courses relate to different career fields.

8. Use case studies to stimulate student career explorations.

CASE STUDY

Profile of a Disadvantaged Youth

Name: Bobby Johnson
Age: 16
Grade: 10
School: Cedar River High, Cleveland, OH

Background

Bobby is from an economically disadvantaged family. He repeated third grade because of excessive absenteeism and because his family moved in the middle of the school year. His grades in school have been at the C and D level but Bobby can get better grades when he tries. Standardized achievement test scores show that Bobby has the ability to achieve. Bobby has untapped potential for academic success in school. This year, unfortunately, Bobby has been failing most of his academic subjects.

Assessment Information

The results of a group intelligence test indicated that Bobby's overall level of intellectual functioning was in the above average range (IQ 118). The results of the Stanford Achievement Test from last year were as follows:

Subtest	Percentile Rank
Word reading	43%
Reading comprehension	37%
Number concepts	60%
Math computations and applications	52%
Spelling	50%
Vocabulary	45%
Listening comprehension	22%
Reading	40%
Total reading	41%
Total math	52%
Total auditory	21%

Bobby was identified as a potential dropout after missing school frequently during the ninth grade. Bobby was placed in vocational education in the ninth grade and then put in a special dropout prevention vocational education program in the tenth grade. This program features a work-study program in which students are placed on a job by the school. The students have their schedules arranged so that they can leave school early to go to work. The students receive assistance in getting a job and some follow-up help after placement.

Bobby was fired from his first work-study job and arrangements have just been made for him to start on another. Bobby told one of his teachers that he was "going to quit school and get his own job." He said that he "could make more money and wouldn't have to hassle with school no more."

Classroom Behavior

Bobby's classroom behavior and emotional development seem normal. His behavior in school is satisfactory except for his extreme passivity and lack of interest in school this year. He has stopped doing all of his homework, participating in class, and he doesn't try to finish in class work or tests.

Case Questions

1. How would you work with this student as a career counselor in terms of your theoretical approach and philosophy of intervention?
2. What additional assessment and other information would you need to obtain in order to provide career counseling services? How would you obtain this information quickly and efficiently?
3. How can the assessment information that is provided be used? Is additional assessment information needed? If so what?
4. What type of career testing would be appropriate to give to Bobby? How would the results be used?
5. What are some specific techniques for motivating students who miss school frequently?
6. Why is career counseling an important educational service in this situation? What does career counseling provide that other educational programs and services don't provide?

SUGGESTED READING

Stern, D., & Eichorn, D. (Eds.). (1989). *Adolescence and work: Influence of social structure, labor markets, and culture.* Hillsdale, NJ: Lawrence Erlbaum.

The book covers topics such as adolescent vocational development, preparing youth for work, dreams and aspirations in the status attainment model, classroom lesson strategies and orientation toward work, cultural boundaries and minority youth orientation, career development in adolescence, adolescents and work, characteristics of high school students' paid jobs, employment experience after graduation, the job market for adolescents, adolescent personality, women's work patterns, and competence in work settings.

CHAPTER

7

COMMUNITY COLLEGE, COLLEGE, AND POSTSECONDARY STUDENTS

After graduation from high school, students tend to enter the work force full-time or have a moratorium and seek further education or training before entering the career field of their choice. Junior colleges and 4-year colleges tend to have student personnel services available to help young adults with their career development and job-seeking skills through career counseling centers and placement services. Trade and technical schools also provide the needed placement services.

The 18- to 25-year-old young adults face a number of problems in their transition from school to work. Certain groups find the transition more difficult than others, such as dropouts and minority group members. There have been a number of programs established to help students in at-risk groups in their career and educational development. Many support systems are available, both public and private, but many times the young adults who need help do not know the resources that are available.

LEARNING OBJECTIVES

After reading this chapter, you should be able to do the following:

- Understand the social, psychological, and cognitive factors that affect career development of college-aged adults
- Discuss the problems of career development of college students and types of educational and counseling interventions possible
- Discuss the problems of the noncollege youths and the types of educational and counseling interventions possible
- Identify successful job-seeking skills and strategies

POSTSECONDARY STUDENTS

Twenty-eight percent of the population in 1955 was in the 18-21-year-old age bracket, 46% in 1975, but only 17% in 1990. A total of 19.8 million college graduates are projected to enter the labor force between 1990 and 2005 (Shelley, 1992). Traditionally this has been the age bracket that attended college, but the proportion of students over 25 entering college or some type of postsecondary education has been steadily increasing. This chapter focuses on the 18- to 25-year-old group who attend community college or 4-year college or some type of postsecondary educational experience.

LIFE STAGES AND LIFE CYCLE

There have been many conceptualizations of the life cycle and life stages that help us to understand the personal and social characteristics of each age group. Buehler (1962) identified five life tendencies: need satisfaction, adaptive self-limitation, creative expansion, establishment of inner order, and self-fulfillment. She concluded that the 18- to 25-year-olds were dominated by their tentative self-determination of an adult occupational role in response to the second tendency, adaptive self-limitation. The life stages are caused by both biological and social events that occur in a person's life. Human behavior and personality do change as individuals grow older. Adult development can be seen as a process of adaptation.

Levinson (1986) characterizes the period as a point when the young adults tend to leave the family and get into the adult world. Gould (1980) has identified two stages: leaving parents/breaking out and leaving parents/staying out. Sheehy (1976) calls this period pulling up roots. Adolescence is viewed as a critical stage in career development because students make commitment to educational and career choices.

DEVELOPMENTAL TASKS

Havighurst (1972) has proposed a set of developmental tasks for the adult years: the physiological, psychological, and social demands adults must satisfy in order to be judged by others and to judge themselves to be successful and happy individuals. He sees failure to achieve these tasks as contributing to later difficulties, unhappiness, and social disapproval.

McCoy (1977) has translated developmental tasks more explicitly for the different stages. She identifies both tasks and outcomes and several interventions or programs that would enhance the achievement of the developmental task. She labels the period of 18 to 22 years as leaving home, and identifies nine tasks.

The first is breaking psychological ties. This facilitates strengthened autonomy of the young adult, and can be accomplished through personal development activities such as assertiveness training workshops.

The second task is choosing a career. The goal is to have the young adult make appropriate career decisions. This goal can be enhanced if the young adult attends career workshops, values-clarification workshops, uses career counseling, and receives appropriate occupational information.

The third task is entering work. Young adults need to successfully complete their educational experiences and enter an appropriate career field for them. They have to choose the appropriate education and career preparation. They need to complete the prerequisites for the career they choose.

The fourth is handling peer relations. Young adults need to develop effective social interaction. Human relation groups and other types of social and/or religious groups that foster the development of communication and caring skills enable young adults to accomplish this goal.

The fifth is managing home. Young adults need to be informed consumers and have a healthy and positive home life. Any type of education and homemaking skills enhance the achievement of this goal.

The sixth task is managing time. Young adults need to make wise use of their time. There are numerous workshops and seminars held on time management as well as tapes available at book stores or the library. There are many programs on the use of leisure time and leisure activities.

The seventh task is adjusting to life on own. Young adults need to develop autonomy and self-fulfillment as a single or as a couple. There are a number of seminars and workshops on living alone. Churches and other social organizations have support groups for singles as well as young married couples.

The eighth task is problem-solving. Young adults need to develop successful problem-solving skills. There are courses and workshops available on critical thinking and problem-solving skills as well as many self-help publications.

The ninth task is managing stress, which accompanies change. Young adults need to develop successful stress management strategies. Cooper, *Euthenics: A Stress Reduction Worktext* (1992), provides useful exercises. There are many seminars and workshops on stress management, biofeedback, relaxation, and transcendental meditation. There are many self-help books, tapes, and videos available on this topic, also.

Chickering and Havighurst (1981) identify four developmental tasks for late adolescents and youths aged 16 to 23: Achieving emotional independence, preparing for marriage and family life, choosing and preparing for a career, and developing an ethical system. Youths have to learn to be willing to risk loss of friends, approval, and status to be themselves, be able to pursue their interests, and to stand by their beliefs.

Preparing for marriage and family is more complex because of the many different types of arrangements accepted by society today. The sex roles are changing. Most young adults do plan to marry and have a family but they are concerned about financial as well as job stability.

Chickering and Havighurst (1981) see choosing and preparing for a career as the most challenging developmental task for the late adolescent and young adult. The meaning of work and career have changed. Young adults take jobs and start work and realize that they may have to change jobs or career fields several times during their lifetime.

Young adults begin to examine their values and beliefs and modify them to fit the careers, life-styles, and larger social context in society today. They create their own system of beliefs and behaviors based on the complex contexts in which they find themselves.

Psychosocial Development

Erikson (1963) calls the developmental crises of young adults intimacy versus isolation. In order to experience satisfying partnerships at this stage of development, young adults need to establish an intimate relationship with another person. If young adults fail to do this, they will feel a sense of isolation.

Intellectual Development

Eighteen- to 25-year-olds are still working on attaining their intellectual skills, and now have to apply them to their personal goals and goals of society. They have to use social intelligence in establishing relationships with spouses, peers, and employers. They have to apply their cognitive and practical intelligence in the workplace. They are still at the achieving stage as far as developing and expanding their capabilities. Most young adults have reached the formal stage of cognitive development.

Coping Skills

Coping skills become important during this period and are complex. Blocher and Rapaza (1981) state that from later adolescence on, vocational and personal development emerge in ways that make them virtually inseparable. The period from 15 to 19 years is labeled *later adolescence,* in which the tasks are to develop identity as a potential worker—learning to move from group to individual relationship—achieve emotional autonomy, and produce in work situations. The coping skills used in this period are reciprocating, cooperating, and separating. Social roles are needed to relate to peers and romantic partners. The exploration period encompasses the decade from 20 to 30 years, and is characterized by marriage and career roles. The development tasks involved are intimacy and commitment: developing generativity; learning to commit oneself to goals, career, and partner; to be an adequate parent; and finally to give unilaterally. The coping skills are sexual relating, risk taking, and value clarifying.

In reviewing the research on college students, Blocher and Rapaza (1981) concluded that the process of vocational development during the college years is more a function of the college experience than a function of antecedent conditions. Research findings support the concept of the college as a learning environment that enhances students' self-awareness and awareness of others and helps them form commitments to career and work, provides information about their strengths and weaknesses, and provides them experiences with people in a wide variety of roles.

Career Development

Ginzberg, Ginsburg, Axelrad, and Herma (1951) have developed a model of the realistic period, which follows the transitional period. It normally extends from ages 18 to 22 or 24. The range is variable because different education and training periods require different amounts of time.

The first stage in the realistic period is the exploration stage. Youths begin to narrow their goals. Many youths are in college but they are still somewhat indecisive and their interests may still change. They realize that they will have to make definite decisions in the near future and are somewhat anxious of making the wrong decision.

The crystallization stage follows the exploration stage. Young adults have definite ideas of what they want to do and not do. Most students reach this stage by the time they graduate from college. Sometimes young adults act as if they have made their choices, but the decision is not stable.

The specification stage is the last stage in the realistic period and follows the crystallization stage. The young adult selects a specific job or graduate school.

Super (1990) also has a developmental life-stage model. The stage from about 15 to 24 years is labeled the exploration stage, and is subdivided into the fantasy, tentative, and realistic phases. The tentative or transition stage usually takes place from 18 to 21 years and the realistic or trial stage from 22 to 24 years. In Super's (1963) model he labeled the period of 18 to 21 years as the specification stage and 21 to 25 years as the implementation stage. In the specification stage adults develop an awareness of the need to be specific and work toward limiting their choice. They are aware of the factors that they need to consider and the factors that may affect their goals and they continue to sharpen their interests and values and choice. They seek information on their preferred occupation, plan for entering that field, and develop more confidence in themselves and their choice.

The goal of the implementation stage is to obtain an entry-level position. Young adults move toward finalizing their plans and set a timetable for entry. Ornstein and Isabella (1990) concluded that neither Super's nor Levinson's developmental stages fit women's careers. Blustein, Walbridge, Friedlander, and Palladino (1991) pointed out the contribution of psychological separation and parental attachment to the career development process. They found that college women's career development was influenced by their general and specific abilities, role models, willingness to take risks, genetic characteristics, and feminist and family-related orientation. These factors helped to predict their career orientation, mathematics orientation, and career choice.

COLLEGE WOMEN

One of the major counseling goals for college women aged 18 to 22 years old is to help them integrate their professional and personal lives because they have a double adjustment to make with potential marriage and career. They can be helped to prepare for the conflicts and dilemmas they will face in the near future. Young women need to be alert to the influence of sex stereotypes and bias that operate in their occupational choices. Sharf (1992) noted a tendency for career choices of college students to be sex-stereotypical, although there has been a decrease in the proportion of young women choosing sex-traditional careers. Cook (1991) recommended that counselors need to be alert to the possibility that women's career choices often do not optimize their abilities and interests.

Swanson and Tokar (1991) identified a wide variety of career-related barriers that differed across career stages. Counselors can run workshops on dual-career families, time management, coping with stress, communication skills, and the like. Counselors need to know the programs available and the requirements for graduation as well as admissions standards for graduate schools. Individual counseling might be necessary to help women with their educational and career choices and to make them aware of new avenues as well as the possible discrimination that they might face in job-seeking efforts. Poe (1991) reported, however, that as the vocational identity of a woman increased the need for occupational information decreased.

DEVELOPMENTAL ADVISEMENT

Developmental advisement is the type of advisement system that is founded in the developmental theories presented at the beginning of this chapter and is advocated for community college and 4-year college students. It is defined as "a systematic process based on a close student-advisor relationship intended to aid students in achieving educational, career, and personal goals through the utilization of the full range of institutional and community resources" (Ender, Winston, & Miller, 1984, p. 19).

The emphasis on this systematic approach is to help young adults accomplish their life goals, acquire the skills and attitudes necessary for promoting intellectual and personal growth, and share concerns for one another.

In order for developmental advisement to be effective, there are seven conditions that need to be agreed on (Ender, Winston, & Miller, 1984). Academic advisement has to be seen as a continuous process in which there are numerous personal contacts that are purposeful and meaningful. Second, advisement needs to focus on quality of life issues and the quality of the college experience for the student. Third, advisement should be goal related, where the goals are established and owned by the student and include academic, career, and personal development areas. Four, advisers need to take the responsibility to establish caring human relationships. Five, advisers should be positive role models for students by demonstrating behaviors that lead to self-responsibility and self-directiveness. Six, advisement needs to be comprehensive and seek to involve and integrate the services and expertise of both academic and student affairs professionals. And last, advisers need to be aware of and be current in information about and use as many campus and community resources as necessary.

ADVISEMENT-ORIENTATION STRUCTURE

There are a number of different types of advisement structures used on campuses, including centralized and decentralized structures. Centralized structures have usually an advisement center for the whole college division. Decentralized structures usually have a coordinator whose major function is to pass on information to students and faculty.

The organizations have a variety of staffing patterns. Some are staffed by faculty members who have some time released from their teaching service and research activities to do advisement (Poe, 1991). Others are sometimes staffed by paraprofessionals, students, or nonstudents who are trained to be information givers and help with course scheduling. Many schools consider the role extremely important and hire professional advisers who have training and education in counseling and educational and career planning.

Advisement centers are advocated by Crockett (1982) for colleges because they are easier for students to access and are staffed by better trained and better supervised personnel. They provide continuity of contact that is student centered rather than content or department centered. They are able to provide more timely and accurate information to students and have the possibility of offering a wide range of advisement services to the students by specifically trained professional personnel. These centers offer more consistent monitoring of student progress and keep more complete records.

MODELS OF ADVISEMENT

O'Banion (1972) proposed a five-stage process model that tries to tie in the significant interrelationship among life planning, career planning, and academic advisement: exploring life goals, exploring career goals, selecting an educational program, selecting courses, and scheduling courses.

Unfortunately, if students see an adviser, it is usually for selection and scheduling of courses, and because of the high ratio of the number of students to advisers, exploration of the first three steps becomes difficult.

Freshman Seminars

Freshman seminars are a formalized way to provide advisement and guidance to students. These seminars can be credit or noncredit seminars. They can be taught by student personnel, professionals, faculty, or counselor educators. Ideally the course should be taught by a team of faculty, career and advisement professionals, student personnel administrators, and students who are trained peer facilitators.

Success in the first year of higher education is critical because it is often filled with anxiety and frustration for students. Students are usually concerned about the expectations of the institution for them. They are dissatisfied with the quality and quantity of faculty-student interaction and academic advisement services. They face pressure in the area of ethics and or substance abuse, sexuality, academic standards, honesty, and integrity.

The goals of freshman seminars are listed in Figure 7.1.

Advisement Process/Intervention Model

Habley (1984) has developed an advisement process intervention model to deliver both career and life-planning services. The services are administered by an academic adviser but use the other support services in the student affairs area.

The adviser has to have a commitment to student development, be willing to participate in the necessary training to implement the model, and be aware of institutional policies and procedures as well as the roles played by student affairs and other support services.

There are eleven tasks. Each task has a feedback loop so that the adviser can return to an earlier task if decisions and actions taken are not supported by the student's actual experiences. Each task provides the student with a series of goals that facilitate the activation of career and life plans. The tasks are presented in Figure 7.2.

---

* Educational planning
* Career planning
* Study skills and learning strategies
* The location of campus and community resources and services
* The achievement of personal goals through a college education
* Liberal arts and general education and specialization: their purposes and relationships
* Personal goal setting, time management, stress management, and other life-management techniques
* Academic policies and procedures
* Personal development activities
* Contemporary issues in college life
* Adjustment to the college environment

FIGURE 7.1
Goals of freshman seminars

TASK 1: Become aware of individuals, abilities, and interests
Activities:
   The adviser can use questions such as, What is important to you? There are value tests and value clarification exercises. The adviser can use placement test results, standardized tests, high school transcripts, and college academic records to have the student focus on his or her abilities and interests.
   The adviser can use the Strong Interest Inventory, Self-Directed Search, COPS Interest Survey, or another standardized test to help the students in gaining insight into their interests.
   Discussion can be held on what activities, hobbies, and leisure activities the students enjoy.
TASK 2: Clarify life goals based on self-awareness
Activities:
   Super and Neville's Salience Inventory helps students focus on their expectations of home, community, school, leisure, and workplace activities. Students can write statements of their expectations on these areas.
TASK 3: Explore relationship between life and career goals.
Activities:
   The adviser initiates deeper discussion of life and career goals using Super's (1976) life-career rainbow. The adviser needs to begin a discussion of how the collegiate experience is used in expanding one's life and career goals.
TASK 4: Explores the world of work
Activities:
   Holland's Self-Directed Search facilitates discussion with students about the relationship between personality and the world of work. Job shadowing, work experience, field trips, and interviews with a number of people in career fields might be helpful. Work experience programs, internships, practicums, and computerized career guidance programs also provide some firsthand experience.
TASK 5: Clarify career goals
Activities:
   This task requires action-oriented decision making by advisees. Advisees have gained self-awareness and information in the first four stages. The adviser has to guide students to synthesize all this information and make a decision. If students have previously made a decision, they need to reevaluate it.

FIGURE 7.2
Advisement/intervention tasks

STRATEGIES FOR CAREER AND LIFE COUNSELING

There are a number of strategies to help students in their career and life planning. To have an effective program the options have to extend well beyond the services offered by the advisement center or career planning and placement service; they have to involve the faculty and the community.

   One of the major ways of delivering career and life-planning services to students is through formal courses. The course focuses on a specific career field. McGovern and Carr (1989) reported on the development of career planning for

TASK 6: Explore educational combinations leading to life and career goals
Activities:
  The curriculum and programs at the institution of higher learning enter the career and life-planning process for the first time.
TASK 7: Select the educational combination
Activities:
  The adviser discusses with students the possible majors and minors and sequence of courses that are available to meet their goals. If the proper program is not offered, the adviser explores the possibilities of students' transferring to another school.
TASK 8: Explore elective courses
Activities:
  The value of the selection of elective courses is discussed in the context of providing students an opportunity to explore new subject areas, investigate subjects that may not be directly related to their program of study, or begin to learn new areas of interest.
TASK 9: Sequence and select courses
Activities:
  The role of the adviser is focused on helping students learn what the requirements are for general education, their major and minor, and the prerequisites and required courses.
TASK 10: Schedule courses
Activities:
  The adviser needs to know alternative strategies and/or courses if some of the required courses are closed.
TASK 11: Evaluate experiences for confirmation or redirection
Activities:
  The adviser and students need to evaluate the outcomes of the course work and discuss whether the courses are meeting the goals of the students. The students may have to reevaluate their career goals or the balance between life and career goals.

FIGURE 7.2, *continued*

undergraduate psychology majors. The course includes seminars on careers in psychology, workshops on job-seeking skills, and applying to graduate school.

There have been other similar courses offered with titles such as "Introduction to the Helping Professions" and "Psychology as a Profession." Many introductory courses have units on the various career fields open to majors in that discipline. These courses are usually offered on three levels, at the beginning level, at the beginning of a major at the junior year, and at the end of a program.

The exploratory courses are designed to assist students in understanding the basic concepts of the career and life-planning process. They also are designed to help students in the development of their decision-making skills. Because many students have not had courses in group activities in high school, these courses are popular with beginning freshmen.

The second-level course is usually offered in the sophomore or junior year and is taught by the faculty within a discipline or program. The goals are to help students understand the specific options within a field and the entry requirements and chances for advancement. Additional training or education required is also discussed.

The third level is through internship and work experience programs. Many schools have work experience programs that, for example, provide computer science majors an opportunity to work in a business or industry in computer programming and be paid for the opportunity. Elementary education students complete several preinternships in the schools and then intern under a directing teacher for a semester in their senior year at college. Taylor (1988) concluded that interim experiences can help students crystallize their vocational abilities, interests, and work values.

There are other approaches. There are many extracurricular activities available that relate to majors offered at institutions. These activities help provide students with opportunities to gain self-awareness and to develop their personal and social skills. There are programs such as theater presentations for drama students, newspaper writing and editing for journalism and communication students, photography for yearbooks for arts majors, governance opportunities for political science majors, and the like.

There are work/study programs in which majors can work with or for faculty in their discipline. The career planning and placement service also has information available on part-time employment. Many times there are opportunities related to one's major or career choice. Kane, Healy, and Henson (1992) state that working one's way through college is becoming the rule rather than the exception. This part-time employment may contribute to the career development of these students, but many jobs tend to be of poor quality.

There are also clubs and organizations for majors sponsored by the faculty such as engineering societies, honor fraternities sponsored by subject areas, and student branches of national professional organizations. These clubs and organizations provide students skills in group interaction, decision making, and leadership.

Numerous social, civic, religious groups, public service, and nonprofit organizations seek volunteers. Volunteerism gives students a chance to meet people in their career field or to gain experience in a specific career field.

HUMAN RESOURCES

There are all types of human resources available to assist in the career and life-planning activities of students, such as peers, alumni, retired people, community employers, and interested citizens. These people are often willing to participate in campus programs or seminars and permit students to shadow them for a day.

THE FORGOTTEN HALF: THE NONCOLLEGE YOUTH

There are approximately 20 million in the 16- to 24-year-old bracket who do not plan to pursue postsecondary education. They may have their high school diploma, but many do not. They have a hard time competing for better paying jobs because those require advanced training. Noncollege youths also are in the need of help in the transition from school to career. They are at a disadvantage because our highly competitive technological economy wants workers who have more education and training. The noncollege youths have to compete for low-paying and many times unsteady, part-time jobs. It should be noted that this group also has to compete with college graduates. About 20% of college graduates end up taking jobs that do not require a degree (Shelley, 1992).

The W. T. Grant Foundation Commission on Work, Family, and Citizenship report *Forgotten Half: Non-College Youth in America* (1988) provided the following information on youths:

High school dropouts age 20 to 24 earned 42% less in 1986 in constant dollars than the same group did in 1973. Young males 20 to 24 who had high school diplomas and had jobs earned 28% less in 1986 than the same group in 1973. Whites earned 24% less and African Americans earned 44% less. The number of 20- to 24-year-old males without jobs rose from 7.3% in 1973 to 12% in 1984. Baxter (1992) reports that fewer than half of all high school dropouts are employed. Only 24% of the group are employed full-time and 13% part-time. A quarter of the group are unemployed, 38% are not employed and not seeking work, and 43% of young males had salaries high enough to support a three-member family above poverty level.

The number of youths working in part-time rather than full-time jobs fell from 73% in 1968 to 49% in 1986. Thirty percent of the 3.1 million family households headed by youths under age 25 in 1985 had incomes below the poverty level.

The students who score at the 20th percentile or lower on mathematics and reading tests as compared with students in the top half of the scores are 8.8 times more likely to have a child out of wedlock, 5 times more likely to have an income below the poverty line, and 2.2. times more likely to have been arrested in the previous year.

There are a number of strategies that have been successful in helping students increase their achievement and improve their motivation and responsibility.

1. Use of volunteers for tutoring
   Adult as well as peer tutors have helped many students increase their achievement as well as their career perspectives. Some schools have successfully used senior citizens as tutors.
2. Use of work experience programs
   Cooperative education, internships, apprenticeship, and junior achievement enterprises have provided students with realistic work experience and role models in the workplace. They are guided to see how important what they are learning in school is useful to them in the workplace.
3. Use of course work in vocational and technical education
   Vocational and technical education can provide students with some salable competencies. The hands-on practical approach to learning

helps students to acquire basic skills and competencies they would need to survive in the workplace.

4. Use of community and neighborhood services
    The availability of community and neighborhood services helps to provide students an avenue to learn skills they need to be more effective citizens. This type of activity provides students with an opportunity to help other people and understand some of the needs of other people.

5. Use of career guidance and counseling
    Young adults need to be exposed to the various career options that are opened to them in their state, region, and community. The services need to be extended from school centers to increase the ways students have to find out information. School might have a negative context, and centers in the community might be a more acceptable avenue. Programs also need to try to get parents more involved in the career development of their children.

6. Use of companies and individuals to sponsor an at-risk youth
    Some companies as well as individuals and civic organizations have been willing to guarantee scholarships for further education and training for at-risk high school students. Others have guaranteed if youths graduated from school they would provide jobs for them.

The strategies are most effective when there is cooperation between schools and community, the public sector and the private sector, and parents and teachers. Certainly schools need to consider strategies to improve their ability to accommodate the different learning styles and to ensure that they have established educational goals and plans to help these at-risk students.

The W. T. Grant Foundation Commission on Work, Family, and Citizenship (1988) stated:

> Every state and community should establish concrete school completion goals, youth employment goals, parental involvement goals, and youth community service goals. These goals should be publicly announced and monitored in annual community-school "report cards," along with achievement scores, college admission results, and other measures of school effectiveness. (p. 37)

AVENUES OF ADVISEMENT

Career Information Centers

Career information centers can be a valuable resource to youths. It is impossible to have direct experience in the range of occupations that might be possible for noncollege-bound youths and high school dropouts. They need to have access to written, audio, visual, and computerized sources of information. The possible jobs available for youths are limited and even more so for disadvantaged youths. Most youths find that there are only service jobs available and low-paying with little chance of advancement. Baxter (1992) reported that young workers are more likely to be service workers or laborers than are their older counterparts. The retail trade industry provides the largest proportion of jobs for young workers (30% of 20- to 24-year-olds and 63% for 16- to 19-year-olds).

The New York City Job and Career Center is an excellent model of a career information center. It is open to both private and public school students, as well as unemployed adults and school dropouts. There are exhibits and visual displays as well as videotaped simulated job interviews.

Seminars for Parents

Seminars need to be held for parents on topics in career awareness and career development. Most adolescents value their parents opinions when it comes to careers and work. Parents occupational information, however, is rather limited. Parents with high status jobs might be well qualified to provide their children information and advice, but youths from poor families often do not have parents who are qualified. These seminars could help not only to increase the parents knowledge and interest in careers for their children, but also increase their career horizons.

Community Mentors

Community mentors can provide youths with firsthand experience and knowledge of a wide variety of career fields. Many adults are very willing to serve as mentors to youths on a short-term and sometimes long-term basis. The mentor's role is to provide youths with advice and knowledge.

One of the successful mentoring programs is the Transition to Working Life program sponsored by the Grubb Institute in London. The Grubb program uses small group activities rather than one-to-one relationships. Eight to 10 unemployed youths are assigned to a working coach. They meet in small groups to discuss topics important to the group. The working coaches report to an adviser who tries to help them understand their roles better and help them be more effective. The working coaches are paid by their employer for a half-a-day per week to participate in this program. The program has had success in helping youths get jobs and has proved to be cost effective.

Adopt-a-School Program

The adopt-a-school program is one in which a business or industry forms close relationship with a school. The business may provide funds beyond what the school budget is capable of providing for special projects. They may also provide opportunities for students to gain work experience or provide a network of contacts that facilitate employment contacts for disadvantaged youths.

Community Groups

Community groups can be used to support job-training activities and career education of disadvantaged as well as school dropouts. They have more capability to gain access to these youths more of the time than the schools. The students who have not achieved or have dropped out have a distrust or lack of interest in the schools. These groups can be very helpful in the transition from school to work of this group. They can provide life-awareness, job-seeking, and job-keeping skill training.

Counseling and Guidance Activities

Counseling and guidance activities are helpful if received in a timely fashion to these youths. Many counselors complain because they have limited time to work with either individuals or small groups. They find that they have increasing paperwork, and much time is taken up in helping the college bound group. Some school systems have counselors assigned to work specifically with the potential dropout population and the noncollege-track students. School districts have implemented dropout prevention programs. Counselors need to have additional time and training to be more effective with this group. Intervention needs to be started in the elementary school rather than the high school.

As part of the dropout-prevention program, students have access to job-training specialists who help them locate part-time jobs during the school year and full-time placements during the summer and after graduation. They work with the employers as well as the students to improve the transition between school and work. They also work in curriculum development and develop courses that will be valuable for the noncollege-bound student.

Job Corps–Related Type of Programs

The Job Corps is a 24-year-old-partnership project among the federal government, private contractors, and several governmental agencies. The Job Corps program provides basic remedial instruction, vocational and technical training, personal and group counseling, job placement, and health and nutritional services among others for participants. Fifty percent of the participants come from a pool of youths from welfare families and about 80% are high school dropouts. They read on the average at the sixth-grade reading level. Although about a third of those who enrolled leave in the first 3 months, 75% of those enrolled move on to a job or to full-time study and provide society with a net social return of $1.46

for every tax dollar invested in the program (Committee on Governmental Operations, Job Corps Program, 1986)

There are currently 14 states and 12 cities that operate youth corps. Career counselors of youths need to be cognizant of the federal, state, and local job corps or youth corps programs. There are also a number of national organizations offering youth preemployment training programs, such as the 70001 Training and Employment Institute. They use remedial instruction, job-readiness or pre-employment training, and numerous motivational activities. They operate 60 programs in 23 states.

JOB-SEEKING SKILLS

One of the major tasks of early adulthood is to obtain a job. Campbell and Heffernan (1983) see the tasks that young adults need to follow to obtain a position in their chosen occupation by knowing where to find job opportunities, knowing how to identify the relevant information from descriptions of jobs, by selecting appropriate jobs based on the match between their personal attributes and the jobs they consider and the organizational environment, by developing a plan to secure employment, by preparing resume and other paperwork that might be required, by being competent in interview and negotiation behaviors, by analyzing the employment offers and their impact on life-style requirements, by knowing when to accept or reject the employment offers, and by being willing to repeat the previous steps until the right job is secured.

Young adults need to be aware of the major factors of why workers get hired (Healey, 1982). Employers tend to hire individuals they know or who are recommended directly by a colleague or employee. Also, they tend to hire individuals who can relate their skills and aspirations to the employer's needs. Employers tend to prefer individuals who demonstrate commitment to their occupation and have been previously successful. They tend to hire persons with whom they feel comfortable and for whom minimum accommodation will be necessary.

Individuals who are seeking a job usually have more success if they have a plan to gain employment. The plan should include strategies on how they intend to locate possible jobs. They need to identify the employers who offer opportunities in the field of which they are interested. They need to use placement offices, state employment offices, ads in newspapers, and professional journals. For college students there is the *College Placement Annual* and other similar publications as well as the placement office.

Job seekers might need to seek the help of individuals already working in the organization or occupation. People contacts can be very valuable and lead to a job. Job seekers not only need to devise an access strategy to get into see the employer but also be able to present their qualifications in an attractive manner. They need to be able to sell themselves to the prospective employer. The resume has to be attractively done with significant information included. Job seekers have to be persistent and learn from their previous experiences and interviews.

TYPES OF STRATEGIES

The U. S. Department of Labor (1976) did a study on the uses and effectiveness of job search methods. They found that about two thirds of the workers applied directly to the employer. About half of the workers reported that they asked about jobs where their friends worked and sought job leads from them. Want ads in local newspapers were also an important source and used by 45.9% of the individuals in the survey. Only about 12% of the individuals reported answering ads in nonlocal papers. A third used the services of the state employment office, 21% a private employment agency, and 12.5% a school placement office. Slightly over 15% took a civil service test. Other avenues were a teacher or professor, a trade journal, a professional journal, union hiring hall, and through placement of ads in a professional or trade journal.

The effectiveness rate was computed by dividing the number of job seekers who found work using the method by the total number of job seekers who used the method, whether successfully or not. The most effective method was to apply directly to the employer (47.7%). The second most effective method was through private employment agencies (24.2%), followed closely by answering ads in a local newspaper (23.9%). Other successful procedures were going through the union hiring hall (22.2%), asking friends about jobs where they worked (22.1%), and contacting school placement offices (21.4%). Relatives were also a valuable source (19.3%). It should be noted that the statistics were computed across occupational groups. When methods by category of job seeker were studied, union hiring halls were primarily effective for craft workers and somewhat effective for operatives and laborers. Private employment agencies were primarily effective for managers and clerical workers. Friends were an assistance in all areas except in the case of professional and technical workers and managers. Answering local newspaper ads were effective in all areas except for laborers. School placement offices were effective primarily with professional and technical workers.

SUMMARY

Chapter 7 outlined the basic issues related to post–high school counseling. Career counselors must provide intensive planned career development activities and access to support systems for youth seeking career training or job entry. The range of postsecondary options for youths exiting public schools requires counselors to plan and deliver a career education program with structure and content relevant to the year 2000.

REVIEW QUESTIONS

1. What should the counselor know about the social, psychological, physical, cognitive, and career development of college-aged students?
2. What are the developmental tasks for this age group?

3.   What psychosocial crisis does this age group have to resolve?
4.   What type of counseling services were available at the college you attended? How were the services structured? Did you use the services? Why or why not? What type of program does the school you now attend have?
5.   What are the goals and objectives of freshman seminars? Did your undergraduate college offer a seminar series? What were the topics covered? Did you feel that the program helped you with your life development?
6.   What are the goals of the advisement process? What are some of the effective delivery systems? What impact did your adviser have on helping you with your educational and life plans?
7.   Do we place an overemphasis on the college-bound student and forget the bottom half of the class? What strategies can we use to help at-risk students go on for postsecondary training and education?
8.   What kinds of behaviors do employers look for when they are hiring workers?
9.   How can counselors help individuals develop their job-seeking skills?

SUGGESTED LEARNING ACTIVITIES

1.   Interview six career counselors working in a postsecondary institution. Determine their role and responsibilities, the number of clients they see, and their clients' problems. Report your results to the class.
2.   Interview six employment and career counselors who work with college-aged youths in a noneducational setting and contrast their roles with the roles of counselors working in an academic setting.
3.   Survey 12 students in a postsecondary institution and see if they use the career counseling services or other services of the counseling center and find out what their evaluation of these services are.
4.   Interview or survey college students and find out their current career goals and previous career history. Analyze whether their career development pattern fits with that proposed by Super (1990) or Ginzberg (1984).
5.   Make a review of courses of study of seminars or courses offered by career counselors for this age level. Analyze the common and unique features of these programs. Do these programs take into consideration the developmental characteristics of this age group?
6.   Visit a job corps type of program. Interview the staff and some of the clients. What were the goals and objectives of the program? What types of interventions did they use? How did they evaluate the success of the program?
7.   Interview the other students in your class or those at your place of employment and find out how they got their jobs, both current and past. Did they develop job seeking strategies?

8. Read the self-help books on the shelf in your library or at your book-store and compare and contrast the methods and strategies given to help individuals develop job-seeking skills.

SUGGESTIONS FOR COUNSELORS

1. Network with potential employers and get them to come on campus and meet faculty and students in given programs.
2. Emphasize job-seeking skills in seminars, such as resume writing, interviewing skills, how to dress, and the like.
3. Make sure students and faculty are aware of the services offered by the career and advisement center or counselors. Think of creative ways to market the services.
4. Hold seminars for faculty. Get them interested in infusing career guidance objectives into their teaching.
5. Conduct regular follow up studies and use recent graduates in activities and as leads to employment opportunities. Feature successful alumni in publications. It is important for women and minority groups to see that graduates made it in nontraditional fields, in their own business enterprises, and in the main stream.
6. Encourage students with academic skills deficiencies to seek tutors to help them or refer them to the academic enrichment center.

CASE STUDIES

I Changed My Mind at the Last Minute

I thought I was going to like teaching, but I find now that I can't stand the kids. They are just a bunch of jerks. They do not want to learn. They stuck me doing my student teaching in an inner-city school with about 80% minority group members. I am an education major and if I don't complete student teaching, I can't graduate. I guess I'll have to find another major. I'll be in school all my life.

I Don't Want to Follow in My Family's Footsteps

My grandfather was a lawyer. My father is a lawyer. I guess ever since I was a little boy they expected me to become a lawyer. I hate the prelaw program. I do not want to go to law school. They will probably never forgive me! They probably will stop paying for my college.

A Dime a Dozen

What am I going to do with my major in history now that I have it? They say there are no jobs in teaching and history teachers are a dime a dozen. I have good grades. I am young, good looking, and adventuresome. I'll try anything, but please find me a job.

Good with Numbers and Dislikes It

I know the test scores indicate that I have high aptitude in math and clerical areas and good skills in the other areas. I rank high on the accountant scale. My God, I don't want to be an accountant! I do not want to work with numbers.

What Do I Do?

I do not have the slightest idea of what I want to major in here. My family just assumed that I would be going to college. I have taken the required courses in the core and now I have to declare a major. Nothing really turns me on! Large classes and lectures. Deadly! Boring!

Case Questions

1.   What additional information would you want on each of these students?
2.   What career guidance or counseling approaches would you use to help these individuals?
3.   What kinds of programs would you institute to help these students in their career and life planning?

SUGGESTED READING

Peterson, G. W., Sampson, J. P., & Jr., Reardon, R. C. (1991). *Career development and services. A cognitive approach.* Pacific Grove, CA: Brooks/Cole.

The authors provide valuable strategies for student personnel professionals working with college-age students. Case studies are presented to illustrate the cognitive approach to career counseling with individual groups.

EARLY ADULTHOOD

Developing Career Identity

Chickering and Havighurst (1981) identified the period between 23 and 35 years as early adulthood. By this time most individuals have started participation in the work force and have had several part-time and possibly even full-time jobs. Some are working in career fields of their choice and others have had to go into alternate fields or accept positions that are available or happen by chance or default. Some of the positions turn out to be challenging and interesting, but many are dull, repetitive, and not stimulating. The other areas of a person's life—family, friends, and life-style—may be strongly affected by the choices the individual makes during this period. Russell (1991) identified three of the major program issues in this period as anticipatory socialization, realistic recruitment, and employee orientation programs. There are a number of major events that happen in early adulthood that affect the individual's personality, such as commitment to work, marriage, and the beginning of a family.

LEARNING OBJECTIVES

After reading the chapter, you should be able to do the following:

- Identify the key theories of career, personality, and social development that are essential to understanding the early adulthood years
- Discuss the role of business and industry in providing career guidance services
- Critique the current practices, methods, and procedures used to help young workers in their career development
- Discuss the barriers to job entry for youthful workers and the need for socialization

DEVELOPMENTAL TASKS

Chickering and Havighurst (1981) identified eight developmental tasks for early adulthood: selecting a mate, learning to live with a marriage partner, starting a family, rearing children, managing a home, getting started in an occupation, taking on civic responsibilities, and finding a congenial social group. McCoy's (1977) version of developmental tasks for this age group was included in Chapter 7. Kenniston (1971) characterized these years as a period of economic and personal temporariness and a struggle between interest in self-autonomy and becoming socially involved. Chickering and Havighurst (1981) extended early adulthood from 23 to 35 years, and called early adulthood a period of "special sensitivity, readiness to learn, and multiple challenges" (p. 34).

Personal and Social Development

Erikson (1968) identified the important crisis in the young adult years to be intimacy versus isolation. The young adult establishes an intimate relationship with another person. If young adults fail to develop intimacy, they begin to feel a sense of isolation. It should be pointed out that young adults may not have resolved some of the previous crises such as identity versus role confusion.

Sullivan (1953) reminded us that peers, although important in personality development, tend to be supplanted by partners. The circle of friends of individuals in early adulthood is generally reduced as they move into more intimate roles as adults.

Physical Development

The period between 18 and 30 years is one of peak physical status. Health also peaks during this time often, but some develop poor health habits. It is estimated, for example, that half of the population is overweight. Part of a sound career counseling program should include seminars on health, nutrition, exercise programs, and diet. Stress in the career field can be handled if one maintains psychological and physical health.

Cognitive Development

Many young adults finally reach the formal cognitive operations stage, but many only use the formal operations in some areas, and others never or rarely use them. Labouvie-Vief (1982) postulated that young adults enter a pragmatic stage of thought. Schaie (1977) claimed that young adulthood is the achieving stage. Adults apply intelligence to situations that have profound consequences for the achievement of their long-term goals. He concluded that young adults have acquired the intellectual skills necessary to monitor their own behavior and move into the responsibility stage when their family is established and attention is given to their spouse's and children's needs.

CAREER DEVELOPMENT STAGES

Ginzberg, Ginsburg, Axelrad, and Herma (1951) identified the final stage of the realistic period as the specification state. Some young adults never achieve this stage of career development. Research by Ginzberg (1988) suggested that a person's occupational choice does not end necessarily at young adulthood, but might recur at some other time in the individual's life or work situation.

Super (1969a, 1990) conceived the period beginning around 25 years as the period of trial and stabilization, and between the ages of 25 and 45 as the period of establishment. The latter period can lead to frustration, advancement, or consolidation. The period from 21 to 25 years is the implementation stage, in which the final step is for the individual to obtain an entry-level position.

Super (1957, 1984) concluded that career patterns of men are applicable to women if modified to take marriage and child bearing into consideration. He has identified a number of different patterns women follow: stable homemaker, conventional (working while homemaking), interrupted (working, homemaking, and working while homemaking), unstable, and multiple trial. Super concludes that women make their decisions on the basis of their circumstances, self-concept, academic, social, and career skills. Fitzgerald and Crites (1980) stated that although the career development process for women is not essentially different from men, it is more complex for women because of the differences in socialization, and in the combination of attitudes, role expectations, behaviors, and sanctions that constitute it. In short, it is still difficult for women to balance home, children, marriage, and career in a society where promotion and advancement are tied to job productivity or performance. Exiting one's career field to raise children for a specific period of time is still harmful to career advancement.

Okum (1984) concluded that the first year on the job for any young adult is a period of trial and error. The young adult might not have used effective problem-solving skills or have developed proper self-awareness. Okum (1984) identifies nine specific developmental tasks that are necessary for young adults to check whether their job choice is worth continued pursuit—extensions of the general developmental tasks to one's work experience, and are included in Figure 8.1.

These tasks require the development of certain requisite skills such as learning, self-assessing and evaluation, developing functional and technical skills, and refining personal work habits.

Levinson (1978) pointed out the importance of finding a mentor or sponsor, and a number of corporate assistance programs do provide mentors. Beginning teaching programs in many states provide the beginning teacher with a peer teacher as well as another educator to provide constructive feedback relative to job performance.

The entry-level period is a phase of experimentation on the part of the young adult as well as exploration (Levinson, 1986). The young adult needs to

* Learning to perform effectively the job requirements
* Accepting responsibility for one's performance
* Accepting the subordinate status of the job within the company, business, or profession
* Getting along with supervisors and bosses and coworkers
* Demonstrating job-keeping skills
* Finding and making use of a mentor or sponsor
* Setting boundaries between the job and outside relationships and interests
* Assessing and evaluating the feedback on the job and performance with one's goals, work experience, and opportunities
* Being able to handle one's feelings of disappointment, frustration, failure, and/or success

FIGURE 8.1
Developmental tasks necessary for young adults in world of work

reflect on the experience as a valuable learning encounter as it relates to the testing of early career choices. Learning about the job in ways other than the expected is an important lesson, also.

Establishment Stage

Super (1969a, 1990) identified the period beginning at about age 25 as the establishment stage. Levinson (1986) views this stage as crucial to entering adulthood and a settling down to job tasks. The individual has three major developmental tasks at this period: the exploration of occupation and marriage or other relationship possibilities offered by the adult world, the establishment of a preliminary self-definition as an adult, and the creation of an initial or entry-life structure that bridges the gap between the identified self and the more global adult world. There may be sex differences in when the period starts for females if they postponed entering the job market because of marriage and children; however, for both men and women, career and occupation interest become a central part of life.

Okum (1984) lists five career developmental tasks for adults in the establishment period: moving to more independence on the job and showing less need for supervision and monitoring, developing high standards of performance and projecting an image of self-confidence, deciding on whether to become more specialized or remain a generalist, assessing future opportunities in order to plan for the next step in one's career, and developing a reputation within one's field beyond the working setting.

In this period workers tend to want to move up the ladder or advance within the organization. Some individuals opt for managerial and administrative roles within their organization. Others evaluate future trends and move toward specialization within their field. Russell (1991) concluded that early-career experiences pose two major tasks for employees: establishment and achievement.

In our technological society it is hard to remain competent and learn new skills without additional education and training to keep current with trends and other career options. To move into other fields, young adults need to continue their training and education as they explore personal dimensions of growth.

In the establishment period, young adults like to see themselves appreciated and rewarded for their work, but find many times that they are not rewarded and not noticed by their supervisors. Feldman (1988) found that early-career-period employees are more likely than other employees to voluntarily leave the organization, possibly because their jobs do not meet their expectations. Young adults need to learn to project an image of self-competence and need to take the responsibility for communicating their worth and value to the organization.

Autonomy and independence are strong motivators of workers at this stage (Drummond & Stoddard, 1992). Workers begin to take on more responsibility. Sometimes they become responsible for supervising others. They may find out that they do not like to be in a supervisory role even if they have the technical competency to be a supervisor. These developmental tasks require interpersonal and communication skills, supervisory skills, technical skills in their career field, decision-making and problem-solving skills, public relations skills, organizational skills, and tact in dealing with others.

Tiedemann and O'Hare (1963) identified seven stages of career decidedness, which require synthesis, analysis, and evaluation skills. The two stages most often faced by young adults are induction (21 to 25 years old), when young adults are entering their career field of choice and experiencing the reality of this choice, and reformation (26 to 30 years old), when young adults are deciding whether or not to pursue the initial choice or to modify it and make a completely different choice.

SELF-CONCEPT DEVELOPMENT

The self-concept of young adults is influenced by their occupational choice and job experiences. On the job there are roles and activities they have to perform that influence how they look at themselves. Dalton (1989) reported that values contribute to workers' job satisfaction. Their relationship with other workers and supervisors also affects how they feel about themselves. A job's economic returns and the values and beliefs fostered by the job affect self-concept. The dissonance, if any, between the young adult's values and those fostered on the job might cause the individual to unconsciously accept those on the job. Jordaan (1963) postulated that occupational choice of individuals is a function of their self-concept at the time of decision. Super (1990) concluded that people go through a series of stages of career development in which the self-concept becomes successively redefined.

CAREER DEVELOPMENT SERVICES FOR EMPLOYEES

Career development services are made available for employees in many organizations and industries. With the number of mergers and acquisitions and the economic competition both within and without the country, organizations find it economically necessary to maintain a productive and competent work force. Jackson and Vitburg (1987) concluded that if companies do not undertake career development services the lack of the services "will imperil their ability to perform effectively and compete for top employee talent" (p. 54).

There are benefits to both the employees and the organization. The organization can benefit by discovering workers with leadership potential and can increase their organizational effectiveness through the optimal use of people. They can develop a highly motivated work force, and the workers can realize their personal goals (Haskell, 1993). Haskell stated that career workshops can help employees manage their careers, learn to make career decisions, select career goals, create career options, and seek career planning information.

Employees can gain by learning to identify their personal strengths and to make realistic career plans. They can learn to follow through on career opportunities, feel they have greater responsibility and control over their futures, and gain increased visibility that enhances their ability to get promotions and raises. Russell (1991) advocated the use of socialization programs such as internships and CO-OPS to help individuals in developing accurate and realistic expectations. Employees also get to know the organization better and career opportunities within the organization.

TYPES OF CAREER DEVELOPMENT SERVICES

There are many different types of career development services offered by organizations that provide both personal and career related services, in addition to many times being responsible for and facilitating both internal and external training. These services provide employees with career exploration services, career ladder information, career counseling, outplacement counseling, and life and career planning workshops. They train supervisory staff in career counseling. Morrison (1991) found that most of the companies surveyed tended to use the human resource development staff or supervisory personnel to conduct individual career counseling and life development services, but sometimes they relied on outplacement services, external referrals, or specialized staff. Many organizations also offer personal counseling services such as alcohol and drug counseling, personal financial planning, marital and family counseling, workshops on human relations, and workshops and counseling on retirement preparation (Morrison, 1991).

The services include assessment centers, psychological testing and assessment, testing and feedback regarding aptitudes and interests. The centers help individuals with self-analysis and planning and organize support groups for single parents, minority group members, women, workers with stress, and time-management problems. Walker and Gutteridge (1979) found the most frequent service was support for external training (83%). Alcohol and drug counseling was second (57%), and retirement planning was third with 56%. A study by Morrison (1991) reported services such as interpersonal counseling (49%), job performance/development (42%), retirement preparation (34%), supervisory counseling (25%), and life and career planning (11%) services as highly important to workers.

Jackson and Vitburg (1987) investigated a number of corporations and cited the following principles that companies use in developing training programs. They believe that people have enormous capacity to develop their innate potential. If employees fail, the reason may be that a failure is the fault of the manager or supervisor, and that individualized coaching or mentoring would enhance the individual's development. Second, there are creative ways of helping the organization increase productivity and employee satisfaction and commitment. Third, being action oriented, it is easier to generate the type of knowledge needed, motivate employees to action, and cut down the fear of risk and fear of participation. Fourth, using feedback and communication, and encouraging workers to focus on outputs and results rather than on job roles and titles, strengthens creativity and ownership and helps improve job satisfaction and performance. Last, working on strengthening the self-image of the worker and the overall image of the organization facilitates both the personal goals of the workers and the goals of the company.

CAREER DEVELOPMENT SERVICE EXAMPLES

Jackson and Vitburg (1987) describe the career development efforts used by General Electric's Transportation Systems Business Operation in Erie, Pennsylvania. The changing direction of the market was going to affect the company dramatically, and many of those who would survive the changes would have their jobs downsized.

A 2-day career development workshop was held and consisted of two groups of 20 each. Participants were involved in workbook processes, role-playing, and training in a new career-management approach. The outcomes of the workshop were to reaffirm the career relationship with the company to encourage collaboration rather than accusation, to see how their talents and experience would mesh with the future directions of the company, and to make them more personally responsive to opportunities that might not have been announced as specific jobs. The results were encouraging in that employees felt a sense of commitment from the corporation to communicate and assist them with career planning.

Kodak has also delivered 2-day training workshops for their manufacturing workers that stress personal career responsibility, self-assessment, clarity of job targets, conflict resolution, self-presentation, and understanding Kodak's goals.

CAREER GUIDANCE WORKSHOPS

Career guidance workshops designed to promote the growth of employees can be beneficial both to the company and the individual. Haskell (1993) outlined steps to create a career workshop with the following topics: assess what participants expect from it, get them to think about their career planning, and reassess career goals and how to achieve them. Examples of the typical goals that are included in these workshops are listed in Figure 8.2.

ACTIVITIES AND MATERIALS FOR CAREER EXPLORATION

Career counselors in organizations can help workers in their career exploration by both formal and informal activities. The purpose of the activities is to lead to a better understanding of the employee's needs, skills, and competencies. The activities listed in Figure 8.3 are designed to help them learn more about themselves and their environments.

Career exploration is crucial at all stages of career development—the decision stage, the establishment stage, and the mid-career transition stage.

BARRIERS TO CAREER EXPLORATION

There are a number of barriers that often prevent thorough career exploration, not only by young adults but also by older adults. Many times employers do a slipshod job of career exploration. They sometimes do an inadequate search

---

* To present an overview of the organization and its future, how the employees fit in, and how they can contribute to the organization in the future
* To help workers develop responsibility for their career development and feel that the company will be a partner on the process
* To identify possible careers or jobs that they would consider worthwhile
* To explore what excites, satisfies, and motivates them, and consider how to maintain this element in their work and learn to enhance it
* To understand the relationship between their life and work
* To increase their ability to cope with change and develop skills and competencies to adapt to the changes within the organization
* To learn the procedures to apply for positions within the company
* To develop their verbal and written ability to communicate their career aspirations
* To increase their knowledge of entrepreneurship and the relationship between job satisfaction and entrepreneurship

---

FIGURE 8.2
Examples of goals for career guidance workshops

* Have the individual complete a career planning workbook or specific learning exercises from a planned program
* Invite the worker to participate in career planning seminars and workshops
* Go through evaluation in an assessment center
* Take a battery of career aptitude, interest, value, and life-style inventories
* Become involved in a growth group or individual career counseling activity
* Find a mentor in the company who is willing to work with them
* Discuss with family, friends, peers, and the counselor their interests, skills and competencies, and life-style preference
* Have them seek feedback as well as evaluate their job performance
* Read books and articles on occupations and the role of these occupations in different types of businesses and industry
* Learn more about the company for which they are working by reading their promotional materials and annual reports
* Interview appropriate resource people in the company and other companies hiring similar workers
* Talk with people working in related job fields and others outside the company about different types of jobs, companies, and so on and study these job descriptions
* Attend seminars on specific career fields
* Study job descriptions
* Observe workers in specific area of interest

FIGURE 8.3
Activities to help young adults in their career exploration

because they are too anxious or afraid or feel the situation is out of control and that it is hopeless. They rely on what others say—supervisors, friends, peers, family—and many times see no real need on their part to do any career exploration.

Sometimes workers feel that they have been coerced to participate in workshops or seminars or group sessions. They are not psychologically ready to cope with this learning experience. This is extremely important when counseling adults. If adults perceive a real threat to personal life-style and job security, they are more apt to enter career exploration seminars with purpose and commitment.

One method of exploring different fields is securing employment from a temporary help service. Newlon and Silvasi-Patchin (1992) stated that this type of participation gives individuals the opportunity to select the type of work environment in which they will be the most productive. Not all individuals will find this type of experience productive. Those who do usually value work variety above job security, love challenge, like to change jobs, like to see a project through to completion, and then move to something else. This type of person has an entrepreneurial approach to work, but does not want the hassle of self-employment.

Many employees follow a random exploration approach that is unfocused and ineffective. They need to be guided in an organized systematic approach to career exploration. Young adults want the process to be convenient and comfortable. However, if the process is not monitored and a systematic, well-organized and planned approach used, the exploration may not be a good learning situation.

The counselor needs to be alert to defensiveness and anxiety because these factors can hinder learning. People, especially when reviewing information and if not perceived as positive to themselves and their performance, might tend to become defensive (Minor, Slade, & Myers, 1991).

The exploration of self-awareness should not just focus on the individual in the work environment but include factors such as family, personal life, community involvement, leisure pursuits, and even religious practices. Employees should not limit their focus to just their current job or organization. With increasing corporate takeovers and a need to maintain a competitive edge, many positions now are being eliminated or a number of positions are being downsized. Employees might need to focus on what opportunities there are outside of their present company and also should consider how their current jobs could be redesigned and improved.

CAREER COUNSELING WITHIN ORGANIZATIONS

Workers need to thoroughly explore the environment and identify alternatives by in-depth evaluation of the best alternatives (Hicks & London, 1991). Counselors in industries need to provide information about the opportunities available within the organization, help individuals tailor-make their career paths, encourage employees to develop career paths, and encourage them to make formal plans and systematize their decision making. Counselors need to provide positive reinforcement, guide workers to appropriate training and development programs, and provide opportunities for achievement.

Morrison (1991) identified six human resource planning elements of concern that need to be addressed:

1. *Legal* aspects—knowledge of labor laws, equal employment opportunity legislation, and affirmative action, and the like
2. *Economics*—labor market costs for different geographic segments, salaries, wages, and benefits
3. *Competition*—recruitment, employment, and career development policies and practices
4. *Technological trends*—computerization, automation, robotics; labor force demographics such as surpluses and shortages, geographic mobility, educational level, sex, minority groups, age and the like
5. *Human resource policy*—developmental opportunities, promotion, training, and mobility
6. *Organization*—culture, philosophy, size, growth; work-force characteristics, such as skills, age, length of service, adaptability, performance, and the like

STRATEGIES TO PROMOTE CAREER EXPLORATION

Management and career development specialists should make sure they are providing a program that attempts to overcome the barriers listed in the previous section. A checklist that can be used in planning seminars is included in Figure 8.4.

JOB ENTRY

The organization has to initiate an action program at the start of a worker's career to help ease the job entry of the new worker. The first several months are a challenging learning experience for both the new worker and management per-

---

Before Program

___ Conduct needs assessment to find out areas of interest and possible times for scheduling
___ Write letter describing possible outcomes, type of activities, and so on.
___ Conduct orientation session for managers, supervisors, and executives
___ Develop brochure for program, include description in newsletter, and so on
___ Order materials, catalog materials to be used
___ Secure appropriate location for career information materials, and so on
___ Schedule room for seminars/workshops

During the Program

___ Remind participants that the program is voluntary
___ Provide extensive opportunities for self-exploration, assessment instruments, learning exercises, and career planning workbooks
___ Use small groups for participants to share their goals, insights, and concerns
___ Involve members of management and supervisors to provide information about the organization and feedback on the performance of the workers
___ Provide information on jobs, job ladders, alternate career paths, and so on
___ Involve family in the exploration process to provide information and collaborate on the self-assessment
___ Be available for individual counseling sessions
___ Have employees set goals and action plans for themselves

After the Program

___ Have participants evaluate the process, the materials, the speakers, the room, the time, and so on
___ Have participants identify additional workshops or seminars they would like to attend or additional areas, materials, and so on they would like to explore
___ Follow up on the goals and action plans

FIGURE 8.4
Checklist for planning seminars on career development

sonnel (Wanous, 1980). The research evidence points out the scope of this problem. Ten percent of all newcomers are either fired or strongly encouraged to leave the organization within the first 6 months of their employment (Kennedy, 1986). Fifty percent of newcomers will leave their jobs within the first 5 years' employment (Dalton, 1989). The number one reason for this turnover is that the new worker fails to adapt to the organizational culture. Career counselors within organizations are expected to help with the transition or the socialization process.

OUTCOMES OF SOCIALIZATION

The goals of the socialization process are to have the workers define their roles, maintain their role behaviors, and develop the necessary attitudes for the maintenance of the organization (Hall, 1990). The outcomes are for employees to develop commitment to the organization, to be satisfied with their jobs, to be motivated to do their work, to have high performance standards, and to want to remain with the company. In the process negative outcomes such as stress and overconformity are to be avoided. The initial orientation session can provide career guidance to new workers (Hicks & London, 1991).

The formal socialization process calls for formal orientation sessions, training and development activities, and job assignments. The orientation programs should be designed to make the new workers feel welcome and communicate clearly how the organization expects them to perform their jobs. The sessions explain the mission and goals of the organization. Training and development programs are often required to teach the knowledge, skills, and abilities that the workers need to perform their jobs successfully. Challenging and interesting work tends to hold new employees within the organization.

In making job assignments the company needs to convey the high expectations it has for workers, who often perceive their value by their work assignments. Informal socialization takes place through the interaction of the worker with supervisors and mentors, co-workers and peers, and subordinates and staff (Hall, 1990). Subordinates and staff can be excellent sources of information. They usually have lower rank within the organization and are less threatening to the new worker. Peers and co-workers are most likely to have the greatest influence on the new workers' behavior because they are in contact with them more often than with supervisors or mentors.

The socialization process can help new workers focus on the salient aspects of their job and can facilitate the development of their self-confidence. If workers perform well and receive positive reinforcement, they will be satisfied with their job and develop internal motivation and commitment to the organization.

SPECIAL PROBLEMS OF WOMEN

Sometimes women have a challenge in the labor market because of stereotyping and covert discrimination. The seminars previously outlined can help women to expand their horizons. To assess your understanding, answer the questions on women in the labor market in Figure 8.5. (Circle the correct response.)

Subich (1989) pointed out that there is a need for career development specialists to help women in expanding their life roles and improving their quality. She reminded us that women continue to have difficulty entering specific occupational fields and attaining well-paying jobs that provide opportunities for advancement. Lee (1989) thought professionals were needed to help women and minority group members achieve the type of life-style they want. He stated that the "professional must be a career development advocate who possesses the awareness, knowledge, and skills to transcend boundaries of ethnicity or sex in his or her career development interventions" (p. 218).

SUMMARY

The period between 23 and 35 years old is labeled early adulthood. The roles of the individual, such as worker, family member, citizen, leisurite, and learner, take on new dimensions and meanings. Super calls this phase the period of trial and stabilization. The first year on the job for a young adult is a period of trial

---

Circle the correct response.

True False 1. Two thirds of women are employed in the lower paying fields of education and the health professions.

True False 2. About one million families are headed by women who are either divorced, separated, widowed, or never married.

True False 3. Fifty-five percent of employed women work in the clerical and service fields.

True False 4. Women between the ages of 20 and 35 have higher self-esteem than women 50 to 65 years old.

True False 5. Working women are more satisfied with life than nonworking women.

True False 6. Women 20 to 35 years old are less aggressive and achievement minded than women 40 to 55 years old.

True False 7. The average age women married in 1983 was 23.

True False 8. Women hold about 50% of jobs in the skilled trades.

True False 9. Working women feel that they have less influence in the home than nonworking women.

True False 10. The top 10 jobs held by women include several in the high-tech field.

Answers 1. T, 2. F (10 million), 3. T, 4. F (lower), 5. T, 6. F (more), 7. T, 8. F (25%), 9. F (more), 10. F (conventional).

FIGURE 8.5

Questions on women in the labor force

and error. Levinson sees this period as a time of experimentation as well as exploration. Individuals are faced with career development tasks such as developing more independence on the job, showing less need for supervision, and developing high standards of performance. This is a period when young adults have to decide whether to keep with their initial choice, modify it, or make completely different choices. This is complicated by the changes in the world economic and labor market. The decision is affected by downsizing in many companies. Many corporations provide career counseling and career development activities for their workers.

REVIEW QUESTIONS

1.   What should a counselor know about the personal, social, cognitive, physical, and career stages of young adults to be able to facilitate their career development?
2.   What are the developmental tasks for young adults? What tasks do young adults have to master for the world of work?
3.   Can we really separate career goals from life goals? How do you look at your short-term and long-term goals?
4.   Have you participated in career development or exploration seminars at your place of work? What topics were presented? What did you learn from your participation?
5.   Why do industry and business conduct these seminars? What activities and strategies should be included in these seminars? Should all workers be required to attend?
6.   What strategies and techniques would you propose to use if you were the career development specialist for a company and were charged with helping new employees to become better socialized?
7.   What strategies and techniques can the counselor use to help young adult women enhance their career development and maturity?

SUGGESTED LEARNING ACTIVITIES

1.   Conduct a survey of local businesses and industry and find out what if any career counseling or guidance services they provide their employees. Report your results to the class.
2.   Interview a career counselor for a business and industry and find out what his or her role and functions are, what type of resources he or she has available for his or her employees, and the type of problems he or she handles.
3.   Design a workshop to help promote the career development of young adult employees.
4.   Design a program to help new employees with their socialization into the workplace.

5. Select several of the self-help books and write a critique of the material included on job-entry skills.
6. Interview a consultant who works with business and industry in conducting career seminars.
7. Interview employees just starting their jobs and find out what problems they identify and what type of inservice assistance they receive at work.

CASE STUDIES

Stuck in a One-Company Town

Let's face it: The only employer in this area is the paper mill, so I took a job as a laborer. My friends live here. My family lives here. I like the paycheck but I just can't see myself doing this stupid job all my life.

Too Busy to Think

I thought I would like working for XYZ Corporation. The job sounded good. I felt good about myself and my competencies to do the work. Their description of what the job would be and what it actually turned out to be are two different things. They said I would be located in Atlanta. I am flying around the country and not even back in Atlanta on weekends except for maybe once a month. I guess my boss is a nice enough person but I hardly ever get to see him. I really wanted to make this job as my career. I do not know whether it would be good for me to quit. I've just been on the job for over a year. The one problem I have is that they keep me so busy and on the road that I don't even have time to look for another job.

Waiting for What?

You counselors are all alike. I took the job at McDonald's because you got to eat and it was there. It helps put food on the table while I think of some other options. You can do anything that you have to do. You make too much about values and roles. One of these days I will be at the right place at the right time and really connect.

Case Questions

1. What additional information would you want to have before deciding how you would work with each of these individuals?
2. What would you say about their stages of career development? Career maturity? Career decision making? Psychosocial development?
3. What types of strategies or interventions would you use in each case?

SUGGESTED READINGS

Gutteridge, T. G., Leibowitz, Z. B., & Shore, J. E. (1993). *Organizational career development.* San Francisco: Jossey-Bass.

    The authors provide case studies of career development systems at 12 exemplary companies and give suggestions for designing and implementing career development programs in business and industry.

Wrightsman, L. S. (1988). *Personality development in adulthood.* Newbury Park, CA: Sage.

    The author looks at three major theoretical perspectives as a framework to focus on aspects of adulthood. There is a chapter on career change.

MIDDLE ADULTHOOD

A Time of Reflection

T he middle adult period (ages 30 to 45) is a challenging phase of life. The age range parameters will vary for this period due to different time frames established in the models cited by this chapter. Much attention has focused on mid-career crises, which quite often occurs during this period. Certainly there is a period of mid-life transition when individuals review and reexamine who they are and what they want to do in life. Individuals tend to reevaluate their life priorities, goals, and relationships in light of prior experiences and impending mortality. Labor market statistics indicate that around 10% of the labor force change jobs during this period. The age period is also the heaviest for divorce. The period is often marked by death of a parent and the youngest child entering kindergarten. Women who have not worked or have worked part-time while raising a family enter the job market again. Mature relationships have been established with associates, friends, and parents. Some people react to the stress of this phase by shifting career fields and jobs and separating from or divorcing spouses. Russell (1991) identified job rotation, downward moves, and personal developmental programs as the three major career issues in this period.

LEARNING OBJECTIVES

After reading the chapter, you should be able to do the following:

- Identify key components of personality, social development, and career development theories essential to understanding middle adulthood
- Discuss mid-career crisis or transition events and identify what counseling approaches are helpful for adults
- Identify and discuss counseling strategies that could be used for some of the major problem areas during this period such as mid-career crisis and displaced homemakers, unemployment, and job dislocation
- Identify problems faced by women reentering the world of work and interventions that can help them with the transition

DEVELOPMENTAL TASKS

McCoy (1977) divides the period covered in this chapter into three stages: 29 to 34 years old, called catch-30; 35 to 43 years, called mid-life reexamination, and 44 to 55 years, called restabilization. There are seven tasks listed for the first stage, none for the second, and 11 for the third. Two common tasks of these stages are problem solving and managing stress accompanying change. The initial stage deals with raising young children, relating to teenaged children, and launching children into the world. The middle stage and restabilization stage have tasks, related to aging parents and handling their increased demands.

Self-appraisal objectives are included at each stage: searching for personal values, searching for meaning and reassessing personal priorities and values, and adjusting to realities of work. There are relationship tasks at each level: at the catch-30 stage; reappraising relationships; at the mid-life reexamination stage, reassessing marriage, and at the restabilization stage, becoming deeply involved in social life. At the restabilization period two additional tasks are added: managing leisure time and participating actively in community concerns. This period is also marked with additional economic tasks, for example, managing budget to support college-age children and aging parents.

The mid-life reexamination period posits searching for meaning, reassessing marriage, reexamining work, relating to aging parents, reassessing personal priorities and values, adjusting to single life, problem solving, and managing stress accompanying change as critical issues. Adults in this phase need personal counseling for self-growth and for setting new life goals.

Chickering and Havighurst (1981) identify three major tasks. The first is adapting to a changing time perspective. Adults during this period begin to see that the future is not unlimited and they do not have time to do everything. They feel that time is running out with many things unaccomplished, unseen, and unexperienced.

The second is revising career plans. Many times, adults feel that by this stage in their life they have mastered the roles and routines. They think about whether they want to do the same things for the next 20 years. The older the adult becomes, the harder it is to change. Many people decide it is more practical and easier just to stay in the same position, job, or career. Hall and associates (1986) stated that the major tasks facing employees in the middle career period are to confront and reappraise their early career decisions and goals and to remain productive at work.

The third task is redefining family relationships. Children have usually left home, and both the wife and the husband have to adjust to the new life-style. Sometimes the couple may have had their children as their only shared interest and their relationship ends in divorce or separation. Others feel it is a time of rediscovery and recapturing the freedom they had before the children were born.

The middle adult period is a period in which adults maintain their career or develop a new one. Neugarten (1968) described middle-aged persons as no longer driven, but now the driver or in command. They become more interested in developing helping relationships on the job and become mentors.

Some middle-age men do change career fields. Chickering and Havighurst (1981) reported that about 10% of the men between ages 40 and 60 are career changers. Instead of maintaining roles and skills, they have to learn new sets of competencies and knowledge.

The fourth task is making mature civic contributions. For many this may assume a priority beyond job functioning. Many times, when adults have resolved family and work decisions, they turn their time and energy into civic activities. The new activities provide a new environment for adults and result in new personal relationships and new opportunities for personal growth and problem solving.

Lowenthal, Thurnher, Chiribog, and associates (1975) identified four stages in life, the third of which is middle-aged, a term with negative connotations. Characteristic of men in this period are a narrowed life-style, heightened sense of orderliness, a plateau as far as job advancement, strain and stress and boredom as potential problems, and perceived by family members as the boss.

Women in this period are characterized as having a negative self-concept, being unhappy and absent-minded, having increased marital problems, being critical of their husbands, wanting a simplistic life-style, and anxious over the last child leaving home.

Neugarten (1977) saw the period as a period of reexamination of self when one takes stock and plans ahead. More women work and tend to become more dominant, instrumental, autonomous, self-confident, and more accepting of their aggressive impulses. The last child is usually gone and women's freedom and home satisfaction increases.

Intellectual and Cognitive Development

Schaie (1977/78) conceptualized three stages of intellectual development in the adult period:

1. An achieving stage when the young adult strives for goal orientation and role independence
2. A responsible stage when the adult of middle years is involved in long-term goal integration and increased problem solving
3. A reintegrative stage when the adult of later years sees the relinquishment of occupational and family responsibilities and the simplification of cognitive structures through selective attention to meaningful environmental demands

Most healthy adults show little decline in their performance on intelligence tests until their 50s; some studies show little decline to retirement. Partly, the adults' performance depends on their motivation to develop or maintain particular intellectual abilities.

The individual's cognitive processes in this period also vary in the same ways as the person's intellectual capacities. Adults' life-styles and how they input their information and use their information processing affects their cognitive functioning. There are alternate ways of looking at the stages of cognitive development.

One perception is that there is a regression of the use of logical thought in adulthood. The other is that adults have climbed to a higher stage or more advanced mode of reasoning. Adults differ in how they use their existing thought structures through accommodation from the new experiences they encounter.

Personality Development

Levinson (1986) developed a series of stages of adult life. He concluded that there are life structures, basic patterns, or designs of an adult's life at a given period and that these life structures take place through an orderly sequence. The period from 40 to 45 years is labeled mid-life transition and the period from 45 to 50 years is called entering middle adulthood. The adults have to resolve their disillusionment, the disappointment of not having achieved their dream or life goal. Adults have to cope with this discrepancy and look at what they have achieved and revise their goals to be more realistic. The idea is that adults have to resolve the polarities in their life and achieve balance. The resolutions are complicated because of the changes in the political and social climate of the world, the changes in technology, and the changing family structure.

Erikson (1968) identifies generativity versus stagnation as the crisis of adulthood. Generativity involves adults being creative and productive and developing an interest in guiding the development of the next generation. Adults show caring and concern about people and the environment. Adults who resolve the stagnation conflict become caring and involved individuals. If there is not movement toward generativity, adults tend to suffer boredom, apathy, and have poor interpersonal relationships.

Peck (1975) expanded on the generativity versus stagnation crisis and felt that the accomplishment of generativity is accomplished by the change of valuing physical powers to valuing wisdom, as well as through a movement from rigidity to flexibility, both mentally and emotionally. There is a change in dimensions of human relationship from sexualization to a personal relationship based on friendship and companionship.

CAREER DEVELOPMENT THEORY

A number of career development theorists have proposed progressive career stages. Hall (1976) identified three stages: early, middle, and later career. The middle career period is characterized by training and updating one's skills, learning to train and coach others, and reassessing one's self. London and Stumpf (1982) developed three substages in the mid-career stage: growth, maintenance, and decline.

The growth period is marked by working through the mid-life crisis. Adults are required to evaluate their goals and may modify career direction. There is a fear of stagnation in this substage.

The maintenance stage focuses on adults' realization of the value of job security. They perceive change may be risky. They like to take pride in their professional accomplishments and become mentors within the organization.

The decline stage is beset with feelings of failure and insecurity. Some take early retirement without adequate planning. There is a disengagement from work and life, sometimes brought on by physical or emotional problems.

Schein (1978) identified four stages: entry, socialization, mid-career, and late career. There are two dimensions that are important at these stages. The first is finding career anchors. Adults develop these anchors from perceptions of their talents, abilities, motives, needs, and values. Some of these anchors, for example, are technical competence, managerial competence, security and stability, and autonomy and creativity. The second dimension is the decision to be a generalist or to be a specialist.

Super (1990) sees the period between 25 to 45 years as the establishment stage, which may characterized by advancement, frustration, and consolidation. The period between 45 and 60 years is the maintenance stage, which may be characterized by innovation, stagnation, or updating.

MID-LIFE TRANSITION

Sherman (1987) stated that sometimes counselors of adults tend to infer meaning-of-life events based on their normative views of adult development from a societal perspective. He states:

> [T]here meanings are seen as related to social roles which are supposed to provide normative standards, expectations, and guidelines for social conduct and living in broad areas of life . . . one of the most important roles is occupations which provide both purpose and direction to one's life. (p. 219)

Social scientists have focused on mid-career crises but the meaning of them depends on the individual. How the adult views the meaning of the crisis-laden event will determine whether the event becomes a crisis and how the event will be resolved.

There are many alternate explanations for mid-career and life transitions. The explanations range from mental health problems to economic factors to changes in the salience of the work role at this period of time for adults. The theories of Erikson (1982) and Neugarten (1964) help us to understand some of the personality and development aspects, but there are also sociological and economic aspects.

Rising unemployment rates, which may vary from 5% or less to 25% or more, depending on the geographic region, incur life crises. Rising inflation causes individuals to change jobs in order to get higher salaries. We can see the effects of the global economic conditions and the competition from other countries, which have caused internal competition and lowering of salaries in some fields.

COMPETENCIES NEEDED BY COUNSELORS

There are a number of general and specific competencies needed by counselors working with mid-life career changers. The competencies counselors need to have are listed in Figure 9.1.

Brown (1984) felt that career counseling instead of mental health counseling should be pursued first with the client. He postulated that career counseling may even be an efficient and effective intervention with clients who have problems with depression and loss because the focus of the sessions is on ways of regaining what is lost. Even with other mental health problems, he felt that financial problems are usually major and need to be addressed through career counseling, but did state that there are mental health problems that need to be addressed either preceding career counseling or along with it. Klein, Amundson, and Borgen (1992) pointed out that many times clients have difficulty in meeting the basic survival needs, and when they are unemployed they tend to suffer frustration and depression.

TYPES OF INTERVENTIONS

There are many different intervention approaches that help individuals who face mid-career crises. Many educational and public service organizations offer career

---

* Have a knowledge of adult development
* Understand the adult decision-making process and its role in career choice
* Have an understanding of issues such as age bias, sex bias, and cultural bias
* Be current on the job market
* Have competence in developing employable skills
* Be able to conduct and lead small group sessions
* Know how to develop job-finding network and job clubs
* Be able to guide clients in preparing resumes
* Provide practice and skill development in how to interview
* Have individual counseling skills
* Be able to identify type of counseling individual needs—career or personal
* Know community referral sources

FIGURE 9.1
Competencies needed by counselors working with mid-life career changers

guidance services to adults through seminars and workshops, tutoring programs, group sessions, computer-assisted counseling programs, and assessment centers. Telephone counseling is also available. State employment services can be used. Bibliotherapy or extensive reading on areas of concern are other techniques to deal with mid-career crises.

One counseling method is to discuss with a number of people involved in the intervention session, the client, the counselor, mentors, and peers with similar problems.

Many people want to work their problems out by themselves. These individuals are high on independence and autonomy. They have a high internal locus of control and high self-confidence. There are many well-written self-help books available in bookstores and the public library, for example, *The Career Decision Planner* (Lloyd, 1992) and *How to Find Mr. Right: Say Good-bye to the Mr. Wrong in Your Life!* (Walker & Hittle, 1993).

Others want just a minimal amount of help because they have gone through the awareness and decision stages before. They want to be guided to sources of information, human and printed. Bibliotherapy, computer-assisted guidance and counseling programs, interviewing and observing people in certain jobs, and the like tend to be the type of information they want. These individuals recognize their lack of knowledge in certain areas and their limits, but feel they have the capability of working problems out for themselves.

Some want lots of individual attention and help, possibly due to a lack of self-confidence and partly due to the experiences they have been through. Some want to be told what they should do. They have high deference needs and rely on what people they respect tell them. Many of these individuals have had changes in their life, such as from being married to a single status, children not home anymore, and so on. Individuals with an introverted personality would rather keep their discussions private and confidential. Some are paranoid about others hearing about their problems. These individuals need continuous reinforcement to complete the counseling and are more externally oriented.

Small groups are the best intervention for some individuals. They like to hear other points of view and perspectives on their problems. They do not feel as isolated because they now have a support group. They realize that others have the same type of problems and are working them out.

At different stages of an intervention program, some individuals may seek both individual and group support. They have a fear of not making the right move or the right job change. To help, ask them to do extra readings and study beyond that involved in the counseling sessions.

Another dimension is formal versus informal approach. Some individuals prefer formal sessions on a specific topic such as time management, stress management, or constructing a resume. Others prefer informal groups in which the problems of the moment are discussed rather than a formal topic. Choice of system relates to the individual's cognitive style. Field-dependent individuals prefer flexibility to discuss what is important at the time.

One of the major problems that individuals face during this period is, Are they making the right decisions and the right choices? They do not have the time and money and energy to afford a series of wrong choices. Having a trained professional to guide the individual is a better process than relying on one's own strategies and knowledge. Courses and seminars may provide a general overview to the problem areas, but not really provide the necessary support and information the adult needs in this transitional period.

COUNSELING PROGRAMS

Career counseling programs for mid-career transitions usually focus on reevaluation of self, evaluation of options, and development of action plans. The first component is the reexamination of self, which calls for looking at all dimensions of the self including values, needs, interests, skills, employment history, personal history, as well as skills and competencies. Russell (1991) reported on the development of assessment centers in organizations. Over 2000 organizations including IBM, General Electric, J. C. Penney, and Sears, Roebuck and Company have these centers available for the employees to help them gain a better understanding of their skills and to help them develop their career goals and plans.

The counselor can gain information about the adult in transition by using formal and informal assessment techniques. There are a wide variety of biographical data sheets, standardized inventories, and structured and unstructured exercises that can supplement interview data. There are computer-assisted counseling programs as well as computer adaptive tests available.

The counselor should first find out the personal, social, and work history of the individual. The process for finding this information could be a career analysis, autobiography, a personal autobiography, or a biographic data sheet. Sometimes a graphic presentation provides a more dramatic way of looking at life experiences. The client can be instructed to include on the time line his or her career history, family, personal events, and accomplishments, as well as key personal events. In reviewing the career history line the counselor can help the client identify the reasons for job change, why the job was satisfactory or unsatisfactory and why there is now interest in changing jobs. The family line can be used to discuss and assess family relationships and the personal line can be used to discuss accomplishments and leisure activities.

Values and needs can be addressed through value clarification exercises and through standardized inventories. Scarpello and Ledvinka (1988) reported that tests and inventories have been increasingly used to facilitate employee development. The *Values Scale* and the *Salience Inventory* are examples of two of the types of inventories commonly used. The *Edwards Personal Preference Scale* provides a profile of 15 needs. The individuals in this period need to look at their values and see how they relate to their life-style and work style. Also, the *Coopersmith Self-Esteem Inventory* provides assessment of general orientation to life. The individuals need to identify the variables that cause them satisfaction and dissatisfaction with work. They need to explore whether their proposed changes will correlate with their values and expectations. They need to explore the types of work environments that they feel are positive and they feel are negative. Noe and Steffy (1987) reported that these inventories increased workers' career explorations.

Interests are an important dimension to consider in making any type of career transition. There are numerous interest inventories available that can provide useful profiles for the individual to consider, such as the *Strong Interest Inventory,* the *Self-Directed Search,* and the *Career Occupational Preference System.* The clients can be asked directly what these interests are, or learn from listening to the activities they have preferred or chosen. Interest information can be gained from not only what these individuals like to do at work, but also what they like to do in their leisure activities. Ultimately the counselor needs to help the clients relate these interests to the type of interests demanded by fields they are not considering.

Understanding the knowledge of the skills, competencies, and abilities that one possesses is important to take into consideration when planning a job change. If the career change is just minor and the individual is going to remain in a similar or closely related field, the competencies required are probably going to be basically the same. If the career change is going to be major, a 90-degree turn from the previous position, the competencies, skills, and knowledge the individual has might be inadequate. The person might have to seek additional training and education. There are standardized aptitude tests and achievement tests. The client needs to identify and evaluate skills developed through post-work experiences, as well as through avocations and leisure activities.

The second set of activities relates to evaluation of options. Counselors can help clients develop a knowledge basis for their decision making and establishing of plans. The potential fields need to be studied so that the person in transition knows the type of education and training necessary for success in the job as well as the roles, competencies, and experience necessary for entry into those fields.

Developmental programs involve training and assessment components. Russell (1991) reported that the two most frequently used types of programs were the assessment center and job rotation. Some companies include tuition-refund plans that allow workers to take job-related courses or obtain degrees in local colleges. Many organizations have elaborate training and mentoring programs. Some organizations allow mid-career employees to take sabbatical leaves (Feldman, 1988). Others offer renewal seminars. Organizations have also offered job enlargement and job enrichment programs (Courtney, 1986). Russell (1991) suggests that organizations should promote effective career management among mid-career employees to prevent obsolescence and plateauing by use of frequent skills assessment, performance feedback, increased recognition for good performance and improved reward systems.

There are numerous booklets, pamphlets, books, and guides to jobs available—fastest growing, nontraditional, good paying but risky. If training or more education is required, then the counselor needs to guide the individual to the educational sources of information, guide books on apprenticeships, trade schools, technical schools, 2-year colleges, and the like. There are different modes of presentation of the educational sources available. For example, computer guidance systems have files such as community college and technical schools, 4-year colleges, graduate schools, and the like. DISCOVER and CHOICES are two examples of computer-assisted guidance systems.

Many individuals need financial assistance in pursuing their educational goals. The counselor needs to be able to guide them to financial aid sources, particularly if they are disabled. They might need other types of personal assistance programs. The educational and occupational information needs to be appropriate for the age and educational level of the adult.

There are other effective techniques. Adults prefer to have the opportunity to interview people in the career field or job that they are planning to enter. They also like to observe the individual and explore the work environment, that is, job shadow.

Another technique is to develop action plans. After having adults reevaluate their values, interests, skills, competencies, and experiences, they need to learn the educational entry, roles, and functions requirements of various jobs they would consider. They need to translate goals into short-term and long-term plans. They need to look at the realistic factors that might be involved, such as cost of education and/or training, cost of job seeking, and time required for change. Also adults need to be guided in developing decision-making skills and life-planning skills as they consider alternative goals.

WOMEN'S ISSUES

Professional Women

Many business and professional women are married and have husbands who are also pursuing a career. Some are single mothers. Women often play the role of wife, mother, as well as a career person, and have the responsibility for domestic and child-care duties. They often experience problems with their partners about whose career will take precedence and dilemmas about children (Hall & Ricter, 1988). Fernandez (1986) reported that 96% of the women surveyed wanted half-day vacations and flex hours. Betz and Fitzgerald (1987) also found that dual-career couples experienced role conflict and had difficulties dealing with travel, children, household tasks, job transfers, and their career roles and responsibilities.

Counselors should provide seminars and workshops that will be valuable to this group on topics such as assertiveness training, communication skills, stress management, career pathing, organizational dynamics, and image building. Counselors can also assist this group in finding support groups and help them to network with other women both for support and future job contacts. Counselors in business and industry or in university career centers may also help these women find other women who may be willing to serve as mentors.

Women tend to see as obstacles to moving up the career ladder: financial demands, time and energy demands, their husband's career, the training requirements of the career, and lack of job opportunities in their career field (Rosen,

1982). Women who are part of dual-career couples require different assistance than single mothers (Kossek, 1990). Rosen pointed out the obstacles that women have to overcome to move up the corporate ladder are negative sex-role stereotypes, bias in selection and placement decisions, bias in career advancement decisions, management expectations about women's career priorities, failure to assertively protest inequities, male backlash to affirmative action policies, shortage of executive role models, exclusion, tokenism, harassment, and lack of political skills. Some women when they reach the top are unwilling or unprepared to engage in the type of competition and organizational politics necessary to keep there. However, many organizations attempt to facilitate the career development of women and minorities by providing them additional feedback and career management seminars (Hall and Associates, 1986).

Displaced Homemakers

Displaced homemakers include a wide variety of groups of women. Traditionally it has included middle-aged women who because of divorce or death of husband, needed to give up the role of a homemaker and find work to support the family. Now it includes women who are divorced and need to reenter the work force and women with dependent children whose families need additional financial resources. The other group included in this category is traditional homemakers who want to enter or reenter the world of work. Each group has a different set of problems but the one in common is that they do not have specific vocational preparation or work skills necessary to be competitive in the job market. They also lack the job-search skills.

A compounding problem with the first two groups is the fact that they often have serious financial problems and traumatic decisions to make such as the need or appropriateness of selling property, relocation of residence, and other types of financial decisions.

Another set of problems centers around loss or separation. They have lost their major support system and need the help of support groups, but may have problems knowing how to go about meeting new friends. A major problem for these women is their low perception of self. They feel they do not have job skills, view being a housewife as nonskilled work, and may have had little responsibility in areas such as property maintenance, buying cars, appliances, and even paying the bills each month. To the contrary, being a housewife requires budgeting, planning, organizing, and a strong self-concept to cite a few positive variables that are helpful in the labor market.

The groups of women who have gone through divorce, have been abandoned by spouses, have become widows, or whose spouse was suddenly unemployed may need some personal counseling in addition to career counseling. Personal difficulties will not disappear when they find full-time jobs or begin a training or educational program.

Special Competencies Needed for Displaced Homemakers

Counselors working with displaced homemakers need to have some special competencies as well as general competencies. The list of competencies shown in Figure 9.2 provides a framework for action and personal development.

Palo Alto College in San Antonio, Texas, has a program to increase the skills and employability of displaced homemakers. They provided 150 hours of instruction, training, and counseling, 60 hours of which were in typing, 20 hours in grammar, 20 hours in computer use, 20 hours in job search skills, 10 hours in career guidance, 10 hours in office practice procedures, and 10 hours in personal and professional development. In the personal and professional development areas they spent time on wellness, nutrition, exercise, along with instruction on stress management, time management, and assertiveness.

Houser, D'Andrea, and Daniels (1992) found that when self-efficacy was increased there were significant changes in the participants' cognitive and emotional performance. The clients were able to accomplish their goals more effectively. Stidham and Remeley (1992) reported that job club methodology applied in a work-force setting helped the clients obtain employment, and the process helped them increase their self-esteem, develop a positive work ethic, and improve their decision making.

Reentry Women

Programs were previously mentioned for displaced homemakers, and many of the same activities are appropriate for women reentering the job market. Work-

---

* Ability to assess the current and existing skills of the client
* Knowledge of the local labor market information
* Knowledge of the training and educational programs available to prepare individuals for special jobs within the local job market
* Knowledge of agencies sponsoring job clubs, assertiveness training, and day-care centers
* Knowledge of the federal law requirements under Title VII of the Civil Rights Act of 1984 as well as Title IX of the educational amendments of 1972
* Knowledge of the social service agencies, civic organizations, and charitable foundations that might provide temporary financial support or scholarships for training
* Ability to establish groups to provide displaced homemakers with the information they need for career decisions, skill building, and support
* Ability to conduct individual sessions on self-awareness, decision making, and goal setting

---

FIGURE 9.2
Competencies for counselors working with displaced homemakers

shops and other types of training programs are commonly available, but group and individual interventions are often necessary. Group sessions should be used for information giving, skill building, and interpersonal support. Individual sessions are often necessary to help women in increasing their self-awareness, their decision making and goal setting.

SUMMARY

Chapter 9 has provided a summary of the key issues facing adults at the midpoint of their career. Career counseling programs must consider developmental needs in relation to self-appraisal, career planning, career transitions, and career adjustment.

REVIEW QUESTIONS

1. In working with clients who are in middle adulthood, what should the counselor know about their personal, social, and cognitive development?
2. Compare and contrast the different ways of looking at stages of career development. How is the knowledge of career stages helpful to the counselor?
3. What is mid-career crisis? Does everyone go through this crisis?
4. What are some strategies that counselors can use to help individuals who are in the transition?
5. Who are the displaced homemakers? What interventions can be used to help them?
6. What are some of the problems that career and business women have? How can career counselors help them?

SUGGESTED ACTIVITIES

1. Interview a number of individuals who are in middle adulthood. Find out their views on work. Have they gone through a period of career crisis or mid-career transition?
2. Review several self-help books and commercial materials on career transition. What are some of the common themes? How are the topics different than those presented for other age levels?
3. Interview counselors who are working with displaced homemakers. What do they see the needs of the clients are? What type of training do they provide this group? What type of programs are effective?
4. Do a case study of an individual going through mid-career crisis: a displaced homemaker, a business or professional woman, or a dual-career couple.

5. Write a curriculum guide or outline for a seminar for working with one of the special groups identified in this chapter.
6. Make a critical review of the different programs and literature on one of the special groups identified in this chapter.
7. Write a term paper or a research report on mid-career crisis or mid-career transition.

CASE STUDIES

Returning to Civilian Life

Terry has been in the Navy for 23 years. He is a helicopter pilot and squadron leader. He holds the rank of commander. He graduated from Annapolis and has his bachelor's in electrical engineering. He has decided that he does not want to stay in the armed services any longer but would like to remain in the geographical area. His children are in the local schools. He has not worked in his degree field and has not completed any additional graduate work. Although the base does provide some career counseling help, he decides to seek help from a civilian counselor.

Mid-Life Crisis

Natali has had a progression of jobs in the food services industries, and has progressed up the corporate ladder from a salad preparer to a manager of food services in a large resort complex. Now at 40 she has gone through a divorce. She went to a mental health counselor, and feels that she must make major changes in her life-style and career. She is even considering becoming a counselor to help people go through crises like hers.

Case Questions

1. What counseling strategies/approaches would you use with these clients?
2. What additional information is needed?
3. What type of career and life-style planning is needed by these individuals?

SUGGESTED READINGS

Kanchier, C. (1991). *Dare to change your job—and your life.* New York: Master-media Limited.

This is a paperback book that makes for good reading for anyone contemplating a job change. It guides readers through self-analysis and forces the readers to confront themselves.

Kottler, J. P., Faux, V. A., & McArthur, C. C. (1978). *Self-assessment and career development*. Englewood Cliffs, NJ: Prentice Hall.

This career workbook has a strong collection of self-analysis activities for use by adults in a career study group or working alone.

10

OLDER ADULTS

The Graying of America

As we enter the 21st century, counselors and human service workers will encounter a population requiring somewhat different counseling services. This population of older Americans will require sensitive listening, intense empathy, and a multitude of services to assist with adapting to increased longevity. In their seminal work, *Encounter with the Future*, Centron and O'Toole (1982) predicted that people could live to 150 years. Their prediction was based on improved health care, scientific invention, and conscientious attention by Americans to personal health. We now have over 250,000 Americans who have reached 100 years of age (Hodgkinson, 1985), and people have an average life span of 72 years. We anticipate that science will develop an anti-aging drug that will raise the life span to 100 plus years. The Duke University Survey (Beck, 1993) projected a potential life span of 85 or older for 80 million people by the year 2000, and 160 million people reaching 65 or older by the year 2040. What will be the impact of longer life on gerontological counseling? Career counseling? Perhaps a bit of crystal balling would suggest that a large number of these older citizens will want meaningful occupational endeavors. We suspect that longer life will lead to impact on family structure, couple relationships, and work and personal recreational ventures.

LEARNING OBJECTIVES

After reading the chapter, you should be able to do the following:

- Identify the key theories of career development, personality development, and social development that are essential to understanding the older adult
- Discuss the developmental tasks for older adults and their implications for career counseling and career guidance
- Critique the current practices, methods, procedures, and assessment strategies that are currently in use with older adults
- Describe the special roles, problems, and conditions such as outplacement counseling, inplacement counseling, mentoring, motivating workers at the maintenance stage, and retirement

The period of life from age 50 and above is marked by major adjustments such as retirement, the departure of the last child from home, and the death of a spouse. Individuals begin a gradual change in their physical appearance and intellectual capacity. They have to be able to maintain self-confidence in order to cope with these changes. Jordaan (1974) has proposed that this period is divided into two stages: the mid-40s to retirement is called the maintenance stage and after retirement is called the decline stage. London and Greller (1991) predicted that older workers will find that the norm shifts from emphasis on retirement to continued meaningful employment.

DEVELOPMENTAL TASKS

Chickering and Havighurst (1981) identified two periods: late-adult transition (57 to 65 years) and late adulthood (65 years plus). They saw the major issue in the first stage as preparing for retirement and dealing with issues of life-style, income requirements, and alternate living arrangements. McCoy (1977) expanded this phase to include eight developmental tasks.

The first is to adjust to health problems. Older adults can be counseled to attend workshops and seminars on health and nutrition issues. The second is to develop personal relations that can be accomplished through active participation in social, civic, and religious groups and through growth groups and other types of human relations activities. The third is accepting changes in work capacity and personal roles. Preretirement counseling aids individuals in examining these changes.

The fourth is to expand one's avocational interests through continuing education programs sponsored by educational institutions and social, community, and religious groups. There are all kinds of travel opportunities. Older adults can develop skills and appreciations in the fine and practical arts to broaden their knowledge in these areas, too.

The fifth is to be able to finance new leisure activities. Older adults can attend seminars and workshops on investment, money management, or on consumer behaviors. The sixth is to adjust to loss of a spouse. There are numerous support groups available to help individuals cope with different types of life crises and loss. The seventh is problem solving, which is a continual need across the age span. The eighth is managing stress factors that accompany change. There are numerous seminars, workshops, and continuing education programs to help older adults manage stress.

Chickering and Havighurst (1981) stated that the developmental tasks for late adulthood are adjusting to retirement, adjusting to declining health and strength, becoming affiliated with late-adult age groups, establishing satisfactory living arrangements, adjusting to the death of a spouse, and maintaining integrity. Work has been the primary focus of life for most men and women and the adjustment is often difficult for individuals to make from work to retirement. Greenhaus, Wong, and Mossholder (1987) stated that the major tasks of most late-career employees are to remain productive in work and to prepare for retirement.

Personality Development

Lowenthal, Thurnher, Chiriboga, and associates (1975) identified the period around 60 as the preretirement stage. Women in this stage had a positive self-image, felt competent and less dependent, and tended to be frank and more assertive. Men preferred a more simplistic life-style and have a need for companionship and nurturance. Also, they become more self-protective in seeking to avoid stress. Neugarten (1977) characterized individuals in this period as more contemplative and introspective; time to complete life tasks is important because older adults find that the time left to live is limited. Men become more nurturant and affiliative. Gould (1972) found that older adults see their spouses as increasingly important. They review the contributions they have made in both professional and personal lives from a reflective stance.

Edelstein and Noam (1982) identified patience as the emotion that characterizes this period—the ability to tolerate conflict and to identify with the opposition. They have the ability to understand the long-term consequences of their behavior and find that they have to be effective, compassionate, and patient to meet their own needs.

Stages of Psychosocial Development

Erikson (1982) identified the crises for older adults as ego integrity versus despair. The older adults who are able to accept their own lives and see their life as satisfying and meaningful have developed ego integrity. They are able to adjust to their new roles and are people oriented. Adults who have problems resolving this crisis successfully feel depressed and afraid. They dwell on regrets and guilt and isolate themselves from other people. The resolution of this stage correlates with how well adults have resolved the other stages during their lifetime.

Stevens-Long (1988) found the major motivations of later adulthood to be integrity and self-actualization. Individuals in this age period have to accept their past life history as meaningful and having continuity. They are able to meet their own needs without using others instrumentally. Behavior in this period is characterized by autonomy and the ability to see their own roles realistically, and to tolerate conflict and be able to identify with the opposition.

Physical Factors

Stereotyped conceptions of the physical condition of older adults are that they are weak, infirmed, feeble, and afflicted with recent memory defects, but less than 5% of the adults over 65 in this bracket are so affected. Genetic factors influence the individual's potential life span. There is less physical change between 65 and 75 than between 15 and 25. Visual defects and hearing defects become more prevalent. Individuals become less resistant to stress with age and often neglect exercise and good diet. There are homeostatic imbalances and problems with the immune system. Health can affect the individual's ability to work but many individuals want to work as long as they possibly can.

Cognitive and Intellectual Development

There are changes in the cognitive domain from middle age to old age. Individuals have mastered the necessary cognitive skills and have become self-sufficient and independent in functioning. Schaie and Parr (1981) indicated that adults in this age period, because of both biological and social pressure, assume responsibilities for others: one's mate, children, or some social or educational unit. The stage from 30 to 60 years is called a responsible stage.

Individuals in this age group show growth in their problem-solving skills when measured by meaningful tasks. By age 60 there is a decrease in performance on task-specific situations. Verbal ability, information, comprehension, and judgment are maintained through the 60s. Short-term reasoning and spatial reasoning tend to be somewhat impaired. Older adults have the ability to learn new skills and acquire new information.

Career Development

Super (1990) perceived the period of 45 to 60 years as the maintenance period in which adults may work on updating their skills, being innovative, or becoming stagnant on the job. About age 60 there is a deceleration and retirement and disengagement usually takes place about age 65. Jordaan (1974) perceives the maintenance years as a period in which adults are trying to preserve the status and gains they accomplished during their earlier years. These years are usually the period of highest salary for this group. After resolving their mid-career crises or transition, they move toward a period of maximum growth and productivity.

Crites (1976) found that as adults enter the later years, they begin to derive less satisfaction from their work, their level of performance, and their accomplishments. Partly this is due to the diminishing prospects for advancement and recognition as older workers reach the end of their career.

The length of working life has increased for both men and women since the turn of the century and may tend to increase more because mandatory retirement laws have been eliminated in some states. Also, increasing numbers of adults are not working in the fields they originally started in. Super (1957) found that one half of the workers over 60 had changed the type of work they do. Changes in job are not always a function of dissatisfaction, but sometimes due to technology or changing economic conditions. The recent corporate downsizing in mid-management positions has had a profound impact on career counseling services. Unemployment presents problems to older workers. Although there is supposed to be no age discrimination, older workers tend to have a harder time getting jobs.

CAREER OBJECTIVES

The changing job market, the influence of technology, corporate downsizing and takeovers, and other factors force workers not to just ride out this period to retirement but to set new or revised career objectives. Healy (1982, p. 536) identified the objectives listed in Figure 10.1 as being important for workers at the maintenance stage.

CHALLENGES

Older workers are finding types of challenges on their jobs such as their organization's products or services have changed and they are required to deal with new types of information, people, and equipment. Fyock (1990) stated that keeping older workers productive and challenged in the workplace will become one of the biggest concerns for business and industry. He identified the three most serious problems in this period as career burnout, career plateauing, and career obsolescence. Russell (1991) pointed out that there are different issues for older employees depending on whether they are moving up in the organization or down to another position, or out by retirement or termination. For example, they must learn how to use and deal with computer input and output. Their organization may have changed along with their own roles and responsibilities and authority. The worst challenge might be that their job has been eliminated and they have been laid off. They have to find another job, go for additional training or education, or retire. Lewis (1993) reported that the percent of older "discouraged workers" who drop out of the labor force because they cannot find jobs jumped to 18%, triple the percentage of older workers in the work force. Career counselors will need to develop a series of job-finding seminars for older citizens that focus on specific career adjustment skills, job search techniques, and development of new skills.

The types of jobs are changing. A major development for older workers is that many new industrial jobs now do not require the physical labor of the past because of changes in machinery and assembly methods. There are marked changes in the electronics field as well as in clerical and communications fields. Many older workers see technology as a threat to their jobs and fear or reject the retraining that might be necessary. They do not feel that unions or the govern-

---

* To renew and refocus their motivation and enthusiasm toward work
* To secure the support of their families, friends, and colleagues for efforts toward career improvement
* To get the necessary knowledge base to be a more effective worker
* To update the career decision skills necessary for guiding the direction of their careers
* To reevaluate their career goals so that they are feasible, realistic, and in line with their values and interests
* To focus on enhancing their self-concept, self-esteem, and self-confidence by reviewing their past and current achievements
* To be prepared for crises and to develop alternate career or job strategies
* To redesign their jobs with their employers to increase their job satisfaction
* To be able to change their job or career if necessary

FIGURE 10.1
Career objectives for workers at the maintenance stage

ment support older workers as they should. Organizations have problems finding ways to help all their workers maintain their employability. The Wright State University contract with Chrysler Corporation (Messner, 1993) is an excellent example of a program designed for skilled workers who could shift to other jobs after their current jobs were phased out. The training program is located in the plant and is operated 24 hours per day. At this time 80 employees attend the school for 4 hours per week during their regular shifts. Early findings suggest that cooperative training programs of this nature permit workers to develop new skills—for example, computer technology—for use in other skilled jobs.

Lynch (1980) found that workers in their 60s were concerned about time management, obsolescence, ignorance of their employees, and fatigue. They worried about having to make decisions in areas in which they were not knowledgeable. They felt that there was not enough time to master the new technology both in the computer field and industrial manufacturing.

STEREOTYPES AND MYTHS

Stereotyping in this case is making judgments about individuals based on their age. Sometimes stereotypes are based on other factors such as sex or racial, ethnic, or occupational group. Age stereotypes are influenced by cultural and societal factors, family and peers, depictions in the media and by personal experiences. There are positive stereotypes that picture older workers as trustworthy, honest, and stable, but most have a negative context that older workers lack motivation and are closed to new ideas and are rigid and dogmatic.

Lynch (1980) lists five myths about older workers:

1. Older workers are slow and cannot meet the production standards.
2. They cannot meet the physical demands of their job
3. They cannot be depended on because they are absent from work too often
4. They are not adaptable and will not accept change and if they are hired
5. They increase the pension and insurance costs of the organization (Bird & Fisher, 1986).

To the contrary, older workers have proved to be dependable, less absent, and very prompt in reporting to work. Also, their job performance reflects attention to quality and a concern for meeting all job performance requirements.

Rosen and Jerdee (1988) pointed out the numerous cliches that are commonly used to describe the older worker such as "you can't teach an old dog new tricks," "over the hill," "marking time," "fading fast," "frail and fragile," "on the shelf," "out to pasture," "ready for the scrape heap," "ready for the gold watch," "one foot in the grave" (p. 17).

Fyock (1990) listed many of the stereotyped concepts held by many individuals such as older workers are viewed by customers as being slow and unproductive, they won't be with us long, they don't want to advance, they are inflexible and resistant to change, they don't need to work, they are absent often from work because of illness, they are difficult to work with, they are expensive to train, they raise insurance costs, they are not interested in working, they are more accident prone, they are not adept intellectually, and they lack experience.

Rosen and Jerdee (1988) concluded after reviewing the research on older workers that they have much better attendance and lower accident records than do younger workers. There is no significant impairment of their ability to function in a variety of types of positions. Fyock (1990) summarized the characteristics of older workers based on reality rather than myth. Older workers are as productive as younger workers, remain longer, want to learn and grow, are willing to change and adapt, work because they need the money, have fewer incidents of absence and tardiness, are adept at interpersonal relationships, repay the training investment quickly, are motivated to work, have fewer on the job accidents, and have good problem-solving skills. Career counselors need to present this type of data to older clients and in career information seminars to industrial personnel managers.

LABOR MARKET PROBLEMS

Older workers do face a number of problems in the labor market. These are deficiencies in training that limit their employment opportunities, lack of desirable part-time jobs, inflexible work arrangements, and age discrimination (Bird & Fisher, 1986).

Brandt (1992) found that age discrimination occurs at all levels of employment, from the lowest clerical positions to the highest management positions. Sometimes their problems are not necessarily caused by age discrimination but by other types of factors such as health and low levels of formal education. Another factor is where the worker lives. Many businesses and industries are consolidating and closing offices and moving to areas where costs are lower.

COUNSELING COMPETENCIES

Career counselors need to have skills in the traditional counseling areas, but will need additional skills and knowledge when working with older adults. These competencies are listed in Figure 10.2.

PROBLEMS OF THE SOCIALIZATION PROCESS

Hall and associates (1986) found that there are marked differences in later career socialization than early career socialization. There are fewer promotions or job moves available. Workers have to develop their own personal meaning in their career and develop their own status passages. Howland (1989) reported that older workers tend to be more satisfied and committed to their jobs and less willing to leave than younger workers.

* Knowledge of the social security system such as the level of benefits, the age of eligibility for benefits, the change in benefits that occurs when retirement is postponed a year and the "earnings test" under which benefits are reduced when the retiree earns more money from working
* Knowledge of the barriers faced by older employees such as the negative stereotypes that limit employment, the limited training opportunities, the physical disabilities that may interfere with regular work routine and the limited part-time employment opportunities and knowledge of strategies to help adult workers reduce these barriers
* Knowledge of the provision of the Age Discrimination in Employment Act
* Knowledge of the various governmental, state, and private training programs that are designed to help older workers such as the Senior Community Service Employment Program (SCSEP) and others that are not exclusively for older adults such as the Job Training Partnership Act, and Comprehensive Employment Training Act
* Familiarity with the National Older Workers Information System (NOWIS)
* Familiarity with the various industries and companies and organizations and knowledge of the hiring practices for older employees
* Knowledge of the volunteer organizations who use older adults
* Familiarity with the Tax Equity and Fiscal Responsibility Act

FIGURE 10.2
Competencies needed for counselors in working with older workers

Career development at this level is more likely to be an individual rather than a collective process. Personal choice has more impact on the adult worker's development. The organization is not using the worker as much. The career issues for older adults are adaptability, flexibility, and the avoidance of obsolescence, and developing identity. The real meaning and purpose of one's career becomes more important.

Career counselors working with older workers must recognize that early career experiences may retard later career development. A worker's early success may reinforce the movement toward a narrow focus, or overspecialization. The overspecialization of the worker may cause the individual to resist moving to new areas. Some older workers resent working with and aiding younger workers.

Later career development can also be viewed as a process of correcting some of the problem areas in earlier stages such as overspecialization, reducing overinvolvement in work, correcting burnout, and so on. Older workers tend to restore the balance between work and other life roles and tend to become more self-directed.

STRATEGIES

Corporate and human service organizations need to initiate and promote career development activities for older adults. They need to provide clear communication of position-related norms for productivity and performance expectations and have clear performance-based rewards (Kaminski-du-Rosa, 1984).

MODELS FOR COUNSELING

Rosen and Jerdee (1988) proposed a human resource development model to assist older adult workers. They advocated that management should link life-span career planning with organized human resource planning, which is linked to organizational strategic planning. Supervisors who are responsible for career management programs need to consider questions such as those listed in Figure 10.3.

The model presented in Table 10.1 is one approach for developing a career management plan for older workers. Prior to institutionalizing this model, the school, agency, or college staff should review each element in the proposed steps and determine if internal staff resources will support this effort.

Rosen and Jerdee (1988) concluded that managers need to develop sensitivity to the career problems of older workers, which include dangers of skill obsolescence, job burnout, plateauing, and loss of motivation for work. Flexible work programs have been beneficial for improving the outlook of older workers and retirees, and have been instrumental in saving firms money (Cascio, 1989). Older workers might be anxious about the new roles they have to perform and feel vulnerable to technical displacement. If additional education and training are required, they might feel that the time and money invested will not be a good investment. Systematic health and performance appraisal can provide the worker and supervisor warning of possible career problems.

---

* What organizational changes are likely to change how the unit will operate in the near future?
* What will be the staffing needs with these changes?
* What present employees are likely to need further education and training to keep employable and productive?
* Is it necessary to reassign or redesign jobs in order to have a better match between the individual skills and abilities that will be required in the near future?
* Are there problems such as dual-career families or parents who would be resistant to relocation if that were necessary?
* What are the career aspirations of the employees in the unit? Are the plans realistic within the constraints of the organization?
* What are the retirement intentions of the older adult workers within the unit?
* Given the answers to these questions, are human resource development and career planning to have high priority?

FIGURE 10.3
Questions for career management of older workers

TABLE 10.1
Human resource model to assist older workers

STEP	FACTORS
Corporate Strategic Plans	Acquisitions
	Mergers
	Divestitures
	Automation
	New products/services
	New markets
	Expansion
	Retrenchment
Future Human Resource Needs	Skills
	Training
	Experience
	Equal opportunity
Assessing Current Human Resources	Demographics and characteristics of current work force
	Health assessment
	Past productivity and performance of workers
	Potentials of employees
	Career aspirations
	Interests of employees
	Experiences of employees
	Educational and training background
Assessing External Human Resources	Demographic information on area
	Economic
	Legal
	Social
	Labor market
Developing Human Resource Strategies	Oversupply
	Shortages
	Maintaining steady state
Implement Human Resource Planning	Recruitment
	Selection
	Training
	Motivation
	Compensation
	Transfer
	Retirement
	Termination
Integrating Corporate Strategies	Individual

Outplacement Counseling

Outplacement counseling goal is to assist employees who are terminated to find other jobs or careers (Russell, 1991). The counselor role is to help these individuals cope with the loss of job and to help them build up their self-esteem and self-confidence. The service is provided in some businesses and industries for both executives and hourly employees. The service does not include placement on a new job by the counselor but helps individuals to develop plans for retraining or seeking new positions.

The termination of employees is stressful to both the employee and to the supervisor. The goal of the termination usually is to eliminate workers who are unproductive or mismatched to their jobs. Some corporate downsizing has indicated that some jobs are not really necessary. The employer wants to make the operation of the company more economically efficient and effective.

By providing outplacement counseling the company attempts to help the employee terminated but also creates good will in the community and fosters the image that the company is a caring organization. The companies also want to avoid lawsuits and grievance proceedings. Terminated employees report enhanced self-confidence and greater awareness of alternate jobs and career paths as a result of outplacement programs (Greenhaus, Wong, & Mossholder, 1987).

Corporate Goals

Brammer and Humberger (1984) developed a list of goals for outplacement services that are listed in Figure 10.4.

Many corporations face problems because of a declining economy, reduced profits, and foreign competition. The cost of keeping unneeded and unproductive workers exceeds the costs of outplacement counseling and severance pay.

---

* Reducing the costs for unneeded workers
* Creating an image that the organization cares for people
* Eliminating outdated, overspecialized, and overpromoted personnel
* Maintaining in-house morale
* Assisting organizations with affirmative action, retirement, and personality conflicts
* Helping organizations to cope with corporate guilt
* Saving unemployment taxes
* Enabling candidates to free themselves from inappropriate job placements
* Assisting with corporate reductions and mergers

FIGURE 10.4
Goals for outplacement services

Takeovers, mergers, and divestitures also present needs to eliminate some employees.

Models for Outplacement Counseling

Brammer and Humberger (1984) developed a four-phase model for outplacement counseling: orientation, evaluation, job targeting, and job campaigning. There are four stages to the orientation phase. Stage one is planning and negotiating for outplacement counseling services. Severance pay is an important consideration. The pay period ought to be from 3 to 6 months, long enough to allow the worker to work conscientiously and efficiently on outplacement planning tasks. The contract needs to advise the company on strategies and methods of termination. The firm also needs to have access to the terminated worker's personnel file so they have information on the work record, performance appraisals, and relevant information on why the worker was terminated. Communication strategies are also important and should be handled by one spokesperson and be clear and positive.

Stage two is termination and employee crises counseling. Terminations are a dreaded and distasteful task for most managers but need to be clean, brief, and compassionate. Human resource counselors need to help the company choose the appropriate person as well as the appropriate time to terminate the employee. The person doing the termination needs to be trained in termination procedures. Corporations need to have developed a prepared statement of the severance benefits. Role-playing provides a useful vehicle to give those involved some practice and a critique of how to successfully conduct the termination process.

The company needs to make sure that there are counselors available to talk with employees immediately after the termination takes place because usually the employee will be in a state of shock, depressed, or highly incensed and emotional about the situation. The counselor's job is to challenge the individuals to move on with their plans and life. Timing for this session is critical for the employees mental health.

Stage three is orientation to outplacement counseling. Outpatient counseling is a voluntary program although it is a part of the severance agreement. Employees are given a chance to decide whether they want to take advantage of the service or not and are given an overview of the services provided by the counselor. They are assured that the outplacement process will ease their anxiety and that they will be guided to take stock of their assets and limitations. The process can be an opportunity for a learning experience for them rather than a negative experience. They are encouraged to have positive perceptions of the process and told their expectations will be a factor.

Stage 4 is a general introduction to life and career planning. The introduction to the process helps them know what will be the time table for the counseling and the parameters to be covered. An example of a checklist is illustrated in Table 10.2.

Phase two of the Brammer and Humberger (1984) model is the evaluation process. There are two stages in this phase: testing and self-assessment. The goal of this phase is to help candidates get an accurate and realistic picture of

TABLE 10.2
Checklist for counselors in planning outplacement activities

Outplacement Activity	Scheduled Date	Completion Date
Establishing Personal Network		
Work History Portfolios:		
job achievement		
accomplishment		
job skills/competencies		
job performance evaluations		
avocational skills		
positive reference status		
(previous supervisor's evaluation)		
skills summary		
Values		
Interests		
Needs/wants		
Dreams		
Draft of Resume		
Final Draft		
Draft of Letter to Send Out		
Final Draft		
Self-Marketing Plan		
Strategies and Tactics Plan		
Practice Job Interview		
Difficult questions		
Job interviews		
New Job		

their total selves in dimensions such as interests, values, needs, skills, accomplishments, and achievement. The candidates need to become aware of these areas in order that they can make well-informed choices of their next job or career and preferred future life-style. The second goal is to help the candidates enhance their self-esteem and appreciate their achievements and accomplishments and accept their limitations.

There are numerous instruments and batteries to provide this information as well as assessment schedules and values clarification exercises that the counselor can use. Tests can be used to measure personality, temperament, values, and interests. Some of the dimensions that are commonly used in outplacement counseling and examples of some of the assessment techniques are included in Figure 10.5.

In phase three, Brammer and Humberger (1984) list four steps in job targeting:

1. To review the skills developed in the awareness exercises
2. To review the dream occupation and its limitations, choose the top five skills from the list developed, and match them to specific job functions

Dreams	Incomplete sentences such as:
	If I could be anything I wanted to be, I would _____ .
	I always wanted to be _____ .
	Writing out why you cannot be what you want to be
	Writing out how you could use your present skills and competencies to be _____
Achievements	Reference letters
Accomplishments	Life history
	Listing of accomplishments and achievements in educational, vocational, community, leisure/recreational, and family
Values	Super and Nevill's Values Scale
	Rokeach Value Survey
	Values clarification exercises
	COPES
Interest	Strong Interest Inventory
	COPS
	Self-Directed Search
	Johansson Career Assessment Inventory
Personality Traits	16 PF test
	California Psychological Inventory
	Neo Personality Inventory
	Myers-Briggs Type Indicator
Abilities/Aptitudes	CARS
	GATB
	Bolles Quick Job-Hunting Map

FIGURE 10.5
Assessment techniques used in outplacement counseling

3.   Choose appropriate job arenas and write job objectives
4.   Write job resumes to match each job objective

The counselor can train the worker to use the *Dictionary of Occupational Titles* and the *Occupational Outlook Handbook* to identify job functions. The job arena has a broad definition. It can be a discipline like theology or anthropology, a service such as counseling, an environment such as small business, or a location such as the sun belt. They can formalize their goals as follows:

I desire to seek a job as _____ in the field of _____ in a (setting/environment) at a salary of _____ to start by _____ .

Phase Four is the job campaign phase, which involves obtaining interviews, making the job decision, and evaluating one's progress. In this phase the clients are trained in writing resumes. They are trained to conduct informational interviews of prospective employers to find out the required skills, qualifications, and hiring practices of the organization. They are guided in how to make telephone calls to obtain the interviews they desire. They are instructed also on using personal campaign letters to obtain interviews. They are encouraged to develop networks, including search firms, employment agencies, newspapers, and so on. They practice effective interview techniques and how to follow up on the interview.

Franzem (1987) reported on a model used by the Stroh brewery in Detroit and included as special support services that addressed retirement, personal and family issues, financial problems, income support, health care, relocation, new business assistance, individual counseling, and other supportive service referrals. The program offered outreach services, orientation, job-search skills workshops, help with individual development plans, and ongoing counseling. There were three target terminal goals: retirement, job placement, or full-time student. The education could be in the form of skills training or basic remedial education. The counseling services provided placement activities such as a job fair, job bank, job development, and mass and self-marketing.

Competencies Needed for Outplacement Counseling

Outplacement counselors need to have graduate training and experience in career counseling, have knowledge of the corporate world, know the labor market information, know the hidden job market in the area, know personnel directors in the area, have training and experience in assessment techniques, be skilled in communication, be able to direct groups, and to know how to help people going through sudden crises.

Other Ideas for Outplacement Counseling

Zelvin (1987) proposed that employers institute a job hotline that would present a computerized list of employees being terminated by job description, location, and other useful information. The data could be transmitted to small business employers through a toll-free number.

Support groups are also valuable for workers who have lost their jobs. Group meetings provide these displaced workers an opportunity to help each other, and promote goal setting. The members help to motivate one another. Wolfer and Wong (1988) have written a self-help book that describes a step-by-step procedure of helping individuals pick up the pieces, assess themselves, develop an action plan, and find a suitable next position. They have included a number of exercises grouped into three categories: taking good care of yourself, keeping an eye on finances, and finding that new job.

Inplacement Counseling

Many organizations try to provide counseling services in order to avoid dismissing surplus employees and to salvage employees who are not functioning well in their current jobs. Many organizations find this method is cost effective over time and less expensive than the costs of terminating employees. These employees may be reassigned to other jobs within the organization, retrained, or the work area restructured to accommodate new roles for these workers.

COUNSELING OLDER WOMEN

Many older women reenter the work force when their children are grown, their spouses die, or they separate through divorce. They are often unprepared to enter the work force and need help in job-seeking skills. They also need to update and upgrade their skills and may seek advice on education and training. Older female workers also are moving toward retirement and need workshops and seminars on retirement and financial management. Many are interested in volunteer work and need information about organizations that seek volunteers.

RETIREMENT

Many organizations have preretirement counseling programs for their workers. Russell (1991) stated that preretirement programs are designed to facilitate an individual's adjustment to retirement.

There are many variables to which the counselor needs to attend. Cook (1987) pointed out that retirement has been influenced by demographic changes in the work force and federal legislation. The Federal Age and Discrimination in Employment Act abolished mandatory retirement for most employees making the decision to retire more of a voluntary choice for individuals. In addition to adjustment to retirement and leisure experiences there are other issues such as early retirement, involuntary retirement, and reentering the work force after retirement. Some are practical concerns such as income available after retirement and the worker's financial obligations. The counselor needs to explore the family ties and responsibilities of the worker. The counselor needs to assess the health of the workers and their ability to be involved in post retirement work, and leisure activities. Another important variable is the life-style of the workers and their interests and hobbies. Some workers want to travel or relocate in some other geographic area.

Workshops or counseling sessions need to address the personal variables also (Cook, 1987). Some workers want to take early retirement because they are unhappy with their work assignments and supervisors and generally dissatisfied with their work. Retirees tend to focus on what has been and need to be guided to set plans and goals for after retirement. They need to explore their options and consider the wide variety of things they can do that they claim they never had time to do before.

They want to feel wanted and sometimes become involved in volunteerism and part-time employment. Fischer, Rapkin, and Rappaport (1991) reported that active involvement in work or volunteer roles appears to be beneficial to retirees.

There are a number of federal, state, and local programs that try to tap the expertise of older workers.

Many workers immediately after retirement feel relaxed and elated and express a sense of freedom. Atchley (1975) labeled this the "honeymoon period." Soon the next stage or "disenchantment stage" emerges and the retirees feel a sense of emptiness and disappointment. This stage is followed by the "reorientation state," in which the retiree works on problems of adjustment and maintenance. The "stability stage" follows and is characterized by renewed efforts in decision making and planning to reenter the work force.

Counseling Approaches

Seligman (1980) proposed four steps that a counselor could use in working with older adults. The first is to help clients express and clarify their feelings about the present situation, retirement, bereavement, job displacement, and so on. The second is to develop an accurate understanding of the situation, its options, and limitations. The third is to assess the resources of the clients and especially those in career crises. The fourth is to assist clients to develop plans to resolve the current crisis that draws on these resources. Seligman feels that counseling with older adults should have a longitudinal focus because research has shown that behavior and adjustment during the later years are built on the strengths and attitudes developed in the past.

Healy (1982) proposed a self-exploratory cognitive counseling approach designed to help adults become more aware of how their careers are an expression of themselves. The procedure is based on the rationale and premises that older adults should systematically update their understanding of who they are and are becoming in order to retain control of their careers, and that career counselors can facilitate the self-appraisal so that it is more accurate and comprehensive. Counselors can also facilitate the clients' ability to manage their own careers by actively listening and underscoring insights. Clients are more willing to accept a broader perspective when they feel that the counselor understands them and accepts them. Clients are more likely to use realistic career decision skills when they receive feedback from a counselor they trust.

The counselor actively and attentively listens to the client and asks the client to elaborate to be sure he or she understands what the client is expressing. The counselor repeats or mirrors what he or she has heard to expand the client's understanding. The counselor then encourages the older adult to elaborate in order for the counselor to have more complete information. Lewis (1993) reminded counselors that older job seekers frequently undervalue themselves and have low self-esteem, especially when they have been unemployed for a long time.

The counselor also should encourage the client to express his or her present emotions and feelings on personal life changes/job changes, adjustments in family life, and general physical and mental health as they deal with self-attributes, also. The counselor takes an oral autobiography. Later the counselor has the client focus on his or her career aspirations and life goals.

The general outcome of this process is to guide the clients to expand their self-awareness and increase their certainty about their self-ascriptions, to interpret career forces in their milieu more accurately, and to increase the congruence between their career actions and goals. The clients are guided to express greater satisfaction with the course of their careers and report a greater sense of control over it.

Lewis (1993) reported that word of mouth through networking lands the best jobs. Networking is effective for older workers if they know how to market and package themselves. The American Association for Retired Persons has several publications to help 50 years old and over job seekers find new employment. Older clients should be guided to develop an accomplishment-oriented portfolio that demonstrates work skills, personal interests, and career accomplishments. The portfolio should document specific skills and provide evidence to support the acquisition of these skills.

MENTORING

A mentor is a person who oversees the career and development of another person (Zey, 1984). This process is accomplished through a number of types of roles such as teaching, counseling, providing psychological support, protecting, and at times promoting or sponsoring. LaPorte (1991) found that some companies such as Apple and Procter and Gamble, among others, have established a formal mentoring program to assist women and minority employees advance in the company. Zey (1984) proposed a four-level model of mentoring. Level one is teaching. The protege is provided instruction in the skills and competencies of the job, which sometimes include management tricks and social graces. The primary mentor investment is time.

Level two is psychological counseling/personal support. The mentor has a self-involvement and emotional involvement in his protege. He uses confidence-building experiences, pep talks, and sometimes personal assistance in the protege's personal life.

Level three is organizational intervention. The mentors invest their reputations, use their organizational relationships, and intercede in the protege's behalf or run interference for the protege where needed.

Level four is sponsoring. The protege is recommended by the mentor for promotion and more responsibility.

Kram (1986) subdivided the mentoring role into two areas: career functions and psychosocial functions. The career functions include challenging work, exposure, protection, coaching, and sponsorship. The psychosocial functions include friendship, acceptance and confirmation, counseling, and role modeling.

Mentoring can enable individuals in mid- or later career a chance to pass on their personal values and experiences to the next generation and in turn enhance the self-esteem of the mentors. The older adult workers tend to like this relationship because they enjoy passing on wisdom and experience. They sometimes enjoy the interaction and the opportunity to become reacquainted with their youthful selves. Mentoring also can be a negative experience for some. If the mentor is questioning his or her own identity at mid-career, the process might be unrewarding for both.

One of the advantages for being a mentor is that it does help enhance the individual's career. The protege helps the mentors perform their jobs better and contributes to the increased reputation of the mentors. The protege helps contribute to the information and problem solving. The protege becomes a good sounding board for the mentor. The mentor feels a sense of pride for being involved.

One of the major concerns for organizations is selecting a mentor and making it attractive for the person. Zey (1984) has listed nine key questions that are presented in Figure 10.6.

In order to attract people to be mentors, the protege is going to be closely evaluated for his or her desire to learn, his or her skills and competencies, and his or her ability to get the job done. Mentors look for qualities in a protege such as intelligence, ambition, desire and ability to accept power and risk, loyalty, ability to perform the mentor's job, commitment to the organization, and similar perceptions of the organization and work.

Mentoring Workshop

Individuals who plan to be mentors need training on how to become one. They need to learn how to enhance their communication, listening, and career counseling skills. An outline of a workshop is included in Figure 10.7.

SUMMARY

We reviewed pertinent literature on the role and needs of older Americans who are leaving or entering the work force. A number of strategies for career counselors was presented and a redefinition of roles suggested. Career counselors

FIGURE 10.6
Selecting a mentor for corporate employees

* Is the mentor good at what he or she does?
* Is the mentor getting corporate support?
* How does the organization judge the mentor?
* Is the mentor a good teacher?
* Is the mentor a good motivator?
* What are the protege's needs and goals?
* What are the needs and goals of the prospective mentor?
* How powerful is the mentor?
* Is the mentor secure in his or her own job?

Objectives
* To explore the role of the mentor in career development
* To learn the different roles of the mentor
* To discuss the benefits and limitations of the process
* To study effective communication and interpersonal skills
* To understand career development theory and application
* To study the developmental characteristics of the appropriate age groups
* To develop an action plan for the mentoring process
* To design a plan for evaluating the process both during and at the end of the process

Suggested Session Topics:

Day 1

Morning
   What is mentoring? What is the role of mentoring in career development? What are the roles of a mentor? What are the benefits of mentoring to the mentor, the protege, and the organization?
   What do former mentors have to say about mentoring?

Afternoon
   What type of interpersonal and communication skills are needed?
   Who am I going to work with? What can I expect? What if the relationship is not mutually agreeable or acceptable?

Day 2
   At what skill level am I?
   Assessment of basic mentoring skills
   What should I say if . . . ?
   How do I role-play situations?
   How do I set goals and determine an action plan?
   How do I evaluate the process and my effectiveness as a mentor?

FIGURE 10.7
Workshop for training mentors

should adapt their programs to include a number of approaches for working with aging workers.

REVIEW QUESTIONS

1.   What should the counselor know about the social, psychological, physical, cognitive, and career development of older adults?
2.   What are the developmental tasks of this age group?
3.   What developmental crisis do they have to resolve during this period?
4.   What type of career counseling is appropriate for the maintenance stage?
5.   What are the career and work problems of older adults? How can the counselor help with these problems?

6. Should industry write off older workers or provide career development services for them? If yes, why? If no, why not?

7. What is outplacement counseling? Describe the objectives and procedures of outplacement counseling.

8. What are the goals and objectives of mentoring? What are the roles of the mentor?

SUGGESTED LEARNING ACTIVITIES

1. Interview older adults to find out their attitude toward work, their work environment, and job satisfaction. Report your findings to the class.

2. Interview several older adults and get their job history. How do the job histories correlate with career development theories?

3. Interview counselors who work with older adults and find out the type of problems their clients have and the types of interventions counselors have found effective in working with them.

4. Interview counselors who work in outplacement. Identify the types of knowledge and methods the counselors use.

5. Find several of the self-help books that are available for outplacement counseling. What are some of the common themes and objectives in these books? How are they different?

6. Interview several retired individuals. Identify what stage they are currently in. What is their attitude toward work? Are they currently working part-time?

7. Critique the commercial materials available on one of the following topics: outplacement counseling, inplacement counseling, mentoring, retirement, and so on.

8. Write a paper that reviews the research on one of the topics in the chapter such as mentoring, outplacement counseling, retirement counseling, problems of older workers, and so on.

CASE STUDIES

The Widow

Melodie is a 55-year-old widow who has always been a homemaker and has not had any work experience. She graduated from high school and started her associate of arts degree at a community college but dropped out to get married. Her husband was a used car salesperson who made a steady living but had very little in savings or insurance. Melodie was active in civic and church work. She served as a hospital volunteer. She has two grown daughters who are living on the opposite coast. She feels that she does not want to go to live near them or live with them yet, and wants to remain with her friends.

However, she needs to find work in 3 to 6 months. She feels depressed and says she has no marketable skills.

Down and Out but Willing

John is one of the homeless people in this southern community. He migrated here from the north. He graduated with a degree in management from an Ivy League college and worked his way up the corporate ladder. The work was extremely stressful and he had several mental breakdowns. He was in and out of mental hospitals and halfway houses. He had a series of part-time jobs. When not in a depressive state, he performed quite capably on the job. A social worker stopped to talk to him while John was on the street corner with his sign "will work for food." He agreed to talk to the career counselor at a social agency.

Not Ready for Retirement

Dale is 58 and is a manager of marketing for a regional phone company. He is a recovering alcoholic and has not had a drink for the past 20 years. Although he has been very successful in his work, the company is downsizing and has offered him an attractive severance package. He is used to traveling and likes the contact with people. He feels that retirement would be detrimental to his physical and mental health.

Case Questions
1.   What counseling strategies/approaches would you use with these clients?
2.   What additional information is needed?
3.   What type of career planning is needed by these individuals?

SUGGESTED READINGS

Centron, M., & O'Toole, T. (1982). *Encounters with the future. A forecast of life into the 21st century*. New York: McGraw-Hill.

This book provides a summary of social, economic, educational, and labor market changes and their impact on career counseling.

Messner, P. E. (1993). *Skilled trades cooperative training program*. Dayton, OH: College of Education and Human Services, Chrysler Project.

This is a training project to assist employed individuals develop career cross-over skills. The training occurs on the job and involves university, management, and labor representatives in a team planning model.

CHAPTER

CAREER COUNSELING SPECIAL POPULATIONS

There are approximately 43 million people who have some type of mental or physical disability that may limit their daily activity. The disability is a career or vocational handicap if it interferes or limits the individual's career or job opportunities. The problem has economic, social, and psychological consequences because many graduate or drop out of school without marketable skills. The U.S. Commission on Civil Rights (1983) reports that 50% to 75% of this group are unemployed. A larger percentage of disabled individuals are unemployed, underemployed, and nearer the poverty level than nondisabled workers. A smaller percentage of disabled individuals complete vocational training, get a high school education, or enter college than nondisabled individuals.

LEARNING OBJECTIVES

After reading this chapter, you should be able to do the following:

- Describe the scope, goals, and sequence of career education programs for disabled
- Identify the developmental, physical, psychological, social characteristics, and special needs that might impede the career development of disabled individuals
- Discuss the research on career development of disabled individuals and its implications for practice
- List and describe assessment instruments and techniques that could be used with disabled individuals
- Discuss the competencies and roles of career counselors working with disabled individuals

Career education and counseling programs for disabled individuals have many of the same goals and activities that programs have for nondisabled individuals. Moore, Agran, and McSweyn (1990) reported that many elementary and middle school teachers seldom provide these students with the opportunities to take part in career awareness and career exploration activities. The methods, procedures, and assessment strategies often have to be modified to be appropriate for disabled individuals. Remember that a disabled student is one whose mental or physical condition limits or prevents him or her from succeeding in a regular classroom. A disabled worker is one whose disability prevents him or her from performing work required by a particular job or to function in the work environment.

DEVELOPMENTAL ISSUES

The Division of Career Development of the Council for Exceptional Children (1987) states that career development is an ongoing, sequential process designed to assist children, youths, and adults in achieving meaningful work roles, such as student, consumer, citizen, family member, and employee. One of the key issues is the age at which the disability occurred. If the disability occurred at birth or early in the individuals' development, these individuals could be impaired in their ability to accomplish the developmental tasks at the appropriate time. Mental and physical deficits could also hamper their cognitive and intellectual development. Their interpersonal and communication deficits could affect their psychosocial development.

Lombana (1992) indicated, in general, that the earlier a person becomes disabled, the less traumatic is the adjustment process. She gave the example of a blind person. A person born blind is less likely to have extreme stress about the adjustment than an adult who is suddenly blinded by an accident. She does point out that there are life stages during which the acceptance of a disability or any perceived limitation is especially difficult. Adolescents who tend to be more introspective and insecure might have a hard time accepting their physical self. Joiner and Fisher (1977) found that adults faced with sudden disabilities had a difficult personal adjustment.

Super (1957) felt the time of onset of the disability, whether it is during precareer or mid-career stages, is important as to the effects the disability will have on the vocational self-concept of the individual. Stone and Gregg (1981) called to our attention that a disabled child is sometimes overprotected by parents and community and his or her career awareness is limited and career development usually delayed. The type of disability is also a factor. Bolton (1973) found that deaf adolescents are more limited in career development than nondisabled adolescents. Stone and Gregg (1981) concluded that early onset of a childhood disability such as heart disease or visual impairment could greatly limit an individual's career choice. Smith and Chemers (1981) found that early onset of a disability affects the personality dynamics of the individual, who will be less assertive and independent than nondisabled individuals.

Adults who develop disabilities are often forced to change their career direction. They sometimes lower their educational and vocational aspirations (Thurer, 1980). If they are going through medical conditions causing disabling conditions, even if the conditions are temporary and will improve or stabilize in the future, they will show indecisiveness in their career choice and decisions (Roessler & Rubin, 1982). Roessler (1988) pointed out that some 11 million persons of working age with disabilities remain unemployed or are in jobs that do not use their skills and abilities. Thus, it is important to introduce interventions that will facilitate their career development.

Super (1990) did not feel there is a need for a specialized career development theory for individuals with disabilities but sees a special application for a more general vocational theory. Clark, Carlson, Fisher, Cook, and D'Alonzo (1991) pointed out that Super's assumption was that all youths without cognitive functioning deficits of one kind or degree should parallel nondisabled development. The age range and stages might vary some, but Super feels that growth and development of an individual can be facilitated and enhanced for those with disabilities. Hershenson (1974) disagreed and sees that a study of the disabilities can help vocational development theories in understanding all individuals by focusing on career development theory as a life-long process. The work with the disabled is valuable in that it brings attention to disjunctions and nonmodal career patterns. Disabled workers use a variety of techniques to compensate for their limitations. Hershenson (1974) concluded that the experiences of the disabled are a valuable asset to be considered in extending the range and limits of vocational development theories.

ATTITUDES TOWARD DISABLED

The attitude of the public in general is positive toward the disabled, but still many misconceptions and stereotypes exist. Wehman (1993) reported on a survey conducted by Louis Harris and associates in 1991 that found that 98% of all the people surveyed believed that all people, regardless of their ability, should have an opportunity to participate in the mainstream of society and 92% believed that employment of persons with disabilities would be economically a good thing. However, 77% said they felt sorry for these individuals. The Conference Report of the Americans with Disabilities Act of 1990 states that discrimination toward people with disabilities "continues to be a serious and pervasive social problem . . . and individuals with disabilities continually encounter various forms of discrimination" (p. 3). The Americans with Disabilities act (ADA) was signed by President Bush on July 26, 1990, and prohibits discrimination by employers against qualified individuals with disabilities in terms of the job application procedures, the hiring, advancement, and discharge of employees, job training, employee compensation, and the condition and privileges of employment. Sometimes the negative attitudes others have about the disabled person can be almost as damaging to the individual as the disability. Attitudes of others affect the individual's self-esteem. Counselors in the school system and career counselors in employment agencies or settings need to have a broad understanding of the attitudes, knowledge, stereotypes, and beliefs employers, peers, parents, and teachers have toward the disabled. Weisenstein and Koshman (1991) pointed out how the influence of being labeled disabled has on the employer's perceptions of the worker's traits for successful employment.

In reviewing the research on attitudes toward disabled students Lombana (1992) concluded that sex, age, race, and teaching experiences have relatively little impact on teacher attitudes. Teachers with greater knowledge of disabling conditions have more positive attitudes toward disabled students than teachers with lesser knowledge. Classroom teachers do not favor mainstreaming for seriously disabled students. Also, the labeling of disabled students negatively influences teachers' attitude toward them.

Lombana (1992) also found that students with the least severe or visible disability appear to be more accepted or preferred and emotionally disturbed or mentally retarded students are generally the least preferred. Children feel more strongly about the physical attractiveness of the child; teachers, the ability to conform to classroom rules and routines.

Needless to say, adults who are labeled as disabled face attitudinal barriers to employment. Employers have stereotyped conceptions of the disabled as less dependable because they are apt to be sick more often, as more expensive because of increased insurance rates and possible plan modifications.

AMERICANS WITH DISABILITIES ACT

The Americans with Disabilities Act (ADA) (PL 101-336, 1990) in the area of employment mandates that employers may not discriminate against a person with a disability in hiring or promotion if the individual is otherwise qualified for the job. Second, employers can ask about a person's ability to perform a job, but cannot inquire if a person has a disability or require a person to take tests that tend to screen out persons with disabilities. Employers are required to provide "reasonable accommodations" to individuals with disabilities. This includes steps such as job restructuring and employment modification unless an undue burden would result.

A disability is defined as "a physical or mental impairment that substantially limits one or more of an individual's major life activities." (Examples include specific physical or developmental disabilities, drug addiction, alcoholism, specific learning disabilities, HIV infection.) There must be a record of such an impairment, and the employee must be regarded as having such an impairment.

Wehman (1993) stated that there are millions of people with mental, physical, sensory, and health-related disabilities who would like the opportunity to participate in the community and workplace. Counselors need to remind individuals with disabilities that employers can not ask them about the severity of the disability but can ask them about their ability to perform a specific job function. Working with ADA clients will demand staff training to help counselors develop new skills and philosophy. They will have to be able to mobilize staff opinion, parental attitudes, and those of the business community to get them to accept the employability of clients with no previous work history.

Counselors need to be advocates of the disabled and work aggressively toward them. Wright (1980) reminded us that one of the best methods of changing the attitudes of employers for the disabled is through the placement of a disabled individual who turns out to be a successful employee. Contact with a disabled person is frequently cited as the experience that changed the other person's attitude toward the disabled individual. Contact has to be structured and personal to be effective.

Career counselors can meet with employees who have fears, and provide them information about the type of disabilities and what they need to know about the problems. Many times the counselor has to become a teacher. Lombana (1992) concluded that affective approaches, especially when coupled with more cognitive understandings of disabling conditions and careful structured personal contact with disabled people, appear to represent the most effective means of eliminating attitudinal barriers and developing healthy, positive attitudes. Many times employers will generalize the disability to all areas of behavior; for example, if a person cannot walk, people will say that he cannot do anything. Other times employers will ignore the disability completely as if it never existed.

Career counselors need to look at their own attitudes toward the disabled and also focus on the combination of information, contact, and experiential learning. They need to study the psychology and the etiology of the various disabilities and participate in professional development activities that focus on counseling the disabled and recognize the unique problems. Babbitt and Burbach (1990) reported that physically disabled college students have high career aspirations, but appear to be less optimistic about realizing their employment dreams. Counselors must be comfortable with their attitudes before they can be strong advocates about hiring the disabled and become a positive role model for other people.

The attitude that disabled have toward themselves is just as important as how other people view them. The self-awareness activities have to focus on not only the traditional values, interests, skills, and the like, but also on the limitations of the disability. The counselor needs to guide the individual to an honest acceptance of the disability but with clear recognition of the limitations and with a clear understanding of the parameters that can be done even with the disability. Even though disabled individuals have a restricted repertory of things they can do in comparison with nondisabled, the counselor must help clients frame these perceptions positively yet realistically. Clients need to develop positive self-images. This is sometimes hard to accomplish because of the attitudes that other staff members have toward individuals with certain disabilities (Brown, Berkell, & Schmelkin, 1992).

LIFE-CENTERED CAREER EDUCATION

Brolin (1986) has developed a life-centered career education curriculum that includes a total of 22 student competencies under three categories: daily living skills, occupational guidance, and preparation and personal-social skills. The skills are included in Figure 11.1.

The life-centered career education program tries to involve the special education teachers, regular classroom teachers, guidance counselors, family, community agencies and organizations, and representatives from business and industry.

Special education teachers become the consultants to the other groups involved in the program as well as to monitor each student's progress. Regular teachers and counselors have the major responsibilities in teaching the competencies. Parents can have an important role if they are willing to structure the responsibilities, teach some of the specific skills, and create an environment at

FIGURE 11.1

Life-centered career education goals

Daily Living Skills
* Managing family finances
* Selecting, managing, and maintaining a home
* Caring for personal needs
* Raising children and family living
* Buying and preparing food
* Buying and caring for clothing
* Engaging in civic activities
* Engaging in recreation and leisure time
* Getting around the community

Personal Social Skills
* Achieving self-awareness
* Acquiring self-confidence
* Achieving socially responsible behavior
* Maintaining good interpersonal relationships
* Achieving independence
* Achieving problem-solving skills
* Communicating adequately with others

Occupational Guidance and Preparation Competencies
* Knowing and exploring occupational possibilities
* Selecting and planning occupational choice
* Exhibiting appropriate work habits and behaviors
* Exhibiting manual and physical skills
* Obtaining a specific occupational skill
* Seeking, securing, and maintaining employment

home in which confidence and independence can be fostered. The family is also encouraged to participate in the school in classroom activities. The principle of shared responsibility among all groups is extremely important (Steere, Panscso-fare, Wood, & Hecimovic, 1990)

Civic, church, and service organizations are usually willing to be involved in the career education program of disabled students. The Rotary, Jaycees, Red Cross, and Association for Retarded Citizens are examples of some of the organizations who are willing to participate. Business and industry members are usually willing to be speakers, arrange for field trips and work experience programs. They also are willing to assist in curriculum development.

An example of the groups having responsibility for teaching the disabled is presented in Table 11.1.

The curriculum relies on the people involved in the process, the process the team follows, and then roles and responsibilities in the program. The program is to be accomplished by infusion, which is the process of integrating the career education goals and objectives into the regular curriculum rather than having a separate course in career guidance.

The occupational guidance and preparation competencies are broken down into subcompetencies. For example competency 17 is knowing and exploring

TABLE 11.1
Teaching responsibilities for occupational guidance program in the junior high

Occupational Guidance Competency	Junior High Participants
Career Knowledge and Exploration	Vocational education teachers
	Home economics teachers
	Guidance counselors
Career Choice	Business representatives
	Vocational and technical education teachers
	Guidance counselors
Work Attitudes and Habits	Vocational education teachers
	Basic skills teachers
	Home economics teacher
	Art teacher
Physical and Manual Skills	Physical education teacher
	Vocational education teacher

occupational possibilities. The subcompetencies are to identify the personal values met through work, to identify the societal values met through work, to identify the remunerative aspects of work, to understand classification of jobs into different occupational systems, to identify occupational opportunities available locally, and to identify sources of occupational information.

Under selecting and planning occupational choice are to identify major occupational needs, to identify major occupational interests, to identify occupational aptitudes, to identify requirements of appropriate and available jobs, and to make realistic occupational choices.

Under exhibiting appropriate work habits and behaviors are to follow directions, to work with others, to work at a satisfactory rate, to accept supervision, to recognize the importance of attendance and punctuality, to meet demands for quality work, and to demonstrate occupational safety.

Under physical-manual skills the competencies are to demonstrate satisfactory balance and coordination, to demonstrate satisfactory manual dexterity, to demonstrate satisfactory stamina and endurance, to demonstrate satisfactory sensory discrimination.

Under the competency seeking, securing and maintaining employment are to search for a job, to apply for a job, to interview for a job, to adjust to competitive standards, and to maintain postschool occupational adjustment.

The curriculum guide provides objectives under each subcompetency and includes activities and strategies to help the disabled students accomplish the objectives. The roles of adults and peers are also specified for each objective. A modified example is found in Figure 11.2.

The curriculum also includes forms to rate the competencies and subcompetencies in each area as well as individualized education program forms in which the students' annual goals can be checked, and the specific educational services required, whether they be special services, media materials, or individ-

---

Objective
   Identify three jobs you would like to have after graduation.
Activity/Strategy
* Look at ads in newspapers
* Look at state employment listings
* Use computerized guidance system or *Occupational Outlook Handbook* to read about job
* Share with class the job and why you have interest in it
Adult/Peer Roles
* Parents assist.
* Students in jobs identify possible jobs.
* State employment counselor helps students get information on these jobs.
Chamber of Commerce or Industry/Business Representative
* Discusses jobs available in community

FIGURE 11.2
Identifying jobs of interest

ual implementers. There is also a check sheet for short-term individual objectives that need to be monitored. There are materials available for elementary classrooms, middle school classrooms, and for high schools.

ROLE OF THE CAREER COUNSELOR

There are a number of different roles the career counselor needs to do in order to have an effective program in career education for disabled students. The counselor has to be an effective coordinator and work with teachers, administrators, parents, and the community and business sector to make sure the program is comprehensive and well coordinated. Omizo and Omizo (1992) emphasized the importance of the counselor combining data on career and vocational interests, aptitude, and work-related adaptive habits with data generated from psychological, educational, economic, and social cultural assessments in helping the student in his or her career planning. The school counselor is a team member who works with other school personnel, special needs teachers, health professions, and the like because they have special skills and knowledge that will be helpful. The counselor needs to get the help of special teachers to translate the career concepts to a level that is meaningful and understandable to the students within each program.

The counselor needs to be an effective consultant and be able to be an advocate for the disabled and provide useful information to employers participating in cooperative education programs on how to work effectively with the disabled students as well as to regular education teachers who may be involved. Parents are also an important group (Elksnin & Elksnin, 1990).

The counselor needs to be knowledgeable in the instruments that are available and appropriate for measuring the aptitudes, attitudes, achievements, interests, values, motor skills, personalities, and self-concepts of the disabled group.

The counselor needs to be a job developer and locate businesses, industries, and individuals who might be willing to employ a disabled student. Some employers are willing to be speakers and allow the students to job shadow or make field trips to the place of business to observe.

The counselor also needs to provide both individual and group counseling opportunities for these students. Group sessions might help disabled students to have a support group of individuals with similar problems. Disabled students have their reversals and problems and need access to individual counseling also.

The roles are numerous and complex because the counselor not only has to have knowledge of disabled individuals, their needs, and attitudes, but also a knowledge of the labor market, present and future trends, and the types of jobs that are possible for the disabled. Counselors have to be aware of their own inadequacies and prejudices toward the different disabled groups in order to be effective. Counselors have to be self-confident, enthusiastic, and recognize the need to involve a multidimensional team.

Phelps and Lutz (1977) proposed an eight-stage model to develop career education activities for disabled students. The first area is to identify and assess the learners' needs. They recommended that there should be accurate information on the learners that provide the learning strengths and weaknesses as well as their needs. A review should also be made of instructional strategies and materials appropriate for the learner. The second phase is to identify and inventory the school and community resources available to assist these special needs learners and the instructional staff. Counselors also advocate forming an advisory group to help in identifying community resources.

The third step calls for the career guidance staff to identify and analyze clusters of occupations that would be appropriate for the special needs learner and for instructional content for the career exploration and preparation phases of the program. Counselors need to identify the basic competencies these learners need for employment.

The fourth step is to select an instructional team to help the learner in developing the competencies identified. The fifth step is to plan instruction and to develop an individual educational plan for each of the disabled students. In the sixth step a plan for using out-of-school and in-school work experience is formulated. The seventh step is the implementation stage and does require instructional sequence plans, analysis of instructional materials, behavioral management strategies, and learning environment management strategies.

WORKING WITH REHABILITATION CLIENTS

In working with rehabilitation clients, counselors need to determine the effects of the disability on the individual and look at medical, psychological, social-cultural, and educational factors. Rehabilitation counselors work with a wide variety of medical and health professionals in order to synthesize information and assist their clients in developing plans for rehabilitation that leads to employment or other goals. They must have knowledge of both the medical and psychological aspects of a broad range of disabilities, consumer and environmental assessment techniques, occupational and labor market information, community resources, and job hiring requirements (Rubin & Rubin, 1988).

They need to ask what limitations are imposed on the individual by the disability itself. Then they need to investigate what limitations are imposed on the individual by the individual as a result of the disability and look at the psychological aspects. They also need to look at what limitations on the individual are imposed by family, peers, and the community or others in the immediate environment. Last they need to assess the limitations that are imposed educationally as a result of the disability.

SPECIFIC LIMITATIONS

Maki (1986) identified 14 specific limitations that disability may impose. These are listed in Figure 11.3.

GOALS OF CAREER DEVELOPMENT

Burkhead (1984) identified five major goals or career development programs for disabled individuals:

1.   To facilitate the disabled individual's optimal level of independent functioning
2.   To consider the needs of the whole person in the provision of a program of services
3.   To educate community and business leaders about architectural and transportation barriers and about legislation to eliminate these barriers
4.   To educate employers about disabled workers and about legislation pertaining to employment of disabled persons
5.   To facilitate the disabled client's exploration of career alternatives, assist in clarifying career goals, and to provide services to reach career goals

CAREER DEVELOPMENT THEORY

Most of the major theories of career development fail to look specifically at the career development of individuals with disabilities or vocational disabilities. The theories may provide some understanding of career development but have their theoretical and practical limitations for working with this type of client. Her-

- ∗ Sensory impairment—reduction or incapacity to receive environmental stimuli in the visual, auditory, olfactory, tactile, or taste domains
- ∗ Communication difficulty—reduction or incapacity to receive, process, and transmit messages, either verbally or nonverbally, to or from other individuals in the environment
- ∗ Atypical appearance—physical or behavioral cues emitted by an individual, used to attract the attention of others, that may be interpreted as significantly different from the cultural standards
- ∗ Emotional and behavioral considerations—interpersonal or physical manifestations of affective and/or cognitive processes that interfere with an individual's ability to function effectively in the environment
- ∗ Unapparent limitation—no cues are overtly transmitted to others in the environment and the person is considered to be nondisabled by the general public, but disability is present
- ∗ Cognitive and learning difficulty—an impaired ability to obtain, process, or retain information potentially affecting the individual's ability to attend, conceptualize, abstract, judge, problem solve, or gain from interaction with the environment
- ∗ Substance dependency—physical or psychological need for and use/misuse of chemical agents over a period of time either on a prescribed or self-regulated basis
- ∗ Pain sensitivity/intolerance—the physical or psychological sensation of pain exceeds the individual's threshold of tolerance affecting the life-style and ability to concentrate, learn, effectively interact, or physically maneuver within the environment
- ∗ Consciousness—inability to maintain a condition of mental awareness of the environment at any given point in time
- ∗ Debilitation—progressive, though usually gradual, deterioration of physical, emotional, or intellectual capacities
- ∗ Motion deficit—partial or total restrictions in movement or coordination in the limbs or trunk of the body affecting the individual's ability to maneuver within and to manipulate the environment
- ∗ Mobility—inability to interact within the total context of the environment as a result of physical barriers, when factors may be present that cause or exacerbate the disabling condition, when the individual would be a threat to self or others if permitted to interact, or if a controlled environment is required in the treatment of the debilitating conditions
- ∗ Uncertain prognosis—inability to predict with any degree of certainty the duration, severity, and/or probable final status of a disease or mental disorder
- ∗ Special considerations—unique implications of a situation that if unattended would result in less than optimal rehabilitation outcomes for any given individual

FIGURE 11.3
Specific limitations of disabilities

shenson and Roth (1970) proposed a model of vocational development that was based on the assessment of the physical and psychosocial background of individuals, their work personality, motivation, vocational self-image, work competencies, behaviors, skills, interpersonal relations in the work setting, work choice, and work adjustment. They postulated that the disabilities that most directly affect the work competencies and the client's adjustment to the disability depends on the prior nature of these constructs and their interrelationships. The time of the onset and the impact of the disability on the individual's life-style have to be considered. McMahon (1979) also provided us with a framework for understanding the career development and work adjustment of individuals with disabling conditions especially in the mid-career stage. He stated that work adjustment is the goodness of fit between the job dimensions and the worker dimensions. Worker dimensions are defined as needs and competencies where as job dimensions are the job reinforcers and job demands. McMahon felt that one can predict both mathematically and subjectively the worker/job fit, the worker's understanding of the realities of the job, and the worker's level of assessment. He postulated that mid-career physical disability is important only to the degree that it alters the needs or competencies of the worker or the reinforcers or demands of the job. He sees the worker/job fit before becoming disabled as the primary factor in predicting vocational redevelopment. Schmitt, Growlick, and Klein (1988) pointed out that the Minnesota point of view (trait-and-factor approach) has emphasized the individual's need to achieve and maintain correspondence with the environment that is becoming more complex because of the technological advances and the age of information.

CAREER COUNSELING SERVICES

There are a number of career counseling delivery systems that are available to help individuals who are disabled, including schools, state and private vocational rehabilitation services, and social service agencies. Schools under PL 94-142 and PL 94-482 provide education as well as vocational training for all disabled students between the ages of 3 and 21. Many community colleges have specific educational and training programs for the disabled. The state and federal vocational rehabilitation programs provide assistance as well as coordinate services to the disabled. The Veterans Administration has a wide range of medical, educational, and vocational benefits and services available to disabled veterans. There are a number of agencies administered under the Goodwill Industries of America, the National Easter Seal Society, and the National Association of Jewish Vocational Services that provide vocational evaluation, vocational training, and job placement services to moderately and severely disabled individuals. There are many proprietary rehabilitation companies also that provide career counseling services to assist their clients in identifying appropriate career goals, preparing for the career, and attaining a suitable adjustment on the job. The groups provide consultation and expert-witness testimony regarding the impact of the disability on a client's career and earning potential in worker's compensation or personal injury cases.

CAREER COUNSELING INTERVENTIONS

There are a wide variety of counseling interventions the career counselor can use with disabled individuals. Individual counseling is quite often one of the main strategies because the counselor needs to help facilitate the client's career decision making. It is necessary for the counselor to discuss the problems and barriers the clients might face in their situations. Robinson and Mopsik (1992) provided valuable suggestions on establishing and maintaining the proper environment for counseling disabled individuals and creating appropriate experiential situations for the client. Their guidelines have applicability across developmental levels and call for the counselors to use multisensory approaches, structured tasks, and an environment that is not distracting. Counselors are reminded to communicate concretely, avoiding verbal generalities and abstract relationships, and speak using short, concise, explicit sentences. They are encouraged to use consistent repetitions. The counselor might have to deal with a lack of family support and self-confidence as well and needs to monitor the case closely until the individual is adjusted in his or her training or work setting. A number of transitional strategies are widely used to help individuals with disabilities adjust from school or training to the world of work. Transition needs to be planned effectively and individual transition plans developed for the clients and interagency agreements negotiated (Heal, Copher, & Rusch, 1990).

Vocational training is one of the most widely used interventions. The purpose is to help clients develop the knowledge, skills, and behaviors required to achieve their career goals. There are many options available including colleges and universities, business and trade schools, apprenticeship programs, adult education, and vocational and technical schools (Szymanski, Hanley-Maxwell, & Asselin, 1990).

Work adjustment programs are also available to help clients develop general work behaviors and skills such as personal hygiene and grooming, attendance and punctuality, interpersonal behavior on the job, quality or quantity of work, and other skills that may be required for success on the job. This training is often available through rehabilitation facilities and agencies. The individuals perform real work. The work environment can be adjusted to meet the special needs of the clients.

Traditional employment programs are another approach. The clients are trained to fill positions and are placed on a job and supervised by the agency. They are used to promote appropriate work habits and to help clients build up their self-confidence. The agency may have several sites available that they have contracted to fill, and the jobs might provide a progression from one level to another as the client's skills, behaviors, and confidence increases.

On-the-job training is similar to the previously mentioned types of work programs but the focus is on helping clients learn the knowledge and specific skills necessary for a given occupation. This type of program is an alternative to vocational training in schools. The individual quite often is hired by the company if the job performance is satisfactory on the completion of the training.

Job placement is a goal of many counselors for the client. Placement often is difficult because employers often overestimate the impact of the disability on the individual's job performance and underestimate the capabilities of the individual who is disabled. They express positive attitudes but do not end up hiring many. Job placement requires the individual to be employable. Success often depends on whether the job placement is consistent with the client's career goals and job adjustment.

The counselor has to offer either individual or group instruction in job-seeking skills. Usually in these sessions the counselor covers such topics as how to identify job leads, making inquiries about job openings, identifying and describing vocational assets, answering difficult questions about disabilities and personal or employment problems, completing job applications, and handling job interviews.

The job club (Azrin & Besalel, 1980) has been applied to disabled individuals. The job club provides group instruction in job-seeking skills and is used as a buddy system. The club meets daily until placements are achieved. The group members share job leads and transportation as well as become a support system for each other. The counselor can provide supervision and instruction to help facilitate the goals of the group.

Job development, job modification, and/or job restructuring might be necessary to accommodate an individual with disabling conditions. Whatever the need, the adjustments depend on the cooperative interaction among employer, counselor, and client. Job restructuring and job modification often require the assistance of industrial or rehabilitation engineers to modify the equipment or working environment.

The counselor sometimes has to consider all the employment options. Some individuals with severe disabilities might not be able to function in a competitive employment situation. They might only be able to perform at a reduced rate, and the counselor might have to help negotiate for some waivers in the production demands. Some workers will only be able to function in segregated employment such as in sheltered workshops. Some workers who cannot function in other types of settings because of their disabilities might be able to function in homebound employment, such as mail order sales and telephone solicitation. Some who are more entrepreneurial might be able to develop a business of their own and make some type of product or provide some special type of service.

MODELS OF CAREER COUNSELING SERVICES

Schmitt, Growick, and Klein (1988) developed a model to assist learning disabled students in their transition from school to employment, and from adolescence to adulthood. These individuals have difficulty in making the adjustment because of their learning disabilities. These disabilities also cause problems in the home and in the family besides in the school. These individuals usually have average to above average intelligence and have different orientation for receiving and processing information. They are not as directed toward the future opportunities in their career and education as their nondisabled peers. Their comprehensive delivery plan called for the following steps:

- Development of an individualized transition plan that is based on a comprehensive assessment of vocational, academic, and interpersonal functioning
- Evaluations that will identify the individualized learning styles resulting in the maximum use of program information and facilitate planning and delivery of services
- Vocation exploration and career education that include a planned career exploration using an interactive computer program and counseling services
- Employability training skills that address the vocational, social, and emotional skills necessary to enter the training step of the model. The interpersonal skills include listening, problem exploration, goal setting, problem solving, and decision making. Assertiveness training and conflict management skills are also provided the learning disabled youth.
- Interpersonal skills including a variety of behavioral, cognitive, and cognitive behavioral skills such as self-instruction, cognitive restructuring, cognitive rehearsal, cognitive modeling, imagery, and stress testing experiences
- Extrapersonal skills including the development of skills to gain access to and effectively use community resources
- Supported job search and placement follow-up that includes job-seeking skills, job clubs, and business and industry linkages
- Parent and agency cooperation and involvement that includes active, structured involvement and participation of parents and schools, agencies, and business and industry

SUPPORTIVE EMPLOYMENT APPROACH

Supportive employment is a paid employment experience for clients with severe disabilities who require long-term support to sustain employment, and is offered in settings that provide integration with individuals without disabilities who are not paid caregivers (Moon, Inge, Wehman, Booke, & Barcus, 1990). Supportive employment programs have common features, such as employment as the desired outcome, ongoing support, or follow-up, paid jobs as a primary focus rather than services for job preparation. The philosophy is that all individuals, regardless of the severity of the disability, have the capacity to work if they receive appropriate ongoing support. The emphasis is on social integration with nondisabled individuals who are not paid caregivers, and a variety and flexibility of job and support possibilities (Helms, Moore, & McSweyn, 1991). Wehman (1993) concluded that although the ADA does not specifically address the concept of supported employment in its laws or regulations, the underlying theme of ADA is competitive work in a nondiscriminatory work environment and is highly consistent with supported employment.

Szymanski, Buckley, Parent, Parker, and Westbrook (1988) presented a six-phase model that includes the initial assessment phase, plan development phase, job placement phase, training phase, ongoing support phase, and periodic assessment phase.

The detailed steps of the initial assessment phase are presented for an overview of the model. There are two phases, client attributes and job market attributes, that are outlined in Figure 11.4.

Client: identify or evaluate
* Past work experience
* General work-related interest areas
* Work hours available or preferred
* Social survival skills
* Mobility/transportation skills/availability
* Previous service history
* Relevant medical or psychological information
* Specific occupational skills or deficits
* Financial status, potential disincentives
* Work attitude/motivation
* General level of independence
* Parent or guardian level of support for employment
* Probable nature and level of ongoing support necessary for continued employment
* Potential reinforcers and relative strengths

Job market: Identify, perform, and document
* Nature and scope of local work opportunities
* Specific jobs and work settings appropriate for supported employment
* Specific business and job requirements and flexibility
* Job analysis of potential supported employment jobs
* Specific job characteristics, such as wages, benefits, hours, level of social integration, and potential transportation
* Potential for job accommodation
* Number of potential supported employment placements feasible or desired by employer
* Receptivity of employer to integration with co-workers and public
* Employer-specific hiring orientation and training process
* Job/employer—specific limitations on support/intervention

FIGURE 11.4
Schedule for assessing client and job market attributes

ASSESSMENT ISSUES AND PROCEDURES

Assessment is an important phase of career counseling for individuals with disabling conditions. Rehabilitation counseling follows mainly a medical model, and diagnosis is one of the important steps in the process and role of the counselor. Hartlage (1986) provided a four-stage model, including the following:

- Determination of the relevant issues and questions
- Development of necessary background data
- Selection of appropriate assessment instruments
- Use of assessment into action plans

The first two steps are necessary to help the counselor gain the necessary information to make the selection of instruments that will be valid and appropriate to answer the questions that need to be addressed. He felt that in the assessment intelligence, academic skills, hemispheric dominances, and special characteristics such as interests and aptitudes should be measured. The major question to be answered is, Has the diagnosis led to findings that will be of maximum value to the client? He stated that whether or not the assessment did a good job of classifying, diagnosing, describing, or helping understand the client is secondary to the issue of whether the assessment actually helped the client.

Berven (1986) pointed out that in counseling disabled individuals, a wide variety of sources and types of assessment data are used. He mentioned four major types of procedures. The first is the interview. The second is the use of tests and inventories. The third involves simulated and real work experiences. The fourth involves the use of functional assessment scales.

He stated that the interview is probably the most widely used technique to collect data, and the procedure could be enhanced if the counselor follows more comprehensive and systematic interview procedures. Under tests and inventories he included tests of maximum and typical performance. Under the former category he included intelligence tests, multiaptitude batteries, and tests of specific aptitudes. Under the latter he included tests that are relevant to determining how an individual may be expected to typically behave in given situations and the vocational interests, attitudes, values, and personality tests in this category. Simulated and real work situations as assessment tools have long been some of the most widely used and accepted approaches to vocational assessment in rehabilitation counseling. Work samples use simulations of tasks actually performed in occupations or clusters of occupations. Situational assessment used the work environment rather than specific occupational tasks. Job try-outs or on-the-job evaluations use actual community job sites where the person's performance is observed and evaluated for a period of time. Functional assessment scales are instruments used to systematically describe an individual's functioning in terms of skill, the "can do" skills, and behaviors, the "does do" behaviors. Some of the instruments are in the form of checklists and are based on direct observation, and others are self-report inventories given to the client to complete.

EXAMPLES OF ASSESSMENT USED WITH THE DISABLED

There are a wide variety of instruments that have been used and validated with different disabled groups and some that were designed for certain targeted groups. The Joint Standards for Educational and Psychological Tests has some explicit standards for the proper use and interpretation of standardized tests for the disabled group that counselors need to know.

USES Non Reading Aptitude Test Battery (NATB)— United States Employment Service

This test was designed for use with disadvantaged and semiliterate individuals, grade 9 to 12, and adults. It measures intelligence, verbal, numerical, spatial, form perception, clerical perception, motor coordination, finger dexterity, and manual dexterity.

Adult Basic Leaning Examination (ABLE)— The Psychological Corporation

This test was designed for adults who have not completed eight grades of formal education and measures vocabulary, reading, spelling, arithmetic computation, and problem solving.

Wide Range Achievement Test (WRAT)— Jastak Assessment Systems

The test can be administered to individuals 5 years to adult, measures spelling, arithmetic, and reading, and is best used in a clinical setting as a screening device to determine approximate educational achievement levels.

Reading-Free Vocational Interest Inventory— Elbern Publications

The test is designed to provide information about the vocational preferences for persons with mental retardation and learning disabilities through the use of pictorial illustrations of individuals engaged in various occupational tasks.

Wide-Range Interest Opinion Test—Jastak Assessment Systems

The test measures vocational interests and assesses the levels of self-projected ability, aspiration level, and social conformity. The test is appropriate for use with culturally disadvantaged, mentally retarded, learning disabled, and the deaf. The picture titles can be read to the blind.

MESA—Valpar International

The test is designed to provide baseline data for the development of an individual educational, training, or employment plan, and is used with individuals contemplating entering the labor market or changing fields of work. The test consists of a number of computer-assisted tests measuring a number of aptitudes.

Wide Range Employability Sample Test— Jastak Assessment Systems

The test measures a person's ability to work at routine manual tasks and helps determine the feasibility of competitive employment of the severely disabled. The test is used for placement in sheltered workshops or daily activities programs.

VCWS Range of Tests

VCWS1-Small Tools, VCWS2 Size Discrimination, VCWS4 Upper Extremity Range of Motion, VCWS7 Multi-Level Sorting, VCWS8 Simulated Assembly, VCWS9 Whole Body Range of Motion, and VCWS11-Eye-Hand-Foot Coordination are some of the work-sample type of tests that can be used with retarded hearing impaired and visually impaired individuals.

SUMMARY

Career counseling of special populations is usually part of special education programs in the schools and rehabilitation services in the public and private sector. The purpose of career counseling with this group is to help them to enhance their career self-concepts and make appropriate career and educational decisions. With proper guidance and help they can make good decisions about their life and career goals. Counselors need to be familiar with the legal rights of the disabled and be proactive advocates with schools, business, and industry.

REVIEW QUESTIONS

1. What are the important developmental issues that affect the career and personal adjustment of disabled individuals?

2.   Do you feel that there should be a specialized career development theory for disabled individuals? Why or why not?

3.   What are some of the misconceptions and stereotypes individuals have about the disabled individual?

4.   What is your attitude toward disabled individuals? What experiences have you had in working with people with disabilities?

5.   How would you go about changing the attitudes of employers toward disabled individuals if they had negative ones?

6.   What goals and objectives would you include in a career guidance program for disabled youth in elementary school? In middle school? In high school? In college?

7.   What factors do the career counselor have to consider when working with rehabilitation clients?

8.   What are some of the career counseling interventions that have been successful with disabled youth and adults?

9.   What model of assessment would you use with rehabilitation and disabled clients? What types of assessment instruments would you use?

SUGGESTED ACTIVITIES

1.   Review curriculum guides for career education and counseling programs for the disabled. What are some of the common goals and objectives found in these guides? What are some of the differences you found?

2.   Construct a Likert type of attitude scale on attitude toward the disabled and give it to your classmates or some other group. (A Likert scale is a 5-point scale with the following categories: strongly agree, agree, uncertain, disagree, and strongly disagree.) Analyze the results and report them to the class.

3.   Write a paper or report on a type of disabled clients you might work with in the future.

4.   Interview personnel directors of some of the major businesses and industries in your community. Find out if they employ disabled workers. In what type of jobs? Do they actively recruit individuals so classified?

5.   Interview several individuals with the same or different disability. Discuss their job history and their goals for the future. How do their patterns of career development fit Super's conceptualization?

6.   Make a file of agencies and individuals who provide career counseling for the disabled. Report your findings to the class.

7.   Make an annotated bibliography of career tests and assessment techniques that would be appropriate for disabled individuals.

8. Interview several rehabilitation counselors and find out the type of problems their clients have, the types of interventions they use, and their successes in job placement.

9. Interview several resource room and special education teachers. Discuss how they approach career education in their work with their students. Also interview a school guidance counselor and find out what type of career guidance program is conducted for special needs students.

CASE STUDY

Profile of a Nonvisually Disabled Student

Name: Tim Bellinger
Age: 16
Grade: 11
School: Pines High School, Boston

Background

Tim was placed in a learning disabilities class when he was in third grade. He was diagnosed as having a severe reading disability due to visual processing and visual perceptions problems. He is an auditory learner with good listening skills and good verbal skills. For example, if a class test is read to him, he makes a higher score than if he has to read the test himself. His learning disabilities teacher has recommended that he be given all tests orally as an accommodation for his disability. This accommodation is part of his written individual education plan (IEP).

Because Tim has good verbal and listening skills his disability is not apparent in most settings. He has developed excellent coping strategies in reading and processing visual information. These coping strategies have presented problems for Tim because some of his teachers expected him to achieve the same as a nondisabled student based on his verbal skills.

Assessment Information

The results of a recent intelligence test indicated that Tim's overall level of intellectual functioning on the WISC-III was in the low average range (IQ 85, Verbal 92, Performance 79). Tim's adaptive behavior on the Adaptive Behavior Scale was average for his age. The results of the Stanford Achievement Test from last year were as follows:

Subtest	Percentile Rank
Word Reading	27
Reading Comprehension	18
Word Study Skills	22
Number Concepts	47
Math Computations and Applications	52
Spelling	30
Vocabulary	35
Listening Comprehension	52
Reading	21
Total Reading	23
Total Math	50
Total Auditory	53

Educational Placement and Goals

Tim is mainstreamed for most of his classes, which include mathematics, science, physical education, and business education. He receives special instruction in English and learning strategies in a resource room for students with learning disabilities. His grades in English and math are C's; in science, his grades are D's and F's.

Tim plans to enroll in a high school work-study program during his senior year. This will involve placement in a part-time job in which he will leave school early each day to go to work. Tim has had no previous work experience.

Classroom Behavior

Tim's classroom behavior and emotional development seem normal. His behavior in school is satisfactory except for three incidents of misbehavior in science class. During an informal interview, one of his teachers indicated concern about Tim's self-concept and felt that he may have a low sense of self-worth due to academic frustration. His parents have reported that Tim sometimes indicates his frustration with school by saying things such as "I'm dense," and "I won't ever get it." His teacher also observed that Tim is attentive in class but is usually one of the last students to finish his work.

Case Questions

1. How would you work with this student as a career counselor in terms of your theoretical approach and philosophy of intervention?
2. What additional information would you need to obtain in order to provide career counseling services? How would you obtain the information quickly and efficiently?

3. How can the assessment information that is provided be used? Is additional assessment information needed? If so, what?
4. How should Tim's learning style and coping strategies be accounted for in career counseling?
5. What types of career counseling services would be most beneficial to this student?
6. What types of part-time jobs would best fit this student's needs?
7. Tim is a junior. When should he receive career counseling?
8. How does career counseling for students with disabilities like Tim's differ from services for nondisabled students?

SUGGESTED READINGS

Gostin, L. O., & Beyer, H. A. (1993). *Implementing the Americans with Disability Act: Rights and responsibilities of all Americans.* Baltimore: Paul H. Brookes.

The book presents an in-depth look at the ADA legal requirements and social issues. There are chapters on employment issues. Questions that can be asked in interviews and job descriptions and requirements are just a few of the important topics covered.

Moon, M. S., Inge, K. J., Wehman, P., Brooke, V., & Barcus, J. M. (1990). *Helping persons with severe mental retardation get and keep employment.* Baltimore: Paul H. Brookes.

The authors cover topics on supported employment issues and strategies. A number of guidelines for career counselors are presented to work with the group.

12

MULTICULTURAL CAREER COUNSELING

T here are many different cultural and ethnic groups in our country. Many from these groups are underemployed or unemployed. Youths from these groups face a struggle in getting jobs even if they are high school graduates. Counselors have to be aware of the economic, political, and legal issues that affect the employment of these people. Counselors need to develop multicultural awareness and be able to focus on the needs of the culturally different, who frequently have language, educational, and prejudice barriers to overcome. These clients represent a wide variety of ethnic backgrounds that challenge career counselors to change their personal views of the groups and to try to understand their perspectives.

LEARNING OBJECTIVES

After reading this chapter, you should be able to do the following:

- List and discuss the major minority and ethnic groups and the role of the career counselor in working with these groups
- Identify the major barriers to employment for these groups and strategies to overcome these barriers
- Discuss counseling strategies that would be effective in helping these groups
- Identify career assessment instruments that would be appropriate for these groups

TRENDS IN THE JOB MARKET

Hoyt (1989) pointed out some startling statistics for the career counselor to consider:

- Five out of six new entrants into the labor market between 1989 and 2000 will be women, immigrants, and people belonging to minority groups.
- Seventy-five percent of the workers who will be employed in the year 2000 are in the labor force today. The upward mobility of minorities will be severely limited.
- The new jobs will be in service-producing not goods-producing industries, a great number of these jobs will be in low-wage occupations, and the percent of minority persons living in poverty will increase.

Many of the new jobs will demand more education than those now existing. Unfortunately there is a decrease in the number of minority group members finishing high school in some states or entering college. Minority youth tend to be concentrated in large urban school districts in which the educational offerings are sometimes not as good as those offered in the suburban areas.

Both African Americans and Hispanics are overrepresented in the slow-growing or declining occupations, but underrepresented in the fastest growing occupations (Hoyt, 1989). Smith (1983) concluded that the interest in ethnic minorities has grown because of the increasing awareness of the uneven distribution of the races and sexes in the labor market and the inequality of underrepresentation of racial minorities and women in the labor market. Legislation has been enacted to help to reduce the educational, attitudinal, and employment handicaps that hinder minorities and women in their employment efforts. Meier (1992) concluded in his review on vocational choice and decision making that problems such as stereotyping and restriction of career opportunity occur with people of color.

Another problem has been the high unemployment rate of minority youths. Many minority youths will have a hard time gaining security of career mobility because they cannot get the work experience needed to help them in their transition from adolescence to adulthood and school to work. If jobs are not available, crime and delinquency become more of an option for this group. Minority groups such as African Americans and Latino Americans have higher unemployment rates than do Anglo-Europeans (Bureau of Census, 1990). When employed, ethnic group members tend to be overrepresented in slow-growing or declining occupations but underrepresented in the fastest-growing occupations (Kutscher, 1987).

Glasgow (1980) pointed out that the underclass is obsolete, undereducated, jobless, and without the social skills and social credentials necessary to gain access to mainstream life. The underclass are people who are removed from the mainstream of life and do not share the American Dream and have given up or refused to work.

WHO CONSTITUTES MINORITY GROUPS?

Kinloch (1979) provided us several ways of looking at minority groups. The first way is to differentiate a group by physiological type, that is, women, young people, old people, students, and the like. The second is by cultural type, that is, African Americans, Hispanics, Native Americans, and Asian Americans. The third is to classify economic types, such as poor, lower class, or upper class. The fourth is by behavioral type, such as mentally ill, delinquents, criminals, and the like.

African Americans

African Americans are the largest racial minority in the United States and constituted in 1990 almost 12.1% of the population or approximately 30 million African Americans. It is projected that this group will increase 22% or by 6.6 million people by 2000. The group is very young with the mean age in 1980 of 23. Their career development in the past was influenced by slavery. African-American men were employed primarily as agricultural workers and African-American women, as domestic workers. About 80% of African Americans live in urban areas and slightly over 50% live in the south.

The largest proportion of African Americans is employed as blue collar workers. Although there is an increasing number of African Americans entering professions and the technical fields, the percentage is very small.

Asian Americans

Asian Americans consist of Chinese, Japanese, Filipinos, Koreans, Hawaiians, and Indo-Chinese. The 1990 Census included 7.3 million Asians and Pacific Islanders from 32 distinct cultural groups, or 2.9% of the total U.S. population. Most of Asian Americans are located in California and Hawaii. Outside of the Indo-Chinese refugees, Asian Americans have accommodated and adapted well to the existing American society and are viewed as hard workers and skilled in math and science. Most of the groups, except for the Vietnamese, came to America voluntarily. They maintained their ties with their countries, kept large portions of their cultural heritage, and were able to maintain their families as a unit. Many Asian Americans were able to use their educational attainments to move up the career ladder. The 1970 census data show that Japanese, Chinese, and Filipinos were more likely to be found in professional and technical occupations than Anglo-European or African Americans. Asian Americans also have one of the lowest unemployment rates. Mayhovich (1976) concluded that the career development of Asian Americans has been influenced by their culture. They tend to view education as a means of acquiring a salable skill and major in business administration, engineering, or science, not in the liberal arts. Leong (1993) reminded us that not all Asian Americans have Asian values.

Hispanic Americans

Hispanic Americans include Mexicans, Cubans, Puerto Ricans, and refugees from the Central American countries and Haiti. In the 1990 census there were 22.4 million persons of Spanish origin. There are three major subgroups: Mexican Americans or Chicanos (62%), Puerto Ricans (13%), and Cubans (5%), which account for 80% of the Hispanic-American population. There are 16 other Spanish-speaking countries represented from South America, and 8% of the population is from Spain. They are at present the second largest ethnic grouping in the United States and growing rapidly. There are distinct ethnic groups but share in common their Spanish heritage. Hispanics have a higher unemployment rate than Anglo-Europeans but lower than African Americans. Contrary to stereotypes, only 5% of Hispanic men work in farm occupations. Fifty-eight percent is employed in blue collar jobs, 24% in white collar work, and 13% in service occupations.

Native Americans

Native Americans are clustered primarily in five states, Arizona, California, North Carolina, New York, and Oklahoma. The 1990 census reported that there are slightly less than 2 million Native Americans/Native Alaskans, but some experts feel that this underestimates the group and that there are twice as many. Although many live on reservations in rural sections of the country, more are moving to urban areas to find employment. This move has made a change in the attitudes, customs, life-style, and occupation of Native Americans. Richardson (1981) described the life of the Indian as one of hardships, incarcerations, and degradations. He quoted some statistics, such as 44 is the life expectancy of Indians, 25% to 35% of all Indian children are separated from their families, and their suicide rate is 7 times the national rate.

Native Americans have some career development problems. Many live on the reservation and are isolated from the mainstream American culture. They also have several cultural traits or values that conflict with that of the prevailing majority. They choose careers that are in close proximity to or on their reservations whenever possible.

RELEVANCE OF CAREER THEORIES FOR MINORITIES

Two opposite views of the value of career theories for minority groups exists: One is that they are valuable; the other, of little importance. Smith (1983) summarized the criticisms into five themes.

The theories (Super, 1990; Holland, 1985) were based on biased sampling that was restricted to the Anglo-European population; the theories are based on some faulty assumptions such as a continuous, uninterrupted, career pattern.

The theories are not meaningful for minority populations, as the theories tend to not reflect the world in which minorities live; and the theories are static and tend to ignore the changing economic and social changes. In short, a new theory of career development is needed that accounts for specific group behaviors of Asians, Hispanics, Native Americans, and African Americans. Cheatham (1990) criticized existing career theories and measures for failing to account for African Americans' experiences with discrimination and the unavailability of career information and guidance for this subgroup.

The critics feel that the life-stage development for ethnic minorities applies more to the most successful members of the group and are not real for other members. Minority members have a hard enough time surviving and are not able to focus on career planning for life. Herbert (1990) reported support for Levinson's theory of stages of adult development.

Mitchell and Krumboltz (1990) felt the process of career decision making is the same across all cultures, even though career choice is heavily influenced by such factors as race, gender, and culture. Brown (1990) gave counterarguments such as there is no compelling evidence that current theories predict any less well for women and minority groups than they do for Anglo-European males. He also states the importance of comprehensive theories as contrasted to minitheories, but recognizes that gender and race influences socialization and the career development process. He felt differences can be accommodated in the existing theories.

Warnath (1975) points out that most career theories assume that there exists a free and open labor market, but for many minority groups the market is neither free nor open. The overemphasis on self-awareness activities and changing the attitudes and motivation of minority group members might not be in their best interest. This is especially noteworthy when economic and social conditions are at the root of the problems.

Career theories do not deal with attribution of cause. Griffith (1980) observed that African Americans respond on three levels to the American opportunity level: the ideal, the perceived, and the real. Equal opportunity symbolizes the ideal. The perceived represents what is thought to be obtainable. The economically disadvantaged ethnic minority member will focus on the perceived and real opportunity structure.

Osipow (1975) also pointed to deficits in career theories for minority group members. He felt that career theories represent the ideal career development of people at the upper level of professional and vocational activities. He also suggested that the occupational environments postulated by Holland are not equally available to many minority members. They are channeled into low-level realistic and conventional types of positions. Top-level jobs are not often available to minority groups because of economics, racial discrimination, and social and educational factors.

Dickens and Dickens (1982) posited that African-American career development has four stages: entry (feels as if he or she has it made because of having a job, naivete about norms and culture and race relations, tries to fit in and does not make waves), adjustment (dissatisfied with lack of mobility, Anglo-Europeans' moving ahead, anger/rage appears, low self-confidence), planned growth (realizes that getting ahead means expending more energy, feels self-confident, sets goals), and success.

Self-concept development is also different for minority group members, but there is much variability across environmental and social class variables (Cook, 1991). They often separate their work self-concept from their personal self-concept. Other groups have greater importance to them than their work groups. Osipow (1975) believed that many minorities who enter lower entry-level positions are not able to integrate their self-concepts with their lives and jobs. Osipow felt that career development as a process of implementing one's self-concept is not realistically possible for most minority members. Dunn and Veltman (1989) found that career maturity scores for minority students were higher after they participated in a summer program. Leong (1991) found that Asian-American students were lower in career maturity and higher in independent decision-making skills and extrinsic and security values than Anglo-European students.

Smith (1983) also questioned the value of the concept or construct of career maturity. The construct is based on the premise that we have shared agreement on the concept of career development. Some feel that the career life-stage development can be generalized to most groups in our society. All people have common vocational tasks they must master and if they do it will enhance their likelihood of making the right career choices.

OCCUPATIONAL INFORMATION

Smith (1983) concluded that the amount, level, and type of occupational information clients have influences their career behavior. Studies have shown that African Americans, Hispanic, and Native Americans know less information than Anglo-Europeans. Davidson (1980) concluded the African-American youths are hampered by their lack of information on job availability. Gottfredson (1978), in his analysis of the 1973 to 1974 assessment of career and occupational development conducted by the National Assessment of Educational Progress, found that African American males and females had trouble in naming things a person should consider when choosing a job. Bowman (1993) recommended that career literature and programs should be presented in the language of the audience.

CAREER ASPIRATIONS

Career counselors feel that career aspirations are an important component in the career development process and provide goals for attainment for individuals when they become adults. Counselors like to see a congruency between expectations and aspirations and educational attainment. There has been considerable research on the career aspiration of African Americans with sometimes contradictory results. Frost and Diamond (1979) found that young African-American girls tended to choose more low-status and traditionally feminine occupations than Anglo-European females. Smith (1983) concluded the differences found are a function of the lack of controls for socioeconomic status and class in the study, and that if these aspects are controlled, African-American aspirations are generally as high or higher than Anglo-Europeans.

Kuvelsky and Juarez (1975) reported that Mexican-American youths held high educational and career aspirations. They feel that too many experts are advocating solutions such as raising the aspirations of disadvantaged and minority groups, building up their self-images, teaching mainstream values, and requiring more compensatory education. They feel these ideas create more stereotypes and problems than do good. Arbona and Novy (1991) compared occupational aspirations and expectations of 866 African-American, Mexican-American, and Ango-European freshmen and found more gender than racial or ethnic differences. Arbona (1990) found Hispanics have high occupational aspirations but lower expectations. Career progression and work values of college-educated Hispanics were similar to Anglo-Europeans, and that educational attainment varied by national origin, generational status, and social class.

CAREER CHOICE

In reviewing studies on career choice, Smith (1983) concluded that minority youths are not participating in a broad range of occupations and tend to cluster their choice in a limited segment. African Americans, for example, tend to be overrepresented in the social sciences and underrepresented in the technical and natural sciences. Almost a half of the students get their degrees in education, social sciences, or business. Gottfredson (1978) pointed out that there is a shortage of minority group members, especially African Americans, entering fields demanding enterprising and investigative skills. Smith (1980) called for a national effort to encourage minority students to consider jobs in nontraditional career fields. Drummond and Hansford (1992) found that African-American parenting teens tended to think about codes having social, conventional, and enterprising careers. They did not select the fastest-growing jobs in the state and nation. They did not aspire to high technological jobs requiring advanced education, but chose many types of jobs in which they would only be able to earn a marginal salary. In studying rural underachieving minority students, Medina and Drummond (1993) found that the students tended to select law, medicine, teaching, or nursing as their career choice rather than the fastest growth occupations in the states or the jobs with the largest openings in the region and state.

ASSESSMENT OF MINORITY GROUPS

The assessment of minority groups with scholastic aptitude, cognitive, noncognitive, or nonintellective measures has been an area of controversy. The validity of tests such as the *Strong Interest Inventory*, Holland's *Self-Directed Search* and the *Vocational Preference Inventory* have been questioned. The question raised is whether these tests are biased toward minority groups. Do these tests measure accurately the interests of American ethnic minorities? There has also been debate about the efficacy of scholastic aptitude, general aptitude, and intelligence tests for minority groups.

Harrington and O'Shea (1980) tested the *Career Decision-Making* (CDM) instrument with different groups of Hispanics and found that the CDM and Holland's personality types were applicable to Spanish-speaking high school students.

Job Programs for Minority Youth

There have been many federal, state, local, and private attempts to help minority youth attain employment, such as the National Supported Work Demonstration Program, Job Corps Program, and the like.

The group of minority youth has the highest unemployment rate for the age bracket and the highest school dropout rate. Youths involved in these programs receive counseling and support and temporary job placement. They tend, however, not to continue their work activity after the program ends. One notable result of these job programs is the achievement gains these youth have made in both reading and mathematics. Smith (1983) concluded that many of these programs were too simplistic for a complex problem. These programs have done more to help middle-class professionals to get jobs helping these individuals than they have helped the youths for whom the programs were intended (Gottlieb, 1979).

Miller and Cunningham (1992) developed a successful work experience program for minority students that provided students with a personal awareness of careers, helped them relate current academic preparation to future requirements of careers, provided them with job-related experiences, and introduced them to effective job-seeking skills. This was accomplished through informational seminars, career luncheons with role models, graduates and representatives from business, job fairs, career tours, job shadowing, and individual counseling.

ASSESSMENT INSTRUMENTS

There are problems in using assessment instruments and tests with minority group members if tests have not been developed, validated, or normed for that group. The examiner needs to have had experience in testing the particular ethnic group. Fouad (1993) stated that culture plays a large role in vocational assessment, and counselors must be careful that the results of assessment do not perpetuate cultural stereotypes. Standard use of certain assessment instruments may be inappropriate for some racial/ethnic groups. Even when tests are translated into the native language of the client, the test still might have problems because certain questions or problems make no sense in their culture. Nazzaro (1979) identified some common problems relating to the assessment of ethnic minority clients:

- People from certain cultures fail to pay attention to the demands of a timed test.
- Individuals from other cultures may not be familiar with the content of the items, which may not make any sense in their culture.
- Test takers fear that low scores will dishonor their families.

Oakland (1982) pointed out that examiners need to recognize some potential features that might bias the results of the tests.

Language—The examinee's ability to understand and communicate in English is very important. Conventional measures requiring high levels of competence in English are not appropriate.

Test wiseness—The examiner cannot assume that the examinee can understand directions, go through proper test-taking procedures, and be involved and attentive during testing.

Motivation and anxiety—The examiner may find an examinee who refuses to cooperate or is too anxious. The examiner needs to consider the attitudinal characteristics of the examinees and attempt to get them to do their best.

Cultural differences—A minority examinee may come from a restricted environment in expectations, language experiences, formal and informal learning experiences, and upbringing. The examiner needs to know what the background of the examinee is and whether the test is appropriate.

There are many tests that are available in different languages. The Rokeach Value Survey is available in many languages including Czech, Chinese, French, German, Hebrew, Hungarian, Japanese, Lithuanian, Russian, Spanish, Swedish, and Vietnamese.

The *Self-Directed Search*, the *Sixteen Personality Factor Questionnaire*, the *General Aptitude Test Battery*, the *Strong Interest Inventory* and the *World of Work Inventory* have Spanish versions. There is a Vietnamese version of the *Self-Directed Search*.

There are also some achievement, intelligence, and general aptitude batteries available in languages other than English.

CAREER DEVELOPMENT NEEDS

A number of authors have identified these career development needs of minority groups members (Smith, 1983; Lee & Simmons, 1988; Drummond & Hansford, 1992; Medina & Drummond, 1993) and they are summarized in Figure 12.1.

* Need for systematic program that emphasizes self-awareness and career awareness to start in early childhood
* Need to use a broader model to look at skills and abilities, such as Gardner's types of intelligence
* Need to relate academic skills to everyday life and career fields
* Need to reinforce achievement in mathematics and quantitative thinking
* Need for greater occupational awareness
* Need for more accurate occupational information on the local, state, and national levels
* Need for good role models
* Need for role models in nontraditional and diversified fields
* Need for fewer environmental constructs that limit career development
* Need for fewer constraints that limit career development of minority members
* Need to be cognizant of current labor market trends
* Need to help minority groups to diversify their interests and choices

FIGURE 12.1
Career developmental needs of minority group members

COUNSELING IMMIGRANTS FOR EMPLOYMENT

Tinglin (1985) stated that the key issue for the counselor who works with immigrants is how the work fits into the broader context of the person's life situation. An overriding problem becomes the immediate demand to get the individual settled in the new country in a job. Employment provides the individual a link to the past and reduces the individual's feeling of uprootedness. The job also helps the individual feel accepted and provides economic basis for successful settlement. Tinglin identified some basic goal orientations for these clients: to help them gain employment in the same occupation in which they had been engaged in their country of origin and to help them identify an alternative or accessible occupation when their chances of pursuing the intended occupation are perceived to be very poor. Also there is a need to help them establish a career especially when they are entering the work force for the first time. Other possibilities are to help them in self-employment such as beginning a family business enterprise. Another goal is to help them gain occupational advancement and mobility in their job.

Tinglin identifies five stages of occupational development:

1.   Initial contact—The immigrant seeks information about the job market and suitable contact points for gaining entry.
2.   Exploration stage—The immigrant makes applications, seeks interviews, follows up leads, and the like.
3.   Transition stage—The immigrant does things such as occupational retraining or language training to facilitate reentry into a previously

practiced occupation, or seeks training to meet the requirements of a new area of interest.

4. Rooting—The immigrant goes through a settling-down process and develops a commitment to work in that particular occupational area.

5. Establishment—The immigrant achieves professional status and recognition within the chosen occupation.

The third dimension in Tinglin's model is relating needs, skills, and resources. He includes 17 areas in this area such as having basic understanding of the mainstream working environment, knowledge of the sources of information and help, how to access them, and the ability to conduct an effective job search. Minimum job skills and experience are necessary to meet the survival needs, and workers need to have skills or competencies in all the 17 areas to achieve any of the other goals such as occupational continuity, establishing first career, occupational change, career advancement, or self-employment. Westwood and Ishiyama (1991) identified barriers and challenges faced by immigrant minority clients, including handicaps in areas of language, racial prejudice, lack of cultural knowledge of finding a job, and interviewing techniques. They also have stress from the cultural adjustment to a new society and problems of racial and ethnic discrimination and intolerance. Minority immigrants are generally at a disadvantage because they lack the social networks necessary to connect them to a wide range of employment opportunities. Relatives and friends many times are not much help. This group is often not well informed and is also poorly connected to social networks or the job market. Language is an additional obstacle to gaining employment and understanding the information available on the job market. They find problems in marketing themselves. In some cultures the values prized are modesty and deference to others. The minority group members not only have to learn the process for job search but also have to sometimes make cultural adaptations. Problems arise in interview situations because the interviewer and immigrant generally come from different cultural perspectives. Miscommunication arises because each participant is not tuned into the other's frame of reference. The interviewers may be influenced by negative attitudes or stereotypes of the applicant. Language training needs to be made readily available for those not having proficiency in English. There may be built in barriers and discriminatory practices that limit the hiring of these minority groups. The minority group members also might have stereotype conceptions of America and Americans and have a hard time in adapting to the new culture.

COUNSELING INTERVENTIONS

Amundson and Borgen (1985, 1992) provided several counseling intervention approaches for working with immigrants. They pointed out that it is common for unemployed immigrants to be frustrated by their lack of knowledge of effective ways to find employment and their lack of resources to help them become more successful. Typically they will make statements such as, "At first I was full of hope. America seemed to be a land of opportunity and getting a job seemed to be a matter of trying hard." Or, "I looked everywhere, but I just opened my mouth and people moved away. Maybe my English is so bad they don't like me. They refuse to talk to me when I go to look for work" (p. 272).

Borgen and Amundson (1985) stated that successful interventions with unemployed immigrants require two factors: accessing their cultural group for psychological and social support and understanding successful job search strategies within the new culture. Westwood and Ishiyama (1991) pointed out that it is difficult for the counselor to know what are the most culturally appropriate interventions and approaches to use with immigrants.

Loganbill, Hardy, and Delworth (1982) proposed a system for classifying interventions that includes five categories:

- Facilitative interventions that form the basis of the counseling relationship and involve unconditional regard and warmth, respect, and empathy
- Confrontive interventions that involve a comparison of the person's functioning with the oral statements that are made
- Conceptual interventions that are designed to offer a cognitive understanding are important to a situation. The counselor provides relevant information and encourages the clients to use other perspectives when viewing their particular circumstances.
- Prescriptive interventions that provide the client with a specific plan of action to use in a particular situation when immediate action is required or when a client needs clear directions to lower anxiety
- Catalytic interventions that promote change or get things moving with a minimum of direct counselor involvement. The counselor is able to focus attention on key issues by assuming a low profile and using skillful questioning, probing, or exploring techniques.

The counselor needs to be familiar with the cultural group being counseled and have a high level of cultural awareness to provide effective use of the interventions.

Borgen and Amundson (1985) also pointed out that interventions can be categorized in several other ways such as the primary focus, that is, whether it is remedial, preventative, or developmental. Remedial interventions can be accomplished on a one-to-one basis in which the counselor helps in addressing the immediate problems of the individual. Preventative interventions involve counselors working with the environments of clients to help them alleviate potential problems. Developmental interventions require working with the clients in the development of their life skills and attitudes that are necessary for them to cope with future problems.

The target does not have to be limited to minority group members. The counselor works with minority group members and their employment problems. The counselor also works with potential employers and other helping professionals who are involved in working with culturally different workers to help them develop a greater awareness of culturally diverse workers. The counselor also works with the group on enhancing their career development and job-seeking and job-keeping skills and helps clients learn how to conduct themselves when interviewing with a prospective employer.

Borgen and Amundson (1985, 1992) suggested that the first phase of the counseling process ought to include conceptual and facilitating interventions. It is important at the start of the counseling session to make sure there is a shared understanding of what the sessions are about. The counselor has to gain an understanding of the cultural group of which the client has membership. The counselor has to spend time to gain this information before using it to work with the client toward the problem at hand. Clients have to merge previous cultural perspectives from their culture with those of the new culture. The counselor may use confrontation, conceptual, and prescriptive interventions.

Clients have to understand the limits of the counseling and be encouraged to be creative and persistent in their job-search strategies by learning effective job-seeking techniques. The clients need to practice their job-seeking skills before trying them out in real-life situations. Counselors may find that they have to do some direct teaching and provide supervised practice. The clients need to have support services and have debriefings after they get some feedback from employers. Counselors need to follow up on their clients systematically.

USE OF JOB-SEARCH SUPPORT GROUPS

The use of job-search support groups is a valuable part of the intervention process. A cohesive group helps the minority group members in a variety of ways. The members help each other understand other people's point of view, and can share concerns and ideas with other clients who face similar problems and learn from the interaction. Members can be aided in their problem solving because they have ideas from others in the group on how they approached, handled, or solved a similar problem. They grow because they receive support and encouragement from the others in the group and gain in knowledge and relevant information. Counselors have to feel competent and at ease with a crosscultural group. They need to develop a broader cultural awareness and have the ability to facilitate the group process by taking into consideration the particular cultural values of the minority group members. Culturally homogeneous groups provide a better environment for trust and support for most members. Heterogeneous groups provide the counselor with an excellent opportunity to confront and challenge the group members about how they see their situations. Nevertheless, despite many suggestions on interventions with minority populations, Meier (1992) concluded that there has been little research to evaluate the effectiveness of these interventions.

DOUBLE MINORITY-STATUS CLIENTS

A small percentage of clients has a double minority status, such as being physically disabled and also a member of a minority group. People not only have developed attitudes toward the group membership but also about disabled individuals. Combined negative images concerning poverty, gender, and minority issues can create problems. Counselors are faced with working with clients who have major inferiority and identity problems. Different cultural groups will define disability differently, and clients feel that the counselor does not understand them from two perspectives: the cultural group and the disability. Clients also have trouble understanding themselves because they are receiving inconsistent messages both from the dominant group and their own group and usually have other compounding problems such as language differences between them and counselors, different cultural values of the middle-class majority culture, and the culture-bound definitions of what are normal or abnormal.

Westwood and Vargo (1985) suggested that the first step is to make sure that the client knows what the counselor's role is. Many people have had minimal contact with counselors and have little information on what a counselor does. The counselor needs to introduce and explain the role of counseling to the new client before any rapport can be established. In order to do so, the counselor has to be viewed as knowledgeable about the clients' cultural groups and about their various types of physical disabilities. Counselors need to be aware of their attitudes toward the minority group and their attitude toward disabilities so that they can maintain objectivity and be effective in helping the client.

The counselor has to understand the degree of acculturation the client has made to the dominant culture and to what degree the identity with the minority group remains. Counselors need to understand the clients' own views of their disabilities and the degree of support the individuals have from family and friends.

Assessment becomes a problem because many people are not fluent in English and many of the assessment tests are not valid. Also their disability may interfere with their performance and make vocational assessment difficult. The clients' choices are limited because of lowered expectations based on minority group membership and the functional limitations of the disability.

DEVELOPING MULTICULTURAL AWARENESS

Dana (1993) advocated that counselors not only need to be culturally sensitive but also culturally competent. Sensitivity starts with awareness of other cultures based on knowledge and firsthand experience. Cultural competence begins with the acknowledgment and acceptance of cultural difference. Harris and Moran (1991) indicated that it is important for professionals to learn within the context of each culture how to convey respect, personalize knowledge, show empathy, be nonjudgmental, develop role flexibility, demonstrate reciprocal concern, develop tolerance for ambiguity, and how individuals process knowledge. Wigglesworth (1991) pointed out that these characteristics are important for not only counselors but also for managers, teachers, other employees, and students. It is important to be aware of the cultural diversity in the workplace, have knowledge of the culture of others, and have the ability to apply the knowledge and insights of other cultures into our profession. In order to accomplish this, we have to have an awareness of our own values and value system.

Stone (1984) advocated that counselors use these multicultural competency strategies and suggestions to increase their awareness, sensitivity, and knowledge of ethnic cultural groups:

- Learn all you can about multiethnic and multicultural concepts such as ethnic groups, race, minority, culture
- Make a study of onomastics or surnames
- Be cognizant of ethnic and cultural demographics such as statistical data regarding population, income, employment, education, fertility, and mortality rates
- Learn about the different predominant ethnic religions
- Study and experience ethnic folkways in terms of food, dress, dance, medicine, folklore, and folk music
- Study literature, music, art, dance, history, and drama by authors of ethnic cultures
- Learn about the significant ethnic, cultural, and historical dates, events, and holidays
- Participate in growth and encounter experiences with members from different ethnic groups
- Demonstrate multicultural competencies in group and individual counseling situations

MULTIETHNIC STAGES OF DEVELOPMENT

Banks (1979) stated that individuals working with ethnic groups should be aware of the stages of ethnicity in order to ensure greater success with multiethnic clients who possess multicultural backgrounds. The five stages are: ethnic psychological captivity, ethnic encapsulation, ethnic identity, biethnicity, and multiethnicity. Jones (1985) modified the five phases in which phase one is characterized by ethnically dominated behavior whereby the individual avoids other ethnic cultures whenever possible. Stage five is characterized by a more transcendent worldview. Individuals see themselves as members of the ethnic groups of the world, sharing a common culture as well as a unique culture. Atkinson, Morten, and Sue (1989) developed a five-stage model that includes a conformity stage, dissonance stage, resistance and immersion stage, introspection stage, and synergetic articulation and awareness stage.

In the conformity stage, the minority member is self-deprecating and prefers to identify with the dominant cultural values. In the synergetic stage the individual accepts his or her cultural identity and develops selective appreciations of the dominant culture.

SUMMARY

Our society is characterized by cultural heterogeneity. Minority groups will become the majority group in the next century. Career counselors need to recognize the career development needs of minority group members and the types of interventions that are successful in working with these groups. Counselors need not only to be culturally sensitive but also culturally competent. Sensitivity begins with the awareness of other cultures based on firsthand knowledge and experience. Cultural competence begins with the acknowledgment and acceptance of cultural differences. Swanson (1993) summarized the main chapter themes well and states that a multicultural perspective is a vital viewpoint because of the more diversified career counseling clientele we have and the changing demographics in our country. She sees the need for a heightened awareness of the importance culture plays in career choice and the career counseling relationship.

REVIEW QUESTIONS

1. What are some of the important problems minority group members face in our society today?
2. Who constitutes minority groups? In what ways can we classify groups?
3. Which are the major minority groups in the United States? What are some of the unique problems of each group?
4. Are career development theories inappropriate and unreal for minority groups? Why or why not?
5. How can we increase the career knowledge and aspirations of minority group members?
6. What are some of the important career development needs of minority group members?
7. Who are double minority-status group members? What can be done to help these individuals?
8. How can counselors develop greater multicultural awareness, sensitivity, and knowledge?
9. What are some of the aspects involved in using assessment instruments with minority group members?
10. What do you know about the minority groups in your community?

SUGGESTED ACTIVITIES

1. Interview career counselors who work with minority group members. Find out what problems they have in working with different groups and the intervention strategies they find effective.
2. Conduct a study on an ethnic or minority group. Review their religions, literature, music, art, and the like. Study the demographic sta-

tistics on the group. Learn about their customs, food preferences, clothing styles, and the like. Read what the literature says about working with this group.

3. Participate in a growth or encounter experience with a person from an ethnic group or minority group or a recent immigrant. Describe your experiences.

4. Interview several minority group members and find out about their career histories. Report on how this information fits into current career development theories.

5. Make a file on index cards of career assessment instruments appropriate for different minority groups.

6. Survey career choices of students in the junior high, senior high, or community college. Compare the choices by ethnic or minority group membership. Write a report of the results from your study.

CASE STUDY

A Job for Eva

Name: Eva Goode
Current occupation: Vehicle loader
Time at current job: 6 months
Previous jobs or occupations: Electronics tech, carpenter,
    antiques dealer, framer, engineering assistant
Age: 31
Education: B.Ed. Vocational Education
Holland Code: RAI
Myers-Briggs Type: ISTP
Values Scale: High values—creativity, way of life, personal development, economic returns. Low values—risk, physical activity, social relations, social interaction, working conditions

On the Adult Career Concerns Inventory, Eva's highest scores were on the three scales of the exploration stage: crystallization, specification, and implementation, all 5.0 scores. On the establishment stage she averaged 4.5. On the maintenance stage, she was greatly concerned with keeping up with new knowledge, equipment, and methods in her field, and having refresher training to keep up. The disengagement stage items were all rated of none or little concern.

Eva scored the following on the Salience Inventory:

Participation
   High: working
   Moderate: studying, community service
   Low: family, leisure

Commitment:
 High: leisure, home and family, studying
 Moderate: community service
 Low: working

Value expectation
 High: home and family, leisure
 Moderate: community service, studying
 Low: working

On the Job Satisfaction Scale, Eva rated 15 of the 20 items "1," *not satisfied.* She circled "dissatisfied" to the question about her overall career progress to date. She checked that she was considering a new field and was trying to get started in it. She checked "yes" on the following items on the Job Involvement Scale:

Most things in life are more important than my work.
I am so involved in my work that it is hard for me to take vacations.
Most of my life goals are not job related.
I feel depressed when I fail at something connected with my job.
I'll stay overtime to finish a task, even though I'm not paid for it.
Sometimes I'd like to kick myself for the mistakes I've made in my work.

Case Questions
1. What approach would you use to counsel Eva if she were African American? Latino? Asian American? Native American? Would they be different?
2. How would you interpret the scores to the individual?
3. Do you feel the assessment instruments and techniques would be valid for each of the four groups mentioned in question one?
4. How would you summarize the assessment data in language that the client could understand?
5. What types of approaches, interventions, and the like would you use to help Eva?

SUGGESTED READINGS

Atkinson, D. R., Morten, G., & Sue, D. W. (1989). *Counseling American minorities: A cross cultural perspective* (3rd. ed). Dubuque, IA: William C. Brown.

The authors discuss why counselors should understand a crosscultural perspective. They have a series of chapters on the American Indian client, the Asian-American client, the African-American client, and the Latino client.

Dana, R. H. (1993). *Multicultural assessment perspectives for professional psychology.* Needham Heights, MA: Allyn and Bacon.

The goal of the book is to stimulate the awareness of helping professions of the four major cultural/minority groups in America and provide the tools necessary to develop cultural acceptance.

PART

THE NATURE OF CAREER INFORMATION

13

CAREER INFORMATION SOURCES

I ndividuals in a rapidly changing society need career and occupational information to guide their career planning. They have not had the experience or
opportunity to learn about this information through other ways and they
may want to know where specific programs are located or what schools have a
major in a given discipline. They may have scored high on a certain occupation
scale on an interest test and have no idea what people in this occupation do.
Information about careers and occupations and various education programs
can help individuals at any stage of development in their career and educational decision making.

Counselors and career development specialists also need to be alert and
knowledgeable about educational, career, and occupational information, and
not only need to know the sources but also the techniques of getting the information they need. Counselors as well as their clients may need local, regional,
state, national, or international information. They may have a good grasp on
local school and college programs, but have little knowledge of other educational opportunities in the state or region. In addition, counselors may know
the job opportunities in their local community but not in the state.

In this information age we are bombarded with myriad information in all
types of forms. The question arises, How accurate and reliable is the information? Is it biased? Is it appropriate for the use we want to make of it?

Career information is viewed by career theorists as an important variable
in the process of career development. Yet many people do not know where to
find the information they need. Also, much of the material is unrealistic,
poorly organized, or just plain dull. Little research is found in the literature on
the effectiveness of the different types of information sources in career decision
making. We do know that direct experience through an apprenticeship or
internship experience has more direct impact on a person's career decision
making than reading an occupational monograph.

LEARNING OBJECTIVES

After reading the chapter, you should be able to do the following:

- Identify the major information sources in career counseling and discuss their strengths and limitations
- List and describe the major types of information sources available to helping professionals
- Locate, select, and evaluate the information sources available on a given career or occupational field
- Design a plan to set up staff and maintain a career resource center
- Design a professional continuing education plan to maintain skills about the information sources needed to be an effective career counselor

CAREER COUNSELING MODEL

A six-stage process is proposed to evaluate career counseling and information sources. The first step is to identify the goals and objectives for the information. The question to be asked is, Why is the information needed? The information might be necessary for clients to have in order to investigate a certain occupation or to identify what schools offer training in a given field.

The second step is to identify who needs the information. Is the information for an individual or group? What are the characteristics such as educational level, learning style, and the like of the individual or the group who is going to use the information?

The third step is to consider the context of where the information is going to be used. The information could be used in a group session as exercises or information could be used in a one-on-one counseling session. The counselor could also be ordering materials for a library or a resource center. The counselor might use the information for planned purposes, or the information might just be available for clients who might be interested and choose the information source by chance or because it is the only source available. Individuals might get the information from a bookstore or some agency on their own.

The fourth stage of the model is the type of format. Is the information to be used in printed format, video, computer-assisted or some other type of format. The question is, What type of format would be most appropriate for the stage of career development and the learning type of the individual? What type of format is most appropriate for the developmental level and needs and learning style of the individual?

The fifth stage of the model focuses on the cost of the information. Is the information free or is there a fee? Many sources of information from professional organizations or governmental sources are free or at a minimum cost and other sources vary in cost. For example, some of the job-shadowing and internship types of programs are high in the time involved but not costly for the client involved. Some types of simulated experiences cost a considerable amount of money.

The sixth stage of the model is evaluation, which is tied to each of the previous steps of the program. The counselor needs to evaluate whether the goals set for using the information were appropriate. The clients must evaluate whether the information source provided the information they needed. The counselor has to determine that the right type of delivery approach was used to work with the client and that the information was provided in the best setting.

In a school career guidance program there might be a formal class and a career resource center available. In an outplacement counseling program, there would be workshops on career and occupational information for the workers, but the workers might have access to information without any formalized introduction to the sources. The type of individual and the developmental needs of the individual have to be taken into consideration in selecting the best approach. Also, cost has to be considered because public/private schools and nonprofit organizations have tight budgets and limited resources. Computer hardware and career guidance software might take time to acquire and are expensive.

It is important to evaluate the goals and objectives and determine whether the information source chosen is appropriate for the purpose. It is also important to determine whether the information source is appropriate for the individual or individuals using it. Is the source appropriate for group situations or just for one-to-one situations? The next important consideration is whether the information source is practical. It may be theoretically sound, but may be too expensive, too time consuming, may demand computer equipment that is not available, or there may not be enough computer terminals or stations to have more than one individual work at a time.

The last aspect of the model is to evaluate the evaluation procedures. Evaluation should be consistent and continuous. Clients or individuals using the materials must evaluate them as well as the counselors selecting them. The arrangement of the materials in a career resource center must also be evaluated.

INDIVIDUAL LEARNING STYLES

There are a number of different ways of conceptualizing learning style. Keefe and Monk (1988) defined learning style as

> the composite of characteristic cognitive, affective, and physiological factors that serve as relatively stable indicators of how a learner perceives, interacts with, and responds to the learning environment. It is demonstrated in that pattern of behavior and performance by which an individual approaches educational experiences. (p. 3)

Cognitive styles relate to how individuals process information. In selecting an information source, it is important to take into consideration how a person prefers to perceive, think, and remember the information. If the source used does not correlate with the individual's processing habits, will the information really be assimilated?

Affective styles relate to the approaches that motivate the individual and relate to the factors such as attention, expectancy, and incentives. Griggs (1991) broke the emotional factors into four components: motivation, persistence, responsibility, and structure. In selecting information sources counselors must take into consideration the sources that motivate the individual to act on and use the information. Some types of information sources may just turn off the individual and be ineffective, for example, providing print material to an individual who is more of a visual or auditory learner. The career information impact analysis in Figure 13.1 provides the career counselor directions for using different modes of career information with clients.

Physiological styles refer to the biologically based modes of responses that are partly based on personal nutrition, health, sex-role differences, and accustomed reaction to the physical environment. Partially, the structure of the context in which the information is located and used will have an effect. The loca-

Extent of	Classifications	
10	On-the-job tryout: part-time, summer jobs, work-study programs	Provides direct contact with actual work situations
9	Direct exploratory experience: work samples, work evaluation tasks	
8	Direct observation: visits to work settings	
7	Synthetically created work environ-ments: combination of stimuli and environmental manipulations, virtual reality	Simulation of work settings and occupational roles
6	Simulated situations: career games, role-playing	
5	Interviews with workers/experts: sessions with workers and personnel directors, mentors at the work site or during career days	Information is processed by and adapted to the needs of the individual.
4	Computer Career Guidance Systems: computer systems that store, retrieve, and process occupational data in response to individual requests	
3	Text materials: self-help books, guided workbooks	
2	Media: videos, films, slides, audio-tapes	Information is in fixed format, and is designed for general use.
1	Printed materials: books, pamphlets, career biographies, and so on	

FIGURE 13.1
Career information impact analysis

tion of the career resource center and how it is structured might encourage the use by some individuals and discourage it by others.

Some clients are high in the visual perceptual style of information process-ing and have a bias for receiving information in visual, pictorial, or graphic rep-resentations of experience. Others are high in auditory perceptual styles and like to listen to others talk about experiences. The former individuals prefer their information through videos, field trips, pictures, or cartoon types of presenta-tion. The latter prefer their information through tapes, interview situations, group discussions, lectures, and the like.

Others are high on emotive perceptual modes and respond to new informa-tion in terms of feelings. These individuals react initially to the physiological or emotional tone of an experience. These individuals are receptive to information from inspirational and motivational tapes. They probably enjoy more physical involvement in the process and the environment should be conducive to them to learn.

Gregorc (1988) identified four types of learning styles that are primarily cognitively oriented: cognitive sequential, abstract sequential, abstract random, and concrete random. Concrete sequential individuals are task oriented, prefer details, are organized, and like to have the facts. They prefer hands-on approaches, workbooks, data-gathering activities, how-to-projects, and computer exercises.

Abstract sequential individuals are analytical, theoretical, intellectual, and prefer convergent thinking. They prefer to acquire their information through conventional means such as lecture and text material.

Abstract random individuals are affective oriented and view themselves as imaginative, flexible, emotional, and holistic in approach. They prefer group work, media presentations, personalized examples, and role-playing.

Concrete random individuals are independent and divergent thinkers, like to experiment, and do not mind taking risks. They prefer simulations, games, and problem-solving situations. They like to brainstorm and find alternatives.

TYPES OF CAREER DECISION INFORMATION

There are a variety of format types through which career information is presented.

Printed Format

The most common format of career decision information is in printed form. There are all types of printed material, such as pamphlets and brochures, periodicals, journals, magazines, books and encyclopedias.

Audiovisuals

A second major category is audiovisuals, such as movies, slides, and tapes. There are a wide variety of commercially produced as well as noncommercially produced audiovisual materials available. Many are free or inexpensive, especially those produced by professional organizations to provide orientation to individuals about career opportunities in a specific field.

Computer-Based Systems

A third major source of information is the computer-based systems such as Guidance Information System, Discover, CHOICES, and SIGI. Computer uses in career counseling is discussed in more detail in Chapter 14. There are numerous computerized systems, varying from statewide network systems to systems on disks for personal use.

People

People are an important source of career and educational information. Most schools and training programs have advisors who are available to explain the program, the requirements for entry, the cost, the time commitment, the jobs available for those completing the program, and related information. Human resource directors are also an important source of information about the types of jobs available within an organization and the criteria used for hiring. Workers in specific career fields are an invaluable source to find out about the type of work they do and their perception of the field as a potential career opportunity for the interviewer. State employment counselors and career counselors in private or public organizations also are important sources of information on the current job situation.

For counselors wanting to obtain additional career information, other counselors are an important source of information. Counselors need to continually network with professionals in their field as well as professionals in business, industry, education, and training. Publishers representatives can provide leads on new information in many fields. Career fairs and job fairs are conducted by most high schools, junior colleges, colleges, and universities. The business/industry plant visitation guide is one process for developing contacts with human resource directors (see Figure 13.2).

Simulation

Simulation exercises are another type of source of information that permits a more interactive approach. Many types of simulated approaches are available today in the form of computer games on certain types of jobs and career fields to in-basket techniques and games. The simulation allows an individual some first-hand opportunities to see what some of the job parameters and demands are. Games are appropriate for adolescents beginning their career exploration to acquire preliminary exploration of the career field. There are also simulations valuable for workers at other stages of career development. For example, the American Banking Association has a simulation exercise in which an individual can manage a bank for a week.

Realistic Job Preview

Many people have a better idea about whether they would consider a job in a given company or organization if they had an opportunity to observe individuals

The following questions are intended to serve as a guide for a visit to a business or an industry in which you focus on some of the "human" aspects of work. As you visit these places, take a look at the psychological impact of the work organization on the worker and the workers' product. Write your observations of and reactions to the business or industry, using the following questions merely as a frame of reference.

About the Organization
1. What is the main function of the business or industry?
2. How is the general staff organized?
3. How many levels and what kinds of jobs are represented?
4. How many employees are in the organization? How many males, females, minorities? What is the company doing to achieve equal opportunity for minorities and women?
5. What kinds of training are required for the jobs represented?
6. What are some of the main concerns of management (productivity, equal employment, absenteeism, turnover, etc.)?
7. How democratic or authoritarian is the organization? To what extent are workers at all levels involved in decision making?
8. Is the business/industry unionized? What impact does the union have?
9. What are the communication patterns? What does morale appear to be like in the company?
10. What kinds of job-enrichment programs have been developed?

Questions of Workers
1. What do you like about this work setting?
2. What is satisfying about your job? What about the job is stressful? Dissatisfying?
3. What kind of life-style is associated with this job (overtime, evening work, time for leisure, travel, set hours, own boss, etc.)?
4. Do you get most of your satisfactions off or on the job?
5. What kinds of affiliations do you have in connection with this job?
6. To what extent is this kind of work the kind of thing you like to do?
7. Do you see this work as a lifelong one or as a stepping stone to some other job or occupation? What are the opportunities for advancement on this job or in this company?
8. To what extent does this occupation provide the economic resources for you to live the kind of life you like?
9. Did you plan for this kind of work or did you get it by chance?
10. From whom did you get help in planning or preparing for this field?
11. If you were to start over, would you choose the same kind of work? If not, what kind of work would you most like to do?
(Add your own questions here.)
12.
13.

FIGURE 13.2
Business-industry visitation guide

on the job. Field trips, job shadowing, and other similar procedures provide the individual a chance to see firsthand what is involved in a given job. There are a number of techniques that can be used to provide additional experience for individuals who want more of a feel of what the job is like, such as cooperative work experience programs and other types of on-the-job training experiences. Many courses and training programs involve laboratory experiences or a field component. Many individuals learn through doing whether they like some types of jobs or not. There is no substitute for firsthand experience. Companies often feel this way, also. For example, someone interested in a potential management position in a grocery chain has to go through training as a stock boy, bagger, worker in produce area, clerk in the fish counter, butcher, cashier, a baker, frozen food and dairy custodian, and personnel. Working for a temporary employment agency also provides firsthand experiences in a number of different career fields.

Counselors can use many of the previously mentioned steps to gain the information they need to be more effective counselors. They should interview employers in the areas to find out what jobs are available and what the entry requirements. Community surveys are a valuable way to gain specific information about possible openings.

SOURCES OF INFORMATION

There are many sources of career and educational information available. Counselors need to know how to access local, regional, national, and even international sources. One way to become more familiar with local sources is to design and implement a community survey. Counselors must have firsthand information on the cost, time of training, financial aid available, time programs are offered, entry requirements, and contact person for the educational opportunities available and the type of anticipated openings in different jobs and occupational fields. Sometimes small businesses are neglected and only large employers are assessed by career counselors. We recommend a file be created of small businesses within a 25-mile radius and the type of entry-level jobs for high school graduates in the specific firms.

School counselors should conduct a needs assessment of their students to investigate what their educational and career plans are in relation to long-range life planning. Counselors can compare the aspirations of the students to the local labor market information. If they find discrepancies, this information might be valuable to use in workshops for the students or for group counseling sessions to help students get a broader picture of the possibilities in other areas, nontraditional career fields, and the like.

State departments of labor, state manpower commissions, as well as the U.S. Department of Labor provide projection of needs in all occupational areas for a 5- to 10-year period. In addition, current census data provide information on employment trends.

Counselors also may be interested in following up their graduates or their clients who have gone through career counseling to find out what they currently are doing. Graduates or previous clients often are willing to serve as a source of information and to talk with individuals who might be considering their field as a possible career field. Graduates of local schools and training programs are often willing to help individuals find placement and are willing to be interviewed, observed, and even provide limited hands-on experiences for a client or student.

Major Federal Sources

The U.S. Department of Labor is the major source of labor market information. The Bureau of Labor Statistics and the Employment and Training Administration are the two components of the bureau that provide information sources most often used by career and employment counselors. The Bureau of Labor Statistics publishes the *Occupational Outlook Handbook,* the *Occupational Outlook Quarterly,* the *Occupational Projections and Training Data,* the *Occupational Employment Statistics Survey Operations Manual* and the *Occupational Employment Statistics Dictionary of Occupations.*

The Employment and Training Administration section of the U.S. Department of Labor publishes the *Dictionary of Occupational Titles,* the *Guide for Occupational Exploration,* and *Selected Characteristics of Occupations Defined in the Dictionary of Occupational Titles.*

Other publications that might have value to career and employment counselors are the *Military Career Guide: Employment and Training Opportunities in the Military,* published by the U.S. Department of Defense division on Manpower Installations and Logistics. They also print a volume entitled *Military Occupational and Training Data.*

The U.S. Department of Commerce, International Trade Administration publishes the *U.S. Industrial Outlook,* a valuable source for projected growth. The Bureau of Census has publications such as *U.S. Census of Population, 1990: Alphabetical Index of Occupations and Industries* and *U.S. Census of Population, 1990: Classified Index of Industries and Occupations.*

The U.S. Department of Labor also provides a wide variety of special reports on labor market information, data on youths, women, veterans, and minority group members, and other information on employment and unemployment. The *Occupational Outlook Quarterly* includes articles on these topics, too.

An important federal agency that provides guidance to each states' career, occupational, and labor market information is the National Occupational Information Coordinating Committee (NOICC). NOICC facilitates coordination among the various agencies that produce and use occupational information and provides funds and assistance to the states for developing systems of using and disseminating the career information. NOICC works with the Bureau of Labor Statistics and the Employment and Training Administration of the U.S. Department of Labor, the National Center for Educational Statistics, the Office of Vocational and Adult Education, the Rehabilitation Services Administration, Office of Bilingual Education and Minority Language Affairs of the U.S. Department of Education as well as with the U.S. Departments of Defense, Agriculture, and Commerce.

Some of the major governmental publications are listed and summarized in Figure 13.3.

Source:
  Occupational Outlook Handbook (Bureau of Labor Statistics, U.S. Department of Labor)
Description:
  Contains detailed information on about 200 occupations including descriptions on working conditions, employment, training, other qualifications, advancement, job outlook, earnings, and related occupations
Counseling Uses:
  Good readable reference source for clients and counselors

Source:
  Occupational Outlook Quarterly (Bureau of Labor Statistics, U.S. Department of Labor)
Description:
  Contains articles on new occupations, job and labor market, training opportunities, and studies completed by Bureau of Labor Statistics
Counseling Uses:
  Good readable reference source for clients and counselors

Source:
  U.S. Industrial Outlook (U.S. Department of Commerce)
Description:
  Contains reviews and forecasts as well as current situations for 250 industries
Counseling Uses:
  Excellent source for counselor in identifying growth and nongrowth industries and understanding trends in industry

Source:
  Military Career Guide: Employment and training opportunities in the Department of Defense
Description:
  Contains 134 clusters of occupations common to the Army, Navy, Air Force, Marine Corps, and Coast Guard, and describes typical work tasks, work environment, physical demands, training, and civilian counterpart
Counseling Uses:
  Good guide for counselors and clients to explore career fields within the military services

Source:
  Dictionary of Occupational Titles (DOT) (U.S. Department of Labor)
Description:
  Contains definitions and classifications for about 20,000 occupations using a nine-digit code number
Counseling Uses:
  Good source for counselors on types of tasks, job functions, and groups of related jobs

Source:
  Vocational Preparation and Occupations (U.S. Department of Education)
Description:
  Contains explanation of classification systems and crosswalk tables for eight vocational areas
Counseling Uses:
  Good source for counselors and students to identify which programs to enroll in and which occupational skills to acquire

FIGURE 13.3
Major governmental career information sources

Nongovernmental Sources

A number of nongovernmental agencies, professional organizations, private organizations, and foundations develop and disseminate career information. Some of the commercial firms that research and publish labor market information are the Wharton Econometric Forecasting Associates, Merrill Lynch, Chase, and Data Resources, Inc. The U.S. Chamber of Commerce also disseminates information that is of value to the career counselor. Professional organizations in engineering, the sciences, and social sciences also publish useful information.

State Sources

Labor market information is also produced by federal agencies for each state. The reports available focus on historical, current, and projected information on employment, unemployment, and occupational trends. The reports focus on the make-up of the labor market and include statistics on the characteristics of those unemployed, the economically disadvantaged, and special groups. Information is available on turnover and wages. The occupational labor market information includes information on the characteristics of occupations and jobs and the current and projected labor supply as well as information on salaries and fringe benefits. Affirmative action updates contain statistics on women and minorities in the work force and general population.

All states have state occupational information coordinating committees (SOICC), which are made up usually of representatives from the state employment security agency, state employment and training council, vocational rehabilitation, economic developmental, education and human services, and corrections. These committees are charged with assimilating the job market trends and information needed by economic planners and legislatures. Another group within SOICC is charged with designing and implementing a state career information delivery system (CIDS). The goals of the state system are to provide current, accurate, and locally relevant occupational, career, and labor market information and to facilitate transition from school to work, or from one job to another job, or from home to work.

CIDS have five objectives for the system (National Occupational Information Coordinating Committee, 1990):

1.   To help students and clients learn about the various career opportunities available to them now and in the future
2.   To help those entering the work force develop an awareness of occupations they would find satisfying
3.   To encourage adolescents and adults to seek out career information on their own
4.   To provide students and clients information about the educational and training opportunities available for careers or jobs that interest them

5.   To be a resource base for career education, career and employment counseling, employment and training, and educational decision making

Most include in their data base occupational and education information specific to their state, and some systems include regional and national information. Military files are also a part of almost all of the systems. Besides delivering local, state, and national career information to counselors and users, they are able to sort and select occupations according to variables identified by students and clients. Most systems use on-line computer data bases that are also available for the microcomputer. Many of the systems also include financial aid information. The state CIDS are used by a wide variety of users, such as secondary schools, vocational and technical schools, colleges and universities, rehabilitation centers, job service offices, libraries, correctional facilities, and state and federal employment training programs.

In addition to the computer data bases, some states produce information in the form of booklets, microfiche, and needlesort.

Commercial Publishers

Many publishers publish print materials for use in career counseling and career education programs. The number of publishers and publications in this field has dramatically increased since the 1970s. At the 1993 American Counseling Association's annual meeting, over half of the exhibitors displayed career materials that they are trying to market. A representative list of publishers is included in appendix B of the text with a brief annotation of the types of materials available.

There are a wide variety of types of printed materials available from the publishers such as the following:

1.   Biographies and autobiographies—These works present a life history of successful people in given fields. They present the problems and pitfalls, as well as the personal qualities, and education and preparation necessary to be in the career field.
2.   Fiction or novels about people in career fields—These works present individuals in different roles, describe the duties and preparation necessary, and relate the values and working environment deemed important.
3.   Career encyclopedias and books about careers in specific professions, businesses, and industry as well as in career clusters—These sources usually describe the entry requirements, starting salaries, geographic location of jobs, chances for advancement, and job prospects in the immediate future and 5 to 10 years from now. There are all types of books available on topics such as nontraditional jobs, jobs for women, high-paying jobs, high-risk jobs, and so on.
4.   Directories—There are all types of directories available: trade schools, colleges, graduate schools, for example, Barron's *A profile of American colleges.*

5.   How-to books—There are books on how to write your resume, how to interview for a job, how to be assertive, and how to conduct one's own job search.

Professional Organizations

Many professional organizations publish and distribute career and educational information; for example, the American Psychological Association prints *Graduate Study in Psychology*. Professional organizations also sponsor clubs for high school and college students and offer discounted rates on their publications. Counselors will find these publications useful and will be able to identify the programs that are accredited by professional associations. Counselors and clients also need to be aware of the possibilities that the information might be biased, presenting the glamorous side of the career and not mentioning the negative features. Other materials may tend to present the negative side of work and the restrictions in order to discourage individuals from entering the field.

Industries and Businesses

Industries and businesses publish a considerable amount of printed materials. Many of these publications are used as recruiting tools and emphasize the benefits and values of selecting a career within a certain business or industry. Even some of the promotional materials and annual reports have useful information that might help individuals gain some awareness and understanding of the career possibilities within these organizations. A caution: Counselors should seek to verify the career information presented to ensure accuracy.

Educational and Training Institutions

Most educational and training organizations have myriad publications from general brochures on types of programs, entry requirement, costs, whom to contact, and how to apply to specific brochures and booklets or catalogs on specific programs and training fields. Trade schools, technical schools, and specific community college and university programs often include a section on the types of jobs graduates of their programs can anticipate.

Periodicals

A number of professional journals as well as popular periodicals focus on career development and career education. Some of the journals are sponsored by divisions of major professional organizations such as the American Counseling Association and the American Psychological Association.

The following journals were cited in Jepson's (1992) review of career counseling and development:

American Journal of Sociology
Applied Psychology: An International Review
Career Development Quarterly
The Counseling Psychologist
Educational and Psychological Measurement
Journal of Applied Psychology
Journal of Applied Social Psychology
Journal of Career Development
Journal of College Placement
Journal of College Student Personnel
Journal of Counseling and Development
Journal of Counseling Psychology
Journal of Employment Counseling
Journal of Genetic Psychology
Journal of Marriage and the Family
Journal of Multicultural Counseling and Development
Journal of Occupational Behavior
Journal of Occupational Psychology
Journal of Vocational Behavior
Measurement and Evaluation in Counseling and Development
Psychological Reports
Psychology of Women Quarterly
School Counselors
Sex Roles
Work and Occupations

In addition to these widely cited journals, some of the governmental periodicals include *Monthly Labor Review* (U.S. Department of Labor), *Occupational Outlook Quarterly* (U.S. Department of Labor), and *American Education* (U.S. Department of Education). Some of the more popular magazines include *Career World*, *Glamour*, *Mademoiselle*, *Seventeen*, and *Reader's Digest*.

It is extremely important that career counselors establish a consistent professional development plan that includes regular reading, attendance at career seminars, and continuing education.

Bibliographies and Indexes

Numerous bibliographies and indexes help counselors keep abreast with the many materials available. Some are published by professional organizations such as the National Vocational Guidance Association, others by public service organizations such as the B'nai B'rith Career and Counseling Service, and others by commercial publishers, such as Chronicle Guidance Publications.

The ERIC Counseling and Personnel Services Clearinghouse (CAPS) publishes a number of valuable resources:

Periodicals

Career Development
Programs and Practices
Counseling for Career Change
Career Resource Centers
Mid-career Change
An Overview of Counseling Practices and Programs
Educational Advising and Vocational Choice
Vocational Counseling of Disadvantaged Students

Monographs

Gysbers, N. C. (1987). *Career development today: An overview.*
Knowdell, R. L., McDaniels, C., Hesser, A., & Watz, G. R. (1983). *Outplacement counseling.*
Pyle, K. R. (1986). *Group career counseling: Principles and practices.*

They also publish *Spotlight,* a 4″ by 9″ information brief on important topics. These provide a brief synopsis of the topic and issues and a list of three to five references.

One such *Spotlight* is "Computer-Assisted Career Guidance Systems." They also have *Highlights,* an 8½″ by 11″ sheet printed front and back. For example, one fact sheet is entitled "Selecting a College: A Checklist Approach." The following titles indicate what kinds of topics CAPS covers:

"Starting with a List of Objectives"
"Using Computer Programs and Guidebooks"
"Acquiring More Information"
      "College Catalogues"
      "College Representatives"
      "College Visits"
      "College Students, Faculty, or Recent Alumni"
      "High School Counselors"
      "Parents and Friends"
      "College Fairs/College Nights"
      "Commercial Guidebooks"
"Applying for Admission"
      "Application Fee"
      "Academic Records"
      "Admission Test Scores"
      "Letters of Recommendation"
      "Essay"
"Responding to Admission Offers"
"In Summary"
"Resource Documents"

Saterstrom, M. H. (Ed.). (1990). *Educators' Guide to Guidance and Education Materials.* Randolph, WI: Educators Progress Services is a volume listing free materials, printed and audiovisual, available to counselors and educators and is updated each year.

Career Index. (1990). Moravia, NY: Chronicle Guidance Service is an annual compilation of occupational and educational materials from a number of different organizations.

Counselor's Information Service. Washington, DC: B'nai B'rith

The counseling information review of Career and Counseling Services publishes a newsletter that contains an annotated bibliography of current literature on educational and vocational guidance. Areas on special populations such as rehabilitation, disability counseling, aging, and adult education receive attention.

Educational Information

Many sources of educational information are available in most schools, public libraries, universities, and college career centers. Some occupations require specific courses or training, and other areas require just general preparation, so the training or education requirements are not always spelled out in the occupational literature. There are many guides published annually to different types of secondary preparation: from apprenticeship programs, technical and trade schools, 2- and 4-year colleges to graduate programs.

Technical and Trade Schools

A number of guides are available on technical and trade schools, but they are not as comprehensive as those for colleges and universities. Not all technical and trade schools are accredited and many are for-profit operations; therefore, some go out of business or drop programs that are not running in the black.

Some examples of guides to technical and trade schools include the following:

> *American Trade School Directory.* Queens Village, NY: Corner Publications.
> *Directory of the National Association of Trade and Technical Schools.* Washington, DC: National Association of Trade and Technical Schools.
> *Directory of Post-Secondary Schools with Occupational Programs, Public and Private.* Washington, DC: U.S. Government Printing Office.
> *Lovejoy's Career and Vocational School Guide.* New York: Simon and Schuster.
> *Technical, Trade, & Business School Data Handbook* (by geographic region) Concord, MA: Orchard House.

Most of these schools will have brochures or flyers available; some, catalogs.

One publisher, Orchard House, publishes *Technical, Trade, & Business School Data Handbook. Northeast/Southeast.* The current edition provides information on 3,600 schools. For each school, the name, address, telephone number, accreditation information, and enrollment data are given. There are also separate sections entitled academic, expenses, placement, admissions, financial aid, and student life.

The academic section describes the faculty, degrees, major fields of study, the academic calendar, and the academic curriculum along with information on the average school week and special programs and facilities. The academic experience paragraph provides information on the enrolled students' probability of academic success.

Under admission the criteria used for evaluating applicants is discussed, the step-by-step application procedures outlined, and the percentage of applicants selected along with information on their high school rank. Under student life things like the location of the school and accessibility to public transportation are discussed. Attendance policies and expected dress codes are mentioned.

Don't forget the yellow pages of the telephone book (see Figure 13.4 for an example from the Jacksonville, Florida, phone book).

Colleges and Universities

A wide variety of sources of information can be found about colleges and universities. Many libraries have college catalogs available or the college catalog on microfiche, but the most up-to-date source of information about colleges and universities is their catalogs and other specialized publications.

There are many directories available, including the following:

The College Blue Book. New York: Macmillan.
The College Handbook. Princeton, NJ: Educational Testing Service.
Barron's Profiles of American Colleges. Barron's Educational Series
Lovejoy's College Guide. New York: Simon and Schuster.
Peterson's Annual
Guides to Graduate Study

These are only a few of the many sources. For example, Orchard House, in Concord, Massachusetts, publishes *College Admission Index of Majors and Sports.* This volume lists the majors offered and the colleges and universities that offer each of these majors. They also have a list of sports and universities and colleges that field teams in each of these sports. They also list colleges and universities by their religious affiliation if they are connected with a church denomination. They provide tuition information. The listings are arranged by state.

Media Sources

A wide variety of media materials are available for counselors to use. There are posters, slides, films, records, cassettes, microfilm, microfiche, transparencies,

FIGURE 13.4
Examples of trade and technical schools

Florida College of Medical and Dental Careers
    Medical assistant
    Dental assistant
    Medical office management
    EKG/Lab assistant
    Pharmacy assistant
    Nursing assistant
Advanced Career Training School of Travel
    Travel agencies
    Airlines
    Computer training
    Tour and cruise operators
Florida Technical College of Jacksonville
    Computer applications specialist
    Electronics technology
    Computer applications specialist
Elkins Institute
    Radio broadcasting
    Electronic technology
    Data entry
    Word processing
Stenotype Institute of Jacksonville
Teller Training Institute
Amaro School of Modeling
Barbizon School of Modeling
Bartending at Professional Services Schools
Beauty Care Academy of Cosmetology
Cleveland Institute of Electronics
Columbia School of Broadcasting
Construction Educational Services
Contractors Exam School
Dave Buster's School of Construction
Dental Laboratory Training School
Flagler Career Institute
Flight Preparation Inc.
Florida Beauty College
Florida Community College at Jacksonville
    Trade and industrial
    Industrial technology
    Criminal justice
    Printing
    Marine trade programs
    Occupational programs
Florida School of Massage
International Centers for the Study of Electrolysis
Lodging Industry Training Center
National Educational Center
    Electronics
    Commercial art
    Computer-assisted drafting
    Engineering drafting
National Truck Drivers and Heavy Equipment Operators School
Normandy Beauty College
Problem Hair Design College

and videos on career fields, career awareness, and self-awareness topics. *The Educators' Guide to Free Guidance Materials* previously cited lists free films, filmstrips, slides, and tapes. There are film and video libraries that provide career and vocational videos and films free of charge for a given show date. One such company is Modern Talking Picture Services, Inc., Scheduling Center, 5000 Park Street, N., St. Petersburg, FL 33709-2254. Many universities have media libraries and rent media. A number of commercial producers offer rentals as well as sales. Some films or videos are produced by governmental organizations such as the Peace Corps, the National Science Foundation, the National Oceanic and Atmospheric Administration, and other professional organizations. Some examples of titles are shown in Table 13.1.

Media approaches appeal to visual learners, to adults, as well as to low-motivated clients. Reading usually is not involved. With films, slides, and videos caution has to be taken to preview the media before using it. The scenery and styles may be out of date even if the material presented is appropriate. In the information age and with the competition of television, students and counselees are turned off quickly by out-of-date media.

People

People are an important and major source of career and educational information. Admissions counselors, former graduates, department chairpersons, and students within programs can provide individuals information about educational programs. People can be an important source of information for finding out about jobs available and the qualifications required. Career counselors should make a systematic attempt to find out what their students or clients need to know about the local employment opportunities. It is also useful for students and clients to interview a worker in a given field they are planning to select. Also in outplacement counseling situations, clients often are advised to contact employers to see if the type of qualifications needed, the scope of operating the work environment, and so on would be something they might consider if an opening existed.

TABLE 13.1
Some governmental and professional organizations and sample film and video titles

Title	Sponsor
Challenge of Manufacturing	Society of Manufacturing Engineers
Box Business	International Corrugated Package Association
Race Against Time	Society of Manufacturing Engineers
New Engineers	National Science Foundations
NOAA Corps	National Oceanic and Atmospheric Administration
Your Future: Careers	Instrument Society

It is important for counselors to try to build bridges with the employers in their area so that they will receive notices when vacancies exist as well as be able to call on these individuals or their representatives to participate in career seminars, job fairs, career fairs, and the like. An index of human resource directors in a 25-mile radius is essential for developing personal contacts with potential job sites.

The type of questions counselors would want to have information on are included in Figure 13.5. Counselors could record the information on a floppy disk of a data management program and use a desktop publishing program to make a neat-looking booklet for distribution to counselors, teachers, and clients, or they could publish a newsletter for counselors and clients, feature job prospects on bulletin boards, and the like.

Many times a counselee wants to talk personally to persons who are working in a field they are considering. A file of graduates who are working in the field or a contact person in a business or industry who can recommend an individual is essential. The client may have to call a personnel director and ask him or her to set up an appointment or see if the person is willing to accept a telephone call. Examples of the types of questions are included in Figure 13.6.

```
Name of company _____
Address _____
Name of contact person _____
Title _____
Description of business _____
_____
_____
Number and type of employees _____
              Full-time _____        Part-time _____
Entry-level jobs for high school graduates and salary range
Entry-level jobs for community college graduates and salary range
Entry-level jobs for technical/trade school graduates and salary range
Entry-level jobs for college graduates and salary range
Current job openings
Expected job openings 1 year from now
Expected job openings 5 years from now
Jobs for disabled/women/minority workers
Inservice and professional development programs
Opportunities for advancement/career ladders
Work environment and conditions
Fringe benefits
Trends and changes anticipated
Additional information
```

FIGURE 13.5
Employer information form

1. What is your present position in the company?
2. What is your job description and/or roles and responsibilities?
3. How long have you been in this position?
4. What type of education and training does this job require?
5. What do you like most about your job? Why?
6. What do you like least about your job? Why?
7. Why did you choose this field?
8. How did you prepare yourself for this job?
9. What advice would you give a person who is planning to enter this field?
10. What do you think the job outlook for this field will be 5 years from now? Ten years from now?
11. What would you and your employer look for in a person whom you might hire for this type of position?
12. How have your job responsibilities changed from when you started in this field or position?
13. Do you have much flexibility and variety in your position?
14. Please describe your activities and schedule for a typical day.
15. Are there other people in your field whom you might think would be willing to speak to me about this field?
16. Would you be willing to allow me to observe you or shadow you for a day?

FIGURE 13.6
Interview sheet for career interview

It is important to have a structured set of questions because there may be a limited amount of time available for an interview or session. Job and career fairs provide interaction with people in given occupational fields as college nights or fairs do for given educational areas. When there is a presentation, limited time for sessions, and more than one counselee or student involved, there may be problems in the scope and type of information presented. Presenters might allow limited time for questioning and possibly present a biased or selective view of the career field. Career nights and fairs should be considered as an orientation or awareness session and time allotted for more individual study and information gathering such as reading more about the career and interviewing individuals who are currently working in the field.

APPRENTICESHIPS

Many types of careers demand an apprenticeship. The Bureau of Apprenticeships of the U.S. Department of Labor has some general information for counselors and clients, but more specific information can be obtained through local union or Department of Labor offices. The yellow pages can also provide partial information. For example, in the Jacksonville, Florida, yellow pages, the following training programs were listed:

Painter's and decorator's
Carpenter's
Jacksonville electric joint apprenticeship
Sheet metal workers
Plumbers and pipefitters

The local committee for each apprenticeship can provide information about the availability and requirements for such programs.

JOB ANALYSIS

A more detailed approach to finding out about given jobs is completing a job analysis. Individuals can identify categories by using one of the systems to classify work described in Chapter 3.

Fine (1986) categorized job analysis procedures into three groups: task-based, attribute-based, and behavior-based. The task-based approach requires the individual to look at worker functions in relation to data, people, and places. The attribute-based approach focuses on aptitudes, interests, and physical demands required by the job. The behavior-base approach focuses on the functions the worker has to do in relationship to people, data, and things.

For example with data an individual might be required to (1) compare, (2) copy, (3) compile and compute, (4) analyze, (5) coordinate or innovate, and (6) synthesize. With people the continuum ranges from (1) taking instructions and helping or serving to (7) mentoring.

The *Occupational Outlook Handbook* uses 16 dimensions in which to compare jobs. These are included under three categories: job requirements, work environments, and occupational characteristics, as shown following:

Job Requirements

1. Leadership/persuasion
2. Helping/instructing others
3. Problem solving/creativity
4. Initiative
5. Work as part of team
6. Frequent public contacts
7. Manual dexterity
8. Physical stamina

Work Environment

9. Hazardous
10. Outdoors
11. Confined

Occupational Characteristics

12. Jobs concentrated geographically
13. Part-time
14. Earnings
15. Employment growth
16. Entry requirements

After interviewing and observing individuals in the field and reading literature on the job, the potential candidate might want to fill out a check sheet as found in Figure 13.7 comparing these attributes and needs with those of the job.

Job analyses are often completed in assessment centers or in the counselor's office. Students and clients are not often motivated to do an in-depth study of an occupation on their own but will tend to complete the analysis and discuss the careers in a group setting. Individuals considering career fields need to make decisions on whether they will accept or work toward meeting the

	My Skills/Needs/ Achievements	Job Skills/Needs
Educational training Requirements		
Skills People		
Skills Things		
Skills Data		
Special aptitudes		
General aptitudes		
Communication skills		
Physical attributes		
Motivation and energy		
Experience requirements		
Values		
Salary and benefits		
Working conditions Environment		
Working environment		
Hours/schedule		
Work location Transportation to/from work		

FIGURE 13.7
Assessment worksheet

requirements for a specific day and therefore consider whether they would go through the training or education required for the job, whether they like the type of work they are doing all day and where they would be required to work, and whether they feel the earning potential is what they desire.

CAREER RESOURCE CENTERS

Many schools, colleges, universities, as well as corporations have career resource centers. The specific functions are illustrated in Figure 13.8.

A career education center that is conveniently located and attractively arranged will be used more often than one that isn't. Mamarchev and Pritchett (1978) outlined eight steps necessary to establish a career resource center (CRC):

1.   To plan thoroughly after conducting a needs assessment, and to include immediate, intermediate, and long-range goals
2.   To consider the physical design carefully. Questions such as is the location accessible, is it attractive, is the space allocated efficiently arranged, does the set-up encourage unsupervised use, can existing facilities be remodeled for CRC use?
3.   To determine the staff needs and role of each staff member
4.   To determine how the resource materials and information sources will be catalogued and arranged. There will be educational, vocational and personal-social types of information. There might be computers and other audio visual equipment and material.
5.   To develop a plan for publicizing the availability of the CRC. This might include newsletters, bulletin boards, career days, open houses, and involvement of advisory committee members.

```
PROGRAM ACTIVITIES————————————————MATERIAL DEVELOPMENT
    Speakers                                   Briefs
    Tours                                      Curriculum guides
    Career counseling                          Research reports
    In-service training                        For staff
    Outreach function
    Staff training
                        Research and development
                        Worker needs
                        Projection and trends
                        Translation function
```

FIGURE 13.8
Career resource functions

6. To assist individuals in their career planning, decision making, and personal assessment
7. To have a plan of evaluation in place to assess the effectiveness of the program and to demonstrate the accountability of the CRC
8. To provide fiscal budget for CRC operation

Brown and Brown (1990) pointed out that the four major concerns in establishing such a center are assessibility, attractiveness, ease of operation, and adaptability.

Counselors involved in CRC have to recognize the importance of identifying the needs that users have and making sure that the activities and materials meet the needs of the users. The center needs to be open at times other than class periods or work or school hours, which means before school or work hours, during lunch periods, and after school or work hours. The operation of the center must be easy for the clients who will use it. This means simple procedures for coding and organizing the materials so that they are easy to locate and easy to file back.

There is also the need to determine whose responsibility it is to develop and maintain the CRC. In most cases the CRC might be a part of the library or media center of a school, so it usually is the counselor's or media specialist's responsibility to develop and run the center. In postsecondary institutions it may fall on the student personnel division and in business on the human resources department. There is also a need to coordinate the CRC operation with teachers, administrators, counselors, and media specialists. For a CRC to be effective the effort has to be a joint enterprise. Last, there is a need to determine the operating policies of the CRC. Questions such as can the material be borrowed, how long, and the like are important to answer. The question of security of the resources also must be addressed.

Criteria for Selecting Material

There are a number of criteria that need to be considered in selecting the information sources for the CRC. Questions such as the following need to be asked:

1. Who are going to be the users of the information? Is the information going to be used by students, teachers, displaced homemakers, the unemployed? The group determination is important in determining the type of material as well as the reading level of the material or verbal level of the presentation. The range and scope of the material might be a limiting factor if, for example, the group were mentally disabled or a homogeneous group of accountants.
2. What are characteristics of the community being served? If people tend to remain in the area, then possibly the materials should emphasize the career fields available in that area. In other communities,

there is high mobility and people move in and out of the community rapidly.

3. What uses will be made of the materials? If the materials are only going to be used as a supplement to individual counseling, a wide variety of single copies of materials is needed. If the information sources are going to be used in groups, possibly multiple copies as well as more media sources are needed.

4. What sources are already available? Many times there are a wide number of information sources already available. Counselors might have some sources in their bookcases. Others might be with other personnel such as teachers or in the media center. Many times librarians order materials they think will be of general interest to the users.

5. What budget is available for materials? The amount of materials will be somewhat influenced by the amount of money budgeted for materials. The cost of printed materials and audiovisuals is rising and this limits the number of items that can be purchased. Unless there is up-front funding and a good amount budgeted, the collection probably will be limited and the counselor will not be able to update annuals and keep the information up to date. Look for the wide variety of free and inexpensive career guidance materials available.

SUMMARY

Career information sources can facilitate career development and decision making. Counselors must know the important sources of career and educational information as well as the advantages and disadvantages of each type. The information has to be processed through the sensory registers and encoded from short-term to long-term memory. Counselors need to be able to evaluate which type of format would be most effective for the client—printed material, audiovisuals, computer systems and software, simulations, or realistic job preview.

REVIEW QUESTIONS

1. What factors need to be considered by the career counselor in selecting career information sources for clients to use?

2. List and discuss the different types of formats used to disseminate career information. What are the advantages and disadvantages of each type of format?

3. What techniques and procedures should the career counselor use to find out about the local job market?

4. What are some of the major sources of career information published by the federal government? Your state government? Describe the type of information provided and how you would use it as a counselor.

5. What are some of the other sources of career information that are readily available to the counselor and client? Discuss the advantages and disadvantages of each type of source.

6. What is job analysis? How and when would you use this in your career counseling?

7. How would you arrange a career resource center? How would you go about selecting the resources? What staff and budget will you need?

SUGGESTED LEARNING ACTIVITIES

1. Visit a career resource center. Talk to the director and find out how it is set up and why. Who uses it? How are the materials selected? Make a report of your findings to the class.

2. Make a bibliography of free or inexpensive materials that would be helpful to you in your career counseling.

3. Interview several individuals using materials from the career resource center. Get their reaction to the center and the material they were using.

4. Interview several career counselors and have them identify the information sources they feel are the most valuable to them. Report your results to the class.

5. Choose a theme and secure career information on the topic. Make a presentation to the class using the different types of formats and get them to discuss what they liked and disliked about each.

6. Conduct a career guidance needs assessment with your students or fellow workers and design your data-gathering instrument, pilot it, and analyze the results. Present your results and reactions to the class.

7. Get a group of your classmates to work with you on a project in your community to identify local resources and sources of information. Report your findings to the class.

8. Select an occupation and make an analysis of the job. Compare the different approaches. Write a report of your analysis.

CASE STUDIES

Finding the Big Picture

Eric came into the career planning and placement office and said: "I want to research what I am going to do after I graduate. I know it is sort of late. I majored in political science because I like the instructors and the courses are interesting. I have read that there is a tight job market for college graduates and I am going to graduate in May. I know I am good and have competencies employers are looking for. I think that I need to get the big picture and find out what jobs there are out there for me."

Teaching Related Life Skills

Ms. Fletcher, a middle school (science, mathematics, social studies, English, physical education, art, music) teacher wants to show students what they are learning is related to skills that they need not only in every day living but also after they graduate in the workplace.

Case Questions

1. What sources of information would you use in these two situations?
2. What additional information is needed?
3. What counseling strategies/approaches would you use with these clients?

SUGGESTED READING

Ghorpade, J. V. (1988). *Job analysis: A handbook for the human resource director.* Englewood Cliffs, NJ: Prentice Hall.

The book presents detailed information on job analysis, job information, methods and systems of job analysis, job descriptions, worker specification, and uses of job information.

14

COMPUTER APPLICATIONS IN CAREER COUNSELING

T he computer is one of the most widely used tools in schools, homes, and businesses. The cost of the hardware and software has been declining and the number of applications to counseling and guidance has been increasing. Two of the major uses have been computer-assisted counseling and computer-managed counseling. Career guidance and counseling computer-assisted systems have been developed and used extensively and allow for selection and retrieval of career and educational information. Many of the major information sources such as the *Occupational Outlook Handbook* and the *Dictionary of Occupational Titles* have been made available on disk.

Computer-managed counseling helps counselors reduce their clerical and administrative tasks. The computer can be used for maintaining records, keeping activity logs, scheduling, and word processing. The computer has been used in computer-assisted testing and computer-adaptive testing. Many achievement, aptitude, and personality tests, including interest tests, are administered, scored, and interpreted by the computer.

However, not every counselor or client is enamored by the computer. A number of counselors feel that the computer programs are dehumanizing the counseling process, and think that the computers are used many times inappropriately and are poor substitutes for the counselor. Also there are problems about maintaining confidentiality and the possible problems of unauthorized access.

LEARNING OBJECTIVES

After reading this chapter, you should be able to do the following:

- Discuss the advantages and disadvantages of computer information systems
- List the sources of information on computer systems and software available for counselors
- Identify uses that career counselors make of the computer
- Identify the characteristics of good career guidance software

COMPUTER-ASSISTED CAREER GUIDANCE SYSTEMS

One of the major computer applications to the career guidance field has been the development of a large number of computer-assisted career guidance systems (CACGS). They can be used as an information system to provide information on specific careers and educational programs or used in an interactive mode in which the client can choose alternatives based on self-assessment. There are usually five components to a computer system of self-assessment: assessing the aptitudes, interests, skills, and values of the client and identifying the careers related to the patterns of these constructs. The career counseling approach is to narrow the list of careers initially identified, review the skills, aptitudes, and educational level required by the jobs generated in the shorter list, and plan strategies to help users to implement their career plan.

ADVANTAGES AND DISADVANTAGES OF CAREER GUIDANCE SYSTEMS

A comparison of the advantages and disadvantages of computerized career guidance systems can be found in Figure 14.1.

ADVANTAGES
* Users react positively to the system.
* Users gain increased knowledge about themselves.
* Users develop more specific career plans after using CACGS.
* Users are motivated to use other career information and planning sources.
* Users learn more about career exploration resources.
* Users find the systems helpful, understandable, and enjoyable.
* The system can be effectively used to provide services that used to be provided by counselors.
* The systems deliver the same services to all clients and are not subject to conscious or unconscious biases of the counselor.
* Counselors have more time to do other aspects of their work.
DISADVANTAGES
* The hardware and software may be expensive.
* Counselor intervention is needed to provide reinforcement, clarification, and support for decision making.
* Counselors may know better information sources on the local and regional level than those provided by the CACGS.
* Career counseling may become mechanistic and lose the human touch.
* Clients may not discuss findings with the counselor.
* Budget may not allow for the periodical updates and annual franchise fee.

FIGURE 14.1
Advantages and disadvantages of CACGS

SOURCES OF COMPUTER INFORMATION

Several good sources for computer software that contain reviews for counselors have been published by professional organizations, and others have been published by commercial publishers.

Counseling Software Guide (Walz & Bleuer, 1989) contains a description of over 500 counseling-relevant software programs and 93 intensive software reviews. The guide is broken into three sections. Section one deals with trends and developments and has five papers on topics such as software for personal counseling, software for career counseling, software for academic advising, software for testing, and software for administration.

Section two contains software descriptions in five categories: software for personal counseling, software for career counseling, software for academic advising, software for testing, and software for administration.

Section three, software for career counseling, has two categories: self-assessment and guidance, which includes a description of systems, assessment, and career exploration software; and finding and keeping a job, which contains descriptions of software, job-search skills, resumes, applications and cover letters, interviewing, placement, and job-success skills.

The guide also contains a list of publishers of computer software in Appendix A, computer compatibility in Appendix B, and a computer software evaluation checklist in Appendix C. The annotated list of sources includes a brief summary, a description of the hardware, intended users, contacts, cost, and description.

The reviews were generated partially through a selected group of software users and having them evaluate their reaction to the software and partially through a careful evaluation of the software using the software evaluation checklist. The guide has not been updated, however, as of 1993.

The Psychware Sourcebook is compiled and edited by Samuel E. Krug (1992). The directory describes computer-based products for assessing or modifying human behavior. The products are listed both in numeric order by products code and in alphabetic order by title. Each listing includes eight types of information: product number, name, supplier, category, applications, sales restrictions, pricing, and product description. The categories selected were career/vocational, cognitive/ability, interest/attitudes, motivation, neuropsychological, personality, structured interview, and utility.

Applications were also classified among behavioral medicine, clinical assessment/diagnosis, educational evaluation/planning, individual counseling, learning disability screening, marriage/family counseling, personnel selection/evaluation, training/development, and vocational guidance/counseling. Five indexes are reported: title product category, product category, product application, service, and supplier. A unique feature of the guide is that reproductions of samples are provided for more than half of the products described in the directory.

The Computer Use in Psychology: A Directory of Software is in its third edition and is published by the American Psychological Association (1993). The materials listed are test software packages for test interpretation, career guidance systems, adaptive tests, and the like.

HOW TO EVALUATE SOFTWARE

Maze (1989) recommended that users evaluate the software themselves. The reviews are opinions of the authors who wrote them. Counselors should send for promotional literature and compare the literature to the reviews. The findings indicate that companies are willing to send representatives to provide on-site demonstrations or at least provide demonstration disks.

When having an on-site demonstration, Maze suggested having other people at your site use the program and watch the number of times the demonstrator guides the user. The purpose of this procedure is to receive another person's opinion on the usability of the software besides yourself. Another suggestion was to have a sample of the program's contents printed so you can compare similar programs; for example, ask for the printouts of the same three occupations from each program. Maze suggested that counselors ask for written information about the sources of the data and try out the program themselves and see if they can confuse it by hitting wrong keys, ask the program to print when no printer is available, and reboot the computer in the middle of an operation.

When ordering less expensive software, Maze recommended trying it for the 10- to 30-day approval period and see what programs are worth keeping. Instead of "whenever everything fails, read the directions," begin by reading the directions and following each step listed in the manual. The counselor should have some users try the program and ask whether they understood the procedures and directions and what they liked and disliked about it. Sampson and Reardon (1990) pointed out that counselors need to evaluate the features of the systems and costs in the context of their client population and the type of organization they serve. They concluded that there is no one best computer-guidance system.

Types of Software for Career Counseling

A wide variety of types of software is available to help clients in assessing their self-awareness. Programs are also available on career interests, work values, skills assessment, comprehensive career search systems, and banks of information about jobs. Programs have also been designed to help individuals search for jobs and write resumes. There are many types of programs available on schools and colleges, scholarships, and degree programs. Some programs present just instruction and others provide instruction and practice. Programs available to aid clients to write resumes, participate in interviews, and make career decisions need to have a practice component.

Some CACGS programs measure dimensions of the entry behavior, which may be career maturity or aptitude, before the start up of the program. The counselor and the client decide where to start in the program. The comprehensive career guidance systems allow users to retrieve information from a large data base on careers and career fields and often allow the users to delimit the search by selecting a number of different criteria such as work values, expected salary, education requirements, type of work environment, and the like.

Positive Features of Software Packages

In reviewing the critiques of career software packages in the *Counseling Software Guide,* Bridges (1989) identified eight positive features of the packages for career guidance:

- The flexibility of some software allows the user to move freely between sections or modules, to change answers, and to get feedback.
- Career counselors and developers coordinate some software packages so that it is theory based and linked to the career counseling program at the site.
- The documentation provided by the software is thorough and clear and provides follow-up activities, books to read, and information on the reliability and validity of the program.
- The scope of the printouts makes available the answers and results of data-base searches to the counselee and counselor.
- The use of the computer capabilities makes the program attractive and motivating.
- The time required by the program fits into a class period or counseling session.
- The information on start-up use includes the exact hardware requirements and the procedures for installing and starting the program.
- Help is available from the publisher on problems that might arise or on replacement of problem disks.

Primarily the strengths viewed were technical features of the software and features of the computer. Only one related to coordination or correlation with counseling and career theory.

Negative Features of Software Packages

Bridges (1989) listed 10 negative features by reviewers:

- How programs responded to answer changes was inappropriate (some required users to reanswer all).
- The program bombed out when the wrong key or return was hit at the wrong time.

- The time some programs took to sort or process information was too long.
- The time some programs take to complete and report analysis decreases usefulness and loses the user's interest.
- The program was too simple or too complex for the users.
- The time it takes to learn or use the program was not worth the output.
- The number of assessment questions was too small to be useful.
- The instructions were not clear or sufficient to understand how to use the software.
- The screens were hard to read, possibly because of too much data or little use of graphics.
- The program did not store information for later counseling sessions.

Bridges calls for close cooperation between career counselors and developers. She feels that developers should work with an advisory committee and seek consultation from graphic artists and professional writers. The software should be closely edited to ensure the information is up-to-date and the program is using current computer technology.

Ideal Career Guidance Software

Walz and Bleuer (1989) list 10 characteristics of ideal software:

- The software provides detailed and accurate information on the hardware requirements, the type of capacity, the printer support, type of monitor, type of graphics card.
- The software is available for both IBM and compatible computers and Apple.
- The software is available for reasonable try out before purchase.
- The publisher provides revisions and updates at no or minimal cost to the original purchaser.
- The program or modules of the program can be completed within a 50-minute time period.
- The program makes attractive use of graphics and color.
- The program involves the user in an interactive role.
- The program allows the user to change answers and move between sections.
- The program allows users to save information and provides also printed feedback.
- The program is designed to minimize the consequences of errors.

COMPUTER INFORMATION SYSTEMS

Computer career guidance systems are available both for the personal computer and for use with the mainframe and terminals. Four of the widely used systems are computerized heuristic occupational information and exploration system (CHOICES), DISCOVER, the Guidance Information System (GIS) and System of Interactive Guidance and Information (SIGI). Some systems provide both occupational information along with educational information. A detailed description of several systems is provided in the next section with an annotated list of several other programs.

The Guidance Information Service

The Guidance Information Service (GIS) is produced by the Educational Software Division of the Houghton Mifflin Corporation. The cost of an annual license fee is approximately $2,000 and in the career decision making system, an interest inventory is added to the system, about an additional $400. The system requires IBM PC or compatible with a minimum of a 10MB hard drive with 256 RAM. The system requires DOS 2.1 or higher and supports a monochrome or color graphics printer. Guidance Information Service is also available on a variety of other computers, including several mainframes and microcomputers.

Guidance Information Service contains six major file systems: occupational information, Armed Services occupational information, 2-year college information, 4-year college information, graduate and professional school information, and financial aid information.

The two career files describe more than 1,000 occupations and 200 armed services careers. Each of the civilian occupations includes a job description, the employment outlook, the average starting salary in the United States, the geographic location of jobs, and the course of study and/or training required to enter the field.

The college files provide information on 1,700 2-year colleges, 1,700 4-year colleges, and 1,500 graduate and professional schools. The system reports on 900 characteristics of the institutions and programs, providing details about admissions data, athletic programs, campus life, and residency requirements.

Guidance Information Service also has a financial aid file and lists about 600 national sources with information about loans, scholarships, and grants. There are regional and local data bases on vocational and technical schools as well as for regional and local data on financial aid. Customized lists of local occupations are sometimes available.

Houghton Mifflin sends updates twice a year to users. There are over 4,500 sites in the United States that use GIS. Houghton Mifflin also provides free to GIS users a series of college recruitment videotapes cross referenced to its 4-year college file. GIS provides back-up sources for the counselor. There is a GIS resource and activities book that includes how-to instructions, classroom lesson plans, strategies for working with students with special needs, plus other suggestions on using the information files. There are supporting guides for indexing occupations, financial aid opportunities, graduate and professional schools, and colleges. The users can have printed short profiles or long-form (in-depth) reports. A user's guide, resource and activities book, and a counselor's manual are available. GIS is self-instructional for the user, and a tutorial program is available to guide the user and a menu system.

The program will accept scores from the *Strong Interest Inventory*, the *Self-Directed Search*, the *Career Assessment Inventory*, or the *Harrington-O'Shea Career Decision Making System*.

In his review of GIS, Allbritten (1989) stated that the program is a mature product that is reflected in its refinements. GIS is a recommended information retrieval tool. Allbritten recommended that the quick reference card should be kept handy along with the manuals because the command system although intuitive is lengthy.

DISCOVER

DISCOVER is a system that combines career guidance and search strategies to provide users self-knowledge and to tie that information with occupational and educational information. The system is marketed by Eureka and the American College Testing Program and was developed by Bowlesby (1984). There are several versions for postsecondary students and adults in career transition, for high school students, and for junior high and middle school students. Versions are available for a variety of types and makes of computers with 256K RAM. A 10MB hard disk is required. Software is also available for the Apple II and some TRS-80 models. The licensing fee is about $1,800. The cost for the middle and junior high level is $325.

DISCOVER for postsecondary students and adults contains nine modules. The first module is beginning the career journey and is designed to instruct the user in effective career planning. Learning about the world of work provides an overview of the conceptual model developed by ACT for organizing occupations and relating personal attributes to job families. Learning about yourself, the third module, has users assess their interests, abilities, values, and experiences. The relationship of these personality and cognitive variables to the world of work is demonstrated in this module. The inventories can be taken on the computer or by pencil and paper except for the aptitude area, which is based upon self-ratings.

Finding occupations is the fourth module in which user's characteristics assessed in the third module are compared to careers and jobs that match those characteristics.

Learning about occupations, the fifth module, provides information about selected occupations and guides the user to narrow the list to ten or fewer occupations. Making educational choices, the sixth module, helps users select the major program or training needed for the list of occupations developed in step five.

Planning the next steps, the seventh module, helps users identify specific schools that offer the training needed. The information can also be correlated to military occupational specialties. The module also provides information on financial aid. Nontraditional methods of being awarded credit such as CLEPT and other similar exams are indicated. Job-hunting skills are also introduced.

Planning your career, the ninth module, guides people to consider their career rainbow, Super's conceptualization of the roles individuals are involved in during their life span and the roles' relative importance to the users. The last module is making transitions, which has users assess the stress that is part of their career transition.

Allbritten (1989) stated that the typical client requires three to four 1-hour sessions plus a follow-up session with the counselor to get the most out of the system. He feels that the counselor needs to have several hours of personal work with the system and attend workshops sponsored by the publisher.

DISCOVER for high schools contains seven units rather than nine. Planning your career and making transitions were not a part of the high school package. The modules are beginning the career journey, learning about the world of work, learning about yourself, finding occupations, learning about occupations, making educational choices, and planning next steps.

As with the DISCOVER program for postsecondary students and adults, the system can be used to provide information quickly about various jobs, schools, military programs, financial requirements, and nontraditional ways of earning college credit and job-seeking skills. The system can also provide guidance plus information.

Users in the third module enter their scores on interest inventories such as the self-directed search or on aptitude tests such as the differential aptitude test or rate themselves. There are inventories of values, experiences, and interests that are included in this unit.

As for adults, the information given by the user in module three is used along with the level of education the user wishes to attain to identify the specific jobs or careers that fit that pattern under the world-of-work map developed by ACT.

Sampson (1989) rated DISCOVER as a flexible and enjoyable program to use even though some minor technical problems were encountered.

The adult-level programs and the high school programs provide information on 45 occupations and cover 4,300 vocational and technical schools, 1,400 2-year colleges, 1,700 4-year colleges, 1,200 graduate schools, 100 external degree programs, and 200 military programs.

DISCOVER for junior high and middle schools includes three major modules plus an introduction and exit module. The first is entitled you and the world of work and features the world-of-work map. Students learn about the world-of-work map through guiding Moxey the mouse in a maze. The students are required to answer questions about worker tasks to aid Moxey in reaching the cheese. Exploring occupations, the second module, helps students to learn about the relationships of occupational clusters with worker tasks. The third is planning for high school and allows the counselor to put the local graduation requirements into the program.

Bronk (1989) found DISCOVER for junior high and middle school to be a most comprehensive and systematic approach to career awareness and the process of planning. He liked how it helped students to understand how abilities and work lead to success in life, but had some concerns about the flexibility of the program and the limited access to job information and graduation requirements.

SIGI

System of Interactive Guidance and Information (SIGI) is an individualized career guidance program that teaches users the process of career planning and decision making, and provides up-to-date career information. The system is appropriate for use by high school and college students and adults. Users are asked to identify their values and occupations, plan educational and training programs, and are guided to make informed career decisions.

The system has been expanded and now called SIGI Plus. The system is available for most different microcomputers with hard disk and the license costs about $1,400 per year. The publisher of SIGI Plus is the Educational Testing Service. SIGI has nine different sections: introduction, self-assessment, search, information, skills, preparing, coping, deciding, and next step. The introduction provides the user an overview of the system and provides guidance on how to use the system. Users analyze and rank their values, interests, and skills in the self-assessment section.

In the search section, users identify desirable and undesirable work characteristics. The information section provides a description of the skills, characteristics, potential salary, and future in the field. Users rate themselves on the skills required in the jobs described in SIGI. In the preparing section users take a look at job-preparation paths and can estimate their likelihood of achieving success in completing the preparation. The coping section covers the practical issues about career preparation. Career decision-making strategies are included in deciding. The last section is entitled next steps, and includes suggestions on how users can achieve their career goals.

In his review of SIGI Plus, Gonzalez (1989) indicated that the system is a complete career decision-making and planning software tailored to the individual needs of the users and aids them to acquire career decision-making skills.

SELF-UNDERSTANDING SOFTWARE

A number of software programs are available to help people in understanding themselves. Some are comprehensive programs, and others have a single focus or theme. A brief annotated list is provided of a sample of the many packages available.

> Title: Guidance and Counseling Software
> Publisher: Conover Co.
> Level: Junior and senior high
> Computer: Apple II

There are four areas included in the guidance system software: Self-evaluation series, you and other series, values clarification series, parent-adolescent series, my plus and minus qualities, self-image inventory, what do I value, successful communication skills are among the programs included in this series. The programs are used with individual students as a basis for either individual or group sessions.

Title: Life Coping Skills Series
Publisher: Society for Visual Education
Level: Middle school and up
Computer: Apple II

There are four programs in this series: building relationships, forming positive behavior, increasing self-esteem, and communication. Emphasized skills include those that help students look at themselves and see what effect their attitudes and actions have on others.

Title: Master Budget Calculator
Publisher: CIASA Wintergreen Software
Level: Adolescents and adults
Computer: IBM and Apple

The program has three parts: expense totaller, week/month/year converter, and budget formulator, which provides users an idea of how their money is spent in relation to their values represented by 12 types of expenses.

Title: Understand Yourself
Publisher: Dynacomp, Inc.
Level: Late adolescent through adults
Computer: IBM, Apple, Tandy

The program contains 10 tests of which the following are self-administered assertive test, conscience test, a test of marital adjustment, measurement of personal adjustment.

Title: Tool Box for Emotional and Social Growth
Publisher: Peak Potential
Level: K–12
Computer: Apple II

The Tool Box contains activities, games, and role-playing exercises for counselors to use to help social and emotional growth of students.

SELF-MANAGEMENT SOFTWARE

A number of software programs are available to help people cope with stress and reduce tension and anxiety and are available across age levels. A second major theme that appears in this software is decision making. There are also packages to help children and adults improve their self-concept and understand their motivation.

Some examples of these programs are the following:

Title: Job Stress and Burnout: Coping and Prevention
Publisher: Cambridge Career Products
Level: High school to adults
Computer: Apple II

The program contains 10 exercises to help users enhance their jobs and reduce their stress and potential burnout. The last unit takes the information the user recorded from previous units to help users formulate a behavioral contract.

Title: The Idea Generator
Publisher: Experience in Software
Level: High school and adult
Computer: IBM and compatibles

The idea generator is designed to help users deal with personal, career, and academic problems and goals.

Title: Spectrum I
Publisher: Institute for Personality and Ability Testing
Level: Adult
Computer: IBM and compatibles

Spectrum I is a computerized assessment tool to measure four motivational factors—accomplishment, recognition, power, and affiliation—and is useful in placement and selection decisions and in career development.

Title: Be a Winner: Set Your Goals
Publisher: Microcomputer Educational Programs
Level: Middle school and above
Computer: IBM or Apple

Be a winner is an interactive computer program to assist students in looking at their abilities, values, and aptitudes and how they relate to their personal goals.

CAREER SELF-ASSESSMENT

Other career assessment programs are available besides GIS, CHOICES, DISCOVER, and SIGI Plus that are less comprehensive or are targeted to special groups.

The Career Planning System developed by the Conover Company is a career-exploration system designed for special need students. It was field tested with special needs students capable of reading at the 3.5 grade level. There are two modes of operation: direct entry access and full management system. The full management system stores student input but also does data-base sorts. There is a short version of this program and an interest assessment program that helps students identify their vocational interest based on the activities that are familiar to them.

Career point is a comprehensive career development system that uses the Self-Directed Search of Holland to assess the occupational values, skills, and interests of its users. The career point program also has modules on setting goals and your development plan.

C-LECT is a comprehensive career guidance program published by the Chronicle Guidance Publications, which has three modules: occupational, educational, and financial aid. The data base for C-LECT includes profiles of 701 occupational profiles coded by Holland's codes, the *Dictionary of Occupational Titles,* and the *Guide for Occupational Exploration (GOE).* There are 3,000 related occupations in the data base, 103 with military cross-reference in the educational module. There are over 8,000 institutions, including 1,821 4-year colleges, 2,245 2-year colleges, and 4,127 vocational schools.

C-LECT has financial aid information available for both college-bound and noncollege-bound students. The program is targeted for junior high through college-level students. C-LECT, Jr. is the self-assessment and career exploration program available for junior high students.

Another occupational and educational data system available for students and adults is COIN published by Educomp, Inc. There are six career modules: interest, working conditions, career clusters, educational levels, physical strength, and physical demands. The program is targeted also for people changing careers, displaced workers, and military service candidates.

Career Search 1, 2, 3, 4, and 5 is a software package by occupational awareness designed to help learning and physically disabled students match their interests and abilities to possible careers.

Exporacion de Carreras is a career exploration system in Spanish that presents materials on over 300 occupations published by Cambridge Career Products.

Labor Market Access published by E and F Vocational Services is designed to help vocation counselors compare a disabled client's pre- and postaccident access to employment. It is targeted for counselors who work with clients who are involved in personal injury, wrongful death, career decision making, and with spouses involved in divorce.

Pictorial Inventory of Careers (PIC) has a version that includes filmstrips and tapes targeted to assess the vocational interests of disadvantaged, emotionally disabled, physically disabled, and academically disabled vocational students.

Occupational Outlook on computer is produced by CFKR Career Materials, Inc., and is a computerized version of the *Occupational Outlook Handbook* produced by the Department of Labor. It also incorporates information from the

Dictionary of Occupational Titles, Guide for Occupational Exploration, Dictionary of Holland Occupational Codes, Classification of Jobs, and the *Occupational Outlook Quarterly.*

COMPUTERS IN CAREER TESTING

There are many computer applications in career testing. One major use is computer-assisted testing. Thompson (1989) reported that computer-assisted testing software is used for three major functions: as a way to administer a test, as a means to score pencil-and-paper tests, and as a means to generate diagnostic and prescriptive reports.

On-Line Computer Administration

An increasing number of tests are now available in on-line computer versions. Often the items are multiple choice and are presented one item at a time on the full screen. The examinee is first given instructions that are presented visually on the screen. The instructions often call for the examinees to press a key to record their answer. Sometimes light pens are available to use. Practice items are usually provided and the examinee has a chance to become familiar with the test format. Some programs ask the examinees to check to see if they recorded the right or proper answer before letting the users go to the next item.

Masden (1986) reported seven advantages of administering tests on a computer terminal:

- Relatively low equipment costs are required if the testing volume is low.
- Computer-assisted tests reproduce closely the instructions and presentation formats of pencil-and-paper versions.
- Testing at a terminal has proved to be as cost-effective as traditional testing after initial equipment costs are covered.
- Positive client response to computer-assisted testing is common.
- Evidence is beginning to show that computer testing does not affect the reliability of the test instrument over a wide range of special clients and situations.
- The collection of ancillary test data is now possible on variables such as response time and patterns for items and scales.
- Adaptive testing, in which selection of the next question is based on the test taker's responses to previous items, is a near-perfect example of computer-assisted testing adjusted to suit the needs of the examinees.

Thompson (1989) reported that there has been a dramatic increase in the number of microcomputer-based test software packages in the last several years. He indicated that the more advanced test programs provide for administration of the test at the computer terminal and the scoring of the test almost immediately with the report generated within minutes of the individual completing the test. Comprehensive reports might use graphs and profiles along with the narrative.

Masden (1986) also described some of the major limitations. There are increased costs if equipment has to be purchased or augmented to run the program. If computer availability is limited, the counselor might encounter scheduling problems. Some users have problems using the equipment and have developed strong negative attitudes toward the computer. Test makers find that it is sometimes difficult or impossible to adapt certain types of tests and item formats for the computer. Another technical problem is that many tests do not have normative data. The same basic problems characteristic of pencil-and-paper formats on interest tests and personality tests operate often on the computer versions. Test takers are influenced by response set and social desirability factors. They can cheat or come out with any score they want to on some tests.

Jackson (1985) suggested that there are some major areas of differences between standard and computerized types of tests. The method of presentation of the stimulus materials differs not only in arrangement but also in size. Usually only one nonverbal item is presented on the screen rather than a double column of many items as on a pencil-and-paper test. The type of task required of the test taker is often different; for instance, the tests may not permit the opportunity to review previous responses to items. The method of recording responses is also different; also, the method of score interpretation.

Computer Scoring

Computer scoring is one of the signs of the changes in technology over the years. Test-scoring equipment has been available for over 50 years. Thompson (1989) stated that the first computerized test interpretation packages appeared in the early 1960s. Since then, a large number of scoring and interpretative packages have been developed for the major tests. When the tests were not administered by the computer, data entry was done through optical scan equipment or batch entry of scores into a terminal. Sometimes the responses of each test taker for each item were typed into a data set.

Computer Adaptive Testing

The computer allows more adaptive test formats. On adaptive tests the item selection is sequential. The items selected by the computer is based on how the test taker did on the previous item. Thompson (1989) found this to be one of the advanced approaches because the tests used the capacity of the computer to customize the test to the unique characteristics of the individual test taker. The computer can store banks of items and accept rules for selecting items using a branching process. The process allows presenting each test taker items based on what is most appropriate for their level of performance. For example, test takers would not have to deal with low-level items if they showed that they had mastered higher-level material. Testing time is reduced along with the frustration level of the test taker. Some aptitude and achievement tests are now being developed using this format.

Computer-Aided Personality Tests

The computer is widely used to test personality and cognitive dimensions. Jackson (1985) listed nine advantages of personality testing:

1. The saving of time of the counselor or psychologist
2. The possibility of using trained assistants to monitor test administration
3. The short time lag between administering the test, scoring it, and interpreting it
4. Elimination of human scoring errors
5. The programming capabilities of the computer to combine rules and complicated processing
6. The standardization of interpretation, eliminating different points of view
7. The potential for systematically collecting and developing normative data bases
8. The ability of the computer to perform complex scoring procedures
9. The ability to use computer-based assessment with special populations for which standard pencil-and-paper procedures are not feasible

Career Inventories

There are some career inventories that were originally published in pencil-and-paper form available on the computer, such as the *COP System Interest Inventory*, the *Strong Interest Inventory*, the *Career Development Inventory*, the *Career Psychological Inventory*, the *Ohio Vocational Interest Survey II*, the *Self-Directed Search*, and the *Vocational Preference Inventory*.

Scoring and Interpreting Systems

There are many different programs available to help counselors in the scoring and interpretation of test results. The programs sometimes call for the counselor to enter the individual item responses or the scores of the subtests in other cases. Data can be fed to the computer by optical scan equipment if it is available. There have been some cases of copyright infringement by some of the firms that offer computerized scoring programs. Counselors should check to see if the company is authorized by the publisher to score, interpret, and generate test reports. For example, the National Computer System provides programs for the scoring and interpretation of such tests as *Strong Interest Inventory, Career Assessment Inventory, Guilford-Zimmerman Temperament Survey, Millon Adolescent Personality Inventory, Millon Behavioral Health Inventory, Minnesota Multiphasic Personality Inventory, Sixteen Personality Factor Questionnaire, Hogan Personality Inventory, Hogan Personnel Selection Series, Vocational Information Profile,* and *Alcohol Use Inventory.*

Self-Awareness Tests

There are many test companies that provide software to administer, score, and report results of self-awareness tests commonly used in career guidance. The Consulting Psychologists Press has software for the *Myers-Briggs Type Indicator* and the *Adjective Check List.* Multi Tech has software available for the *Adult Personality Inventory.* The *Neo Personality Inventory: Computer Version* is published by Psychological Assessment Resources, and the interpretative program relates scores on the test to vocational interests.

Computer Adaptive Tests

The *Differential Aptitude Test: Computer Adaptive Edition* measures test taker's aptitudes in verbal reasoning, numerical ability, abstract reasoning, mechanical reasoning, space relations, spelling, language use, and clerical speed and accuracy. The test usually takes about 90 minutes rather than over 3 hours. The computer adapts the test to the test taker's ability level as they progress through the test and eliminates the questions that are too hard or too easy. The test is administered and scored by the computer and an individualized score report can be printed immediately after each test administration.

The *Microcomputer Evaluation Screening Assessment: Short Form* (MESAF2) is a 1-hour program that uses gamelike exercises to measure skills of motor coordination, academics, problem solving, size and shape discrimination, and memory. The test consists of 12 computer-administered tests, one pencil-and-paper test, and three hardware exercises to students. The examiner records the times, answers other than those taken on the computer, and the observations to generate the report form. The report form reports the *Dictionary of Occupational Titles'* Qualification Summary. The test was designed for the computer originally and criteria-referenced adaptive testing methods were used. The difficulty level of the items is adjusted to the test taker's ability.

The issues of the reliability and validity of this form of testing are usually raised because testing time is much shorter and not all test takers are given the same set of items. Each individual's test may be unique. The counselor needs to check the data presented on the validity and reliability of the test.

COMPETENCIES NEEDED

Career counselors need to develop competencies in using the computer. They need to have basic computer literacy. Walz and Bleuer (1989) point out the need for counselors to know what software is available for use in their work and how to evaluate counseling software. They conclude that budgets that provide for extensive hardware and software may not correlate highly with how well computers are used in counseling programs. Some counselors are overwhelmed and develop an aversion to the computer. Some counselors, with limited resources available, are able to use cheap and inexpensive programs effectively. They concluded that the effective use of computers is tied to leadership and that research has shown that if counselors are committed to using computers and persist in their use, the use will be more effective. Sampson, Reardon, and Lenz (1991) recommended that counselors receive more training and that video systems outline and describe the skills needed.

SUMMARY

Krumboltz (1990) summarized the impact of technology very well by stating "computerized approaches to helping the career counselors do not make the job any easier, but they do make it possible for the job to be done better" (p. 135). Major computer-assisted career guidance systems as well as individual software is now readily available to counselors and clients and is rated highly by both groups. The programs need to be carefully evaluated to ensure that the material presented is accurate, that they meet the developmental needs of the clients, and that they are user friendly and free from technical problems.

REVIEW QUESTIONS

1. What are the advantages and disadvantages of computer-assisted career guidance systems?
2. What sources would you use to locate career guidance and counseling software? What are the limitations of these sources?
3. What features do a career counselor need to consider when evaluating software?
4. What are the major career information systems? What features do they include? In what ways should a counselor use these systems?
5. What is computer-assisted testing? What is computer-adaptive testing? How are these two types of testing used by the career counselor?
6. What type of computer skills and competencies do career counselors need to have to function today?
7. What are the characteristics of ideal software?

8. Have you used a CACGS? Which one or ones? What was your reaction to the system? If you used more than one, compare and contrast the systems.
9. Have you taken a computer-assisted or computer adaptive test? Compare these formats with the traditional pencil-and-paper format. What version of the test did you prefer? Why?

SUGGESTED LEARNING ACTIVITIES

1. Interview several people who have used the CACGS. What did they like about the system? Dislike?
2. Interview several counselors who consistently use CACGS in their work. When do they use CACGS? With whom? Why? What is their evaluation of the CACGS?
3. Arrange to use DISCOVER, GIS, SIGI, or CHOICES. Experiment with the interactive feature. What was your evaluation of the system? How would you use it as a counselor?
4. Evaluate a software package that would be appropriate for career guidance using the evaluation procedures in the *Counseling Software Guide.*
5. Conduct a research study involving using the computer in one type of intervention. Have one group use CACGS, another have group sessions with the counselor, and a third group who receives no information at all. Test the three groups both before and after the sessions. Analyze your results and see if there were any significant differences in knowledge or self-awareness by group.
6. Take both the pencil-and-paper and computer form of one of the career tests. Which version did you like best? Did you have the same profile of scores on both forms? Did the mode of presenting the items differ?
7. Make a bibliography of appropriate software available for use in your work.

CASE STUDIES

The Wrong Assessment

John came out of the office after completing CHOICES, sat down in the chair by your desk and, said, "You told me that this was an excellent information source. People say that the computer is never wrong. Hah! The information about paralegal was all wrong. Why I researched carefully this job in the *Occupational Outlook Handbook,* looked at the current national, state, and regional statistics from the Department of Labor and Manpower, and the data in the program were way off. Why even the educational requirements were wrong. Why you can't get a job in the field without. . . ."

A Funeral Director?

Mary stood in front of your desk and said, "I was an undergraduate major in psychology and have almost completed my master's degree in career counseling and the computer tells me I should be a funeral director. Why weren't counselor and psychologist not on the list of the top ten career fields? I know you are going to tell me that a funeral director is one of the helping professions, but I question the validity of the system."

Biased Systems

Mohammed said this system is all biased. It does not provide minority students with realistic choices. Everything is geared to the white middle class male.

Computers Are Boring

"I hate computers," Mona said. "They are so impersonal. You can't talk to them and discuss things with them as you're going through the program. It is boring to sit in front of the tube. There have to be better ways than this."

Case Question

1.   How would you reply to each of the people in these cases?

SUGGESTED READINGS

Sampson, J. P., Jr., & Reardon, R. C. (Eds.). (1990). *Enhancing the design and use of computer-assisted career guidance systems.* Alexandria, VA: National Career Development Association.

The book contains chapters by a number of well-known authors in the field, such as J. Harris Bowlsbey, who wrote a chapter on career-based guidance systems: their past, present, and possible future.

Other organizations such as the Association of Computer-Based Information Delivery Systems for Career Information Clearinghouse have newsletters and other publications.

15

ASSESSMENT IN CAREER COUNSELING

A ssessment has had an important place in the history of career counseling. The trait-and-factor approach relied heavily on matching the requirements of an occupation with the individual's characteristics. The Minnesota group, among others, developed many tests to help simplify the process, such as the *Minnesota Spatial Relations Test, Minnesota Clerical Test,* and the *Minnesota Rate of Manipulation Test.* The creation of many tests was stimulated by the career counseling movement.

Group intelligence tests became widely used in schools, business, and industry because of the success of the *Army Alpha* and *Army Beta* examinations during World War I. World War II stimulated the use of multiaptitude tests. Then, we began to reevaluate tests and issues such as cultural and gender bias and the validity of the tests for the situations they were used.

At present assessment has ventured into new directions. One is in the use of the computer. There are many computer-assisted and computer-adaptive tests that have been developed. Test interpretation has become much easier and more elaborate with computer-generated test reports. Informal assessment procedures are used in many of the career guidance systems rather than formal standardized test instruments. More emphasis is placed in some systems of assessment on description rather than prediction.

Nevertheless, assessment instruments are still widely used in career counseling contexts. They have also become increasingly relied on for other purposes, such as licensure and certification. Assessment information has helped to document the success of these programs.

LEARNING OBJECTIVES

After reading this chapter, you should be able to do the following:

- Discuss the major reasons tests are used in career counseling
- List and explain the different types of tests used in career counseling
- Explain the process of locating and evaluating tests
- Identify appropriate strategies to interpret test data to clients or students

USE OF TESTS

The task force of the American Association for Counseling and Development (1980, 1989) identified four major uses of testing: for placement and selection purposes, predicting behavior and performance in many different situations, describing individuals and providing diagnostic information, and providing a picture of growth.

In education, business, and industry tests are used for placement and selection purposes; for example, certain colleges require the *CEEB Scholastic Aptitude Test* for admission to the freshman year. Now the trend is to move away from the use of testing for prediction purposes, partly because of the low correlations found between test scores and success in most educational and occupational fields. More emphasis is being placed on the use of tests to describe the individual. Criterion-reference tests allow people to see what skills and competencies they have mastered. The interpretation is in terms of learning outcomes mastered, for example, rather than how the individual compares to a norming group. The diagnostic use of test results help learners in improving their performance from knowing their strengths and weaknesses. The accountability movement has influenced the use of experimental design, pre- and posttesting to investigate growth in career maturity, assertiveness, self-confidence, and the like. The question asked is, Did the program lead to gain in the student's scores?

Sundberg (1977) identified three major purposes of assessment in image forming, decision making, and theory-making contexts. In image forming the counselor takes a sample of behavior in order to construct a model of the client. In decision making the test information is used to help the client make decisions or for the counselor to make decisions about the individual. In theory building the information from objective or formal measurement of clients is used to build theoretical concepts of behavior.

Prediger (1974) saw three major purposes of assessment in counseling. The first is to help clients stimulate, broaden, and provide focus to their career exploration. The second is to help the individual in self-exploration. The third is to help individuals identify various career options. Tests are viewed as a source of information that can help people to expand their outlooks.

Zunker (1994) saw assessment data as providing diagnostic, predictive, and comparative uses in career counseling. He felt that the diagnostic information can be used to increase individuals' self-awareness and to help individuals identify their strengths. The data have predictive values also and can yield information regarding the probable course of action the individual might take; for example, do the scores have to be admitted to college or graduate school? The information on some interest tests is often compared to different occupational groups. Herr and Cramer (1992) stated that tests in career counseling help clients understand their interests, values, and personality characteristics.

In summary, the functions of the assessment can help clients gain new insights, explore and modify their career interest and concepts of self, and allow them to make comparisons with norming and occupational groups. The procedure is an efficient way of collecting data and helps stimulate a broader focus on themselves and career possibilities. The counselor and client have to decide whether formal assessment techniques, such as standardized tests, or informal techniques, such as structured interviews, would provide the most valid information for the purposes it was needed.

DEVELOPMENTAL ASSESSMENT MODEL

Super (1990) proposed a new model of assessment for career guidance. The model consists of four steps: preview, depth-view— further testing?, assessment of all the data, and counseling.

Step One

In step one counselors begin by reviewing their clients' records and then interview them. Then counselors make a counseling plan based on their preliminary assessment. In the interview the counselor asks the client about the importance of work and the values the client hopes to realize through the worker role. The counselor ascertains the counselee's readiness to assess his or her abilities and interests and to make self- and occupational matching decisions.

Step Two

The counselor assesses the work salience, work values, and career maturity of the client. Super, Osborne, Walsh, Brown, and Niles (1992) have developed instruments to measure these three constructs. The Work Salience Inventory measures the relative importance of five diverse roles in the individual's life— study, work and career, home and family, community service, and leisure activities. The instrument looks at the individual's participation in each role, the commitment to each role, and knowledge of each role.

The *Values Scale* measures 21 values that are either extrinsic or intrinsic, such as prestige, creativity, altruism, social interaction, and the like. The *Career Development Inventory* can be used to measure the client's stage of career maturity. Super and Thompson (1979) identified four aspects of career maturity: planfulness, exploratory attitudes, decision-making skills, and information.

Planfulness is a tendency to plan based on a sense of control, an awareness of the past and anticipation of the future, and a sense of self-esteem (Nevill & Super, 1986). Exploratory attitudes are characterized by "a habit of asking questions about the various roles of life and the developmental tasks to be encountered" (p. 7). The test scores do not provide all the information that the counselor needs. The counselor needs to compare the clients/aspirations with labor market information and ability or aptitude tests.

Steps Three and Four

The counselor and client need to be able to synthesize and understand the information from the tests so that they know where they are in the developmental process. The client needs to understand the relation of the role of work with the other life roles and how these values fit together.

The counselor guides the client in exploration, or crystallization, or where the client is developmentally. An outline of steps two and three are included in Figure 15.1.

FIGURE 15.1
Super's development assessment model

Step Two: Depth-view—further testing?
    A. Work salience
        1. Relative importance of diverse roles
            a. Study
            b. Work and career
            c. Home and family
            d. Community service
            e. Leisure activities
        2. Participation in each role
        3. Commitment to each role
        4. Knowledge of each role
    B. Values sought in each role
    C. Career maturity
        1. Planfulness
        2. Exploratory attitudes
        3. Decision-making skills
        4. Information
            a. World of work
            b. Preferred occupational group
            c. Other life-career roles
        5. Realism
    D. Level of abilities and potential functioning
    E. Field of interest and probable activity
Step Three: Assessment of all data
    A. Review of all data
    B. Work salience
    C. Values
    D. Career maturity
        1. Individual and occupations
        2. Individual and nonoccupational roles
    E. Planning communication with counselee, family, and
        so on

OTHER MODELS

There are other models or approaches for counselors to use to look at assessment. Brooks (1984) stated that career theories look at career problems in one of four ways:

1. Matching the client's interests, needs, and skills with the appropriate occupation (Holland, 1985; Bordin, 1990; Roe, 1956)
2. Looking at developmental approaches to career maturity and decision making (Super, 1990; Ginzberg, 1988; Super, Osborne, Walsh, Brown, & Niles, 1992)
3. Focusing on the decision-making process (Tiedeman & Miller-Tiedeman, 1984; Krumboltz, 1979)
4. Identifying barriers or obstacles posed by the social environment (sociological approaches)

The assessment procedures to support each approach are available. The social environment approach is used probably less often but there are instruments to measure locus of control, attribution, and dimensions of the psychosocial environment of the individual.

Drummond (1992) advocated that counselors use a decision-making model to determine what assessment tools and techniques would be needed. The first step is preparation, which involves the following:

- Specifying the judgments and decisions to be made
- Describing the information needed
- Locating the information already available in files or records
- Deciding what information is still needed and when and how this information can be obtained
- Selecting data—gathering instruments and tests to be used and reviewing the instruments for validity, reliability, usability, and interpretability

The second step of the decision-making process is data collection, which involves the following:

- Securing the needed information through testing, observation, and other appropriate methods
- Recording, analyzing, and interpreting the information

The third step of the decision-making process is evaluation, which involves the following:

- Forming hypotheses
- Making decisions or judgments
- Reporting those decisions and judgments

SOURCES OF TEST INFORMATION

Many sources of test information are available to counselors. Of special interest to career counselors are the following:

> Kapes, J. T., & Mastie, M. M. (Eds.). (1988). *A counselor's guide to career assessment instruments* (2nd ed.). Alexandria, VA: American Association for Counseling and Development.

The volume presents a review and analysis of 43 of the most commonly used career instruments and an annotated listing of 126 other instruments. The multiple aptitude batteries, interest inventories, work value instruments, career development and maturity instruments, personality measures, as well as combined assessment programs and instruments for special populations are included in the volume.

> Educational Testing Service. (1987). The *ETS test collection catalog: Volume 2: Vocational tests and measurement devices.* Phoenix, AZ: Ornx Press.

The volume contains the description of more than 1,400 tests that cover such areas as work sample tests, career choice, and planning aids, vocational interest and aptitude instruments, and personal evaluation instruments.
There are many other annotated list of tests.

> Mitchell, J. V., Jr., (Ed.). (1983). *Tests in print III.* Lincoln: Buros Institute of Mental Measurements, University of Nebraska–Lincoln.
> Sweetland, R. C., & Keyser, D. J. (1986). *Tests* (2nd ed.). Austin, TX: Pro Ed.

The Educational Testing Service (ETS) has one of the largest libraries of tests—more than 13,000 from America and selected foreign test publishers—and publishes annotated bibliographies of tests. Following are examples of bibliographies that would be of interest to career counselors:

> Occupational Attitudes and Job Satisfaction
> Adult Basic Education
> Vocational Measures for the Handicapped
> Clerical Aptitude and Achievement
> Employment Interviews
> Mechanical Aptitude and Knowledge
> Occupational Knowledge and Skilled Trades
> Professional Occupations
> Vocational Choice-Perception-Development
> Vocational and Industrial Aptitude
> Vocational Interests
> Vocational Ratings and Selection Forms

TEST REVIEWS

Several sources of test reviews other than the Counselor's Guide to Career Assessment Instruments are readily available. The classics in the field are the *Mental Measurements Yearbooks*. The 11th yearbook is the latest one in the series.

> Kramer, J., & Conoley, J. (Eds.). (1992). *The eleventh mental measurements yearbook*. Lincoln: Buros Institute of Mental Measurements, University of Nebraska–Lincoln.

The yearbooks come out every few years and contain usually two critical reviews of the tests listed. The Buros Institute has developed an on-line data base so that current test reviews are provided to professionals and the information is available to users through BRS Informational Technology Services. New test critiques are reviewed each month by the institute and then entered, if acceptable, into the data base.

A new series that provides useful and practical information on tests published by the Test Corporation of America is the *Test Critiques Series.* There are now 10 volumes of the critiques available and volume eight is in press. These reviews are geared to the practitioner and discuss both applied and theoretical issues. A comparison of the advantages and disadvantages of each test information source can be found in the June 1988 issue of the *Journal of Employment Counseling* (Drummond, 1988).

TYPES OF TESTS

The primary types of tests used in career counseling are aptitude, achievement, interest, vocational maturity, values, and career development. Sometimes self-concept, locus of control, and personality tests are given.

Aptitude Tests

Aptitude tests measure an individual's capacity, or potential, for a given skill or task, and are used to predict and describe behavior. There are multiaptitude batteries and specialized batteries. Four of the most widely used multiaptitude batteries are the *Armed Services Vocational Aptitude Battery* (ASVAB), the *Differential Aptitude Battery* (DAT), the *United States Employment Service* (USES) *General Aptitude Test Battery* (GATB), and the *Career Ability Placement Survey* (CAPS).

ASVAB

The ASVAB was first developed in 1966 and has gone through several revisions since then; Form 19 is the current edition. The ASVAB measures aptitude in general academic areas and in career areas that encompass most of the civilian and military world of work (U.S. Department of Defense, 1992). The ASVAB has 10 subtests and takes 3 hours to complete. The scales are general science, arithmetic reasoning, word knowledge, paragraph comprehension, numerical operations, coding speed, automobile shop information, mathematics knowledge, mechanical comprehension, and electronics information. The test yields three composite scores:

> Academic ability: word knowledge, paragraph comprehension, and arithmetic reasoning
> Verbal: word knowledge, paragraph comprehension, and general science
> Math: mathematics knowledge and arithmetic reasoning

The ASVAB has three occupational composite scores:

> Mechanical and crafts: arithmetic reasoning; mechanical comprehension; and auto, shop, and electronics information
> Business and clerical: word knowledge, paragraph comprehension, mathematical knowledge, electronics information, and general science
> Health, social, and technology: word knowledge, paragraph meaning, arithmetic reasoning, and mechanical comprehension

Differential Aptitude Test (DAT)

The DAT is used for vocational and educational guidance with students in grades 8–12. The test takes 235 minutes and contains eight subtests: verbal reasoning, abstract reasoning, mechanical reasoning, numerical reasoning, spelling, sentence structure, clerical speed and accuracy, and spatial relations. The *Career Planning Questionnaire* can also be used with the test. There is also a computer adaptive version available that is discussed in Chapter 14 on the use of the computer in career counseling.

USES General Aptitude Test Battery

The GATB is one of the most widely used batteries for assessment in vocational counseling. The test takes 150 minutes and measures nine dimensions: verbal, numerical, spatial, form perception, clerical perception, motor coordination, finger dexterity, manual dexterity, and general learning ability. The test has good supporting materials available such as the *Guide for Occupational Exploration*, *Dictionary of Occupational Titles*, and the *Bridge of the World of Work*.

Career Ability Placement Survey

The CAPS is a 50-minute battery used to assess abilities for jobs in 14 occupational clusters and contains eight tests: mechanical reasoning, spatial relations, verbal reasoning, numerical ability, language usage, work knowledge, perceptual speed and accuracy, and manual speed and dexterity.

The authors of CAPS state that the test can be used for the following purposes:

- Classroom career exploration units, matching individual student's abilities with occupational requirements
- School course training program selection
- Career development with the COPSystem, Interest Inventory, and COPES, a values profile
- Curriculum evaluation
- Employee evaluation

The aptitude batteries have many subtests or scales that are similar but differ primarily in coverage in the practical, dexterity, and mechanical areas. The target group for each test also differs. Some are more for adults, others primarily for high school students.

Specialized Aptitude Batteries

There are some specialized batteries to measure specific aptitudes. There are tests designed to measure clerical ability, mechanical ability, psychomotor ability, artistic ability, musical aptitude, and computer aptitude. Both the multifactor and special aptitude tests are useful to career counselors who are helping their clients gain a better self-awareness and understanding of their own special abilities.

Achievement Testing

Achievement test information is also valuable to the career counselor to help clients in making educational and career decisions. Achievement tests measure acquired knowledge and skills. There are a variety of types of achievement tests, for example, survey achievement batteries, which measure knowledge and skills in reading, mathematics, language arts, social studies, and science. Sometimes the tests measure study skills and survival skills. There are single-subject achievement tests such as in algebra, chemistry, and the like. There are criterion-referenced tests that measure knowledge and comprehension of a specific set of skills or competencies or learning outcomes. There are minimum-level skills tests that measure objectives or skills identified as the minimum skills to

be achieved in order to pass from one level or grade to another or to pass a specific cause at the high school level. There are also individual achievement tests
that are administered individually across a wide age or grade range to measure
achievement usually in reading, mathematics, and the language arts. Diagnostic
tests are tests used to assess the strengths and weaknesses of students in a given
subject area by measuring a limited number of skills thoroughly.

Adult Achievement Tests

The *Test of Adult Basic Education* (TABE) measures adult proficiency in reading,
mathematics, and language. A locator test is first administered to determine which
is the most appropriate form, and then a practice exercise is available to reduce the
test taker's anxiety. The first form is on the second- to fourth-grade level; the second form, fourth- to sixth-grade level, and the third form, sixth- to ninth-grade
level. The reading test measures vocabulary and reading comprehension. The
mathematics test assesses computation skills, knowledge of concepts, and problems solving. The language test measures mechanics, expression, and spelling.

The *Wide Range Achievement Test-Revised* (WRAT-R) is used both with
children and adults to measure basic skills of word recognition, spelling, and
arithmetic. The WRAT-R provides information to aid the counselor in educational placement, vocational assessment, and job placement and training.

Achievement tests are valuable to the career counselor for four major reasons according to Seligman (1980). These provide an objective measure of how
much an individual has learned, to show the relative standing of the individual
in relation to different reference groups (e.g., class, school, nation), to indicate in
which educational areas a person is in need of remediation, and help identify the
areas in which the individual has most strength.

Interest Assessment

Interest tests and assessment devices have been used since Miner in 1918 developed one of the first interest questionnaires and Strong published in 1927 the
Vocational Interest Blank.

There are a wide variety of techniques and instruments used to measure
interests. Some of the most widely used scales are the *Self-Directed Search*
(SDS), the *Strong Interest Inventory* (SII), the *Kuder Occupational Interest Survey*, Form DD, (KOIS), revised, and the *Career Occupational Preference System*
(COPS).

The *Self-Directed Search* is one of the most widely used interest inventories. The SDS is 16 pages in length and can be administered to high school students and adults. The SDS is designed to provide immediate feedback to the
examinee and can be self-administered and self-scored. Specifically the examinees are asked to list their daydreams, activities that are liked or disliked, competencies, occupations of interest, and self-appraisals in mechanical, scientific,

teaching, sales, and clerical fields. The SDS yields a summary code of three letters representing the three highest personality types from the six—realistic, investigative, artistic, social, enterprising, and conventional. There is a version, Form E, that is available for people with a fourth-grade reading level and that yields a two-letter code rather than a three-letter code. There is also a computerized version of the test.

The Strong Interest Inventory

The SII used Holland's typology as a basis for interpreting the scores by including these as six general occupational themes. The SII includes 207 occupational scales and 17 new nonprofessional or vocational/technical occupations. The authors give the following purposes for the test: to aid students in making occupational choices, to serve as a stimulus for exploring life-styles and vocations, and be a catalyst in student-parent discussions.

The manual also states the values it has for use with employees: to aid them in employment decisions, to help adults considering mid-career evaluation and change, to aid in identifying and advising managerial candidates, to help clients understand job satisfaction and dissatisfaction, and to aid in preretirement and retirement planning. The test can be computer-administered and scored or sent to a scoring service for results.

Career Occupational Preference System (COPS)

COPS measures interests and uses a modified version of Roe's classification system in the profile. The scales on the test are as follows:

Science professional	Business skilled
Science skilled	Clerical
Technology professional	Communication
Technology skilled	Arts professional
Consumer economics	Arts skilled
Outdoor	Service professional
Business professional	Service skilled

COPS is an integrated system that also contains a values inventory as well as an aptitude inventory. There are correlative materials available for use by the clients to help them find out more about the different occupations within a category. Clients are urged to consider career groups for which interest, aptitude, and work values are all high.

There are many other interest inventories available. The counselor needs to be familiar with how the instruments organize the interest information and the type of occupations or job clusters included and the type of client taking the test. The educational and intellectual level of the examinee also needs to be considered. There are several picture interest inventories, some of which are available on videotape.

Interest inventories are used for three general purposes according to MacAleese (1984): to identify the unknown interest of the client, confirm the stated interests of the client, and to identify the discrepancies between aptitude and interest.

Values Inventories

Values are an important part of the assessment process in career counseling. Values show the relative importance people place on activities. There are many different approaches to appraising values from general inventories measuring global values to more specific inventories measuring specifically work values. *Rokeach Value Survey* includes two sets of 18 values. The first set of values is called terminal; the second, behavioral. The terminal values include comfortable life, exciting life, sense of accomplishment, world at peace, world of beauty, equality, family security, freedom, health, inner harmony, mature love, national security, pleasure, salvation, self-respect, social recognition, true friendship, and wisdom. The behavioral values include ambitious, broad minded, capable, clean, courageous, forgiving, helpful, honest, imaginative, independent, intellectual, logical, loving, loyal, obedient, polite, responsible, and self-controlled. Test takers are asked to rank order the two sets.

Several tests measure work values. The *Career Orientation Placement and Evaluation Survey* (COPES) measures personal values that have been observed to be related to the type of work one chooses and the satisfactions derived from the work one does. There are eight dimensions:

Investigative vs. accepting
Practical vs. carefree
Independence vs. conformity
Leadership vs. supportive
Orderliness vs. noncompulsive
Recognition vs. privacy
Aesthetic vs. realistic
Social vs. self-concern

Both self-scoring and machine-scoring forms can be given from seventh grade through adulthood. The test takes approximately 40 to 50 minutes and self-interpretative profiles and guides can be used with the test.

Super has two values scales, the *Work Values Inventory* and the *Values Scale*. The *Work Values Inventory* (WVI) measures 15 extrinsic and intrinsic values important to the world of work. There are 45 items that people are asked to rate as to their importance on a 5-point scale. The WVI includes scales such as altruism, aesthetics, creativity, intellectual stimulation, independence, achievement, economic returns, security, prestige, management, surroundings, supervisory relations, variety, and way of life.

A longer scale measuring 21 values rather than 14 is the *Values Scale.* There are 106 items on the scale and test takers are asked to rate the importance of the items on a 4-point scale. It was developed for use in a crosscultural study and includes some of the same values as on the WVI, but some different ones such as risk, physical prowess, and personal development.

Career Development Instruments

There are many career development inventories that have been developed to help counselors assess dimensions such as role salience, career attitudes, career knowledge, career maturity, career stage, and career decision making.

Two of the tests which Super and his associates have developed to support his developmental theory are the *Career Development Inventory* (CDI) and the *Salience Inventory.* The CDI is a 120-item pencil-and-paper test assessing eight dimensions of occupational decision making: career planning, career exploration, decision making, world of work information, knowledge of preferred occupational group, career development knowledge and skills, and career orientation. The test yields scores in career development attitudes, career development-knowledge and skills, and career orientation total. One disadvantage of the test is that it has to be sent to be machine scored by the publisher.

The *Salience Inventory* (SI) is a test developed to measure the relative importance of the roles of study, work and career, home and family, community service, and leisure activities on a person's life and the values the individual seeks in each role. The first component in the SI is anticipation, what the individual actually does or has done recently. The second component of the SI is commitment, how the individual feels about the different roles. The third component is value expectations. Test takers are asked which values they seek in each of the five major life roles such as ability utilization, achievement, aesthetics, altruism, autonomy, creativity, economics, life-style, physical activity, prestige, risk, social interaction, variety, and working conditions.

The *Career Maturity Inventory* (CMI) is authored by John O. Crites and published by CTB/McGraw-Hill. The CMI has two parts, an attitude scale and a competency test. The attitude scale measures five areas: decisiveness in career decision making, involvement in career decision making, independence in career decision making, orientation to career decision making, and compromise in career decision making. The competency test has five subscales: self-appraisal, occupational information, goal selection, planning, and problem solving.

The CMI measures attitudes and competencies important for career decision making. The test is untimed and takes on the average about 3 hours. The CMI can be machine or hand scored and was developed for use with 6th- to 12th-grade students.

The *Adult Career Concerns Inventory* (ACCI) is authored by Donald E. Super, Albert S. Thompson, and Richard H. Linderman and published by Consulting Psychologists Press. The test measures Super's theory of life stages (exploration, establishment, maintenance, and disengagement). The test also has a career change status scale.

TEST ADMINISTRATION

The AACD (1980, 1989) standards emphasize the importance of following the proper test administration procedures. Counselors need to make sure that the test is presented consistently in the manner specified by the test developers and/or used in the standardization, and that the people being tested have orientation and conditions that maximize their opportunity for optimal performance.

To get the best results as a result of testing, the client has to see the importance of the experience and be motivated to take the tests. The counselor has to know all about the test before giving it, specifically, the content of the test, the type of items, and the directions for administering the test. The AACD (1989) position statement stated that effective administration of the test requires the counselor to have knowledge of and training in the actual instruments and the process of presentation.

TEST INTERPRETATION

There are some general guidelines that counselors should follow in interpreting tests. Shertzer and Linden (1979) recommended the following:

- Describe the test and test results in nontechnical terms
- Explain the type of test scores used in reporting the results
- Provide a simple and organized presentation of the results and don't overwhelm the test takers with too much information at once
- Present the results clearly and honestly in terms of a perspective the client can understand
- Encourage the clients to express and explore their reactions to the test results and their feelings and attitudes toward the scores

There are a variety of types of interpretations that the counselor might use. Zytowski (1981) gave the following examples:

Unadorned—"Your interests are most similar to a school counselor." Or, "Your three high point codes on the SDS are SAI, social, artistic, and investigative."

Extrapolative—"Your interests are most similar to a school counselor. You also might want to consider social worker, psychologist, and personnel worker." Information is added that helps clients in their interpretation of the results.

Synthetic—"You seem to like to work in careers that are helping professions." "Your SDS code was SIA." "Your scores on the achievement and aptitude test show you have excellent communication skills and problem-solving abilities. You need these skills in the helping professions." The counselor provides general ideas that the clients can incorporate into their image of themselves.

Predictive—"Ninety-five people out of 100 who have scores similar to you on the SAT are successful in this program." The counselor uses test data to offer a prediction to the client in this approach.

Evaluative—"It appears to me your best bet would be . . . " The counselor uses test results to suggest to their clients what they should do.

Genetic—"It appears that your problems in information processing relate to your learning disability." The counselor in this approach uses information from assessment to explain how the individual got to be a certain way.

Personological interpretations—"I bet you like to work in groups better and that you don't like competition." The counselor infers personality descriptions from scores on tests intended to measure other domains. Here the counselor saw high scores on the social worker scale.

In reviewing new developments in test interpretation such as counselor guided, self-directed, and computer-produced reports Zytowski and Borgen (1983) concluded that the clients prefer human intervention even though the other methods might be as beneficial.

OTHER METHODS OF ASSESSMENT

A variety of other types of self-appraisal instruments and techniques other than standardized pencil-and-paper type of inventories can be used. Some of the computer-assisted approaches are discussed in chapter 14. Other techniques involve the use of card sorts, interview procedures, guided fantasy, self-rating scales, and observational techniques. Super and Crites (1962) identified four techniques that can be used to measure interest: expressed interests—what clients say their interests are; manifest interests—what clients are observed actually doing; testing—what clients know about various fields; and interest inventories—what clients check about their interests and preferences.

Many of the self-help books contain a wide variety of self-appraisal exercises to help clients organize their own characteristics and how they relate to the world of work. They are asked to identify their skills through the context of their achievements. The approach presents problems to individuals who have not achieved or had the opportunity to learn skills.

Use of Myers-Briggs in Career Counseling

Miller (1992) found that the combination of the SII and Myers-Briggs Type Indicator (MBTI) provide clients with "within" occupational information and could provide the catalyst for the client to consider how his or her preferences related to the many settings in which a given occupation group work. He stated that as clients begin to understand why certain occupations are more appealing to them, they become more motivated to the task of finding the needed pieces of career-related information. Hummerow (1991) indicated that both instruments are used in career counseling because they give a fuller picture of a client. He also summarized the relationship between the MBTI types and those of Holland. For example, males whose high point code is social tend to have extraversion, sensing, and feeling preferences, and females tend to be high on the extraversion, perception, and intuitive scales. Hammer (1993) listed each of the 16 types on the MBTI and provided a list of the 10 most attractive or popular occupations for that type. For example, the most attractive occupations for a ESFJ (extraverted feeling with sensing) are teacher, administrator: student personnel, manager: office, religious-oriented occupations, dental assistant, child-care worker, home economist, hair dresser or cosmetologist, receptionist, and food service worker. ESFJs tend to like to set up effective procedures, are defensive, keep what works, have skills, and are skilled at building consensus. Hammer (1993) provided a table for each type that explores how they set goals, gather information, make contacts, and make decisions, lists their preferred methods, the potential obstacles, and tips to improve the exploration and decision making of this group. ESFJs prefer immediate and tangible goals to long-term goals. They tend to collect just enough facts to make a decision rather than focus on the long-term outlook. Although they usually have an extensive network, they may spend valuable time in unproductive networking. They usually use a subjective, person-centered approach in making their decisions and avoid at times considering the logical consequences of each alternative. Hammer's (1993) publication is *Introduction to Type and Careers* and guides clients through career exploratory activities and is designed to help individuals choose a new job or career, change their job or career, or increase their satisfaction with their present career.

Guided Fantasy

Many career counselors use guided fantasy in their repertory of assessment tools. Jones (1984) identified three major components of guided fantasy: relaxing the clients, leading them through the fantasy exercise, and then helping the clients examine and reflect on the experiences.

Example of an Exercise

"Picture yourself at work 10 years from now. Relax and let your ideas flow. You are videotaping highlights from a typical day. Describe to me . . ."

Checklists and Rating Forms

Many of the workbooks and workshop materials include self-rating scales. Clients are asked to check the descriptors or behaviors that apply to them or rate each item on a 3- to 5-point scale.

Example:

Check an *x* before the statements that sound like something that you might like to do or think.

> fix things for myself
> make things with my hands
> help people with their personal problems

Career Portfolio

The career portfolio provides authentic assessment of an individual's growth and development and has the potential for providing career direction that is stronger and more effective than traditional career counseling (Bernhardt, Cole, & Ryan, 1993). The portfolio becomes part of the process of developing reflection among students and adults as they make career decisions. The use of portfolios by career counselors provides access to students' thoughts regarding career plans, educational results, and career exploratory activities. Portfolios offer a less than traditional process for analyzing a person's growth in the career area that is different from traditional test inventories, computer simulations, and face-to-face individual counseling. The career data in the portfolio give career counselors an opportunity to analyze client thought in a broader context (e.g., reflecting on values, questioning decisions, and exploring alternatives). It is authentic self-analysis with reflection.

A variety of approaches can be used by career counselors as they work with clients. The following portfolio model is provided as an example for use at the high school level (see Figure 15.2). The content areas were developed by a team of high school teachers in a moderate-sized midwestern community. The particular group of students in this setting were identified as being in at-risk category, hence the area of self-esteem was given more attention in each individual portfolio.

The following are potential areas in which portfolios can be used by career counselors in either institutional or private practice settings (Bernhardt, Cole, & Ryan, 1993):

- Individual counseling to examine career goals and plans in-depth
- Group counseling sessions that would permit participants to share portfolio content with others
- Career fairs where portfolios could be used for display of career growth and development to potential employers. An executive summary of one or two pages should be developed for each client.

FIGURE 15.2
Career portfolio model

1. **Introduction**
   A. Title page
   B. Prereflections on why and importance of doing daily journal
   C. Postreflection on why and importance of doing daily journal
2. **Student Self-portrait**
   A. Attendance goal 90%
   B. Topics for daily log
   C. Rate attitude (1–4) (manners, willingness to work, completes assignments on time)
   D. Daily log—student's reflection on the day
3. **Education plan**
   A. Proficiency test, drug survey, self-esteem test results
   B. Intake forms, test of adult basic education results
   C. Student goals
   D. Copies of exceptional work
4. **Career plan**
   A. Career and education plan
   B. Short-term and long-term goals
5. **Conclusions**
   A. Reflection—goals for career planning
   B. Evaluation of short-term goals
   C. Expectations for future

- Individual employers that clients could call on individually. The portfolio could be left with the employer to review and return at a later time. Our experiences suggest that this is a very effective process.
- Immediate family members, spouse, or other significant adults who could review, discuss, and validate career plans

Scoring of portfolios in comparison with traditional practices requires considered use of professional judgment by the career counselors. Portfolio outcomes are tied to assessing the clients' progress on developing a set of career goals that are appropriate for them. The portfolio does not assess all clients on the same aptitude dimensions; rather, it captures the richness of each individuals' unique goals, values, and aspirations. A scoring process might include acceptable/unacceptable global ratings on the part of the career counselor. Each career counselor will need to decide a scoring process that will reflect the level of career maturity presented in the portfolio reflection. For example, Client A, who states, "I want to be an engineer. My father is.", demonstrates a low level of reflective thought. Client B, who states, "My goals are to enter the engineering field with a major in electrical. This is consistent with my strong vocational interest inventory and differential aptitude test scores that were taken in the junior year. Also, my grades in mathematics and science have been at the A level. During the Career Fair I discussed training and educational opportunities with several colleges and it reinforced my plans.", demonstrates above-average reflective thought. In short, scoring portfolios required considerable judgment on the counselors part.

SUMMARY

Test and assessment instruments are just one tool to help clients gain greater self-awareness and knowledge of their interests, aptitudes, values, and achievement. Counselors need to be knowledgeable about the instruments and be trained in test administration and interpretation. Counselors need to make sure that the tests and assessment instruments are valid and reliable for which purposes they intend to use them.

REVIEW QUESTIONS

1. What career guidance tests have you taken? What was your reaction to these tests? Why were they taken? Did you find the results useful?
2. What role do you think career assessment has in career counseling?
3. Identify several career development theories. What type of assessment instruments were developed as part of those theories?
4. What are some of the important sources of test information? What types of information does each source provide?
5. What types of tests do career counselors use? Why?
6. What factors should a counselor consider in administering tests to clients?
7. What are the important guidelines to follow in interpreting test results to clients?
8. Discuss the different types of test interpretations. When would you use each of the types? Why?
9. What other types of assessment techniques do career counselors use? Give examples of when you would use each type and why.

SUGGESTED LEARNING ACTIVITIES

1. Do a critical review of one of the widely used tests in the career counseling field. Discuss the technical qualities of the tests, the practical values, and what the experts think about the test. What is your personal reaction to the test?
2. Interview counselors in different contexts and find out what tests they use and why. Compare the similarities and differences across settings.
3. Administer one of the career guidance tests, score it, and write an interpretation of the results. Tape the session when you report the results back to the test taker and play the tape to the class.

4.   Make a bibliography of career guidance tests that would be appropriate for use at the level on which you plan to work.

5.   Review some of the computerized test reports. What are some of the common features of the reports? How do they differ in format?

6.   Construct a short nonverbal (picture) interest test and try it out on several individuals. What was their reaction to the test?

7.   Construct a card sort, a fantasy exercise, and so on and administer it to several individuals. What was their reaction to the assessment technique?

CASE STUDIES

Rita

Rita is 30 and a single parent. She has a daughter 5 years old. She has graduated with a B.A. in elementary education, and is currently a severe learning disability Resource Teacher K–5. She wants to change job fields and has come into the career planning and placement office to get some help.

She lists as her strengths working well with people, having good communication skills, being creative, ability to work well independently, and being analytical. She lists as her weaknesses being a procrastinator, being a poor speller, taking things too seriously, and being unsure of herself in public speaking situations. She lists as her top values: honesty, harmony, money, responsibility, and self-worth. When asked to list her five top job interests, she names counseling, physical therapy, occupational therapy, arts/crafts, and child development. On the Myers-Briggs she is an ENTJ. On the Strong Occupational Themes Scale, she is moderately high on social and average on the other five. Her interests were found to be most similar to individuals in the following social occupations: guidance counselor, speech pathologist, YWCA director, special education teacher, recreational leader.

Her strongest basic interest areas were adventure, mathematics, writing, social service, public speaking, mechanical activities, art, teaching domestic arts, and merchandising. Her interests were similar to people working as YWCA directors and moderately similar to people working as dietitians, special education teachers, recreation leaders, store managers, guidance counselors, speech pathologists, personnel directors, and IRS agents.

Her interests were very dissimilar to people working as an athletic trainer, physicist, mathematician, physical education teacher, emergency medical technician, physical therapist, nurse, and LPN.

Her academic comfort score falls in the average range. Her score on the introversion-extroversion scale falls in the extroverted direction.

Case Questions
1.   How would you describe Rita's interests?
2.   ENTJs tend to work as management consultants, human resource personnel, computer professionals, family physicians, sales managers, credit investigators, marketing professional, educational administrators, and health administrators. How do those fields fit in with Rita's expressed interest and those identified on the SII?
3.   On the MBTI, Rita's potential strengths are ability to get things organized, problem solving at a systems level, being decisive, being analytical, and have long-range vision. How would you guide her to think about her career development?
4.   What other types of information would you like to have to guide Rita to make her career and educational decisions?
5.   If you were Rita, what decisions would you make?

Charles

Charles is a 24-year-old male who graduated from a state university with a major in English. He could not find a job where he could use his degree, and finally found work as a waiter at a local upscale restaurant. For the past couple of weeks he reports that he has been feeling depressed because he feels that his life is at a dead-end. He wants to get a professional job, but does not know what to do next. He feels that he might have made the wrong decision about his major. He is considering going back to school to get another degree. He took the *Values Scale*, the *Salience Inventory*, the *Adult Career Concerns Inventory*, and the *Self-Directed Search*.

His total scores on the SDS were as follows:

Realistic	27
Investigative	25
Artistic	7
Social	21
Enterprising	32
Conventional	23

His code would be ERI. He looked up occupations with similar codes and found the following occupations: chemical equipment sales engineer, director of research and development, manager of bulk plant, revenue agent, sales engineer mechanical equipment, special agent, superintendent logging, and superintendent drilling. His scores on the Values Scale are as follows:

On the Values Scale	Raw Score
Ability utilization	16
Achievement	18
Advancement	12
Aesthetics	8
Altruism	13
Authority	11
Autonomy	18
Creativity	13
Economic returns	15
Life-style	20
Personal development	11
Physical activity	16
Prestige	13
Risk	10
Social interaction	9
Social relations	10
Variety	11
Working conditions	8
Cultural identity	7
Physical prowess	8
Economic security	13

On the *Adult Career Concerns Inventory*, he rated the first 15 items "5" (having great concern). The items make up the exploration stage and consist of three substages: crystallization, specification, and implementation. On the establishment stage, Charles was concerned with items dealing with settling down in a job he could stay with but rated the other item of little or some concern. The maintenance and disengagement stage items were all rated of none or little concern.

On the *Salience Inventory*, Charles rated home and family highest, then followed by studying, leisure activity, working, and community service.

Case Questions
1. Give a brief description of Charles.
2. What would you advise him to do?

3.   What additional information would you like to have to help in your counseling of Charles?
4.   What do you think Charles will end up doing?

SUGGESTED READINGS

Comer, J. (1991). *Using the Strong Interest Inventory and the Myers-Briggs Type Indicator together.* Palo Alto, CA: Consulting Psychologists Press.

The author goes through a case study using a five-stage model of career development.

Drummond, R. J. (1990). *Appraisal procedures for counselors and helping professional* (2nd ed.). Columbus, OH: Merrill/Macmillan.

The author presents a general overview of models for test use and selection, basic competencies needed, types of tests and assessment procedures, test takers and their needs, test administrators and their roles, test utilization in different settings, and current issues and trends.

Hammer, A. L. (1993). *Introduction to type and careers.* Palo Alto, CA: Consulting Psychologists Press.

The author guides readers through looking at their type, establishing goals, how to increase job satisfaction, reaching goals, and the career development process for each of the 16 types.

PART

CONTEMPORARY AND FUTURE PRACTICES, TRENDS, AND ISSUES

16

COUNSELING STRATEGIES

C areer counselors use a wide variety of counseling strategies. They work one-to-one with some clients, and use group methods or other strategies with others. The type of clients and their needs partially determines the approach the counselor will use. Career counselors need not only to have a repertory of counseling skills but also a knowledge of the developmental stages and knowledge of the world of work.

The type of approach will depend on who is the target of intervention: an individual, a small group, or an extended group. The purpose can be different. The counseling may be developmental, preventative, or possibly remedial. The intervention selected might be computer-assisted counseling, realistic job preview, direct counseling, or participation in seminars or workshops. The type of approach will also depend on the theoretical orientation of the counselor, for example, whether one has preference for psychoanalytic, or client-centered theory. The type of problem will influence the approach that counselors will take in a given situation. In addition the type of setting and type of agency will possibly restrict the type of clients who use the services as well as possibly determine the type of intervention to be implemented.

LEARNING OBJECTIVES

After reading this chapter you should be able to do the following:

- Identify types of problems faced by clients and approaches to helping them
- Identify strategies and techniques to help people at different developmental stages
- Discuss practices and techniques that work
- Apply group and individual counseling techniques to career counseling

CAREER COUNSELING PROBLEMS

A wide variety of career counseling problems arise. Certain types of problems tend to occur more at one stage than another. The presenting problems are not always the true problems of the client, and can cover a wide range—from a lack of information to inappropriate personal goals. The type of client and the type of problems faced by counselors are also a function of the counselors' work setting, whether it is a mental health clinic, a state employment service, a school or college placement or career center, a rehabilitation center, a sheltered workshop, or halfway house. Brooks (1990) pointed out that theories tend to explain problems in one of four ways. Difficulties are caused by problems of matching the interests, needs, and skills of the individual with the "right" occupation (see discussion of the trait-and-factor theory by Holland, 1985; Bordin, 1990; & Roe, 1956). Difficulties are caused by problems of development and/or vocational immaturity (Super, Osborne, Walsh, Brown, & Niles, 1992). Career problems can arise from the career decision-making process (Tiedeman & Miller-Tiedeman, 1984; Krumboltz, 1979). Last, problems occur from obstacles and barriers of the social environment (sociological perspective).

There have been a number of approaches used to categorize the types of problems career counselors face with clients. Williamson (1939) identified four general categories of problems: individuals who had no idea about their vocational plans or choices, individuals who were uncertain about their choice, individuals who were making unwise choices, and individuals who had a discrepancy between their aptitudes and interests. Williamson followed the trait-and-factor model, which emphasized match between the individual's characteristics and those required by the job. Hahn and McLean (1955) expanded the discrepancy dimensions to include appropriate field–inappropriate level, inappropriate field–appropriate level, and inappropriate field–inappropriate level. In working with the client a counselor needs to place his or her career choice in one of the dimension categories.

The perception of categories of problems is influenced by the theoretical orientation of the counselor. If the counselor used a psychoanalytic approach in his or her counseling (Bordin, 1990), the categories would be of psychological constructs rather than purely career choice constructs, for example, dependency, self-conflict, and choice anxiety. Holland (1985) stated that maladaptive career development equals the failure to develop a personality pattern that is consistent and differentiated, a clear sense of vocational identify, or a failure to establish a career in a congruent occupation. Maladaptive career development occurs as a result of one of the following:

- A person has had insufficient experience to acquire well-defined interests, competencies, and self-perceptions.
- A person has had insufficient experience to learn about the major kinds of occupational environments.
- A person has had ambiguous, conflicting, or deprecative experience about his or her interests, competencies, and personal characteristics.

- A person has acquired ambiguous, conflicting, or deprecative information about the major work environments.

These and other deficiencies make it difficult to translate personal characteristics into occupational opportunities. All four probably contribute to a diffused sense of identity so that choosing an occupation or changing jobs within a career is more uncertain. In addition, many other variables make the translation task difficult or very time consuming. Some people simply have a slow rate of personal development and have not developed a well-defined profile of interests and competencies, or they may be so alienated that they are uninvolved with work or deny the need to choose. And for a few people, neuroticism and pathology make job choosing, changing, and holding precarious; these tasks, like the other major problems of life, require effective interpersonal skills and some emotional stability.

Individuals experiencing difficulty with defining a career choice may fit one of the following:

- Some persons lack the personal, educational, or financial resources to carry out their plans.
- Some persons with consistent and differentiated profiles, and with a clear sense of identity, are unable to find congruent work due to economic or social barriers. The availability of work of different types is determined by the sociotechnical nature of the economy, cultural values, stages in the economic cycle, and traditional definitions of sexual or ethnic roles. And, hard times reduce both job opportunities and career assistance resources of all kinds.

Byrne (1958) expanded Bordin's categories to emphasize interpersonal conflicts such as immaturity, lack of problem-solving skills, lack of insight, lack of information, lack of assurance, and domination by authority, person, or situation.

Severinsen (1973) classified career counseling problems into five categories. These categories and typical types of statements made by clients include the following:

No Goals

I really don't know what I want to do. Nothing seems to interest me. I just try to survive one day at a time.

Choice Conflict

I would like to be a counselor or a psychologist. They both work with people, don't they? What is the difference between the two? Are there differences in what courses I need to take?

Failure

I was turned down for veterinarians' school. I guess I didn't have good enough grades or test scores. I had my mind set that was what I wanted to do. I am depressed.

Need Information

I see that paralegal workers will be in great demand. What do they do? What salaries do they make? Who hires them? Is there any future in that field?

Indecision, Indecisiveness

My mother says I should prepare to be a teacher. My dad says I should go into law. I don't think I like either one. Dad will be disappointed because he is a lawyer . . . and he will be paying for my college, but I don't think I would like either career.

STAGES OF COUNSELING

The Initial Interview

Counseling can be thought of as consisting of stages. The initial interview is a crucial stage in the counseling process. The first interview provides an opportunity for the counselor and client to explore a potential relationship and to assess the probabilities of success. Although the specific format and sequence of the initial interview may vary from counselor to counselor, one important goal is to develop and establish a good working and counseling relationship. The second goal is to observe the client directly, validate information if some preassessment was done, and begin collecting supplemental information that might be valuable to know in working with the client. The third goal is to provide and clarify what the structure will be for the counseling session. The counselor discusses the respective responsibilities of the client as well as the counselor.

The counselor must develop a gestalt of the presenting problem and have clients be open about why they came. The counselor attempts to open up the psychological realms of feelings and attitudes in the person.

Establishing Rapport

The counselor's first major challenge is to establish rapport with the client. The counselor must create an environment in which the client feels safe to explore conflicts, ideas, and options without being pressured to agree or to make decisions. The counselor wants clients to feel that they have been heard, understood, and it is safe to return for additional sessions. Spokane (1991) reminded us that the client brings a certain amount of energy and anxiety into the first session, and the principal therapeutic task of the counselor is to establish the context, set expectations, and to provide structure by informing the client what will or will not happen during counseling.

Basically, the counselor needs to get off to a good start, so the opening minutes of the first session are critical. Attention needs to be directed toward procedures such as the type of initial greeting and self-introduction and little things such as where to sit and where to put one's coat or packages or books. Sometimes a degree of small talk is necessary to cut the ice and break tension or anxiety; other times it is not necessary. The counselor needs to be alert to physiological cues of anxiety such as nervousness or hesitancy in speech.

The counselor can pause and see if the client is ready to start the interview. The counselor might ask a question such as "What brings you to the career counseling center?" or "How can I or the center help you?" or "Would you please tell me why you asked for an appointment at the career counseling center?" We cannot stress enough the importance of trust in dealing with all clients. Our clients seek our help and in effect put their lives in our hands. Counseling ethics require we treat this trust with respect and a sense of humility as we seek to assist clients to find meaning in life.

Client Opening

When asked why they are coming to the career center, clients might be cautious at first and conservative. Sometimes their statement might be vague or indefinite such as "I read in the newspaper about your career counseling center" or "My wife said I should come in for counseling." The counselor can probe and use a variety of techniques to seek clarification. The counselor has to be accepting and nonjudgmental to encourage the establishment of rapport and to clarify the problem or issue. Spokane (1991) recommended giving clients a brief handout about the structure of the counseling and information about the intervention process. They are told that they are expected to talk about their situation and share their feelings with supportive people.

Isaacson (1985) identified three levels of opening remarks. The first is when the presenting problem is indefinite. The second is when the statement gives indication that other problems might be present. Examples of these include the following: "I like meteorology but I am not doing well in it." "There are no jobs in my field." "I have to work from 4 a.m. to 4 p.m. as a taxi driver. That is more time than I want to give." The third type of presenting statement definitely relates to career counseling. Some examples include the following: "I am retiring after 20 years from the Navy and want to know what civilian jobs I might qualify for." "I am a sophomore and am doing well in all my classes but have no idea of what I want to major in here at college."

The statements provide insight into the client's problem, but the counselor tries through questioning and reflecting to get the client to expand and clarify the issues.

Structuring

Structuring involves the setting of the parameters of the relationship and includes such factors as the length of the sessions, how often, when they are to be scheduled, the fee, and where they are to be held. If parameters are not set, the client may develop unrealistic expectations and sometimes expects the counselor to immediately find him or her a job or to be able to describe immediately the career openings that are currently available. Spokane (1991) called this the aspiring stage that occurs before clients are willing to look at incongruency and conflict. The exchange will sound like the following:

Client:	Why do I have to bother going through these tests and computer guidance programs? How is that going to help me get a job?
Counselor:	You seem to be somewhat frustrated.
Client:	You betcha! What jobs are available for me? I have been looking for work for 6 months but don't know exactly what I want to do.
Counselor:	You expect me to decide what you should do and what job you should take.
Client:	Well, of course, you are the expert in career development.

The client has different perceptions and expectations of the counselor than what the counselor sees. The counselor finds that the client expects the counselor to take the responsibility and burden for career choice where as the counselor feels that the client should be responsible. This is just one type of problem that can be avoided if the counselor structures the counseling from the beginning and discusses the things the client is responsible for and what the structure of the additional sessions will be.

Data Collection and Diagnosis

Brooks (1990) stated that one of the first challenges facing the counselor is to try to determine the source of the client's problem and to collect data about why the client is having difficulties or problems. There might be an intake form and certain assessment instruments used to collect data beyond what is gleaned from the counseling sessions. A discussion of assessment procedures and techniques is included in Chapter 15. Other sources of information are personnel files in industry or cumulative records in a school. Both formal and informal assessment are focused on the type of individual as well as type and scope of problem.

In classifying a client's problems, Isaacson (1985) identified as important factors the client's presenting statement, the words and statements the client uses, the affective messages these words connote, and the general information about the client—the client's aptitudes, behavioral functioning, educational level, learning style, personality type, and the like.

Crites (1969, 1976) proposed that three types of diagnosis are necessary if one is to get to understand the client:

1. Differential diagnosis
      Purpose: to identify what the client's problem is
      Types of categories:
         A. Problems of adjustment—adjusted/maladjusted
         B. Problems of indecision—multipotential/undecided/uninterested
         C. Problems of unrealism—unrealistic/unfulfilled/coerced
2. Dynamic diagnosis
      Purpose: to find out why the client has the problem
      Data required: developmental and behavioral
3. Decisional diagnosis
      Purpose: to find out how the client makes decisions
      Data suggested: career maturity inventory

Goals and Plans

Krumboltz (1979, 1983) identifies setting goals as an important first step in career decision making. Counselors need to help the client set immediate goals that are easily understood. Clients have to decide whether they will continue in counseling if needed and if they want to keep the same counselor. Intermediate goals can be set more realistically after several sessions. Clients need to know the various strategies or approaches the counselor considers appropriate.

If the client agrees with the diagnosis of the problem, the counselor and client need to establish goals and action plans together. If the client has a problem of indecision between two occupations; for example, the counselor might want the client to interview a couple of people in each field, or possibly schedule some work experience. Establishing an action plan is step two of Krumboltz's DECIDE process (1977).

To be effective the counseling goal needs to be attainable by the client. The goals need to relate to the problem stated by the client and need to be agreed on by both parties. The goals and plans need to be flexible because there may be changes of direction happen as a result of counseling or other circumstances. The goals need to be within the counselees' competency. When clients can translate the information about themselves and their problems into an action plan, their self-confidence and self-worth is increased (McDaniels & Gysbers, 1992). Another approach is relating educational courses taken by high school through the baccalaureate degree to potential career opportunities.

Many times time is a factor because the client may be unemployed and work is necessary for survival. The counselor needs to discuss time, effort, and commitment and have clients prioritized their goal.

Evaluation

Counselors need to evaluate the session and look at their behavior as well as their clients' behavior (McDaniels & Gysbers, 1992). Spokane (1991) provided two major reasons for evaluation: accountability and to ensure treatments led to the welfare of the individuals. One important dimension is the motivation of the client. The counselor needs to evaluate why the client came for counseling at this time. The counselor needs to consider the client's expectations as well as possible sources that might impede change. The question of whether the client is willing to put time into the process is important.

The counselor also needs to assess the amount of information gained through the interview and whether there are any missing gaps, for example, about the client's work history or the client's career development to this point. Peterson, Sampson, and Reardon (1991) advocated the formative evaluation procedures while counseling is ongoing.

The counselor also needs to evaluate the cognitive capacity of the client as well as whether there was any evidence of any abnormal behavior, high anxiety, or pathologies. Emotional constraints such as fear, anxiety, guilt, and pride affect the way a person thinks and behaves.

Yost and Corbishley (1987) cautioned counselors to be alert to statements such as "I hate to do anything new because I always know I'll do it wrong and I feel so stupid and embarrassed." These types of statements might represent a habitual, generalized response to life and an emotional constraint.

They point out that for many clients the most serious constraints are cognitive. There are three broad classifications of dysfunctional cognitions:

> "I can't." Example: "I am not as good as others. I'll fail. I'll blow it."
> "I won't." Example: "It probably won't work out. I can't see myself doing that sort of thing."
> "I shouldn't." Example: "My family won't be willing to move from here to that area. It is not something my parents would allow me to do."

DEVELOPMENTAL COUNSELING

At each developmental stage, there are a number of normal developmental concerns that counselors need to consider. Brooks (1990) stated that the focus of counseling with adults depends on their developmental stage of life and career. The growth stage centers around accurate self-appraisal, social, and school adjustment. At the exploratory stage, issues focus on anxiety about career choices, lack of information, and lack of role models. These concerns usually are typical in the junior and senior high school students.

Concerns about identity and intimacy are a part of late adolescence and early adulthood. Young adults have problems finding jobs and are frustrated by the process.

In the establishment years (21 to 45 years old), clients have problems with settling down and sometimes question their earlier decisions. They reevaluate marriage, and there is a high divorce rate in this period. Many feel that they have not accomplished their life and career goals. Both women and men face mid-life transitions during this period. Many women return to the workplace when the last child begins school and face career reentry problems.

The period from 46 to 65 years is considered the maintenance period, and the normal developmental concerns of this period are feelings of failure, role reversals in marriage, and the recognition of intimacy needs (Srebalus, Marinelli, & Messing, 1982).

GROWTH STAGE COUNSELING

Sharf (1992) saw one of the major roles of the counselor in the growth stage as helping the individuals in gathering, evaluating, accepting, and integrating information about their educational and work selves. Although individuals get feedback from many sources, they need help to process this information. With the movement in the schools toward accountability, less emphasis is placed on students achieving affective objectives. Self-concept is a crucial factor in the development of career maturity (Super, 1990).

The counselor needs to have activities that assist individuals in periodically reviewing their actions and intentions and helping them to focus on the type of people they want to be (Sharf, 1992).

Healy (1982) provided us with eight principles to encourage the growth of self-awareness and self-confidence:

1. Self-awareness increase when individuals are directed and encouraged to experience a wide range of activities and then to reflect on them.
2. Self-awareness increase when individuals learn how to succeed and get positive reinforcement for their efforts.
3. Self-awareness and confidence increase when individuals are encouraged to show initiative and are able to develop expectations that they are competent.
4. Self-awareness and confidence increase when individuals are guided to gather and organize information about themselves in order to teach others about themselves.
5. Self-awareness and confidence increase if individuals obtain and integrate feedback from those qualified to observe them.

6. Self-awareness and confidence increase systematically if the counselor has a planned program grounded in an appropriate model and with appropriate goals and objectives.

7. Self-awareness increases when individuals are guided to observe and reflect on the significant others in their life and their interaction with these figures.

8. Self-awareness increases when individuals are guided to review their records and achievements and deduce their implications in a supportive setting.

These principles could form the basis for a counseling strategy.

Healy (1982) advocated a four-phase model of self-awareness counseling. In the first phase the counselor develops rapport with the clients or students so that they feel open and secure to explore and to share about themselves, and uses open-ended questions and other techniques to stimulate thinking and discussion. With some individuals, especially visual learners and younger children, the counselor can use the chalkboard, paints, puppets, and the like to help them to talk about themselves. The counselor elicits information about how they feel about themselves, the sources of feedback they have received, and the type of support in their lives. Sharf (1992) felt that the use of assessment through test instruments is premature at this level, but emphasis should be placed on acquiring information about self, others, occupations, and the development of a self-concept.

In the second phase the counselor structures an environment for individuals to reflect and integrate ideas about themselves. They learn to evaluate the feedback about themselves for accuracy and for information. They look at test scores and grades. They evaluate their interaction with family and friends. They are asked to use art, drama, or written modes of communication in this process. They are guided to look at negative aspects of their lives, too. The counselor needs to help them devise strategies to overcome concerns without denying the reality of the deficits. Individuals can be guided to role models who have overcome these problems.

During the third phase the counselor works in skill building, helping individuals to build knowledge and interests. Children are provided experiences to help them evaluate how they become more or less interested, more or less knowledgeable, and more or less skilled through doing things. They learn problem-solving techniques and are encouraged to use these techniques in and out of school.

In phase four the counselor helps individuals to integrate their perceptions of self into a coherent whole. Individuals are encouraged to look at their growth, new roles, and new challenges in a positive light. To encourage the integration, the counselor uses a variety of methods such as autobiographies, poetry, drawings, paintings, collages, pantomimes, and monologues.

Individuals can find increasing their self-awareness to be beneficial to them immediately as well as to help them set new goals. The goals of the counselor in these activities are to help individuals increase their self-esteem and self-confidence, to help them develop more complete pictures of themselves, and to be more honest in their self-disclosure. Counselors need to be able to develop individuals' ability to process and interpret information about themselves and to use their strengths and attributes in problem solving.

EXPLORATORY STAGE

Counselors working with clients in the exploratory stage need to help individuals develop career maturity and master the developmental tasks required at this stage, which is many times difficult because of the client's egocentrism and limited experiences (Sharf, 1992). Counselors have roles as coordinators, facilitators, teachers, consultants, as well as counselors. Important at this stage is providing useful information about problem solving and career opportunities. Individuals have to learn about their values and to be encouraged to seek information about careers, the world of work, and career choice and problem solving.

The counselor has career guidance tests and inventories to use and computer-guidance systems. There are many simulation types of exercises available as well as self-help books.

Some of the background principles for counseling at the exploratory stage are outlined by Healy (1982):

- Individuals are more motivated to acquire information, consider alternatives, and interact in small groups if the counselor provides clear and detailed instructions, the expectations for the activity, and uses appropriate role models and multiple media.
- Individuals improve their performance better when they understand the concepts underlying the activity and have a plan for completing the activity.
- Individuals achieve developmental tasks better when they recognize the need for accomplishing them.
- Individuals learn more quickly and completely when their peers are positive and involved and committed.
- Individuals learn more effectively if they receive corrective feedback and positive reinforcement in their efforts.
- Individuals gain confidence if they can see the results of their efforts and can trace their gains and share with others their progress in their career development.

The counselor in individual or group sessions can help individuals and/or the group recognize information they might need for career exploration. The counselor identifies different sources and teaches individuals how to use the sources by going through an example of the information raised by the individual or by a member of a group. Sometimes the information can be best gained through people or experiences. At the end of the session, the counselor should review the types of information needed and get commitments from the individuals to obtain the needed information before the next session so that it can be discussed (McDaniels & Gysbers, 1992).

Simulation is an interesting method to enhance career development (Sharf, 1992). There are a wide variety of computer simulations, games, and exercises. Sometimes case studies are used to discuss with test scores, demographic information, anecdotal information, and the like. Everyone in the group is asked to discuss the type of person he or she is, and his or her goals and problems.

The group also discusses the personal factors in career choice such as the individual's interests, aptitudes, achievement, experience, and physical characteristics. Leisure activities are not only important in helping individuals with acquiring life time leisure options but also to help individuals explore different career fields (McDaniels & Gysbers, 1992). The type of occupational characteristics could also be discussed, such as what types of skills are needed and the necessary work behaviors. If the job considered required additional training, the group discusses the costs, the requirements, and potential success based on the individual's past experiences. They discuss the impact on the client if he or she decided to go that route and look at life-style required, job demands, and possibilities for advancement. The group experience could be in the form of a structured course (Amatea, Clark, & Cross, 1984).

The counselor might find that the individuals prefer more realistic experiences and could start vocational exploratory groups. The groups are guided to look at their abilities and experiences; discuss and share their career aspirations; explore career fields and make a tentative choice; write a plan that would include what they expected to accomplish next year as a student, family member, citizen, leisurite, and worker; and receive feedback from the counselor and the group. In terms of their exploration, they should build in interviews and job shadowing or some type of work experience.

The counselor wants to choose activities that will enhance their skill acquisition and problem-solving ability. Individuals at this stage need to have a greater knowledge of occupations and education programs, which sometimes can be accomplished through courses but many times is not integrated by teachers into what they teach.

TRANSITION PERIOD

The transition from school to work is a difficult period for many individuals because they have not learned job-seeking skills or job-keeping skills, let alone had guidance in their career choice. Super (1990) pointed out that the impetus for any given transition is not necessarily age itself but a function of the individual's personality and abilities as well as his or her situation. Schlossberg (1984) reminded counselors that it is necessary to understand the type of transition the client is going through—expected, unexpected, never occurring, or chronic. One approach for counselors to use is to provide work experience for the individuals. There are distributive education programs and other types of work experience programs in high schools. Many schools and colleges also have work experience programs. The coordination of these programs often is done by a person who has a counseling background. To be effective the program has to provide appropriate environments and models for the individual. The assignments must be appropriate. The individual has to be able to understand the work environment and the ethics and values that operate in that setting.

The general principles of work experience programs are the following: Learning can be facilitated if the individuals have appropriate role models and the individuals can see what type of behavior is necessary for success. Appropriate work skills, habits, and values can be learned if individuals receive constructive criticism of their performance and positive reinforcement when they do a good job. Learning is greater if the placement correlates with their skills and abilities and presents situations that challenge them. Problem-solving skills can be enhanced if individuals are presented practical problems on the job and guided to how to cope with them. Productive work values and practices can be learned effectively if they can see them practiced in the workplace and have a chance to discuss these issues with the counselor and mentors.

Many schools as well as public and private agencies offer job placement services. Many times although these services are available, individuals do not take advantage of them. Some services offer workshops and seminars on interviewing techniques and resume writing.

Interview sessions can be videotaped and critiqued by counselors and members of a support group. There are lists of questions commonly asked. Some schools run support groups for 1st-year graduates and former graduates who still want to be involved.

ESTABLISHMENT STAGE

Developmental counseling at this stage is concerned with enhancing counselees establishment skills and helping them in learning to commit to self, career, family, and country (Super, Thompson, & Lindeman, 1988). Establishment in a selected field is increasingly more difficult because of the impact of the economy and technology.

With individuals reentering the work market or out of work by technology, corporate takeover, or other causes, or with individuals unhappy with their current work status, group counseling is an effective technique. Job club groups, discovery groups, growth groups, or similar type of groups have become popular (Stidham & Remley, 1992).

These groups meet regularly, and the counselor guides the clients through self-appraisal exercises, guided fantasy, and other types of exercises. There are a number of workbooks available with manuals for the counselor. Field trips, visiting speakers, and other types of similar activities are used.

Spokane (1992) emphasized the importance of preintervention assessment to identify those who will benefit most from group intervention rather than indiscriminate assignment to groups. The counselor has to be an effective group leader and knowledgeable in group dynamics so that the group feels free to share, shows positive interaction with others, and is concerned about mutual support. Group members need to be emotionally stable; aware of their interests, values, aptitudes; and have the capabilities and knowledge of how to follow through and obtain and evaluate the career information they need. Clients need to assume responsibility for their behavior and recognize they have a responsibility also to the group.

The group activities are based on principles such as the following:

- The members of the group are interested in aggressively and actively seeking strategies to enhance their career development.
- A wide variety of modalities needs to be used to facilitate exploring and evaluating desired goals from fantasy to hands-on-experience.
- Sharing with the group one's plan to achieve career goals increases the individual's commitment to the plan and provides a model for others in the group.
- Recalling and analyzing the experiences that have been successful help individuals identify their skills and increase their self-confidence.
- Discussing one's strengths and weaknesses is easier in a support group.

DEVELOPMENTAL MODELS IN BUSINESS AND INDUSTRY

Many businesses and industries provide career development interventions for their employees. Some of the approaches are based on Holland's theory (1985) and stress self-assessment, environmental assessment, and action planning. Four basic questions key to the program are as follows:

1. Who am I? (self-knowledge, self-awareness, self-assessment)
2. How am I seen?
3. What are my alternatives and goals? What other jobs could I do? Are there other jobs in the company I could do? What other jobs are available?
4. How can I achieve my goals? How do I find out about training opportunities? How can I redesign my job and get more responsibility and recognition? How can I move up the ladder?

The company career counselor usually uses approaches such as group activities, in which individuals work in groups to learn about and plan for career development; support-oriented activities, in which group members assist each other in career development planning and implementation; or self-directed activities, in which career development activities are undertaken by individuals by themselves.

WORKSHOPS

Gutteridge and Otte (1983) found that workshops were the major form of group activity and were used by 78% of the organizations surveyed. Leibowitz, Farren, and Kaye (1986) have identified the advantages and disadvantages of workshops. These are listed in Figure 16.1.

WORKSHOP COMPONENTS

Leibowitz, Farren, and Kaye (1986) suggested that the workshop focus on the four questions previously identified. To Who am I?, the participants should define their skills, experiences, personal attitudes, and career preferences. They should assess themselves.

To the second question, How am I seen?, employees are encouraged to check out their self-perceptions with others at work, their peers and their superiors.

In the third component members of the management team should present information on the organization and future trends, problem areas, and so on, so employees can see their options.

To address How can I achieve my goals?, discussion of lateral movement, job enrichment, temporary exploratory moves, realignment moves and relocation moves should be discussed. Employees should be encouraged to make their plans.

If career counselors are not available on a continuous basis, mentors from the organization might be made available. Career resource libraries need to be established. Participants can be provided a workbook or an annotated bibliography of self-help books.

Advantages
  Counselors are able to work with a large number of people at one time.
  Costs are lower per worker.
  With small group work, the workshop can inspire development of networks
    among peers, even across job levels and functions.
  The participants learn from one another and about the organization, especially if
    they work in different areas.
  The company and individuals can take advantage of the group-think situation.
Disadvantages
  Not all individuals work well in groups.
  It is hard to individualize to meet the needs of individuals.
  Time may not be sufficient to allow for clarification and understanding.
  Some participants lack the readiness or entry skills required for participation.
  It is hard to schedule workshops to meet the personal needs of all the
    participants.
  Workshops are delivered on a one-shot-basis many times with no follow up,
    continued practice, or learning taking place.

FIGURE 16.1
Advantages and disadvantages of career workshops

There are also computer-assisted programs that can be run on personal computers, which would be helpful in assisting the employees in all phases of their career development.

MAINTENANCE STAGE

Career counselors can assist workers in the maintenance stage to renew their motivation, acquire information that is important to them in their career development, and provide information on updating their skills and competencies. The stage can be one of self-doubt and letting go (Sharf, 1992). Healy (1982) identified eight career counseling objectives. These are shown in Figure 16.2.

MAJOR THEMES

Self-Understanding

Self-understanding is a key component to most theories and models of career development (Mitchell & Krumboltz, 1990). The writers in this area feel clients need to understand their interests, abilities, values, personality type, and traits. Others feel we need to add more dimensions, such as life-style and work preference.

Yost and Corbishley (1987) included four dimensions of work-related preferences: work tasks, working conditions, work location, and work benefits.

They feel that counselors need to explore in an interview with clients their preference of the work-task dimension first because these skills and activities are the things that consume most of the time at work and have the greatest impact

---

* To help individuals renew and sustain their motivation for career improvement
* To help individuals acquire information about how to improve or sustain their career
* To help individuals update and upgrade their skills necessary to be successful in their career
* To help individuals reestablish accurate self-concept, feasible goals, and realistic attitudes toward themselves and their work
* To help individuals develop a positive outlook on past achievements and future prospects
* To help individuals in identifying strategies to use in crises situations at work, at home, and so on
* To help individuals negotiate with employers in redesigning their jobs to obtain greater satisfaction from work
* To help individuals develop strategies for career or employer change

---

FIGURE 16.2
Career counseling objectives for the maintenance stage

on job satisfaction. They suggest categories such as routine work, physical work, work with machines, tools, equipment, and materials, work with numbers, work with words, work with plants or animals, work with people, work with information or ideas, clerical tasks, and creative expression of ideas or feelings.

Working conditions to many individuals are as important as the tasks. Clients are asked their preference as to relationship with people. Does the individual prefer to work alone, in small groups, or in a large team? What age group does the client prefer to work with? Another dimension is movement and time. Some clients prefer to work just in one setting; others don't mind out-of-town travel and being away for a period of time. Performance conditions is another dimension that deals with the degrees of autonomy, independence, responsibility, and supervision the individual might prefer. Variety is the fourth factor in a career selection and in eventual job satisfaction. The working environment is the last factor. In the working environment it is critically important that one likes peers, the culture of work, social interactions, and a feeling of fit with the environment; these are important to job success.

Location is the third area and includes decisions such as indoor/outdoor, geographic location, urban/rural, or special preference (allergy-free, near recreations, etc.).

The last category is benefits, which includes categories on salary and fringe benefits, opportunities, job security, fame/status, valued work, challenge or excitement, enjoyable colleagues, and portability (job in demand almost anywhere). Counselors record their work-related preferences on a summary sheet under each of the four categories. They have columns and record the activities that the client definitely preferred and a column of activities that the client definitely preferred to avoid.

Counselors also find that having the clients do a work history and list the jobs they had on the left, then in the middle column list what they liked about each job and then in the right column write what they disliked about each job. The counselor can review this exercise with the client to see if there is a pattern of interests and preferences across jobs.

Life-style

Life-style information is also another area that can influence career decision making for special groups. The questions that are asked are more holistic and deal with other aspects than just the work context. The counselor can ask questions such as, Describe what your life is like, not what do you enjoy about how you live. What do you want your life-style to be in 5 years?

Career Counseling and Life Planning with Gays, Lesbians, and Bisexuals

Problems of career counseling with gays, homosexuals, and bisexuals can arise from the low self-concept and poor emotional stability of the clients as well as from the homophobia of the career counselors. Homophobia is the fear and lack of acceptance of individuals who are gay or lesbian. Super (1990) pointed out the importance of self-concept to career development. Also, gays, lesbians, and bisexuals are often discriminated against and the brunt of jokes and sarcasm. Heatherton and Orzek (1989) pointed out that this group may have double or triple minority status when homosexuality is combined with other minority characteristics such as gender and ethnic/racial membership.

Heatherton and Orzek (1989) felt that career counselors can be effective in working with gays, lesbians, and bisexuals if they work toward eliminating their homophobic attitudes. Counselors need to know current gender issues and models of gay and lesbian development. A number of tasks such as helping clients with self- and career awareness and knowing job-seeking strategies are common competencies needed for all clients. Elliott (1993) reminded us that career counselors working with gays and lesbians need to be aware of the cultural heritage of the clients, be comfortable with their differences, and be sensitive to their personal circumstances. If theses conditions cannot be met, the counselor needs to refer the client to another counselor who can meet these conditions.

The National Gay and Lesbian Task Force maintains a list of companies that have a stated policy on sexual orientation. Career counselors need to know which businesses and industries have nondiscrimination policies. Also important in helping these clients is having information on the attitudes of managers and workers toward gays and lesbians. Elliott (1993) found that gender discrimination exists within this group, too. Lesbians earn less than gay workers.

Some counselors (House, 1991) concluded that the self-concept and identity integration of gays and lesbians is related to their coming-out stage. In this process they pass through stages of identity confusion to eventually identity integration. They move from a stage of being aware that they are different but confused, alienated, and defensive, to a stage where they have a healthy self-view and focus on age appropriate issues and developmental plans (House, 1991).

With downsizing of companies and the downturn in the economy, many gays and lesbians are in a quandary about coming out and remain in the closet and keep their life-style secret. Some of the successful approaches career counselors have used in working with this group are the following:

- Help them network with the gay/lesbian community
- Provide successful role models with the same sexual preference
- Arrange for them to job shadow gays/lesbians in the career field in which they are interested
- Get them involved in support groups of individuals with the same sexual preference
- Help them arrange interviews with gay/lesbian workers in companies in which they are considering employment
- Have them role-play problem situations on how to handle antigay and lesbian attitudes and homophobia
- Find mentors for them

Counselors must not limit or convey that there are limited career fields in which gays and lesbians can enter, for example, photographer, interior decorator, and the like. Lesbians may be more open to seeking nontraditional employment because they do not conform to the traditional gender role.

Besides having unique problems in career decision making and job discrimination gay and lesbian couples also face conflicts that heterosexual couples face. For example, dual-careers couples may have conflicts when the partner is going to be relocated or wants to change career fields or jobs.

CAREER DECISION MAKING

The counselor may have to provide special assistance to clients who are having difficulties in the career decision process (Spokane, 1992). Yost and Corbishley (1987) identified six major problems commonly experienced by clients:

1. The client has not done adequate research.
2. The client has identified very few options.
3. The options chosen are inappropriate.
4. The client fails to follow through on the tasks required.
5. The client cannot make up his or her mind about which options are best, if any.
6. The client does not like any of the options identified.

For example, for the clients who have incomplete information, the counselor needs to remind them of the importance of their involvement in the process. They need to have control over their lives and take responsibility. The counselor could provide more guidance in the process at the beginning and then reduce the amount of support as the client learns the process. If interviewing is involved, the counselor can have the client role-play interviews and gain confidence in asking questions. Assertiveness training will help some clients.

For the clients who have too few alternatives, the counselor needs to monitor the process and check to see what criteria they are using to reject the options. If they verbalize, why they are rejecting? This information will provide the counselor with ideas of how to encourage the client to consider others.

PLANNING

After the clients have made their career choice, they have to achieve their goal (Jaffe & Scott, 1991). In order to be successful, clients have to plan how they are going to accomplish their career goal. In most cases it is important for clients to develop a step-by-step procedure and include the dates when each step will be accomplished.

The plan may resemble a straight line with steps in a nice neat sequence if the choice is straightforward. Sometimes the plan might contain more than one line if there are alternate choices to be considered. Other times the plan might resemble a flow chart because there might be a number of decisions that have to be made along the way and alternate routes that might be taken.

Yost and Corbishley (1987) felt it is important for individuals to develop a formal plan. A checklist based on the steps they suggest is included in Figure 16.3.

EXAMPLE OF A PLAN

Mary has always been interested in computers and has had a good background in mathematical and logical areas. She has decided to go back to work because her youngest child is now in school. She came in to see you to find out about what schools provide the training as a computer-repair person.

She outlines the tasks she wants to accomplish.

1. Find out about what schools offer programs in PC computer repair
2. Evaluate the cost and time involved and location of the schools
3. Enroll in the program
4. Complete program
5. Complete resume, register in placement office, check employment office and want ads
6. Apply for jobs
7. Interview for jobs
8. Accept a job

_____The beginning point is identified.
_____The end point is identified.
_____The intervening tasks are placed in chronological sequence.
_____The major tasks are divided into smaller substeps.
_____The choice points and how they will be handled are identified.
_____The points at which evaluation and review take place are indicated.
_____The timeline includes tasks and dates when the tasks will be accomplished.
_____The points at which the client will need help and who the helper will be are indicated.
_____The steps are practical and realistic.
_____The steps answer the questions of what, when, where, how, and in what order.

FIGURE 16.3
Checksheet for evaluating a career plan

SYSTEMS

The type of delivery system that the counselors selects is a function of the type of problem, the type of learning styles, the career knowledge and skills, the intelligence, the locus of control, personality type, educational level, age, race, socioeconomic level, and the like. Probably the most widely used and cited approaches in the literature are individual career counseling, group counseling, computer assisted, direct instruction, and self-directed. Five emerging systems are discussed briefly this section: brief therapy, competency profiling, cognitive and cognitive behavioral approaches, psychodynamic, and self-directed.

Brief Interventions/Therapy

In brief therapy the counselor designs a particular approach to problems. The counselor focuses on solvable problems, sets goals, and designs interventions to meet these goals, and evaluates how effective the approaches have been (Cade & O'Hanlon, 1993). The counselor tries to change how clients approach their problems. The therapy is based on the belief that clients produce and maintain problems and focus on observable phenomena.

Budman and Gurman (1988) reported that the therapy is more effective if clients have above average intelligence and psychological-mindedness, a clear problem, and an ability to relate flexibly to the counselor and to collaborate actively in the therapy process. The counselor emphasizes the client's strengths and resources, maintains an adult development perspective, and accepts the possibility that many changes will occur after the counseling sessions are over and won't necessarily be observable. Budman and Gurman (1988) suggested the use of giving the client tasks to carry out between sessions. The involvement of significant others in the process, and the use of self-help and support groups help increase the individual's self-esteem. The therapist has to hit the ground running and make the maximum effective use of a brief time period.

Spokane (1992) stated that computer-assisted career interventions and self-help books can be used effectively by counselors with clients. Self-help books usually guide clients through self-awareness exercises by having them look at their interests and skills. The books also help readers develop resumes as well as help them know how to prepare themselves in interview situations. Most books emphasize action planning and setting short and long term goals. Spokane (1992) concluded that self-help and self-guided interventions are most effective with clients who are high in identity and low in indecision. Brief therapy (Budman & Gurman, 1988) emphasizes the importance of planned follow-up and continuous evaluation. Brief therapy is problem centered and has a specific goal to help a client overcome the current problem and be able (as much as possible) to meet the requirements of daily living (Garfield, 1989).

Competency Profiling

Competency profiling is a process to assist clients in matching their particular career issues with specific occupational environments. In the past most efforts have focused on matching individuals to work environments using interest, personality, or organizational variables (Mirabile, 1991). The counselor has to establish the KSAs (knowledge, skills, and abilities) for the job and know what competencies are essential for success.

Mirabile (1991) proposed an eight-step model for the use of competency profiling. The first step is to have agreement between the counselor and client that this method would be useful. The second step is to narrow the focus to specific industries or occupational environments. The third is to provide a list of competencies required in the industry or job being considered. The competencies should be listed in random or alphabetical order rather than in order of importance. The fourth step is to have the client rate his or her strengths on each of the competencies listed. The fifth step is to collect additional assessment information from supervisors, peers, subordinants, or anyone familiar with the individual and from other assessment instruments. The sixth step is to develop a composite profile of the client's competencies using self- and ratings by others. The seventh step is to compare the individual's competency profile against the one developed for the job. The last step is to look at the discrepancies between the two profiles and develop an action plan to address the gap.

One of the major problems to this method is the time commitment needed to develop the list of competencies. The Human Resource Network has a file of job descriptions. Instruments such as the *Position Analysis Questionnaire* may facilitate the development of the occupational profile.

Cognitive Approaches

Cognitive approaches to career counseling have received more attention since the 1980s. Cognitive theories are characterized by the emphasis on the structural organization of how we think, reason, and solve problems.

Cognitive interventions such as guided fantasy, rational emotive therapy, self-instruction, and cognitive self-control have been applied to career counseling (McDaniels & Gysbers, 1992). Guided fantasy can be used to expand awareness, explore goals, tap inner resources, and increase self-actualization. Cognitive rehearsal can be used to have clients picture themselves as successful in interviews and other situations.

Rational emotive therapy is a strategy that focuses on eliminating the irrational ideas that prevent clients from thinking and acting productive. Some of the career decision-making theories such as Krumbolz and Hammel (1977) challenge and confront irrational beliefs. The purpose of intervention is to help clients develop more rational beliefs systems about themselves and their environment and to guide them to make appropriate decisions. Counselors also try to help clients eliminate dysfunctional cognitive schemas. Many times clients have made decisions on little or no evidence or a single incidence. Some tend to blame themselves for all the problems that arise.

Self-instructional techniques are structured approaches that help individuals set goals, identify enabling activities, look at alternate solutions, avoid barriers to success, and evaluate their progress in meeting their goals. Cognitive self-control is a method to promote career development by having clients seek relevant information and self-reinforcement to develop appropriate behavior. Clients are encouraged to use self-monitoring to eliminate behaviors that are negative or undesirable to their career development.

Spokane (1991) has as one of his postulates that effective career counseling provides the counselee with clear framework, either self-derived or counselor imposed, that offers an intellectual or cognitive structure for understanding career selection and will counteract any inaccurate theories that the counselee may have.

Psychodynamic

Bordin (1990) suggested a psychodynamic model of career choice in which participation in work and career are rooted in the role of play in human life. Some of his postulates help give the essence of the theory. One of his postulates states that the roots of personality development are to be found throughout the early development of the individual, sometimes in the earliest years (postulate five), and postulate six states that each individual seeks to build a personal identity that incorporates aspects of the father and mother yet retains elements unique to self.

Erikson's theories have greatly influenced Bordin as well as Holland, Tiedeman, and Super. The different stages have been described in Chapters 4 through 10. The key stage for Erikson was identity versus identity confusion because it was the crucial stage between childhood and adulthood and reflected how adolescents handle the previous four stages.

Adlerian theories have also been used in career counseling, especially those dealing with basic life tasks, social interest, family constellation, and life-style. Assessment is a key component of the Adlerian model. Counselors use TAT types of tests, autobiographies, card sorts, and the like to help clients understand their life themes and goals (Sharf, 1992). Savickas (1989) used an Adlerian approach that has both an assessment and a counseling phase. In assessment he uses questions to find out the important life goals and asks whom did the counselee identify with and want to be when he or she was growing up. There are three major counseling sessions. The first focuses on the career style or path, decision-making difficulties, and interests of the counselee. In the second, a list of occupations is developed for further exploration. In the third session discussion is held on any difficulties the individual is having in making a career decision.

Self-Directed Activities

Self-directed activities were a part of several of the systems just mentioned. Pickering (1984) concluded that self-study methods were cost effective. Some schools, businesses, and industries set up self-help sections in their information center (Nachreiner, 1987). Vandergoot and Engelkes (1977) found that self-directed approaches were possibly a more efficient way of providing counseling services. Spokane (1991) concluded after reviewing the literature on self-directed approaches that although there have been positive trends in the differential used on self-directed interventions, the results are not conclusive. Clients with low-level career indecision and low goal instability prefer self-directed interventions (Robbins & Tucker, 1986; Fretz & Leong, 1982). It should be noted that the *Self-Directed Search* (Holland, 1985) is the most widely used interest assessment and was designed to be self-administering, self-scoring, and self-interpreting. There are several forms for different types of groups and computer-assisted versions.

GROUP APPROACHES

Group approaches have been popular in career development approaches. Three popular approaches have been the vocational exploration group, the job club, and the life-planning group. The vocational exploration group is usually packaged in a 6-hour workshop, sometimes subdivided into two 3-hour workshops. The purpose is to help individuals gain self-confidence, share job knowledge and resources, understand people-job relationships, and understand job personalization.

The job club focuses on job placement as the prime objective for members. The group meets daily until they are placed in a job. The group focuses on needed skills such as resume writing and interview rehearsal.

The life-planning workshop focuses on systematic planning for examining present and future plans. Usually the workshop is a 1-day program that lasts for 6 or 7 hours. Self-assessment is a major component, and the purpose of the workshop is to help increase the self-awareness and commitment to develop plans for the future.

A component of all the programs are group exercises to develop cohesiveness and for them to get to know each other better. The group is used for a sounding board as well as a support type of group.

SUMMARY

Career counselors have a number of theoretical frameworks and approaches that can be used in helping their clients in making career and life-style decisions. Counselors need not only to have a repertoire of counseling skills but also a knowledge of the developmental stages of their clients. New trends and techniques are constantly being applied and used in career and life-style counseling.

REVIEW QUESTIONS

1. What are some of the typical types of counseling problems career counselors face?
2. How would you counsel individuals who came in with no goals in mind? Choice conflicts? Career indecision?
3. What are the stages of counseling? Are they different for career counselors than for personal counselors?
4. What is developmental counseling? What are the different stages and the common career counseling problems at each of the stages?
5. What approaches to career counseling are used by business and industry?
6. Did you set up a plan when you made your latest job change or career decision? If yes, what did you include in your plan? If no, why did you not set up a plan?
7. Have you participated in any job club or vocational exploratory group? If so, describe your experiences. What was your evaluation of the group? Do you feel group approaches are effective ways of providing career counseling and guidance?

SUGGESTED ACTIVITIES

1. Interview several career counselors and identify the type of problems their clients present and the strategies they use to help them.
2. Review the literature on career counseling strategies and write a report or present your analysis to class.
3. Design a career workshop for a specific group, such as freshmen, high school seniors, employees in a specific company, and so on.
4. Make a report on job clubs, life-planning groups, or a similar type of group.
5. Interview clients who have participated in group or individual career counseling and find out their evaluation of the services. Why did they go? What type of involvement was required?
6. Have the class identify some career counseling problem area, the type of client, the context, and so on. Select individuals to role-play the counselor and the client. Have more than one team role-play the scenario. Discuss the approaches.

CASE STUDIES

Lena

Lena, age 31, was talking to an older woman friend: "I just can't stand my job any more! My boss is so unreasonable. He makes all sorts of silly demands on me. The other women in the office are so stuffy, you can't even talk to them. The men are either very blah or after you all the time, you know, 'on the make.' The pay is good, but I don't think it makes up for all the rest. It's been going on like this for almost 2 years."

Albert

Albert is a poor student who has failed two grades and is considering dropping out of school. His parents are middle class and support his plan to drop out of school. Although his overall academic performance is marginal, a D+ average, he does test high in mathematical aptitude and social skills. He is 17 and in the 10th grade at a rural midwestern high school.

Case Questions

1. What counseling strategies/approaches would you use with these clients?
2. What additional information is needed?
3. What type of career ethics are being illustrated in each of the cases?
4. How do these cases illustrate job/school satisfaction? Dissatisfaction?
5. What type of career planning is needed by these individuals?

SUGGESTED READINGS

Amundson, N. E. (1989). A model for individual career counseling. *Journal of Employment Counseling, 26*(3), 132–138.

   Amundson presents a model for individual career counseling that takes into account psychological, social, and economic factors, and describes decision making as a four-stage process.

Derr, C. B. (1988). *Managing the new careerists.* San Francisco: Jossey-Bass.

   Derr provides an organizational development orientation to understanding and working with individuals in the workplace. Part two includes chapters on five career orientations, management strategies, as well as case studies.

17

CONTEXT OF CURRENT TRENDS AND ISSUES

As we anticipate the future, those in career counseling will be faced with a perplexing question: Can the six billion people who will be alive in the year 2000 find work when so many of the United States citizens in 1994 are unemployed? What new jobs will be available in the next 20 years as old jobs are replaced with information processing systems, robotics, and new technology that only requires one or two individuals to handle the manufacturing process?

It is anticipated that extreme concern about unemployment will continue to be a number one issue for many American citizens. If you want to anticipate the future, you should analyze the continuing trends that are emerging around us and that are a predominant factor in the existing culture in the United States and throughout the world. For example, we now have barely one out of 30 people working in the field of agriculture within the United states. This type of trend is also noted in Europe and Japan, where we now have one out of 20 working on the farm.

We have also noticed a dramatic shift in the manufacturing sector of the United States economy; now one out of three American blue collar workers work in the service arena. This means they do not work in manufacturing anything that will be used by other citizens; they provide service to the machines of industry and people who do the manufacturing in those existing industrial plants.

As has been amply documented, we have shifted to a service and information economy that requires two competing levels of skills. For those in the service industry, the graduation from high school is quite often adequate for performing successfully in a variety of jobs in hospitals, nursing homes, fast food chains, and others of this nature. For those who have completed some type of postsecondary education, at either the community college or 4-year institution, there is a need for people to handle roboticized electronic processing, repair computers, and design more efficient manufacturing processes. It is possible that one of the major jobs of the future will be the robot technician, whose employed numbers could equal about two million in the year 2010 (Cetron & O'Toole, 1982).

As we anticipate the future, the career counselor must anticipate where job opportunities will exist for individuals leaving public schools and postsecondary institutions. A reasonable analysis of the labor market information suggests that there will be continuing employment opportunities for robot technicians, computer programmers, laser technicians, energy conservation technicians, waste technicians, laboratory genetic researchers, paramedics, and fiber optics technicians within communications. The United States Bureau of Labor Statistics has identified 60 jobs that it describes as the fastest growing occupations in the United States. We note that only a few of them will require 4-year college degrees, and several have no educational requirements beyond high school. Several of the "new" jobs that will be available in the year 2010 will be as follows: automobile mechanics, heating/cooling technicians, appliance service people, energy conservation technicians, housing rehabilitation technicians, holographic specialists, and battery technicians.

By focusing on just one of these particular occupations, battery technician, the career counselor must realize that the use of electric automobiles will require individuals who will be able to service the next generation of fuel cells and batteries that will be used to power the cars and homes of the future. Cetron and O'Toole's (1982) *Encounter with Future: A Forecast of Life into the 21st Century* predicted that the economy would require 250,000 of such positions.

In sum, we do not believe there will be a shortage of jobs as we enter the 21st century, only a shortage of skilled and creative counselors to help people anticipate and develop the skills necessary to participate in a rapidly changing labor market.

LEARNING OBJECTIVES

After reading this chapter, you should be able to do the following:

- Identify the major historical contributions that have influenced the career counseling movement
- Discuss the current status of career counseling
- Identify some of the future directions and concerns in the field

HISTORICAL CONTRIBUTIONS

The vocational guidance movement, an outgrowth of the industrial revolution, profoundly influenced career counseling. The changes in manufacturing led to a concentration of the work force in urban areas, and the need for trained individual to make the system effective. Brewer (1942) identified four social forces that led to the development of the vocational guidance movement: the division of labor, the growth of technology, the inclusion of vocation education in the educational system, and the spread of democracy. Early leaders were interested in helping youths in the transition from school to work. Frank Parsons's (1908) book *Choosing a Vocation* exemplifies the early thinking. The approach involved the study of individuals, aptitudes, and occupations.

The psychological testing movement also affected career counseling. Tests became an important tool to screen and classify individuals. Binet developed a scale to identify the children in France who could not profit from regular classroom instruction. The Army Alpha and Beta tests became important screen tools for the armed services in World War I. Technology was more complex in World War II and the single aptitude type of measure was inadequate. Multiaptitude batteries were used by the armed services. The trait-and-factor movement provided a framework for the development of many different types of tests. In career counseling, aptitude and interest tests were highly respected and used by counselors. Counselors used assessment methodologies to conduct individual and job assessments. Assessment is still an important tool for many of the major approaches to career counseling.

The mental hygiene movement heightened our awareness of the mentally ill and emotionally disturbed individuals in our society. We began to recognize that we had to look at the whole person, not just parts such as aptitudes, interests, and so on.

The psychotherapy movement stimulated at the turn of the century by the interest of physicians in mentally ill and deviant individuals also has had an impact on the career counseling movement. Not only were theories of career development influenced by the movement but also practices. Carl Rogers wrote *Counseling and Psychotherapy* in 1942. His work influenced our thinking on counseling approaches and helped us see the importance of self-concept and the locus of decision making.

Counseling psychology emerged as a separate psychological specialty after World War II. Counseling psychologists were hired to help emotionally disturbed veterans obtain and maintain employment after World War II. The early leaders were student personnel administrators from colleges and universities. The *Journal of Counseling Psychology* was founded in 1954 and included many articles on career development and vocational choice.

The National Defense Education Act of 1958 stimulated the guidance movement. One of the major purposes of this act was to identify talented youth and guide them into the right career fields so we could be competitive with the Soviet Union, which had launched Sputnik in 1957. Counselors were trained to work with elementary and secondary school students. The result was colleges and universities received funding to train people to work as counselors and to hire faculty qualified to teach these students. Doctoral-level graduates were needed to fill faculty lines. They were hired in colleges, community colleges, counseling services, and centers.

In the 1960s the egalitarian philosophy of the courts and society led to concern about human potential, equality of opportunity, concern for minorities, disadvantaged individuals, bilingual groups, and women. Humanistic approaches were popular and behavioral approaches on the wane.

In the 1970s the political and philosophical climate changed. Accountability became a central issue. Conservatism replaced liberalism.

In the 1980s technology had a tremendous influence on the role and function of career counselors. Computer guidance systems were commonplace, and there was myriad software to assist counselors in their work. Some of the major figures and events in the history of career counseling are included in Figure 17.1.

MAJOR ADVANCES IN THE FIELD

The National Vocational Guidance Association/National Career Development Association marked its 75th anniversary in 1988. An interesting commentary is an article by Vernon Lee Sheelby (1988) on what our leaders think and comments on 15 past presidents. They were asked what were some of the major advances in the field.

Max F. Baer (1952–1953)

Recognition and identification of career counseling as a separate profession
Concept of career development gave greater emphasis to a continuous process of school and career planning
Clustering of occupations into job families
Projections of supply and demand
Women in higher education and their challenging men in virtually every industry and occupation

Charles E. Odell (1955–1956)

Career counselors' belated recognition that they must become effectively involved in programs of political and social action at local, state, and national levels
The recognition and acceptance of the need for professionally sound and effective vocational guidance, employment, and career development counseling not only for the young, but for all sexes, all ethnic groups, and indeed for some more than others (affirmative action)

```
1886    Bureau of Labor Statistics
1909    Frank Parsons—Choosing a Vocation
1912    Munsterberg—Psychology of Industrial Efficiency
1913    National Vocational Guidance Association founded
1916    Stanford Binet Intelligence Test
1917    Smith Hughes Act
1918    Otis Group Intelligence Tests
1924    Vocational Guidance Magazine
1926    William Proctor—Educational and Vocational Guidance
1927    Strong Interest Blank
1928    Clark L. Hull—Aptitude Testing
1933    Establishment of United States Employment Service
1938    First Mental Measurement Yearbook
1939    George F. Kuder—Kuder Preference Record
        First edition of Dictionary of Occupational Titles
1940    Army General Classification Test
1942    Donald E. Super—The Dynamics of Vocational Adjustment
        Carl Rogers—Counseling and Psychotherapy
1946    George-Barden Act
1947    General Aptitude Test Battery
1949    Occupational Outlook Handbook first published
        Donald E. Super—Appraising Vocational Fitness
1951    Eli Ginzberg et al.—Occupational Choice: An Approach to General Theory
1953    John Holland—Vocational Preference Inventory
1956    Ann Roe—The Psychology of Occupations
1957    Robert Hoppock—Occupational Information
        Donald E. Super—The Psychology of Careers
1958    National Defense Education Act
1959    Robert L. Thorndike and Elizabeth Hagen—Ten Thousand Careers
1970    John Holland—The Self-Directed Search
1971    Project Talent
        Commissioner Marland and Career Education
1973    John O. Crites—Career Maturity Inventory
1984    Carl D. Perkins—Vocational Education Act
```

FIGURE 17.1
Some key authors, tests, and events in vocational psychology

Raymond N. Hatch (1957–1958)

>   The development of competencies as a guide to training and certification
>   agencies
>   The standardization and evaluation of programs and publications
>   The quality and quantity of resources available to the professional field
>   The definition of the counselor's role and programs to interpret that role
>   The integration of efforts to improve the total educational structure

Helen Wood (1961–1962)

The focus on individual development from a psychological viewpoint

Hope for strong emphasis in rapidly changing nature of American world of work, on the rising educational demands in many fields, and the need to understand these demands and meet them more adequately

David V. Tiedeman (1965–1966)

Concerns shifted from career itself to the development of self-consciousness in career during the lifetime

Need to use principles of quantum thinking

S. Norman Feingold (1968–1969)

Field becoming a recognized profession

Need to get politically involved and know movers and shakers at the private and governmental level

Donald E. Super (1969–1970)

Broadened the definition of vocational guidance to cover the life span and to take into account other life roles

Joined with APGA/AACP

Norman C. Gysbers (1972–1973)

Shift to life-span focus

Personalization of the concept of career, relating it to life roles, settings, and events

Carl McDaniels (1973–1974)

Life span

Theories of career development

Improved theory and practice of career decision making

Improvement in career information resources

Multimedia career information systems

Improved assessment techniques—external and self

Career development vocational guidance—expansion of program

Concept of career encompassing work and leisure

Esther E. Matthews (1974–1975)

History
Review of research

Edwin L. Herr (1979–1980)

Extensive theory development
Refinements in assessment techniques
Greater comprehensiveness in the delivery of career guidance across populations and settings

Harry N. Drier (1980–1981)

Moved from a limited view, limited clientele, and a limited vocational guidance assessment concept in the early 1900s to a programmatic view, content, and practice to better assure that all who deserve help can choose and succeed in their life-career pathways
Sophisticated measurement instruments
Career guidance as the key in over 20 major federal laws
Career guidance leads to economic success, increased worker productivity, decreased civil unrest, and better all around mental health

Juliet V. Miller (1982–1983)

General themes of expanded and improved theory, more comprehensive program approaches, and new applications of assessment and technology
From exclusive one-to-one counseling to the adoption of comprehensive programs that involve computer technology
Transition now in sex roles

Sunny Hansen (1985–1986)

Life-long process, occupation only one part of that process—other life choices are important
Technical advancement
Women advanced
Profound global and economic changes
Need career development in school and workplace

Linda A. Pfister (1986–1987)

Importance of career guidance on the lives of all people
Need for employee (organization) career development

FUTURE TRENDS AND ISSUES

Eight trends and issues are presented in this section: economic and labor trends, global career counseling, technology preparation and preparation of workers, career counseling and programs, career education, career theory, minority groups and gender, and research in career counseling.

Economic and Labor Trends

Career planning will be done with a global perspective. We can see with the European Common Market and other changes the increasing influence of the world economy on the labor market. There are trends such as corporate takeovers, downsizing of companies, and mergers that influence career opportunities, career stability, and career satisfaction. Bigger organizations get bigger and tend to swallow the medium-sized organizations. The smaller organizations with 200 or less workers seem to also do well. These trends present opportunities and challenges to the career and employment counselors. More emphasis needs to be placed on helping individuals learn how to start their own businesses.

Individuals need help in redesigning their job. The higher-level positions and upper- and middle-management jobs will become fewer and require more technical training. Counselors must begin teaching entrepreneurship in our educational systems. We need to think of a career matrix rather than a career ladder that clients mount. It is not always possible to climb the career ladder in the organization. You might picture career development of an individual as a matrix. We can make horizontal as well as vertical moves. We can go forward as well as go backward.

Global Career Counseling

Managers in the 1990s who speak of world markets for products, services, and technologies now must think of a world market for labor that demands new roles and strategies. Thus, there will be new roles and strategies needed by career counselors. Johnson (1991) concluded that the world's work force will become even more mobile. Although much of the unskilled and skilled work force is being provided by developing countries, their jobs are low paying and the industrialized world holds the bulk of the well-paying jobs. Johnson predicts that there will be massive relocations of people, including immigrants, temporary workers, retirees, and visitors to urban areas, in the developed world.

Globalization of labor is taking place. With shortages in a number of skilled areas such as engineering, companies have to recruit globally. The United States as well as other countries now have to compete for labor on a global basis. The situation causes problems for workers because of the different laws, mores, and customs of different countries as well as different levels of pay and compensation. Johnson predicts that eventually the globalization of labor will lead to standardization across countries so the same policies are accepted in Budapest as they are in Boston.

Another trend is more overseas assignments of workers by companies. Employment counselors in companies are now required to know about the laws and customs, child-care arrangements, and schooling among other things of the countries where the company has plants or offices in order to counsel workers about the assignment.

Employment counselors are also involved in international recruitment and are responsible for identifying potential applicants for openings in the home country and abroad. They need to have knowledge of the international labor market. They oftentimes are responsible for establishing a mentor program to help these workers make smooth transitions. Career counselors can offer help to overcome the barriers of reassignment. They may have difficulties recruiting foreign nationals to work for their company; for example, Japanese workers may tend to work for a Japanese company rather than a branch of an American company located in Japan. Workers may fear the glass ceiling or not accept the corporate culture.

Counselors are often involved in assessment of the candidates for overseas assignments. Besides maturity, emotional stability, and compatibility with the company's culture, counselors need to consider factors such as opportunities available for the worker's spouse, educational facilities for the worker's children, and the family's ability to adapt to new surroundings (Werther & Davis, 1993).

Counselors also need to counsel individuals concerning compensation, including expatriation and repatriation benefits. International compensation is also influenced by taxes and living expenses.

To facilitate successful transition and integration of international workers into an organization, career counselors can do the following:

- Secure mentors for their international hires
- Provide orientation of the organization's culture
- Provide orientation of local/national culture and customs
- Form support groups for the spouse and children, as well as the worker
- Provide opportunities for language training if necessary
- Guide them in the extensive paper work involved
- Help transfer school, medical, and other necessary records for the worker
- Explain currency exchange, banking procedures, and the like
- Help spouse find employment, get work permit, and the like.

Technology

Technological advances in robotics, computers, and genetic engineering among others have changed the characteristics of the work force, which also have changed the role of the counselor and will do so even more in the future. Business and industry want individuals with specialized technical skills, and those with computer expertise will be in demand.

Computer-guidance systems, computer-adaptive testing, computer scoring and interpretation of results, computer bulletin boards, word processing, spread sheets, and file programs have already made quite a difference in the type of work a career counselor does. More advances in technology will change the role of the counselor. With fax machines, video disk technology, and modems there can be 24-hour access to information systems. Networks with employees, the employment service, and school will be able to provide current information such as on job openings and interview schedules.

Preparation of Workers

Business and industry have expressed widespread dissatisfaction with the academic preparation of our work force. It has been said that the top half of our work force is the best in the world but the bottom half of our work force is the worst prepared. The amount of time and money industries put into their own training and development will increase dramatically. More industries will adopt Theory Z approach to management; a human resource development perspective; provide career, education, and personal counseling; and will focus on the person as a whole. More businesses and industries will work with the educational system and attempt to influence program and curriculum development.

Career Counseling and Programs

There have been some dramatic changes in the role and function of career counselors. Changes will continue. Their struggle for identity will continue. Even though some of the professional organizations and journals have changed their titles or names to fit the contemporary perceptions of the field counselors, change is not always widely accepted. As the workplace and society have changed, the competencies and job roles have also been modified. Career counselors now can receive certification as a career counselor through the National Board of Certified Counselors.

A number of other human resource personnel besides career counselors work in career counseling. Competing programs prepare individuals to work in the field. In colleges of business there are programs to prepare students to work as human resource developers, organization developmental specialists, and personnel managers. In psychology there are programs preparing individuals to be industrial psychologists, counseling psychologists, employee counselors, vocational counselors, and the like. The complexity of the workplace and life may demand that individuals have a background in mental health counseling or substance abuse counseling. Certification of counselors by national board examinations and accreditation of counseling programs provide some credibility. There will have to be marked changes in the academic preparation of career counselors if the field is to remain a viable program.

Career Education

Career education in the schools is not dead but it does not have the support that it had during the career education movement in the 1970s. The accountability movement placed much pressure on the teacher to make sure that students learn the basic skills. The infusion of career education goals and objectives in the curriculum has not had high priority. There have been competing forces operating. President Clinton is supporting the establishment of national goals for education, and there may be world goals for education someday, too. This movement would be contrary to the history of allowing states and school districts to have autonomy to decide what is taught. A counter approach is the movement to empower the teachers and allow them more freedom in what is taught and how it is taught. Because business and industry is concerned about the preparation of future workers, schools will have career education goals and objectives as part of the mainstream of the curriculum. More effort will be placed on developing the work attitudes of students, as well as teaching them job-seeking and job-keeping skills. Technology is now readily available to help students increase their job awareness and job knowledge. More industries and businesses will adopt a school and provide work and other related experiences for at least some of the high-risk students and for students they might want to recruit for jobs within their organization.

Career Theory

Career theories have been reflective of current trends in the behavioral sciences, but have been static because they fail to reflect the fabric of society and the changes occurring in the labor market. Crossdisciplinary approaches and cross-cultural approaches are needed so that researchers from disciplines such as economics, anthropology, sociology, psychology, counseling, education, biology, business, and medicine are all involved in theory development and inquiry. In the past, theories focused on traits and factors, developmental stages, and roles. In the future theories will tend to be more holistic and reflect a world view. With technological advances and artificial intelligence, the computer can become more apart of model and theory building.

Minority Groups and Gender

As the labor market expands to a world view, more workers are needed to fill the needs of the labor market. Many of the candidates will be women and other minority group members, and will experience an increased rate of employment.

Minority group members and women will outnumber white males in the work force. The high rate of participation of women in the workplace reflects the value the modern couple puts on economic returns but often leads to an increased divorce rate in dual-career couples. Most single-parent families are headed by women. A smaller percentage of women today are housewives and homemakers, and the average maternity leave in business and industry is five to six weeks. Careers today are not interrupted as much by marriage and family as they were in the past.

More special efforts will be made to attract minority candidates and women into the labor market. More effort will be made by the schools in early remediation and dropout prevention. Much emphasis is currently placed on cultural diversity in the workplace, and many career counselors are involved in diversity awareness and training activities.

Action and Basic Research

A greater commitment needs to be made to both action and basic research in career counseling and development areas. With the demands of accountability and cost-efficient methods, research becomes increasingly important. Mixed methodology, qualitative studies, as well as quantitative studies are needed and more sharing of case studies and analysis. There have been a number of networks established in the career counseling field by a variety of professional organizations. Research findings are more readily available to counselors through data bases available on the personal computer. Counselors need to do less talking and postulating and more testing things out in reality. More longitudinal research and less horizontal research is needed. Counselors need to team with their colleagues and test and critically analyze interventions, assessment instruments, and the like.

SUMMARY

This chapter presented only some of the issues and trends that will be with us throughout the 1990s. The one dimension that can be predicted with accuracy is the predictability of change. Career counselors have to be change agents but also develop ability to adapt to change. They should not be surprised by change and develop problem-solving approaches. Career counseling will hold an attraction to a number of individuals because work and career are important roles in our lives, and we feel we have learned from our experiences and can mentor or guide people who need help.

In looking ahead at what will be the important issues of career counseling at the turn of the century, we must recognize and understand where we were and where we are now. First we have to look at this in terms of changes in the nature of the work force and the changes in the impact of macroeconomic systems such as the world economy on how we view people and careers. We have moved from an agricultural society to a manufacturing society to a service-oriented society. Second, we have to reexamine our beliefs about how we look at individuals and their behavior. We have had different frameworks, such as behavioral, humanistic, and cognitive to attempt to explain learning. Technology has stimulated changes in the workplace as well as how we conceptualize behavior. We have to recognize that besides different philosophies and theories to look at behavior and career counseling, there are competing delivery systems.

REVIEW QUESTIONS

1. What do you think the major trends and issues will be in career counseling during the 1990s?
2. What impact do you think technology will have on career counseling?
3. What role changes do you predict for the career counselor in the 21st century?
4. What are some of the historical antecedents of career counseling?
5. What issues and trends listed in the chapter do you agree with? Disagree with?

SUGGESTED ACTIVITIES

1. Interview several career counselors and ask them what they think are the future issues and trends in career counseling.
2. Ask counselors what role changes they expect to see in the 1990s.
3. Write a paper or prepare a report on the future of career counseling.
4. Write a letter to the course instructor expressing your concern about the status of career counseling in the United States.

CASE STUDY

Moving Abroad

Medical Technology was founded in 1990 and grew from a regional to an international corporation with $500 million in sales during the last fiscal year. In their marketing surveys they have identified several areas in Eastern Europe, Africa, and Asia where they are going to open small sales offices. They are going to assign existing sales representatives to work in these overseas offices. They do not have many of their staff excited about this new assignment.

Case Questions

1. What strategies would you use to help these individuals in making a decision about taking these assignments?

2. What types of information would be valuable to them to have prior to leaving for their new assignment?

SUGGESTED READINGS

Journals like *Career Development Quarterly, Journal of Vocational Behavior,* and *Occupational Outlook Quarterly* provide perspectives that help counselors understand future directions. Books like *Ten New Directions for the 1990's* by John Naisbitt and Patricia Abourdene give readers a general overview of current as well as future trends.

SELECTIVE LIST OF PUBLISHERS OF CAREER LITERATURE

AGB Association for the Deaf
3417 Volta Place N.W.
Washington, DC 20007

Airline Employees Association
5600 S. Central Avenue
Chicago, IL 60638-3797

American Academy of Child and Adolescent Psychiatry
3615 Wisconsin Avenue, N.W.
Washington, DC 20016

American Academy of Ophthalmology
P.O. Box 7424
San Francisco, CA 94120-7424

American Advertising Federation
1400 K Street, N.W., Suite 1000
Washington, DC 20005

American Anthropological Association
1703 New Hampshire Avenue, N.W.
Washington, DC 20009

American Association of Blood Banks
1117 N. 19th Street, Suite 600
Arlington, VA 22209

American Association for Clinical Chemistry
2029 K Street, N.W.
Washington, DC 20009

American Association of Nurse Anesthetists
216 Higgins Road
Park Ridge, IL 60068-5790

American Association of Zoological Parks and Aquariums
Oglebay Park
Wheeling, WV 26003

American Coal Foundation
1130 17th Street, N.W., Suite 220
Washington, DC 20036

American Dental Association
211 E. Chicago Avenue
Chicago, IL 60611

American Federation of Teachers
555 New Jersey Avenue, N.W.
Washington, DC 20001

American Fisheries Society
5410 Grosvenor Lane
Bethesda, MD 20814-2199

American Historical Association
400 A Street, S.E.
Washington, DC 20003

American Hospital Association
840 N. Lake Shore Drive
Chicago, IL 60611

American Institute of Architects
1735 New York Avenue N.W.
Washington, DC 20006

American Institute of Certified Public Accountants
1211 Avenue of the Americas
New York, NY 10036-8775

American Library Association
50 E. Huron Street
Chicago, IL 60611

American Optometric Association
243 N. Lindbergh Blvd.
St. Louis, MO 63141

American Planning Association
1776 Massachusetts Avenue, N.W.
Washington, DC 20036

American Psychiatric Association
1400 K Street, N.W.
Washington, DC 20005

American Society of Animal Science
309 W. Clark Street
Champaign, IL 61820

American Society of Plumbers
3617 Thousand Oaks Blvd., Suite 210
Westlake Village, CA 91362

Associated Specialty Contractors, Inc.
7315 Wisconsin Avenue N.W.
Washington, DC 20014

Backstage Press, Inc.
P.O. Box 745
Belle Mead, NJ 08502

Bridgewater Press
100 Whitehorne Drive, Suite 302
Moraga, CA 93950

Brooks/Cole Publishing
511 Forest Lodge Road
Pacific Grove, CA 93950

Career Press
62 Beverly Road
P.O. Box 34
Hawthorne, NJ 07507

Career Publications, Inc.
800 Knoll Center Bellevue
500 108th Avenue, N.W.
Bellevue, WA 98004-5560

Career Search Publishing
4626 Amesbury, Suite 251
Dallas, TX 75206

Career Strategies Center
721 Fair Oaks Avenue South
Pasadena, CA 91030

Careers, Inc.
P.O. Box 135
Largo, FL 34294-0135

Channing L. Bete Co., Inc.
200 State Road South
Deerfield, MA 01373

Chronicle Guidance Publications
P.O. Box 1190
Moravia, NY 13118-1190

College Board Publications
P.O. Box 886
New York, NY 10101-0886

Council on Education for Public Health
1015 15th Street, N.W., Suite 403
Washington, DC 20005

Dow Jones Newspaper Fund, Inc.
P.O. Box 300
Princeton, NJ 08543-0063

Facts on File
460 Park Avenue South
New York, NY 10016

Finney Company
3943 Meadowbrook Road
Minneapolis, MN 55426

Garrett Park Press
P.O. Box 190B
Garrett Park, MD 20896

General Aviation Manufacturers Association
1400 K Street, N.W., Suite 801
Washington, DC 20005

GENMET Publishing Company
1763 White Oak Avenue
Baltimore, MD 21234-1526

Getting You a Job Co., Inc.
516/518 Route 80
Guilford, CT 06437-9935

Higher Education Publications, Inc.
6400 Arlington Blvd., Suite 648
Falls Church, VA 22314-2715

International Association of Firefighters
1750 New York Avenue, N.W.
Washington, DC 20006-5395

Iowa State University Press
2121 S. State Avenue
Ames, IA 50010

Island Press
1718 Connecticut Avenue, N.W., Suite 300
Washington, DC 20009

J. G. Ferguson Publishing Co.
200 W. Monroe Street
Chicago, IL 60606

JETS, Inc.
1420 King Street, Suite 405
Alexandria, VA 22314-2715

JIST Works, Inc.
720 N. Park Avenue
Indianapolis, IN 46202-3431

Junior Engineering Technical Society-Guidance
1420 King Street, Suite 405
Alexandria, VA 22314-2715

Master Media Limited
16 E. 72nd Street
New York, NY 10021

Medical Library Association
919 N. Michigan Avenue, Suite 3208
Chicago, IL 60611

Meridian Education Corporation
236 E. Front Street
Bloomington, IL 61701

Music Educators National Conference
1902 Association Drive
Reston, VA 22091

National Association for Music Therapy
505 Eleventh Street, SE
Washington, DC 20003

National Association of Plumbing, Heating and Cooling Industry
P.O. Box 6806
Falls Church, VA 22046

National Athletic Trainers Association
2952 Stemmons, Suite 200
Dallas, TX 75247

National Braille Press, Inc.
88 St. Stephen Street
Boston, MA 02115

National Career Development Association
5999 Stevenson Avenue
Alexandria, VA 22304

National Federation of Opticianry Schools, Inc.
10111 Martin Luther King, Jr. Highway, Suite 112
Bowie, MD 20715-4299

National FFA Organization
5632 Mt. Vernon Memorial Highway
P.O. Box 15160
Alexandria, VA 22309-0160

National Health Council, Inc.
350 Fifth Avenue, Suite 1118
New York, NY 10118

National Newspaper Foundation
1627 K. Street, N.W., Suite 400
Washington, DC 20006-1790

New Account Company
33 Village Square
Glen Cove, NY 11542

Opticians Association of America
10341 Democracy Lane
P.O. Box 10110
Fairfax, VA 22030

Orchard House, Inc.
112 Balls Hill Road
Concord, MA 01742

Peterson's Guides, Inc.
P.O. Box 2123
Princeton, NJ 08540-2123

Prentice Hall
15 Columbus Circle
New York, NY 10010

River Wind Associates
P.O. Box 128
Orland, ME 04472

Rosen Publishing Group
29 E. 21st Street
New York, NY 10010

Shaw Associates
625 Biltmore Way, Suite 1406
Coral Gables, FL 33134

Southern Newspaper Publishers Association
P.O. Box 28875
Atlanta, GA 30358

Special Libraries Association
1700 18th Street, N.W.
Washington, DC 20009

Ten Speed Press
P.O. Box 7123
Berkeley, CA 94707

Texas A & M University
College of Agriculture
College Station, TX 77843-2142

U.S. Army Recruiting Command
Fort Sheridan, IL 60037-6000

United States Department of Defense
Washington, DC 20301

VGM Career Horizons
4255 W. Touhy Avenue
Lincolnwood, IL 60646-1975

Vocational Biographies, Inc.
P.O. Box 31
Sauk Centre, MN 56378

Vocational Central
P.O. Box 206
Hales Corner, WI 73130-0206

W. T. Grant Foundation
Commission on Work, Family, and Citizenship
1001 Connecticut Avenue, N.W., Suite 301
Washington, DC 20036-5541

SELECTED LIST OF TEST PUBLISHERS AND CAREER TESTS

American College Testing Program
2201 North Dodge Street
P.O. Box 168
Iowa City, IA 52244

    American College Testing Program
    Career Planning Program

College Board Publications
45 Columbus Avenue
New York, NY 10023

    Career Skills Assessment Program
    Scholastic Assessment Test

Consulting Psychologists Press, Inc.
3803 East Bayshore Road
P.O. Box 10096
Palo Alto, CA 94303

    Adult Career Concerns Inventory
    Career Development Inventory
    Coopersmith Self-Esteem Inventory
    Myers-Briggs Type Indicator
    The Salience Inventory
    Strong Interest Inventory
    The Values Scale

CTB/Macmillan/McGraw Hill
Delmonte Research Park
2500 Garden Road
Monterey, CA 93940

Career Maturity Inventory
Comprehensive Test of Basic Skills
Kuder Occupational Interest Survey
Test of Adult Basic Education

Educational and Industrial Testing Service
P.O Box 7234
San Diego, CA 92107

Career Ability Placement Survey
COPS System Occupational Preference System
COPS System Interest Inventory

Institute for Personality and Ability Testing
P.O. Box 188
1602 Coronado Drive
Champaign, IL 61820

Sixteen Personality Factor Questionnaire

Psychological Assessment Resources, Inc.
P.O. Box 998
Odessa, FL 33556

Self-Directed Search
Vocational Preference Inventory

The Psychological Corporation
555 Academic Court
San Antonio, TX 78204

Differential Aptitude Test
Edwards Personal Preference Schedule
Ohio Vocational Interest Survey

The Riverside Publishing Company
8420 Bryn Mawr Avenue
Chicago, IL 60631

Work Values Inventory

U. S. Department of Labor
Division of Testing
Employment and Training Administration
Washington, DC 20213

> General Aptitude Test Battery
> USES Clerical Skills Test
> USES Interest Inventory

U.S. Military Entrance Processing Command
2500 Green Bay Road
North Chicago, IL 60064-3094

> Armed Services Vocational Aptitude Battery

REFERENCES

Allbritten, B. (1989). Review of DISCOVER for college and adults. In G. R. Walz & J. C. Bleuer (Eds.), *Counseling software guide*. Alexandria, VA: American Association for Counseling and Development.

Amatea, E. S., Clark, J. E., & Cross, E. G. (1984). Lifestyles: Evaluating a life role planning program for high school students. *Vocational Guidance Quarterly, 32,* 249–259.

American Association for Counseling and Development (AACD). (1980). *Responsibilities of users of standardized tests.* Alexandria, VA: Author.

American Association for Counseling and Development and Association for Measurement and Evaluation in Counseling and Development. (1989, May). The responsibilities of test users. AACD. *Guideposts,* 12–28.

American Psychological Association. (1993). *Computer use in psychology: A directory of software.* Washington, DC: Author.

American School Counselor Association. (1981). *ASCA role statement: The practice of guidance and counseling by school counselors.* Alexandria, VA: Author.

American School Counselor Association. (1984a). *Position statement. Developmental guidance.* Alexandria, VA: Author.

American School Counselor Association. (1984b). *The role of the school counselor in career guidance: Expectations and responsibilities.* Alexandria, VA: Author.

Ames, L., Ilg, F., & Baker, S. (1988). *Your ten to fourteen year old.* New York: Delacorte Press.

Admundson, N. E. (1989). A model for individual career counseling. *Journal of Employment Counseling, 26,* 132–138.

Amundson, N., Firbank, O., Klein, H., & Poehnell, G. (1991). JOBLINK: An employment program for immigrants. *Journal of Employment Counseling, 28,* 167–176.

Apostal, R., & Bildens, J. (1991). Educational and occupational aspirations of rural high school students. *Journal of Career Development, 18*(2), 153–160.

Arbona, C. (1990). Career counseling research and Hispanics: A review of the literature. The Counseling Psychologist, 18, 330–323.

Arbona, C., & Novy, J. (1991). Career aspirations and expectations of Black, Mexican Americans, and White Students. *The Career Development Quarterly, 39,* 231–239.

Arthur, M. B., Hall, D. T., & Lawrence, B. S. (1989). *Handbook of career theory.* New York: Cambridge University Press.

Atchley, R. (1975). *The sociology of retirement.* Cambridge, MA: Schenkman.

Atkinson, D. R., Morten, G., & Sue, D. W. (1989). *Counseling American minorities: A cross-cultural perspective* (3rd ed.). Dubuque, IA: William C. Brown.

Azrin, N. H., & Besalel, V. A. (1980). *Job club counselor's manual: A behavioral approach to vocational counseling.* Baltimore: University Park Press.

Babbit, C. E., & Burbach, H. J. (1990). Note on the perceived occupational future of physically disabled college students. *Journal of Employment Counseling, 27,* 98–103.

Baltes, P. D., Reese, H. W., & Lippsitt, L. P. (1980). Life-span developmental psychology. *Annual Review of Psychology, 31,* 65–110.

Banks, J. A. (1979). *Teaching strategies for ethnic studies.* Boston: Allyn and Bacon.

Baxter, J. (1992). Power attitudes and time: The domestic division of labour. *Journal of Comparative Family Studies, 23,* 165–182.

Beck, H. (1993, October). The gray nineties. *Newsweek,* 65–67.

Belz, J. R. (1993). Sexual orientation as a factor in career development. *The Career Development Quarterly, 41,* 197–200.

Bergmann, S. (1991). Guidance on the middle school level: The compassion component. In J. Capellute & D. Stokes (Eds.), *Middle level education: policies, practices and programs.* Reston, VA: NSSA.

Bernhardt, G. R., Cole, D. J., & Ryan, C. W. (1993). Improving career decision making with adults: Use of portfolios. *Journal of Employment Counseling, 30,* 67–73.

Berven, N. C. (1986). Assessment practices in rehabilitation counseling. In T. F. Riggar, D. R. Maki, & A. W. Wolf (Eds.), *Applied rehabilitation counseling* (pp. 21–33). New York: Springer.

Betz, N. E., & Fitzgerald, L. F. (1987). *The career psychology of women.* Orlando, FL.: Academic Press.

Betz, N. E., Heesacker, R. S., & Shuttleworth, C. (1990). Moderators of the congruence and realism of major and occupational plans in college students: A replication and extension. *Journal of Counseling Psychology, 37,* 269–276.

Bielby, W. T., & Bielby, D. D. (1989). Family ties: Balancing commitments to work and family in dual career households. *American Sociological Review, 54,* 776–789.

Bird, C. P., & Fisher, T. D. (1986). Thirty years later: Attitudes toward the employment of older workers. *Journal of Applied Psychology, 71,* 515–517.

Blau, P. M., & Duncan, O. D. (1967). *The American occupational structure.* New York: Wiley.

Blocher, D. H., & Rapaza, R. S. (1981). Professional and vocational preparation. In A. W. Chickering & associates (Eds.), *The modern American college.* San Francisco: Jossey-Bass.

Block, J. H. (1976). Issues, problems and pitfalls in assessing sex differences. *Merrill-Palmer Quarterly, 22,* 283–308.

Blustein, D. C. (1992). Applying current theory and research in career practice. *Career Development Quarterly, 41,* 174–184.

Blustein, D. L., Walbridge, M. M., Friedlander, M. L., & Palladino, D. E. (1991). Contributions of psychological separation and parental attachment to the career development process. *Journal of Counseling Psychology, 38,* 39–50.

Bolles, R. M. (1991). *What color is your parachute?* Berkeley, CA: Ten Speed Press.

Bolton, B. (1973). *Introduction to rehabilitation of deaf clients.* Fayetteville: University of Arkansas.

Bordin, E. S. (1946). Diagnosis in counseling and psychotherapy. *Educational and Psychological Measurement, 6,* 169–184.

Bordin, E. S. (1984). Psychodynamic model of career choice and satisfaction. In D. Brown, L. Brooks, & associates (Eds.), *Career choice and development: Applying contemporary theories to practice.* San Francisco: Jossey-Bass.

Bordin, E. S. (1990). Psychodynamic model of career choice. In D. Brown, L. Brooks, & associates (Eds.), *Career choice and development* (2nd ed.). San Francisco: Jossey-Bass.

Bordin, E. S., Nachmann, B., & Segal, S. J. (1963). An articulated framework for vocational development. *Journal of Counseling Psychology, 10,* 107–116.

Borgen, W. A., & Amundson, N. E. (1985). Counseling immigrants for employment. In R. J. Samuda & A. Wolfgang (Eds.), *Intercultural counseling and assessment. Global perspectives.* Lewiston, NY: C. J. Hogrete.

Bowlesbey, J. H. (1984). The computer as a tool in career guidance programs. In N. C. Gysbers & associates (Eds.), *Designing careers.* San Francisco: Jossey-Bass.

Bowman, R. P., & Myrick, R. D. (1987). Effects of elementary school peer facilitator program on children with behavior problems. *School Counselor, 34,* 369–378.

Bowman, S. (1993). Career intervention strategies for ethnic minorities. *The Career Development Quarterly, 42*(1), 14–25.

Brammer, L. M., & Humberger, F. E. (1984). *Outplacement and inplacement counseling.* Englewood Cliffs, NJ: Prentice Hall.

Brandt, E. (1992). Discrimination, age. In L. K. Jones (Ed.), *The encyclopedia of career change and work issues.* Phoenix, AZ: Oryx Press.

Brewer, J. M. (1942). *History of vocational guidance.* New York: Harper & Row.

Bridges, M. P. (1989). Software for career counseling. In G. R. Walz & J. C. Bleuer (Eds.), *Counseling software guide* (pp. 15–18). Alexandria, VA: American Association for Counseling and Development.

Brolin, D. E. (1986). *Life-centered career education: A competency based approach.* Reston, VA: Council for Exceptional Children.

Bronk, R. F. (1989). Review of career directions. In G. R. Walz & J. C. Bleuer (Eds.), *Counseling software guide.* Alexandria, VA: American Association for Counseling and Development.

Brooks, L. (1984). Career counseling methods and practices. In D. Brown, L. Brooks, & associates. *Career choice and development: Applying contemporary theories to practice* (pp. 337–354). San Francisco: Jossey-Bass.

Brooks, L. (1990). Recent developments in theory building. In D. Brown, L. Brooks, & associates, *Career choice and development* (2nd ed.). San Francisco: Jossey-Bass.

Brown, D. (1984). Trait and factor theory. In D. Brown, L. Brooks, & associates (Eds.), *Career choice and development: Applying contemporary theories to practice.* San Francisco: Jossey-Bass.

Brown, D. (1990). Summary, comparison and critique of Mayer theories. In D. Brown, L. Brooks, & associates, *Career choice and development* (2nd ed.). San Francisco: Jossey-Bass.

Brown, J. M., Berkell, D. E., & Schmelkin, L. P. (1992). Professional attitudes: A study of group differences among vocational and special educators toward the employability of persons with severe disabilities. *Career Development for Exceptional Individuals, 15,* 13–27.

Brown, S. T., & Brown, D. (1990). *Designing and implementing a career information center.* Garrett Park, MD: Garrett Park Press.

Budman, S. H., & Gurman, J. B. (1988). *Theory and practice of brief therapy.* New York: Guilford Press.

Buehler, C. (1933). *Der menscheleche leb enslaut als psychologisches problem* [The human life course as a psychological subject]. Leipzig: Hirzel.

Buehler, C. (1962). Genetic aspects of the self. *Annals of the New York Academy of Sciences, 96,* 730–764.

Buhrke, R. A. (1989). Incorporating lesbian and gay issues into a counselor's training: A resource guide. *Journal of Counseling and Development, 68,* 77–80.

Bureau of the Census. (1990). *Statistical abstract of the United States, 1990.* Washington, DC: U.S. Department of Commerce.

Burkhead, E. J. (1984). Services for the disabled person. In H. D. Burck & R. C. Reardon (Eds.), *Career development interventions.* Springfield, IL: Charles C. Thomas.

Byrne, R. H. (1958). Proposed revision of the Bordin-Pepinsky diagnostic constructs. *Journal of Consulting Psychology, 5,* 184–187.

Cade, B., & O'Hanlon, W. H. (1993). *Brief guide to brief therapy.* New York: W. W. Norton.

Campbell, R. E., & Heffernan, J. M. (1983). Adult vocational behavior. In W. B. Walsh & S. H. Osipow (Eds.), *Handbook of vocational psychology* (Vol. 1, pp. 223–262): Hillsdale, NJ: Lawrence Erlbaum.

Caplan, R. D. (1987). Person-environment-fit theory and organizations: Commensurate dimensions, time perspectives, and mechanisms. *Journal of Vocational Behavior, 31,* 248–267.

Carnegie Council on Adolescent Development. (1989). *Turning points: Preparing American youth for the 21st century.* Washington, DC: Author.

Carnegie Council on Adolescent Development. (1990). *Report on the taskforce on education of young adolescents.* Washington, DC: Author.

Carreiro, R., & Schulz, W. (1933). Activities of elementary school counselors in Canada. *Elementary School Guidance and Counseling, 12*(1), 63–68.

Cascio, W. F. (1989). *Managing human resources: Productivity, quality of work life, profits* (2nd ed.). New York: McGraw-Hill.

Cetron, M., & O'Toole, T. (1982). *Encounters with the future: A forecast of life into the 21st century.* New York: McGraw-Hill.

Cheatham, H. E. (1990). Afrocentricity and career development of African Americans. *Career Development Quarterly, 38,* 334–346.

Chickering, A. W., & Havighurst, R. J. (1981). The life cycle. In A. W. Chickering & associates (Eds.), *The Modern American College* (pp. 16–50). San Francisco: Jossey-Bass.

Chusmir, L. H., & Mills, J. (1989). Gender differences in conflict resolution styles of managers: At work and at home. *Sex Roles, 20,* 149–164.

Chusmir, L. H., & Parker, B. (1991). Gender and situational differences in managers values. A look at work and home lives. *Journal of Business Research, 23,* 325–336.

Clark, G. M., Carlson, B. C., Fisher, S., Cook, I. D., & D'Alonzo, B. J. (1991). Career development for students with disabilities in elementary schools. A position statement of the division of career development for exceptional individuals, *Career Development for Exceptional Individuals, 14,* 109–120.

Commission on Youth Employment Programs, National Research Council. (1985). *Youth employment and training programs: The YEDPA years.* Washington, DC: National Academy Press.

Cook, E. P. (1991). Annual review: Practice and research in career counseling and development. *The Career Development Quarterly, 40,* 99–131.

Cook, M. F. (1987). *New directions in human resources: A handbook.* Englewood Cliffs, NJ: Prentice Hall.

Cooney, T. M., & Uhlenber, B. (1989). Family building patterns of professional women: A comparison of lawyers, physicians, & post-secondary teachers. *Journal of Marriage & the Family, 51,* 749–758.

Cooper, P. S. (1992). *Euthenics: A stress reduction worktext.* Dubuque, IA: Kendall/Hunt.

Corcos, A., & McChesney, J. (1991). An experiential learning approach to career assessment: Merging co-op and vocational testing. *Guidance and Counseling, 6,* 42–52.

Cosse, W. J. (1992). Who's who and what's what? The effects of gender on development in adolescence. In B. R Wainrib (Ed.), *Gender issues across the life cycle.* New York: Springer.

Cotton, S., Antill, J. K., & Cunningham, J. D. (1990). The work attachment of mothers with preschool children. *Psychology of Women Quarterly, 14,* 225–270.

Courtney, R. S. (1986). A human resource program that helps management and employees prepare for the future. *Personnel, 63*(5), 32–40.

Crites, J. O. (1978). *Career maturity inventory.* Monterey, CA: CTB/McGraw-Hill.

Crites, J. O. (1969). *Vocational psychology.* New York: McGraw-Hill.

Crites, J. O. (1976). A comprehensive model of career development in early adulthood. *Journal of Vocational Behavior, 9,* 105–118.

Crites, J. O. (1981). *Career counseling: Models, methods, and materials.* New York: McGraw-Hill.

Crockett, D. S. (1982). Academic advisement systems. In R. F. Winston, Jr., S. C. Ender, & T. K. Miller (Eds.), *New directions for student services: Developmental approaches to academic advisement, no. 17.* San Francisco: Jossey-Bass.

Croteau, J. M., & Hedstrom, S. M. (1993). Integrating commonalty and difference: The key to career counseling with lesbian women and gay men. *The Career Development Quarterly, 41,* 201–209.

Dalton, G. W. (1989). Developmental view of careers in organizations. In M. B. Arthur, D. T. Hall, & B. Lawrence (Eds.), *Handbook of career theory.* New York: Cambridge University Press.

Dana, R. H. (1993). *Multicultural assessment perspectives for professional psychology.* Needham Heights, MA: Allyn and Bacon.

Davidson, J. P. (1980). Urban black youth and career development. *Journal of Non-White Concerns, 8,* 119–140.

Dawis, R. (1992). Job satisfaction. In L. K. Jones (Ed.), *The encyclopedia of career change and work issues.* Phoenix, AZ: Oryx Press.

Debenedetto, B., & Tittle, C. K. (1990). Gender and adult roles: Role commitment of women in a job family trade-off context. *Journal of Counseling Psychology, 37,* 41–48.

Dewe, P. J., & Guest, R. (1990). Methods of coping with stress at work: A conceptual analysis and empirical study of measurement issues. *Journal of Organizational Behavior, 11,* 135–150.

Dickens, F., & Dickens, J. B. (1982). *The black manager.* New York: Amacom.

Division of Career Development Council for Exceptional Children. (1987). *Position paper on career education.* Washington, DC: Author.

Drummond, R. J. (1988). Sources of test information. *Journal of Employment Counseling, 25,* 86–94.

Drummond, R. J. (1992). *Appraisal procedures for counselors and helping professionals* (2nd ed.). Columbus, OH: Merrill/Macmillan.

Drummond, R. J., & Hansford, S. G. (1992). Career aspirations of pregnant teens. *Journal of Employment Counseling, 29,* 166–171.

Dunn, C. W., & Veltman, G. C. (1989). Addressing the restrictive career maturity patterns of minority youth: A program evaluation. *Journal of Multicultural Counseling and Development, 17,* 156–164.

Eccles, J. S., Midgley, C., Wigfield, A., Bucwanan, C. M., Reuman, D., Flanagan, C., & Maciver, P. (1993). Development during adolescence: The impact of stage-environmental fit on young adolescents' experiences in schools and families. *American Psychologist, 48*(2) 90.

Edelstein, W., & Noam, G. (1982). Regulatory structures of self and "post formal" stages in adulthood. *Human Development, 27,* 166–173.

Educational Testing Service. (1987). *The ETS test collection catalog: Vol. 2: Vocational tests and measurement devices.* Phoenix, AZ: Oryx Press.

Elksnin, L. K., & Elksnin, N. (1990). Using collaborate consultation with parents to promote effective vocational programming. *Career Development for Exceptional Individuals, 13,* 135–142.

Elliott, J. E. (1993). Career development with lesbian and gay clients. *The Career Development Quarterly, 41,* 210–226.

Elwood, J. A. (1992). The pyramid model: A useful tool in career counseling with university students. *The Career Development Quarterly, 41,* 51–54.

Ender, S. C., Winston, R. B., & Miller, T. K. (1984). Academic advising reconsidered. In R. B. Winston, Jr., T. K. Miller, S. C. Ender, T. J. Grites, & associates (Eds.), *Developmental academic advising.* San Francisco: Jossey-Bass.

Erikson, E. H. (1963). *Childhood and society.* New York: W. W. Norton.

Erikson, E. H. (1968). *Identity: Youth and crisis.* New York: W. W. Norton.

Erikson, E. H. (1982). *The life cycle completed: A review.* New York: W. W. Norton.

Etaugh, C., & Nekolny, K. (1990). Effects of employment status and marital status on perceptions of mothers. *Sex Roles, 23,* 273–280.

Etaugh, C., & Poertner, P. (1991). Effects of occupational prestige, employment status, and marital status on perceptions of mothers. *Sex Roles, 24,* 345–354.

Feldman, D. C. (1988). *Managing careers in organizations.* Glenview, IL: Scott, Foresman.

Fernandez, J. P. (1986). *Childcare and corporate productivity: Resolving family/work conflicts.* Lexington, MA: D. C. Heath.

Fine, S. A. (1986). Job analysis. In R. A. Berk (Ed.), *Performance assessment* (pp. 53–81). Baltimore: The Johns Hopkins University Press.

Fisher, K., Rapkin, B. D., & Rappaport, J. (1991). Gender and work history in placement and perceptions of elderly community volunteers. *Psychology of Women Quarterly, 15*(1), 261–280.

Fitzgerald, L. F., & Crites, J. O. (1980). Toward a career psychology of women: What do we know? *Journal of Counseling Psychology, 27,* 44–62.

Florida Blueprint for Career Preparation. (1988). Tallahassee, FL: Author.

Fouad, N. A. (1993). Cross-cultural vocational assessment. *The Career Development Quarterly, 42*(1), 4–13.

Franzem, J. (1987, February). Easing the pain. *Personnel Administration,* 48–55.

Fretz, B. R., & Leong, F. T. L. (1982). Career development status as a predictor of career intervention outcomes. *Journal of Counseling Psychology, 29,* 388–393.

Frone, M. R., Russell, M., Cooper, M. L. (1991). Relationship of work and family stress to psychological distress. The independent moderating influence of social support, mastery, active coping, and self-focused attention. *Journal of Social Behavior and Personality, 6,* 227–250.

Frost, F., & Diamond, E. E. (1979). Ethnic and sex differences in occupational stereotyping by elementary school children. *Journal of Vocational Behavior, 15,* 43–54.

Fyock, C. D. (1990). *America's workforce is coming of age.* Lexington, MA: D. C. Heath.

Garfield, S. L. (1989). *Practice of brief psychotherapy.* New York: Pergamon Press.

Gelatt, H. B. (1962). *Information and decision theories in preparing school counselors in educational guidance* (pp. 101–114). New York: College Entrance Examination Board.

Georgia State Department of Education. (1984). *Secondary school counseling job description. Georgia comprehensive guidance.* Atlanta: Author. (ERIC Document Reproduction Service No. ED 248 432)

Ghorpade, J. U. (1988). *Job analysis: A handbook for the human resource director.* Englewood Cliffs, NJ: Prentice Hall.

Ginsburg, H., & Operr, S. (1988). *Piaget's theory of intellectual development* (2nd ed.). Englewood Cliffs, NJ: Prentice Hall.

Ginzberg, E. (1984). Career development. In D. Brown, L. Brooks, and associates (Eds.), *Career choice and development: Applying contemporary theories to practice.* San Francisco: Jossey-Bass.

Ginzberg, E. (1988). Toward a theory of occupational choice. *Career Development Quarterly, 36,* 358–363.

Ginzberg, E., Ginsburg, S. W., Axelrad, S., & Herma, J. L. (1951). *Occupational choice: An approach to a general theory.* New York: Columbia University.

Glasgow, D. G. (1980). *The black underclass.* San Francisco: Jossey-Bass.

Goff, S. J., Mount, M. K., & Jamison, R. L. (1990). Employer supported childcare, work/family conflict, and absenteeism: A field study. *Personnel Psychology, 43,* 793–809.

Gonzalez, A. W. (1989). Review of SIGI Plus. In G. R. Walz & J. C. Bleuer (Eds.), *Counseling software guide.* Alexandria, VA: American Association for Counseling and Development.

Gorman, M. (1993). Midlife transitions in men and women. In R. J. Wicks & R. D. Parsons (Eds.), *Clinical handbook of pastoral counseling* (Vol 2.). New York: Paulist Press.

Gostin, L. O., & Beyer, H. A. *Implementing the Americans with Disability Act: Rights and responsibilities of all Americans.* Baltimore: Paul H. Brooks.

Gottfredson, G. D., Holland, J. L., & Ogawa, D. K. (1982). *Dictionary of Holland's occupational codes.* Palo Alto, CA: Consulting Psychologists Press.

Gottfredson, L. S. (1978). *Race and sex differences in occupational aspirations: Their development and consequences for occupational segregation.* The Johns Hopkins University, Center for Social organization of schools, Grant No. NIE-G-78-0210, National Institute of Education, Washington D.C.

Gould, R. (1972). The phases of adult life: A study of developmental psychology. *American Journal of Psychiatry, 129*(11), 33–43.

Gould, S. (1980). Need for achievement, career mobility, and the Mexican American college graduate. *Journal of Vocational Behavior, 16,* 73–82.

Greenhaus, J. H. (1987). *Career management.* Chicago: Dryden.

Greenhaus, J. H., Wong, A. G., & Mossholder, K. W. (1987). Work experience, job performance, and feelings of personal and family well-being. *Journal of Vocational Behavior, 31,* 200–215.

Gregorc, A. F. (1988). *Gregorc Style Delineator.* Columbia, CT: Gregorc.

Gribbons, W. D., & Lohnes, P. R. (1968). *Emerging careers.* New York: Teachers College Press.

Griffith, A. R. (1980a). Justification for a black career development. *Counselor Education and Supervision, 19,* 301–310.

Griffith, A. R. (1980b). A survey of career development. *Counselor Education and Supervision, 19*(4), 301–310.

Griggs, S. A. (1991). *Learning styles counseling.* Ann Arbor, MI: ERIC Counseling and Personnel Services Clearinghouse.

Growler, D., & Legge, K. (1989). Rhetoric in bureaucratic careers: Managing the meaning of management success. In M. B. Arthur, D. T. Hall, & B. S. Lawrence, *Handbook of career theory.* New York: Cambridge University Press.

Grubb, W. N. (1989). Preparing youth for work: The dilemmas of education and training programs. In D. Stern & D. Eichorn (Eds.), *Adolescence and work: Influence of social structures, labor markets, and culture.* Hillsdale, NJ: Lawrence Erlbaum.

Guralnik, D. B. (Ed.). (1980). *Webster's new world dictionary of the American language* (2nd college ed.). New York: Simon and Schuster.

Guterman, M. (1991). Working couples: Finding balance between family and career. In J. M. Kummerow (Ed.), *New directions in career planning in the workplace.* Palo Alto, CA: Consulting Psychologists Press.

Gutteridge, T. G., Leibowitz, Z. B., & Shore, J. E. (1993). *Organizational career development.* San Francisco: Jossey-Bass.

Gutteridge, T. G., & Otte, F. L. (1983). *Organizational career development: State of the practice.* Washington, DC: American Society for Training and Development.

Habley, W. R. (1984). Integrating academic advising and career planning. In R. B. Winston, Jr., T. K. Miller, S. C. Ender, T. J. Grites, & associates (Eds.), *Developmental academic advisement.* San Francisco: Jossey-Bass.

Hahn, M. E., & McLean, M. S. (1955). *Counseling psychology.* New York: McGraw-Hill.

Hall, D. T. (1976). *Careers in organizations.* Pacific Palisades, CA: Goodyear.

Hall, D. T. (1986). *Careers in organizations.* Glenview, IL: Scott Foresman.

Hall, D. T. (1990). Career development theory in organizations. In D. Brown, Linda Brooks, & associates (Eds.), *Career choice and development: Applying contemporary theories to practices* (2nd ed.). San Francisco: Jossey-Bass.

Hall, D. T., & associates. (1986). *Career development in organizations.* San Francisco: Jossey-Bass.

Hall, D. T., & Ricter, J. (1988). Balancing work life and home life: What can organizations do to help? *Academy of Management Executives, 2,* 213–223.

Hammer, A. L. (1993). *Introduction to type and career.* Palo Alto, CA: Consulting Psychologists Press.

Harrington, T. F., & O'Shea, A. J. (1980). Applicability of Holland (1973) model of vocational development with Spanish-speaking clients. *Journal of Counseling Psychology, 27*(3), 246–251.

Harris-Bowlsbey, J. (1984). *DISCOVER for adult learners: Professional manual.* Hunt Valley, MD: American College Testing Program.

Harris, P., & Moran, R. T. (1991). *Managing cultural differences* (3rd ed.). Houston: Gulf.

Hartlage, L. C. (1986). *Neuropsychological assessment and intervention with children and adolescents.* Sarasota, FL: Professional Resources Exchange.

Haskell, J. R. (1993). Getting employees to take charge of their careers. *Training and Development, 47*(2), 51–56.

Havighurst, R. J. (1972). *Developmental tasks and education.* New York: David McKay.

Heal, L. W., Copher, J. L., & Rusch, F. R. (1990). Interagency agreements (IAAs) among agencies responsible for the transition education of students with handicaps from secondary schools to post school settings. *Career Development for Exceptional Individuals, 13,* 121–128.

Healy, C. C. (1982). *Career development: Counseling through the life stages.* Boston: Allyn and Bacon.

Heatherton, C., & Orzek, A. (1989). Career counseling and life planning with lesbian women. *Journal of Counseling and Development, 68,* 52–57.

Hecker, D. E. (1992, Summer). College graduates: Do we have too many or too few? *Occupational Outlook Quarterly, 36*(2),13–17.

Helms, B. J., Moore, S. C., & McSweyn, C. A. (1991). Support employment in Connecticut: An examination of integration and wage outcomes. *Career Development of Exceptional Individuals, 14,* 159–166.

Herbert, J. I. (1990). Integrating race and adult psychosocial development. *Journal of Organizational Behavior, 11,* 433–446.

Herr, E. L., & Cramer, S. H. (1992). *Career guidance and counseling through the life span: Systematic approaches.* Glenview, IL: Scott Foresman.

Hershenson, D. B. (1974a). Vocational guidance of the handicapped. In E. L. Herr (Ed.), *Vocational guidance and human development.* Boston: Houghton Mifflin.

Hershenson, D. B. (1974b, November–December). A vocational-stage approach to sheltered workshop practice. *Journal of Rehabilitation,* 26–27.

Hershenson, D., & Roth, R. (1970). A decisional process model for vocational development. In R. Roth, D. Hershenson, & T. Hilliard (Eds.), *The psychology of vocational development: Reading in theory and research.* Boston: Allyn and Bacon.

Herzberg, F., Mausner, B., & Snyderman, B. B. (1959). *The motivation to work.* New York: John Wiley.

Hesketh, B. (1982). Decision-making styles and career decision making behaviors among school leaders. *Journal of Vocational Behavior, 20,* 227–237.

Hetherington, C., & Orzek, A. (1989). Career counseling and life planning with lesbian women. *Journal of Counseling and Development, 68*(1), 52–57.

Hettler, B. (1986). Strategies for wellness and recreational program development. *New Directions for Student Services, 34,* 19–32.

Hicks, N., & London, M. (1991). Career decision making. In R. F. Morison & J. Adams (Eds.), *Contemporary career development issues.* (pp. 121–150). Hillsdale, NJ: Lawrence Erlbaum.

Hodgkinson, H. (1985). *The changing demographics of American education.* Presentation to the Indiana University of Pennsylvania Invocation on Future Planning, Indiana, PA.

Hoffman, J. J., Goldsmith, E. B., & Hofacker, C. F. (1992). The influence of parents on female business students salary and work hour expectations. *Journal of Employment Counseling, 29,* 79–83.

Hogan, R., DeSoto, C. B., & Solano, C. (1977). Traits, tests, and personality research. *American Psychologists, 32,* 255–264.

Holland, J. L. (1984). *A theory of careers: Some new developments and revisions.* Paper presented at the American Psychological Association Convention, Toronto, Ontario.

Holland, J. L. (1985). *Making vocational choices: A theory of vocational personalities and work environments* (2nd ed.). Englewood Cliffs, NJ: Prentice Hall.

Hotchkiss, L., & Borow, H. C. (1990). Sociological perspectives on work and career development. In D. Brown, L. Brooks, & associates (Eds.), *Career choice and development* (2nd ed.). San Francisco: Jossey-Bass.

House, R. M. (1991). Counseling gay and lesbian clients. In D. Capuzzi & D. R. Grow (Eds.), *Introduction to counseling: Perspectives for the 1990s.* Boston: Allyn and Bacon.

Houser, R., D'Andrea, M. D., & Daniels, J. (1992). Fostering financial independence self-efficiency in AFDC recipients participating in a vocational training program. *Journal of Employment Counseling, 29,* 117–125.

Howland, K. L. (1899). *A review of age-related research.* Unpublished manuscript, Kansas State University, Department of Psychology, Manhattan.

Hoyt, K. B. (1988). The changing workforce: A review of projections—1986 to 2000. *The Career Development Quarterly, 37*(1), 31–39.

Hoyt, K. B. (1989). The career status of women and minority persons: A 20–year retrospective. *The Career Development Quarterly, 37*(3), 202–212.

Huffman, R. R., & Nead, J. M. (1983). General contextualism, ecological science, and cognitive research. *The Journal of Mind and Behavior, 4,* 507–560.

Huhn, R., & Zimpher, D. G. (1984). The role of middle and junior high school counselors in parent education. *The School Counselor, 31*(4), 337–365.

Hummerow, J. M. (1991). Using the Strong Interest Inventory and the Myers-Briggs Type Indicator together in career counseling. In J. M. Kummerow (Ed.), *New directions in career planning in the workplace.* Palo Alto, CA: Consulting Psychologists Press.

Iowa State Department of Education. (1986). *Iowa K–12 career guidance curriculum: Guide for student development.* Des Moines: Author. (ERIC Document Reproduction Service No. ED 273 873)

Isaacson, L. E. (1985). *Basis of career counseling.* Boston: Allyn and Bacon.

Isaacson, L. E. (1986). *Career information in counseling and career development* (4th ed.). Boston: Allyn and Bacon.

Ivey, A. E., & Van Hesteren, F. (1991). Counseling and development: "No one can do it all, but it all needs to be done." *Journal of Counseling and Development, 68*(5), 534–536.

Jackson, D. N. (1985). *Computer-based personality testing.* Washington, DC: Scientific Affairs Office, American Psychological Association.

Jackson, D. N. (1991). Computer-assisted personality test interpretation: The dawn of discovery. In T. B. Gutkin & S. L. Wise (Eds.), *The computer and the decision making process.* Hillsdale, NJ: Lawrence Erlbaum.

Jackson, T., & Vitberg, A. (1987, April). Career development part 3: Challenges for the individual. *Personnel, 54–57.*

Jacksonville Community Council. (1990). *Future workforce needs study.* Jacksonville, FL: Author.

Jaffe, D.T., & Scott, C. D. (1991). Career development for empowerment in a changing work world. In J. M. Hummerow (Ed.), *New directions career planning in the work place.* Palo Alto, CA: Consulting Psychologists Press.

Jepsen, D. A. (1990). *Developmental career counseling. Career counseling: Contemporary topics in vocational psychology* (pp. 117–157). Hillsdale, NJ: Lawrence Erlbaum.

Jepsen, D. A. (1991). Annual review: Practice and research in career counseling and development. *Career Development Quarterly, 41,* 98–129.

Jepsen, D. A. (1992). Annual reviews: Practice and research in career counseling and development. *The Career Development Quarterly, 41*(2), 98–129.

Johnson, W. B. (1991, March/April). Global work force 2000: The new world labor market. *Harvard Business Review, 69,* 115–127.

Johnson, W., & Kottman, T. (1992). Developmental needs of middle school students: Implications for counselors. *Elementary School Guidance and Counseling, 27*(1), 3–14.

Joiner, J., & Fisher, J. (1977). Post-mastectomy counseling. *Journal of Applied Rehabilitation Counseling, 8,* 99–106.

Jones, E. E. (1985). Psychotherapy and counseling with black clients. In P. B. Pedersen (Ed.), *Handbook of crosscultural counseling and therapy.* Westport, CT: Greenwood.

Jones, L. K. (1983). Occ-u-sort kit: Educational and career guidance through the library. *Personnel and Guidance Journal, 61,* 628–631.

Jordaan, J. P. (1963). Exploratory behavior: The formation of self- and occupational concepts. In D. E. Super and others (Eds.), *Career development: Self-concept theory.* New York: College Entrance Examination Board.

Jordaan, J. P. (1974). Life stages as organizing modes of career development. In E. L. Herr (Ed.), *Vocational guidance and human development.* Boston: Houghton Mifflin.

Kahnweiler, J. B. (1984). Career development of women. In H. D. Burck & R. C. Rearden (Eds.), *Career development interventions.* Springfield, IL: Charles C. Thomas.

Kaminski-du-Rosa, V. (1984). A workshop that optimizes the older worker's productivity. *Personnel, 61*(2), 47–56.

Kanchier, C. (1990). Career education for adults with mental disabilities. *Journal of Employment Counseling, 27,* 23–36.

Kanchier, C. (1991). *Dare to change your job and your life.* New York: Mastermedia Limited.

Kane, S. T., Healy, C. C., & Henson, J. (1992). College students and their part-time jobs: Job-congruence, satisfaction and quality. *Journal of Employment Counseling, 29,* 138–144.

Kapes, J. T., & Mastie, M. M. (Eds.). (1988). *A counselor's guide to career assessment instruments* (2nd. ed.). Alexandria, VA: American Counseling Association.

Keating, D. D. (1980). Thinking processes in adolescence. In J. Adelson (Ed.), *Handbook of adolescent psychology.* New York: Wiley.

Keefe, J. W., & Languis, M. C. (1983, August). *Operational definitions.* Paper presented to the National Association of Secondary School Principals Learning Styles Task Force, Reston, VA: Author.

Keefe, J. W., & Monk, J. S. (1988). *Manual to learning styles profile.* Reston, VA: National Association of Secondary School Principals.

Kennedy, M. M. (1986). Glamour *guide to office smarts.* New York: Ballantine.

Kenniston, J. (1971). *Youth and dissent: The rise of the new opposition.* New York: Harcourt, Brace, Jovanovich.

Kinloch, G. (1979). *The sociology of minority group relations.* Englewood Cliffs, NJ: Prentice Hall.

Kinner, R. T., Katz, E. C., & Berry, M. A. (1991). Successful resolution to the career-versus-family conflict. *Journal of Counseling and Development, 69,* 439–444.

Klein, H., Amundson, N., & Borgen, W. (1992). The dynamics of unemployment for social assistance recipients. *Journal of Employment Counseling, 29,* 88–94.

Knefelkemp, L. L., & Slepitza, R. (1976). A cognitive developmental model of career development. An adoption of the Perry scheme. *Counseling Psychologist, 16*(3), 53–58.

Kolb, D. A. (1984). *Learning Style Inventory.* Boston: McBer.

Kossek, E. E. (1990). Diversity and childcare assistance needs: Employee problems, preferences, and work-related outcomes. *Personnel Psychology, 43,* 769–791.

Kram, K. E. (1986). Mentoring in the workplace. In D. T. Hall and associates (Eds.), *Career Development in Organizations* (pp. 160–201). San Francisco: Jossey-Bass.

Krug, S. E. (1992). *Psychware.* Kansas City, MO: Test Corporation of America.

Krumboltz, J. D. (1979). A social learning theory of career decision making. In A. M. Mitchell, G. C. Jame, & J. D. Krumboltz (Eds.), *Social learning and career decision making.* Cranston, RI: Carroll Press.

Krumbolz, J. D. (1983). *Private rules in career decision making.* Columbus, OH: National Center for Research in Vocational Education.

Krumboltz, J. D. (1990). Evaluating computer-assisted career guidance programs. *Journal of Career Development, 17,* 133–136.

Krumboltz, J. D., & Hamel, D. A. (1977). *Guide to career decision making skills.* New York: Educational Testing Service.

Krumboltz, J. D., Mitchell, A., & Gelatt, H. G. (1975). Applications of social learning theory of career selection. *Focus on Guidance, 8,* 1–16.

Kutscher, R. (1987, September). *Projections 2000: Overview and implications of the projections to 2000.* Washington, DC: Monthly Labor Review, U.S. Department of Labor.

Kuvlesky, W. P., & Juarez, R. (1975). Mexican-American youth and the American dream. In J. S. Picoui & R. E. Campbell (Eds.), *Career behavior of special groups: Theory, research, and practice.* Columbus, OH: Merrill/Macmillan.

Labouvie-vief, G. (1982). Dynamic development and mature autonomy: A theoretical prologue. *Human Development, 25,* 161–191.

LaPorte, S. B. (1991, January). Twelve companies that do the right thing. *Working Woman,* 57–59.

Lazarus, R., & Folkman, S. (1984). *Stress, appraisal, and coping.* New York: Springer.

Lee, C. C. (1989). Needed: A career development advocate. *Career Development Quarterly, 37,* 218–220.

Lee, C. C., & Simmons, S. (1988). A comprehensive life-planning model for black adolescents. *The School Counselor, 36,* 5–10.

Leibowitz, Z. B., Farren, C., & Kaye, B. C. (1986). *Designing career development systems.* San Francisco: Jossey-Bass.

Leong, F. T. L. (1991). Career development attributes and occupational values of Asian Americans and white college students. *Career Development Quarterly, 39,* 221–230.

Leong, F. T. L. (1993). The career counseling process with racial-ethnic minorities: The case of Asian Americans. *The Career Development Quarterly, 42,* 26–40.

Levinson, D. J. (1978). *The seasons of a man's life.* New York: Knopf.

Levinson, D. J. (1986). A conceptualization of adult development. *American Psychologist, 41*(1), 3–13.

Lewis, R. (1993, February). Networking, new tactics left older job seekers. *AARP Bulletin, 34*(2), 1, 14–15.

Lloyd, J. (1992). *The career decision planner. When to move, when to stay, and when to go on your own.* New York: Wiley.

Locke, E. A. (1976). The nature and cause of job satisfaction. In M. D. Dunnette (Ed.), *Handbook of industrial psychology.* Chicago: Rand-McNally.

Loganbill, C., Hardy, E., & Delworth, V. (1982). Supervision: A conceptual model. *Counseling Psychologist, 10,* 1.

Lombana, J. H. (1992). *Guidance of handicapped students.* Springfield, IL: Charles C. Thomas.

London, M., & Greller, M. M. (1991). Demographic trends and vocational behavior: A twenty year retrospective and agenda for the 1990s. *Journal of Vocational Behavior, 38,* 125–164.

London, M., & Stumpf, S. A. (1982). *Managing careers.* Reading, MA: Addison-Wesley.

Lowenthal, M. F., Thurnher, M., Chiriboga, D., & associates. (1975). *Four stages of life.* San Francisco: Jossey-Bass.

Lowenthal, M. F., & Weiss, L. (1976). Intimacy and crises in adulthood. *Counseling Psychologists, 61,* 10–15.

Ludeman, K. (1989). *The worth ethic: How to profit from changing values of the new work force.* New York: Dutton.

Lynch, E. M. (1980). *Decades-lifestyle changes in career expectations.* New York: AMACOM.

Lynch, M. D., & Lynch, C. L. (1991). Self-concept development through the adult life cycle. *Journal of Research in Education, 1,* (1),13–17.

MacAleese, R. (1984). Use of tests. In H. D. Burck & R. C. Reardon (Eds.), *Career development interventions.* Springfield, IL: Charles C. Thomas.

Maki, D. R. (1986). Foundations of applied rehabilitation counseling. In T. F. Riggar, D. R. Maki, & A. W. Wolf (Eds.), *Applied rehabilitation counseling.* New York: Springer.

Mamarchev, H. L., & Pritchett, B. (1978). Career resource centers. Ann Arbor: University of Michigan, ERIC Counseling & Personnel Services Clearinghouse.

Masden, D. H. (1986). Computer applications for test administration and scoring. *Measurement and Evaluation in Counseling and Development, 19*(1), 6–14.

Maslow, A. H. (1954). *Motivation and personality.* New York: Harper & Row.

Mayhovich, M. K. (1976). Asian Americans—quiet Americans? In H. A. Johnson (Ed.), *Ethnic American minorities: A guide of media and materials.* New York: Bowler.

Maze, M. E. (1989). How to evaluate and select software. In G. R. Walz & J. C. Bleuer (Eds.), *Counseling software guide* (pp. 5–7). Alexandria, VA: American Association for Counseling and Development.

McCoy, V. R. (1977). *Lifelong learning: The adult years.* Washington, DC: Adult Education Association.

McDaniels, C., & Gysbers, N. C. (1992). *Counseling for career development: Theories, resources, and practices.* San Francisco: Jossey-Bass.

McGovern, T. V., & Carr, K. F. (1989). Carrying out the nitch: A review of alumni surveys on undergraduate psychology majors. *Teaching of Psychology, 16,* 52–57.

McMahon, B. T. (1979). A model of vocational redevelopment for the midcareer physically disabled, *Rehabilitation Counseling Bulletin, 23,* 35–47.

Medina, V., & Drummond, R. J. (1993). Profile of rural Reach-Out students. *Journal of Employment Counseling, 30,* 15–24.

Meier, S. T. (1991). Vocational behavior, 1988–1990: Vocational choice, decision making, career development interventions, and assessment. *Journal of Vocational Behavior, 38,* 131–181.

Messner, P. E. (1993). *Skilled trades cooperative training program.* Dayton, OH: College of Education and Human Services, Chrysler Project.

Milburn, L. (1993). Career issues of a gay man: Case of Allan. *The Career Development Quarterly, 43*(3), 195–196.

Miller, D. C., & Form, W. H. (1951). *Industrial sociology.* New York: Harper and Row.

Miller, M. J. (1987). Career counseling for high school students: Grades 10–12. *Journal of Employment Counseling, 24*(4), 173–183.

Miller, M. J. (1988). Career counseling for the middle school youngster: Grades 6–9. *Journal of Employment Counseling, 25*(4), 172–179.

Miller, M. J. (1989). Career counseling for the elementary school child: Grades K–5. *Journal of Employment Counseling, 26,* 169–177.

Miller, M. J. (1992). Synthesizing results from an interest and personality inventory to improve career decision making. *Journal of Employment Counseling, 29,* 50–59.

Miller, M. J., & Knippers, J. A. (1992). Jeopardy: A career information game for school counselors. *The Career Development Quarterly, 41,* 55–61.

Miller, S., & Cunningham, B. (1992). A guided look experience program for minority students. *Journal of College Student Development, 33,* 373–374.

Minor, F. J., Slade, L. A., & Myers, R. A. (1991). Career transitions in changing times. In R. F. Morrison & J. Adam (Eds.), *Contemporary career development issues* (pp. 109–150). Hillsdale, NJ: Lawrence Erlbaum.

Mirabile, R. J. (1991). Competency profiling: A new model for career counselors. In J. M. Kummerow (Ed.), *New directions in career planning and the workplace.* Palo Alto, CA: Consulting Psychologists Press.

Mitchell, J. V., Jr. (Ed.). (1983). *Test in Spring III.* Lincoln: Burk Institute of Mental Measurements, University of Nebraska–Lincoln.

Mitchell, L. K., & Krumboltz, J. D. (1990). Social learning approach to career decision making: Krumboltz's theory. In D. Brown, L. Brooks, & associates, *Career choice and development* (2nd ed.). San Francisco: Jossey-Bass.

Moon, M. S., Inge, K. J., Wehman, P., Brooke, V., & Barcus, J. M. (1990). *Helping persons with severe mental retardation get and keep employment.* Baltimore: Paul H. Brookes.

Moore, S. C., Agran, M., & McSweyn, C. A. (1990). Career education: Are we starting early enough? *Career Development for Exceptional Individuals, 13,* 129–134.

Morrison, R. F. (1991). Meshing corporate and career development strategies. In R. F. Morrison & J. Adams (Eds.), *Contemporary career development issues.* Hillsdale, NJ: Lawrence Erlbaum.

Morse, C. L., & Russell, T. (1988). How elementary counselors see their role: An empirical study. *Elementary School Guidance and Counseling, 23*(1), 54–62.

Nachreiner, J. A. (1987). A self-help education and career planning resource for adult students. *Journal of College Student Development, 28,* 277–278.

Naisbitt, J., & Aburdene, P. (1990). *Ten new directions for the 1990s: Megatrends 2000.* New York: William Morrow.

National Career Development Association Professional Standards Committee. (1992). Career counseling competencies. *Career Development Quarterly, 40,* 378–386.

National Occupational Information Coordinating Committee. (1990). *Status of NOICC/SOICC Network 1989. Administrative report 14.* Washington, DC: Author.

National Opinion Research Center. (1947). Jobs and occupations: A popular evaluation. *Opinion News, 9,* 3–13.

Nazzaro, J. (1979). *Assessment of minority students* (fact sheet). Reston, VA: ERIC Clearinghouse on Handicapped and Gifted Children. (ERIC Document Reproduction Service No. ED)

Neugarten, B. L. (1964). *Personality in middle and late life.* New York: Atherton Press.

Neugarten, B. (1974, September). Age groups in American society and the rise of the young-old. *Annals of the American Academy of Political and Social Science, 415,* 187–198.

Neugarten, B. L. (1977a). Adaptation and the life cycle. In N. K. Schlossberg & A. Entine (Eds.), *Counseling adults.* Monterey: Brooks/Cole.

Neugarten, B. L. (1977b). Personality and aging. In J. E. Birren, & K. W. Schaie (Eds.), *Handbook of the psychology of aging.* New York: Van Nostrand Reinhold.

Neugarten, B. L. (1986). The aging society. In A. Pefer & L. Bronte (Eds.), *Our aging society: Paradox and promise.* New York: W. W. Norton.

Neugarten, B. L., & associates. (1964). *Personality in middle and late life.* New York: Atherton Press.

Nevill, D. D., & Super, D. E. (1986). *Manual for the Salience Inventory.* Palo Alto, CA: Consulting Psychologists Press.

Newlon, B. J., & Silvasi-Patchin, J. A. (1992). Temporary help services: An alternative form of employment. *Journal of Employment Counseling, 29,* 84–87.

Niemeyer, G. J., Pritchard, S., Berzonsky, M., & Metzler, A. (1991). Vocational hypothesis testing: The role of occupational relevance and identity formation. *Journal of Vocational Behavior, 38,* 318–332.

Noe, R. A., & Steffy, B. (1987). The influence of individual characteristics and assessment center evaluations on career exploration behavior and job involvement. *Journal of Vocational Behavior, 30,* 187–202.

O'Banion, T. (1972). An academic advising model. *Junior College Journal, 44,* 62–69.

O'Hara, R. P., & Tiedeman, D. V. (1959). Vocational self-concept in adolescents. *Journal of Counseling Psychology, 6,* 292–301.

O'Toole, J. (Ed.). (1973). *Work in America.* Cambridge, MA: MIT Press.

Oakland, T. (1982). Nonbiased assessment of minority group children. In J. T. Neisworth (Ed.), *Assessment in special education.* Rockville, MD: Aspen Systems.

Okum, B. F. (1984). *Working with adults: Individual, family, and career development.* Monterey, CA: Brooks/Cole Publishing.

Olney, C. W. (1988). The new job outlook: Preparing for the years ahead. *Journal of Employment Counseling, 25,* 7–13.

Omizo, S. A., & Omizo, M. M. (1992). Career and vocational assessment information for program planning and counseling for students with disabilities. *The School Counselor, 40*(1), 32–39.

Omvig, C. P., & Thomas, E. G. (1974). Vocational interests of affluent suburban students. *Vocational Guidance Quarterly, 23,* 10–16.

Ornstein, S., & Isabella, L. (1990). Age vs. stage models of career attitudes of women: A partial replication and extension. *Journal of Vocational Behavior, 36,* 1–19.

Osipow, S. H. (1975). The relevance of theories of career development to special groups: Problems, needed data, and implications. In J. S. Picou & R. E. Cambell (Eds.), *Career behavior of special groups: Theory, research, and practice.* Columbus, OH: Merrill/Macmillan.

Osipow, S. H., & Spokane, A. R. (1987). *Manual for the Occupational Stress Inventory.* Odessa, FL: Psychological Assessment Resources.

Pallas, A., & Alexander, K. (1983). Sex differences in quantitative SAT performance. New evidence on the differential coursework hypothesis. *American Educational Research Journal, 20,* 165–182.

Parker, H. J., & Chan, F. (1988). Information on projected-growth occupations: Its effect on individuals' prestige ratings. *Journal of Employment Counseling, 25*(2), 76–85.

Parsons, F. (1909). *Choosing a vocation.* Boston: Houghton Mifflin.

Peck, R. C. (1975, April). Psychological developments in the second half of life. In J. E. Anderson (Ed.), *Psychological aspects of aging* (pp. 44–49). Proceedings of a conference on Planning Research, Bethesda, MD.

Peer, G. G. (1985). The status of secondary school guidance: A national survey. *The School Counselor, 32*(3), 181–189.

Peterson, G. W., Sampson, Jr., J. P., & Reardon, R. C. (1991). *Career development and services: A cognitive approach.* Pacific Grove, CA: Brooks/Cole.

Phelps, L. A., & Lutz, R. J. (1977). *Career explorations and preparation for the special needs learner.* Boston: Allyn and Bacon.

Piaget, J. (1952). *The origins of intelligence in children.* New York: International University Press.

Pickering, J. W. (1984). A comparison of three methods of career planning for liberal arts majors. *Career Development Quarterly, 35,* 102–111.

Poe, R. E. (1991). Developmental change in vocational identity among college students. *Journal of College Student Development, 32,* 249–252.

Post-Kammer, P. (1987). Intrinsic and extrinsic work values and career maturity of 9th and 11th grade boys. *Journal of Counseling and Development, 65,* 420–423.

Prediger, D. J. (1974). The role of assessment in career guidance. In E. L. Herr (Ed.), *Vocational guidance and human development.* Boston: Houghton Mifflin.

Pugh, N. (1986). *Occupations: A unit designed for grades 4 to 5.* (ERIC Document ED No. 272 445)

Remer, P., & Schrader, L. A. (1981). Gestalt approach to classroom guidance. *Elementary School Guidance & Counseling, 16,* 15–23.

Richardson, E. H. (1981). Cultural and historical perspectives in counseling American Indians. In D. W. Sue (Ed.), *Counseling the culturally different.* New York: Wiley.

Robbins, S. B., & Tucker, K. R., Jr. (1986). Relation of good instability to self-directed and interactional career counseling workshops. *Journal of Counseling Psychology, 33,* 418–424.

Robinson, D., & Mopsik, W. (1992). An environmental experimental model for counseling handicapped children. *Elementary School Guidance and Counseling, 27*(1), 73–78.

Roe, A. (1956). *The psychology of occupations.* New York: Wiley.

Roe, A., & Lunneborg, P. W. (1990). Personality development and career choice. In D. Brown, L. Brooks, & associates (Eds.), *Career choice and development: Applying contemporary theories to practice* (2nd ed.). San Francisco: Jossey-Bass.

Roessler, R. T. (1988). A conceptual basis for return to work interventions. *Rehabilitation Counseling Bulletin, 32,* 98–107.

Roessler, R., & Rubin, E. (1982). *Case management and rehabilitation counseling: Procedures and techniques.* Baltimore: University Park Press.

Rogers, C. R. (1942). *Counseling and psychotherapy.* Boston: Houghton Mifflin.

Rogers, C. R. (1951). *Client-centered therapy.* Boston: Houghton Mifflin.

Rosen, B. (1982). Career progress of women: Getting in and staying in. In H. J. Bernardin (Ed.), *Women in the workforce.* New York: Praeger.

Rosen, B., & Jerdee, T. (1988). Managing older workers' careers. *Research in Personnel and Human Resource Management, 6,* 37–74.

Rounds, J. B. (1990). The comparative and combined ability of work values and interest data in career counseling with adults. *Journal of Vocational Behavior, 37,* 32–45.

Rounds, J. B., & Tracey, T. J. (1990). From trait-and-factor to person-environment-fit-counseling: Theory and practice. In W. B. Walsh & S. H. Osipow, *Career counseling: Contemporary topics in vocational psychology.* Hillsdale, NJ: Lawrence Erlbaum.

Rubin, S. E., & Rubin, N. M. (Eds.). (1988). *Contemporary challenges to the rehabilitation counseling profession.* Baltimore: Paul H. Brooks.

Russell, J. E. A. (1991). Career development interventions in organizations. *Journal of Vocational Behavior, 38,* 237–287.

Sampson, J. P., Jr. (1989). Introduction. In G. R. Walz & J. C. Bleuer (Eds.), *Counseling software guide* (pp. 1–3). Alexandria, VA: American Association for Counseling and Development.

Sampson, J. P., Jr., & Reardon, R. C. (1990a). A differential feature-cost analysis of nine computer guidance systems. *Journal of Career Development, 17*(2), 81–111.

Sampson, J. P., Jr., & Reardon, R. C. (1990b). Evaluating computer-assisted guidance systems: Synthesis and implications. *Journal of Career Development, 17,* 143–149.

Sampson, J. P., Jr., Reardon, R. C., & Lenz, J. G. (1991). Computer-assisted career guidance: Improving the design and use of systems. *Journal of Career Development, 17,* 185—194.

Savickas, M. L. (1989). Annual review: Practice and research in career counseling and development: 1988. *The Career Development Quarterly, 37,* 100–134.

Scarpello, U. G., & Ledvinka, J. (1988). *Personnel/human resource management: Environment and functions.* Boston: PWS-Kent.

Schaie, K. W. (1977). Toward a stage theory of adult cognitive development. *Aging and Human Development, 8,* 129–138.

Schaie, K., & Parr, J. (1981). Intelligence. In A. W. Chickering & associates (Eds.), *The modern American college.* San Francisco: Jossey-Bass.

Schein, E. H. (1978). *Career dynamics: Matching individual and organizational needs.* Reading, MA: Addison-Wesley.

Schlossberg, N. K. (1984). *Counseling adults in transition.* New York: Springer.

Schmitt, P., Growick, B., & Klein, M. (1988). Transition from school to work for individuals with learning disabilities: A comprehensive model. In S. E. Rubin & N. M. Rubin (Eds.), *Contemporary challenges to the rehabilitation counseling profession* (pp. 93–110). Baltimore: Paul H. Brooks.

Sears, S. (1982). A definition of career guidance terms. A national vocational guidance perspective. *Vocational Guidance Quarterly, 31,* 137–143.

Seligman, L. (1980). *Assessment in developmental career counseling.* Cranston, RI: Carroll Press.

Selman, R. L. (1980). *The growth of interpersonal understanding.* New York: Academic Press.

Severinsen, K. N. (1973). *Career guidance: An individual developmental approach.* Columbus, OH: Merrill/Macmillan.

Sewell, W. H., Haller, A. O., & Ohlendorf, G. (1970). The educational and early occupational attainment process: Replications and revisions. *American Sociological Review, 35,* 1014–1027.

Sharf, R. S. (1992). *Applying career development theory to counseling.* Pacific Grove, CA: Brooks/Cole.

Sheehy, G. (1976). *Passages: Predictable crisis of adult life.* New York: Dutton.

Sheeley, V. E. (1988). Historical perspectives on NVGA/NCDA: What our leaders think. *The Career Development Quarterly, 36*(4), 307–320.

Shelley, K. J. (1992, Summer). More college graduates may be chasing fewer jobs. *Occupational Outlook Quarterly, 36*(2), 5–12.

Sherman, E. (1987). *Meaning in mid-life transitions.* Albany: State University of New York Press.

Shertzer, B., & Linden, J. D. (1979). *Fundamentals of individual appraisal.* Boston: Houghton Mifflin.

Shore, L. (1992). Stress. In L. K. Jones (Ed.), *The encyclopedia of career change and work issues.* Phoenix, AZ: Oryx Press.

Siegel, O. (1982). Personality development in adolescence. In B. B. Wolman (Ed.), *Handbook of developmental psychology.* Englewood Cliffs, NJ: Prentice Hall.

Silvasi-Patchin, J. A., & Newlon, B. J. (1992). Temporary help services: An alternative form of employment. *Journal of Employment Counseling, 29,* 84–87.

Small, S. A., & Riley, D. (1990). Toward a multidimensional assessment of work spillover into family life. *Journal of Marriage and Family, 51,* 939–941.

Smith, A., & Chemers, M. (1981). Perceptions of economically disadvantaged employees in a work setting. *Journal of Employment Counseling, 18,* 24–33.

Smith, E. J. (1980). Career development of minorities in non-traditional fields. *Journal of Non-White Concerns in Personnel and Guidance, 8*(3), 141–156.

Smith, E. J. (1983). Issues in racial minorities career behavior. In W. B. Walsh & S. H. Osipow, *Handbook of vocational psychology* (Vol. 1, pp. 161–222). Hillsdale, NJ: Lawrence Erlbaum.

Spokane, A. R. (1991). *Career intervention.* Englewood Cliffs, NJ: Prentice Hall.

Srebalus, D. J., Marinelli, R. P., & Messing, J. K. (1982). *Career development.* Monterey, CA: Wadsworth.

St. Clair, K. L. (1989). Middle school counseling research: A resource for school counselors. *Elementary School Guidance & Counseling, 23,* 219–226.

Steere, D., Pancsofar, E., Wood, R., & Hecimovic, A. (1990). The principle of shared responsibility. *Career Development of Exceptional Individuals, 13,* 143–154.

Stern, D., & Eichorn, D. (Eds.). (1989). *Adolescence and work: Influence of social structure, labor markets, and culture.* Hillsdale, NJ: Lawrence Erlbaum.

Stevens-Long, J. (1988). *Adult life.* Palo Alto, CA: Mayfield Publishing.

Stidham, H. H., & Remley, T. P., Jr. (1992). Job club methodology applied in a workforce setting. *Journal of Employment Counseling, 29,* 69–75.

Stone, J., & Gregg, C. (1981). Juvenile diabetes and rehabilitation counseling. *Rehabilitation Counseling Bulletin, 24,* 283–291.

Stone, W. O. (1984). Serving ethnic minorities. In H. D. Burck & R. C. Reardon (Eds.), *Career development interventions* (pp. 267–291). Springfield, IL: Charles C. Thomas.

Strom, R. D., Bernard, H. W., & Strom, S. K. (1987). *Human development and learning.* New York: Human Sciences Press.

Subich, L. M. (1989). A challenge to grow: Reaction to Hoyt's article. *Career Development Quarterly, 37,* 213–217.

Sullivan, H. S. (1953). *The psychiatric interview.* New York: W. W. Norton.

Sundberg, N. D. (1977). *Assessment of persons.* Englewood Cliffs, NJ: Prentice Hall.

Super, D. E. (1953). A theory of vocational development. *American Psychologist, 8,* 185–190.

Super, D. E. (1957). *The psychology of careers.* New York: Harper.

Super, D. E. (1963). Vocational development in adolescence and early adulthood: Tasks and behaviors. In D. E. Super (Ed.), *Theory career development: Self-concept theory.* New York: CEEB Research Mimeograph No. 4.

Super, D. E. (1969a). The natural history of a study of lives and of vocations. *Perspectives on Education, 2,* 13–22.

Super, D. E. (1969b). Vocational development theory: Persons, positions, and processes. *The Counseling Psychologist, 1,* 2–9.

Super, D. E. (1976). *Career education and the meaning of work. Monography on career education.* Washington, DC: The Office of Career Education, U. S. Office of Education.

Super, D. E. (1980). A life-span, life-space approach to career development. *Journal of Vocational Behavior, 16,* 282–298.

Super, D. E. (1981a). Approaches to occupational choice and career development. In A. G. Watts, D. E. Super, & J. M. Kidd (Eds.), *Career development in Britain.* Cambridge, England: Hobsons Press.

Super, D. E. (1981b). A developmental theory: Implementing a self-concept. In D. H. Montron & C. J. Shimbman (Eds.), *Career development in the 1980's: Theory and practice.* Springfield, IL: Charles C. Thomas.

Super, D. E. (1984). Career and life development. In D. Brown, L. Brooks, & associates (Eds.), *Career choice and development: Applying contemporary theories to practice* (pp. 192–234). San Francisco: Jossey-Bass.

Super, D. E. (1985). New dimensions in an adult vocational and natural center for research in vocational education. *Career Counseling.* Occasional paper No. 106. Columbus, OH: Ohio State.

Super, D. E. (1990). A life-span, life-space approach to career development. In D. Brown, L. Brooks, & associates (Eds.), *Career choice and development* (2nd ed., pp. 197–261). San Francisco: Jossey-Bass.

Super, D. E., & Crites, J. O. (1962). *Appraisal of vocational fitness by means of psychological tests* (rev. ed.). New York: Harper & Row.

Super, D. E., Osborne, W., Walsh, D., Brown, S., & Niles, S. (1992). Developmental career assessment and counseling: The C-DAC model. *Journal of Counseling and Development 71,* 74–79.

Super, D. E., & Thompson, A. S. (1981). *Adult career concerns inventory.* New York: Teachers College Press.

Super, D. E., Thompson, A. S., & Lindeman, R. H. (1988). *The adult concerns inventory.* Palo Alto, CA: Consulting Psychologists Press.

Swanson, J. L. (1992). Vocational behavior, 1989–1991. Life-span career development and reciprocal interaction of work and nonwork. *Journal of Vocational Behavior, 41,* 101–161.

Swanson, J. L. (1993). Integrating a multicultural perspective into training for career counseling and programmatic and individual interventions. *The Career Development Quarterly, 42,* 41–49.

Swanson, J. L., & Tokar, D. M. (1991). College students' perceptions of barriers to career development. *Journal of Vocational Behavior, 39,* 344–361.

Sweetland, R. C., & Keyser, D. J. (1986). *Tests* (2nd ed.). Kansas City, MO: Test Corporation of America.

Szymanski, E. M., Buckley, J., Parent, W. S., Parker, R. M., & Westbrook, J. D. (1988). Rehabilitation counseling in supported employment: A conceptual model for service delivery and personnel preparation. In S. E. Rubin & N. M. Rubin (Eds.), *Contemporary challenges to the rehabilitation counseling profession* (pp. 111–133). Baltimore: Paul H. Brooks.

Szymanski, E. M., Hanley-Maxwell, C., & Asselin, S. (1990). Rehabilitation counseling, special education, and vocational special needs education. Three transition disciplines. *Career Development for Exceptional Individuals, 13,* 29–38.

Taylor, S. M. (1988). Effects of college internship on individual participant. *Journal of Applied Psychology, 73,* 393–401.

Thompson, D. L. (1989). Software for testing. In G. R. Walz & J. C. Bleuer (Eds.), *Counseling software guide* (pp. 23–28). Alexandria, VA: American Association for Counseling and Development.

Thurer, S. (1980). Vocational rehabilitation following coronary bypass surgery: The need of counseling the newly well. *Journal of Applied Rehabilitation Counseling, 11,* 98–99.

Tiedeman, D. V., & Miller-Tiedeman, A. (1984). Career decision making: An individualistic perspective. In D. Brown, L. Brooks, & associates (Eds.), *Career choice and development: Applying contemporary theories to practices.* San Francisco: Jossey-Bass.

Tiedeman, D. V., & O'Hara, R. P. (1963). *Career development: Choices and adjustment.* New York: College Entrance Examination Board.

Tinglin, W. H. (1985). Counseling minority immigrants for employment. In R. J. Samuda & A. Wolfgang (Eds.), *Intercultural counseling and assessment: Global perspectives* (pp. 253–268). Lewiston, NY: C. J. Hogrete.

U.S. Department of Defense. (1992). *Armed services vocational aptitude battery counselor's guide.* Ft. Sheridan, IL: Military Enlistment Processing Command.

U.S. Department of Labor. (1947). *Guide for occupational exploration.* Washington, DC: U.S. Government Printing Office.

U.S. Department of Labor. (1991). *Dictionary of occupational titles* (4th ed. revised). Washington, DC: U.S. Government Printing Office.

U.S. Department of Labor. (1976).

U.S. Department of Labor. (1991). *Dictionary of occupational titles* (4th ed. rev.). Washington DC: U.S. Government Printing Office.

U.S. Department of Labor. (1992–1993). *Occupational outlook handbook.* Washington, DC: U.S. Government Printing Office.

U.S. Executive Office of the President, Office of Management & Budget. (1987). *Standard occupational classification manual.* Washington DC: U.S. Government Printing Office.

U.S. House of Representatives. (1990, July 12). *Conference report: Americans with Disabilities Act of 1990, 101st Congress, 2nd session, Report 101–596,* Washington, DC: Author.

U.S. Office of Education. (1975). *An introduction to career education: A policy paper of the U.S. Office of Education.* Washington, DC: U.S. Department of Health, Education, and Welfare.

Vandergoot, D., & Engelkes, J. R. (1977). An application of the theory of work adjustment to vocational counseling. *Vocational Guidance Quarterly, 26,* 24–53.

Van Hestern, F., & Ivey, A. E. (1990). Counseling and development: Toward a new identity for a profession in transition. *Journal of Counseling and Development, 68,* 524–528.

W. T. Grant Foundation Commission on Work, Family, and Citizenship. (1988). *The forgotten half: The non-college youth.* Washington, DC: Author.

Walker, J. W., & Gutteridge, T. G. (1979). *Career planning practices.* New York: AMACOM.

Walker, P., & Hittle, S. I. (1993). *How to find Mr. Right: Say good-bye to Mr. Wrong in your life.* Dayton, OH: Agape Publications.

Walz, G. R., & Bleuer, J. C. (1989). *Counseling software guide.* Alexandria, VA: American Association for Counseling and Development.

Wanous, J. P. (1980). *Organizational entry.* Reading, MA: Addison-Wesley.

Warnath, C. F. (1975). Vocational theories: Directions to nowhere. *Personnel and Guidance Journal, 53,* 422–428.

Wehman, P. (Ed.). (1993). *The ADA mandate for social change.* Baltimore: Paul H. Brooks.

Weisenstein, G. R., & Koshman, H. L. (1991). The influence of being labeled handicapped has on the employer's perception of the worker's traits for successful employment. *Career Development for Exceptional Individuals, 14,* 67–76.

Werther, W. B., Jr., & Davis, K. (1993). *Human resource and personnel management* (4th ed.). New York: McGraw-Hill.

Westwood, M. J., & Ishiyama, F. I. (1991). *Challenges in counseling immigrant clients: Understanding intercultural barriers to career adjustment, 28,* 130–143.

Westwood, M. J., & Vargo, J. W. (1985). Counseling double-minority status clients. In R. J. Samuda & A. Wolfgang (Eds.), *Intercultural counseling and assessment: Global perspectives* (pp. 303–313). Lewiston, NY: C. J. Hogrete.

Wigglesworth, D. C. (1991). Meeting the needs of the multicultural workforce. In J. M. Hummerow (Ed.), *New directions in career planning and the workplace.* Palo Alto, CA: Consulting Psychologists Press.

Williamson, E. G. (1939). *How to counsel students.* New York: McGraw-Hill.

Williamson, R., & Johnson, H. (1991). *Planning for success: Successful implementation of middle level reorganization.* Reston, VA: National Association of Secondary School Principals.

Wolfer, K. S., & Wong, R. G. (1988). *The outplacement solution.* New York: Wiley.

Wright, G. N. (1980). *Total rehabilitation.* Boston: Little, Brown.

Wrightsman, L. S. (1988). *Personality development in adulthood.* Newbury Park, CA: Sage.

Yankelovich, D. (1982, May). The work ethic is under-employed. *Psychology Today, 8*(6), 5–8.

Yost, E. B., & Corbishley, M. A. (1987). *Career counseling.* San Francisco: Jossey-Bass.

Zaccaro, S. J., & Riley, A. W. (1987). Stress, coping and organizational effectiveness. In A. W. Riley & S. J. Zaccaro (Eds.), *Occupational stress and organizational effectiveness.* New York: Praeger.

Zaslow, M. J., & Takanishi, R. (1993). Priorities for research on adolescent development. *American Psychologist, 48,* 185–192.

Zelvin, A. (1987, February 2). A job hotline can help the pink slip blues. *The Wall Street Journal.*

Zey, M. G. (1984). *The mentor connection.* Homewood, IL: Dow Jones-Irwin.

Zick, C. D., & McCullough, J. L. (1991). Trends in married couples time use: Evidence from 1977–1978 and 1987–1988. *Sex Roles, 24,* 459–488.

Zunker, V. G. (1994). *Using assessment results for career development* (4th ed.). Pacific Grove, CA: Brooks/Cole.

Zytowski, D. G. (1981). *Counseling with the Kuder Occupational Interest Survey.* Chicago: Science Research Association.

Zytowski, D. G., & Borgen, F. H. (1983). Assessment. In W. B. Walsh & S. H. Osipow, *Handbook of vocational psychology* (Vol. 2). Hillsdale, NJ: Lawrence Erlbaum.

NAME INDEX

SUBJECT INDEX